FRANCE AND THE BRITISH ISLES
IN THE MIDDLE AGES AND RENAISSANCE

ESSAYS IN MEMORY OF RUTH MORGAN

This volume examines many facets of cultural relations between France and the British Isles from the eighth to the seventeenth century, with Ruth Morgan's own special interest in historical literature to the fore but embracing manuscript studies and literary criticism as well. The core of the volume is on the central middle ages, including an important study of Henry of Huntingdon's reaction to Geoffrey of Monmouth's *Historia* in the *Letter to Warinus* and an examination of King Arthur and French nationalism. Crusading history is a topic for literary study, on the *Estoires d'Outremer*, and for a discussion of Anglo-French attitudes to the Crusade in the fourteenth century. The volume opens with studies of Insular manuscripts and texts in the Carolingian empire and closes with seventeenth-century exchanges in the fields of drama and hagiology.

Ruth Morgan
Photograph by Philip Gaskell

FRANCE

AND THE

BRITISH ISLES

IN THE MIDDLE AGES

AND RENAISSANCE

ESSAYS BY MEMBERS OF
GIRTON COLLEGE, CAMBRIDGE,
IN MEMORY OF RUTH MORGAN

Edited by Gillian Jondorf and D.N. Dumville

THE BOYDELL PRESS

First published 1991 by The Boydell Press, Woodbridge

The Boydell Press is an imprint of Boydell & Brewer Ltd
PO Box 9, Woodbridge, Suffolk IP12 3DF
and of Boydell & Brewer Inc.
PO Box 41026, Rochester, NY 14604, USA

ISBN   0 85115 487 5

British Library Cataloguing in Publication Data
France and the British Isles in the Middle Ages and Renaissance :
  essays by members of Girton College, Cambridge, in memory of Ruth Morgan.
  1. England. Cultural relations, history with France 2. France.
  Cultural relations, history with England
  I. Jondorf, Gillian II. Dumville, David III. Morgan,
  Margaret Ruth
  303.48242044
  ISBN 0-85115-487-5

Library of Congress Cataloging-in-Publication Data
France and the British Isles in the Middle Ages and Renaissance : essays
  by members of Girton College, Cambridge in memory of Ruth Morgan /
  edited by Gillian Jondorf and D.N. Dumville.
       p.   cm.
  Includes bibliographical references and index.
  ISBN 0-85115-487-5 (acid-free paper)
  1. Great Britain – Civilization – French influences. 2. Great
  Britain – Civilization – Medieval period, 1066–1485. 3. Great
  Britain – Civilization – 16th century. 4. Great Britain – Relations
  – France. 5. France – Relations – Great Britain. 6. France –
  Civilization. I. Morgan, Ruth. II. Jondorf, Gillian.
  III. Dumville, D.N.
  DA47.1.F73 1991
  941–dc20   90–48688

This publication is printed on acid-free paper

Printed in Great Britain by
St Edmundsbury Press Ltd, Bury St Edmunds, Suffolk

Contents

Ruth Morgan

MELVEENA McKENDRICK

On the day when Ruth's family, friends, colleagues, and students packed the University Church of Great St Mary's for her memorial service, more people were moved to grief than is usual on such University occasions. The reason was, of course, in part her youth – the early death of a mother of three young sons and a scholar with so much distinguished work still ahead of her was a tragic waste which was bound to make a profound impact. But the sense of real personal loss, too, was inordinately strong and widespread, for Ruth was a very special person.

She had something of the crisp, precise manner and diction popularly associated with the 'schoolmarm' and it could never have surprised anyone to discover that she was indeed a teacher. But this impression was misleading. In her approach to life in general Ruth was tolerant, amused, and unshockable. It was her highly developed and easily provoked sense of humour which stood her in good stead in the difficult, day-to-day task of combining all her different roles – as wife, mother, scholar, University Lecturer, college supervisor, and Director of Studies – without letting the strain show. She had the gift, essential in successful women, of having her priorities yet seeming to sacrifice nothing to them. Successful women themselves know that this is not a gift at all but a hard-won skill and Ruth never hid from her friends the cost to her of this achievement; one of her outstanding characteristics was her honesty. But she believed absolutely in woman's right to a career and in woman's duty to that career once embarked upon. Her commitment to her teaching and her research was complete. Yet she was by no means a doctrinaire feminist nor, for that matter, a doctrinaire anything else. She made no assumptions about how other people should live their lives.

Surprisingly, perhaps, for a scholar engaged by preference in research of the meticulous, painstaking sort, Ruth had a cheerfully irreverent attitude to the paperwork generated by academic administration. Her great strength in education lay in her relations with her students and in her teaching itself. Here she did show intolerance, but only with the intellectual laziness, sloppiness, and irresponsibility which she so detested. Her standards were exacting and she suffered fools not at all, but she had the born teacher's knack of reprimanding students – often very fiercely – without losing their affection. Her relations with her students were indeed unusually good, in spite of the fact that most never quite overcame their awe of her. She took great pleasure in their company, treating them as equals without feeling the need to adopt a 'Look, I'm one of you' attitude, and with many of them she established close, lasting friendships.

She was the very best sort of colleague: frank, supportive, and loyal, with none of the faults – envy, small-mindedness, meanness of spirit – so often to be found in our enclosed world. She could disagree without resentment, argue without rancour, and her instincts were always generous. She had a remarkably clear, logical mind with an impressive capacity for reasoned thought and lucid exposition which sped along many a meeting threatening to collapse into woolliness. On top of all this, she was excellent company, with an enviable memory for anecdotes and jokes and an endearing fondness for excruciating puns, which enlivened many a combination-room conversation. Essentially a gregarious person, she had a natural ease of manner, which was invaluable in getting tongue-tied new students to relax at beginning-of-the-year gatherings. She was a devout Catholic convert, and her faith as well as her job and her family brought a very wide circle of acquaintances – one was as likely to meet a gynaecologist or a priest as an academic when one went to dinner – to whom she was enormously hospitable. Students, too, who called at her house to deliver an essay often found themselves staying to supper.

Without being an emphatic or self-assertive person, Ruth made a very distinctive impression. Her voice was rich and low, her speech precise and measured, her handwriting neat but bold, her step long, even, and firm. Her true personality was captured more accurately by her crisply curling hairstyle of later years than by the somewhat severe topknot which she used to wear. There was certainly an austere, self-denying side to Ruth – she indulged less in feminine finery than most women – but this was due to her sense of the relative importance of things rather than to disapproval or lack of interest. In fact she liked attractive clothes, and indeed often had things made to her own specifications; she was attached to her pretty pieces of Victorian jewellery; she discarded her spectacles for contact-lenses and even, after years of indecision (and, it had to be said, contradictory advice from her friends), had her ears pierced. Nonetheless, if asked to choose between the gift of a beautiful ring and that of an illuminated Book of Hours, she would not have hesitated to choose the latter.

The courage, dignity and honesty with which she faced her death were a chastening example to us all. She never pretended that she did not mind dying, but neither did she succumb to anger or self-pity. Sustained by her faith, she prepared for death in the outwardly calm, organised way in which she had always coped with life. Her loss is incalculable, and it is no comfort to be reminded that it is the good who die young. It is a comfort, however, to remember what she was and what she added to so many lives. The essays which follow are a tribute to her scholarship and to her contribution to the mediaeval studies to which she was so devoted. But the greater and more lasting tribute will be the special place which she will always occupy in the hearts and memories of those who knew and loved her.

Publications by Margaret Ruth Morgan

SARAH KAY

1969   Dictionary articles in *The Penguin Companion to Literature, Vol. 2: European*, ed. Anthony Thorlby (London 1969)
Articles on: Albert of Aix, Fredegar, Fulcher of Chartres, *Gesta Francorum*, Giles de Paris, Gottschalk, Matthew of Vendôme, Maurice de Sully, Nithard, Oliver of Paderborn, Raymond of Agiles, Robert the Monk, Tudeboeuf, Walter of Antioch

1970   Review: Michael Altschul, *Anglo-Norman England 1066–1154* (Cambridge 1970), in *Notes & Queries*, October 1970, p. 385

1972   Review: *Geoffroy de Villehardouin: La Conquête de Constantinople*, ed. Jean Dufournet (Paris 1969), in *French Studies* 26 (1972), 60–1

1973   Monograph: *The Chronicle of Ernoul and the Continuations of William of Tyre*, Oxford Historical Monographs (London: Oxford University Press 1973). x + 204 pp. Includes Bibliography and Index.

This work of major historical and literary importance was the subject of numerous reviews:
H[ans] E[berhard] M[ayer], *Deutsches Archiv für Erforschung des Mittelalters* 30 (1974), 252–4;
Marshall W. Baldwin, *American Historical Review* 80 (1975), 953;
Steven Runciman, *English Historical Review* 90 (1975), 424–5;
G. A. Usher, *French Studies* 29 (1975), 179–80;
Hans Eberhard Mayer, *Historische Zeitschrift* 22 (1975), 144–5;
John France, *Medium Ævum* 44 (1975), 409–10;
Jean Richard, *Le moyen âge*, 4e série 30 (1975), 527–8;
Suzanne Duparc, *Cahiers de civilisation médiévale* 19 (1976), 185–6;
W. Rothwell, *Revue belge de philologie et d'histoire* 54 (1976), 650–1;
Anne Iker-Gittleman, *Romance Philology* 30 (1976–7), 679–81;
R. B. C. Huygens, *Speculum* 52 (1977), 409–10.

1976   Reviews:
Jonathan Riley-Smith, *The Feudal Nobility in the Kingdom of Jerusalem* (London 1973), in *Medium Ævum* 45 (1976), 135–7

R. F. Cook & Larry S. Crist, *Le Deuxième Cycle de la Croisade. Deux études sur son développement*, Publications romanes et françaises 120 (Geneva 1972) and

Saladin: suite et fin du deuxième Cycle de la Croisade, ed. Larry S. Crist, Textes littéraires français 185 (Geneva 1972), in *Medium Ævum* 45 (1976), 133–5

1979   Article: 'The meanings of Old French *polain*, Latin *pullanus*', *Medium Ævum* 48 (1979), 40–54

Reviews:

J. Dufournet, *Villehardouin et Clari. Les Ecrivains de la IVe croisade*, I (Paris 1973), and Paul Archambault, *Seven French Chroniclers* (Syracuse, NY 1974), in *French Studies* 33 (1979), 58–60

R. F. Cook & Larry S. Crist, *Le Deuxième Cycle de la Croisade* (see above, 1976). *Ibid.*, 324–6

1980   Review: Jonathan Riley-Smith, *What Were the Crusades?* (London 1977), in *Medium Ævum* 49 (1980), 170

1982   Edition: *La Continuation de Guillaume de Tyr*, Académie des Inscriptions et Belles Lettres: Documents relatifs à l'histoire des croisades 14 (Paris: Geuthner 1982). vi + 220 pp.

Reviews of the above (to 1985):
H[ans] E[berhard] M[ayer], *Deutsches Archiv für Erforschung des Mittelalters* 39 (1983), 245;
J. A. Brundage, *Speculum* 59 (1984), 987–8;
Suzanne Duparc-Quioc, *Bibliothèque de l'Ecole des Chartes* 142 (1984), 163–5.

Article: 'The Rothelin continuation of William of Tyre', in *Outremer: Studies in the History of the Crusading Kingdom of Jerusalem presented to Joshua Prawer*, edd. B. Z. Kedar, H. E. Mayer, & R. C. Smail (Jerusalem: Yad Izhak Ben Zvi Institute 1982) 244–57

Review: *Le Voyage d'Oultremer en Jherusalem de Nompar, seigneur de Caumont*, ed. Peter S. Noble, Medium Ævum Monographs, n.s. 7 (Oxford 1975), in *Medium Ævum* 51 (1982), 123–4

Insular manuscripts of Origen in the Carolingian empire

CAROLINE BAMMEL

The first and arguably the most important period of British influence on the continent was that of the Irish and Anglo-Saxon missions of the seventh and eighth centuries. From Columbanus's arrival in Gaul and his monastic foundations at Luxeuil (590) and Bobbio (614), from the missionary journeys of Willibrord and Boniface in Germany to the period of Alcuin's activity as Charles the Great's literary and educational adviser, Irish and Anglo-Saxon monks, missionaries and scholars played a leading role in the cultural life of Europe.[1] The part of their contribution with which the present paper is concerned is their collecting and copying of books and their building-up of libraries.[2] The importance of Insular manuscripts in the transmission of Latin texts has been emphasised more often in connexion with Classical writers than with church fathers.[3] It may therefore be worth looking at the transmission of one of the major Patristic writers, Origen, for signs of Insular influence.

When Cassiodorus drew up a list of the books in the library of his monastery of Vivarium, at Squillace in the far south of Italy, soon after the middle of the sixth century, he was able to include Latin translations of homilies by Origen on Genesis, Exodus, Leviticus, Numbers, Deuteronomy, Joshua, Judges, I and II Kings, II Chronicles, Jeremiah, and the Song of Songs, and commentaries on the Song of Songs and on Romans. He also listed a translation of homilies on Esdras made by Bellator.[4] Of these items the translation by Bellator, the homilies on Deuteronomy and II Chronicles, and all but one of those on I and II Kings are

---

[1] Cf. Levison, 'Die Iren' and *England and the Continent*; Prinz, *Frühes Mönchtum*; Bischoff, 'Il Monachesimo'; also the relevant contributions in *Die Iren und Europa*, ed. Löwe.

[2] Cf. Levison, *England and the Continent*, pp.132ff.; Prinz, *Frühes Mönchtum*, pp. 514ff.; Bischoff, 'Scriptoria e manoscritti', 'Panorama der Handschriftenüberlieferung' and 'Irische Schreiber'.

[3] Cf. Reynolds and Wilson, *Scribes and Scholars*, pp. 77ff. and 226ff.; Bischoff, 'Paläographie und frühmittelalterliche Klassikerüberlieferung', p. 58, n. 8; Reynolds, *Texts*, pp. xx–xxi and 495.

[4] Cassiodorus, *Institutiones*, ed. Mynors, references in the index, p. 191, under Origenes. The numbers of homilies indicated by Cassiodorus do not agree in every case with those of the surviving homilies.

now lost.[5] There survive the remaining translations listed by Cassiodorus (the homilies on the Song of Songs and on Jeremiah translated by Jerome, the rest by Rufinus) and, in addition, translations by Jerome of homilies on Isaiah, Ezekiel and Luke, translations by Rufinus of homilies on Psalms xxxvi–xxxviii and of Origen's *De principiis*, and an anonymous translation of part of the commentary on Matthew.[6] All except the homilies on the Psalms and the commentary on Romans have received critical editions in the Berlin Corpus.[7] Most of these translations were well known in the period of the Carolingian renaissance and widely diffused in ninth-century libraries.[8] Their transmission before that period varies from work to work.

Important for the purposes of the present paper are the homilies on Numbers and on Luke and the commentaries on the Song of Songs and on Romans. The editor of the Old Testament homilies and of the commentary on the Song of Songs, W. A. Baehrens,[9] conjectured that the archetypes of our manuscripts of the homilies on Genesis, Exodus, Leviticus, Numbers, Joshua, and Judges, and perhaps also of the homilies and commentary on the Song of Songs (but not those of the homily on I Kings (I Samuel) or of the homilies on the prophets) were identical with the copies in Cassiodorus's library. This theory was put forward at a time when the attempt to find traces of Cassiodorus's library in extant manuscripts was fashionable.[10] The arguments used to support it, however, are not conclusive, and the evidence from the transmission of the commentary

---

5   The surviving homily on I Kings (I Samuel) is thought to be translated by Rufinus. Rufinus expresses his intention of translating the homilies on Deuteronomy in the epilogue to his translation of the commentary on Romans and again in the prologue to that of the homilies on Numbers (ed. Simonetti, *Opera*, pp. 277 and 285).
6   This translation is thought to have been made by an Arian in the second quarter of the fifth century in north Italy or the Danube provinces: see Frede, *Kirchenschriftsteller. Verzeichnis und Sigel*, pp. 465–6, and *Kirchenschriftsteller: Aktualisierungsheft*, p. 76.
7   Die Griechischen Christlichen Schriftsteller (= G.C.S.). Studies of the transmission of the various works appeared in *Texte und Untersuchungen* (= T.U.). The transmission of Rufinus's translation of the commentary on Romans is examined by Hammond, *The Manuscript Tradition*; Bammel, *Der Römerbrieftext*, pp.104ff.
8   The influence of Origen in the middle ages is discussed by de Lubac, *Exégèse médiévale*, I.221ff. For a general view of the early manuscript transmission, see Siegmund, *Die Überlieferung*, pp. 110–23.
9   His study of the transmission, published in T.U. 42.1 (1916), was somewhat hampered by conditions during the first world war and by the sheer size of the task undertaken. The editions appeared subsequently with briefer, but in some cases improved, discussions of the transmission in their introductions: G.C.S., *Origenes*, vi (1920); G.C.S., *Origenes*, vii (1921); G.C.S., *Origenes*, viii (1925).
10 The theory that the Vivarium manuscripts found their way to Bobbio was propounded in 1911 by R. Beer, *Bemerkungen*. It was rejected by Lowe, *Codices* IV. xxvi–xxvii: 'the entire theory . . . is built on the naive assumption that Cassiodorus is the only man of late antiquity who could have possessed so large and varied a collection'. For a different view, see Courcelle, *Les lettres grecques*, pp. 342ff. (accepting Baehrens's theory and suggesting that Vivarium manuscripts were dispersed via the Lateran library). The manuscript Leningrad Q.v.1.6–10 (Lowe, *Codices*, XI.1614), thought by Dobiache-Rojdestvensky (*Speculum* 5 [1930], pp. 21–48) to be a product of Vivarium, is for the

on Romans, which was also present in Cassiodorus's library, is unfavourable to such a hypothesis, since the earliest surviving manuscript of this work (Lyons, Bibliothèque municipale, MS. 483, *saec.* v) is earlier than the time of Cassiodorus, while others descend independently from a yet earlier archetype.[11] The contents of Cassiodorus's library no doubt represented a selection of what was available in Rome at the time he assembled it, and it would seem a priori more likely that extant manuscripts with similar contents to those he describes share a common ancestor with copies at Vivarium than that they are directly descended from such copies. In the case of the works of Origen the failures to coincide with what now survives are perhaps more striking than the agreements.

Another attempt to link the early transmission of Latin translations of Origen with a known library was made by Paul Koetschau, the editor of Rufinus's translation of the *De principiis*.[12] Manuscripts of one of the two main branches of the transmission of this work (Koetschau's group γ) have preserved copies of subscriptions going back to an exemplar which was owned and read by the deacon Donatus at Castellum Lucullanum, near Naples, in 562. A similar subscription by the same Donatus still survives in the sixth-century Monte Cassino, Biblioteca dell' Abbazia, MS. 150 of Ambrosiaster's Pauline commentary, the lost beginning of which was replaced in the late eighth or early ninth century by a copy of part of the beginning of Origen's commentary on Romans.[13] Koetschau conjectured that the archetype of the *De principiis* manuscripts belonged to the library of Eugippius at Castellum Lucullanum, and Baehrens, following Koetschau and referring also to the subscription in Monte Cassino 150, supposed that the transmission of the translations made by Rufinus originated in Campania and that of those made by Jerome in Rome.[14] It should not be forgotten, however, that both Rufinus and Jerome had strong links also with the area of Aquileia in north-east Italy, that the various translations were made at different times and for different dedicatees, and that both Rufinus and Jerome had friends in various areas who would have been likely to collect copies of their works.[15]

Consultation of the index of E. A. Lowe's monumental work on Latin manu-

---

homilies of Origen on the Song of Songs 'keineswegs die Vorlage der anderen Hss.' (G.C.S., *Origenes*, viii, p. xiv; T.U. 42.1, p.160).

11 Baehrens held the view that the archetypes of the manuscripts of the Old Testament homilies contained double readings derived from a revision in Cassiodorus's library. It would be possible to cite similar evidence for the commentary on Romans, but here it is necessary to argue either that parallel corrections were made independently in different branches of the transmission or that there were double readings already in Rufinus's own copy of the work; cf. Bammel, *Römerbrieftext*, pp.136ff., 160ff.

12 G.C.S., *Origenes*, v (1913).

13 *Ibid.*, p. lx. Monte Cassino 150 is described by Lowe, *Codices*, III.374. Cf. Bammel, 'Products', III, p. 442, n. 2, pp. 445–6, and 'Products', IV, pp. 366–7. Somewhat similar in script to the sixth-century part of Monte Cassino 150 are the Orléans fragments (described by Lowe as south Italian) of Origen on Leviticus, not used by Baehrens: cf. Lowe, *Codices*, VI.819; X, p. 43; Suppl., p. 3.

14 T.U. 42.1, pp. 194, 198, 230.

15 For details of Rufinus's translations, see Hammond, 'The last ten years', pp. 372ff. (with

scripts prior to the ninth century[16] reveals only one Origen item in Insular script. This is Würzburg, Universitätsbibliothek, M. p. th. f. 27 of Rufinus's translation of the homilies on Numbers, in Anglo-Saxon majuscule and minuscule of the second half of the eighth century.[17] It was written, according to Lowe, 'on the Continent, probably in Germany, but hardly at Würzburg'.[18] It may, however, have reached Würzburg by the ninth century, and it is presumably the manuscript or one of the manuscripts referred to by Bishop Hunbert (832–842), who states *habemus Origenem* in a letter to Rabanus Maurus, abbot of Fulda, asking for copies of the latter's biblical commentaries, in particular those on the Heptateuch.[19] Its text is in fact related to that used by Rabanus and may perhaps derive from an Insular manuscript at Fulda. The manuscripts of the homilies on Numbers were classified by Baehrens[20] into four groups plus two individual manuscripts, all going back to a common archetype. Würzburg, Universitätsbibliothek, M. p. th. f. 27 is the oldest representative of Baehrens's group D. The other members of this group are twelfth-century manuscripts at Bamberg and Leipzig and the text used for the extracts from Origen by Rabanus in his commentary on Numbers. Rabanus composed this work, it would seem, at Fulda during the stay there of Lupus of Ferrières (*ca* 828–836), since subscriptions in its manuscripts state that it was collated and corrected by Lupus and Gerolfus in accordance with Rabanus's instructions.[21] Baehrens argued that the archetype of his group D was in Insular script, on the grounds that the Insular symbols for *eius*, *con*, etc., are taken over from this exemplar in the Würzburg manuscript but sometimes supplemented by the first hand with the full forms above. He locates this archetype at Fulda because of the connexion with Rabanus.[22]

There does survive a Fulda manuscript of the ninth century which includes part of one of the homilies on Numbers, but this was not used by Baehrens. This is Kassel, Landesbibliothek, MS. theol. 2° 54, in which the first part of Homily 23 is added to fill a gap on fos 4v–8v. The main text of this manuscript is the

the table on pp. 428–9). Jerome's translations of Origen's homilies on Jeremiah and Ezekiel are thought to have been made about A.D.380 in Constantinople, of those on Isaiah perhaps later, of those on the Song of Songs for Damasus at Rome perhaps in 383, of those on Luke for Paula and Eustochium at Bethlehem about 390.

16 Lowe, *Codices*, Suppl., p. 76.
17 Lowe, *Codices*, IX.1407.
18 A similar view is expressed by Bischoff and Hofmann, *Libri Sancti Kyliani*, p. 10.
19 *Ibid.*, p. 149.
20 Cf. T.U. 42.1, pp. 81ff. and the introduction to his edition, G.C.S., *Origenes*, vii, pp. ix–xix.
21 Cf. Manitius, *Geschichte*, I.483–4.
22 T.U. 42.1, pp. 88–90. He also argues from the fact that errors involving the misreading of *f* and *p* occur in the Bamberg and Würzburg manuscripts, referring to the illustration of the Fulda cartulary in Steffens, *Lateinische Paläographie*, pl. 54, for a script in which these letters are similar. This was written in or after 828, so considerably later than the Würzburg manuscript; see also Spilling, 'Angelsächsische Schrift in Fulda', especially p. 77. The incorrect description of the script as Irish in T.U. 42.1, p. 90, was dropped from the introduction to the edition, p. xiii.

Book of Wisdom in an Anglo-Saxon hand from Fulda of the third decade of the ninth century. The Origen pages are in Caroline minuscule of about the same date. On the outside pages the *Hildebrandslied* was added in two Fulda hands of the fourth decade of the ninth century writing in Caroline minuscule with 'certain insular reminiscences'.[23]

Unrelated to the branch of the transmission just described is the text of a set of extracts from the homilies on Numbers attributed to Jerome and following Jerome on the Psalms in the Insular manuscript, London, British Library, MS. Royal 4.A.xiv.[24] Lowe dated the Anglo-Saxon minuscule script of this manuscript to the end of the tenth century and suggested a connexion with Winchester.[25] The text of the Origen extracts is, according to Baehrens, related to that of his group C, whose earliest members are French manuscripts of the eleventh and twelfth centuries.[26]

Fulda was important also for the transmission of Jerome's translation of the homilies on Luke.[27] In this case the Fulda manuscript itself survives as Florence, Biblioteca Laurenziana, MS. S. Marco 610. This manuscript contains the homilies on Luke only and is written in Anglo-Saxon minuscule script from the beginning of the second quarter of the ninth century:[28] that is, during the period when Rabanus was abbot (and considerably later than the lost archetype of Baehrens's group D of the homilies on Numbers). A twelfth-century copy is preserved in another Fulda manuscript, Kassel, Landesbibliothek, MS. theol. 2° 49, where it is bound together with Origen's homilies on I Kings, the Song of Songs, Isaiah, Jeremiah and Ezekiel in ninth-century Caroline minuscule, and Fulgentius's *Mythologiae*, also in script of the ninth century.[29] A sister manuscript to S. Marco 610 is one of the few surviving manuscripts in the Laon az minuscule

---

[23] On this manuscript (and its adventures after 1945), see Fischer, *Schrifttafeln*, pp. 14*–15*; Bischoff, *Mittelalterliche Studien*, III.87. Lehmann drew attention to this, and other manuscripts not used by Baehrens, in his review of T.U. 42.1. Baehrens included it in a footnote in the introduction to his edition (p. xii, n.1).

[24] Cf. Warner and Gilson, *British Museum: Catalogue*, I.81–2; fo 36 is illustrated in volume IV (Pl. 34). The manuscript was used by Morin in his edition of Jerome on the Psalms, which is reprinted in C.C.L. lxxviii. ii (Turnhout, 1958); cf. pp. xvi–xvii and xxi.

[25] Lowe, *Codices*, II.216 (where the earlier fly-leaves are described and illustrated).

[26] T.U., 42.1, p. 97; cf. pp. 90ff.

[27] The transmission is described by Rauer, *Form und Überlieferung*, and in the introduction to his edition, G.C.S., *Origenes*, ix (²Berlin, 1959). In this second, revised edition Rauer takes up the suggestions made by Paul Lehmann in his review of the first edition in *Berliner Philologische Wochenschrift* 50 (1930), 1475–80.

[28] Its script is described and dated ('wohl zu Beginn des zweiten Jahrhundertviertels') by Spilling, 'Angelsächsische Schrift', with an illustration of fo 1r on p. 81 (pl.19).

[29] This manuscript and a number of other writings of Origen are listed in the sixteenth-century Fulda library catalogues; cf. Christ, *Die Bibliothek des Klosters Fulda*, pp. 92–4, 174ff., 255, 298. Perhaps also copied or descended from the ninth-century Fulda manuscript (E) is the twelfth-century manuscript Admont, Stiftsbibliothek, MS.112 (B). The Kassel manuscript (N) has had corrections added by a later hand from either B itself or the exemplar from which B was copied (according to Rauer, G.C.S.,

script: Cambridge, Corpus Christi College, MS. 334, of the eighth century.[30]
Lowe described this script as 'no more than an offshoot of the Luxeuil minuscule
type', and remarked that manuscripts in it show marked Insular symptoms and
some connexions with Corbie.[31] On the grounds of the Insular influence on the
script and the observation that Insular symptoms occur in two other less closely
related manuscripts of the work (Douai, Bibliothèque municipale, MS. 231, and
Troyes, Bibliothèque municipale, MS. 390 (from Clairvaux), both of the twelfth
century), Paul Lehmann[32] argued for the likelihood that the transmission from
the eighth century onwards derived from an Insular centre or at least was transmitted largely via Irish and Anglo-Saxon manuscripts. He pointed out that the
late ninth-century Bobbio catalogue lists a copy of the work.[33] In view of the fact
that Corpus Christi 334 derives from north France, one possibility is that the
transmission proceeded from Bobbio via north France and on from there to
Fulda.

It is only for the homilies on Numbers and Luke that Insular manuscripts still
survive, but there is evidence of lost exemplars – making use of Insular abbrevia-
tion-symbols – for two other works, the commentary on the Song of Songs and
the commentary on Romans. For the commentary on the Song of Songs in
Rufinus's translation Baehrens was only able to find manuscripts of the eleventh
century and later. He divided the transmission into four groups, the earliest of
which (A) he labelled the Bavarian-Austrian and North Italian group. The
manuscripts of the Bavarian-Austrian subdivision of this group agree in a number
of errors which derive from misunderstanding of Insular symbols (confusion of
autem and *enim*, of *autem* and *hoc*, and of *per* and *post*, omission of *autem*, *enim*,
eius, and *uel*). Baehrens therefore argued that the common ancestor of the A
group was in Irish script or in a script 'mixed with many Irish elements'. He also
suggested more tentatively that the archetype of all four groups was in a script
influenced by Irish practice, supporting this with examples of the omission of
enim and *eius* and confusion of *quod* and *quam* in his group D.[34] In speculating
about centres of Irish influence from which the manuscripts of the A group could
have been disseminated, he took into consideration Sankt Gallen and Bobbio.[35]
Identification of the commentary on the Song of Songs in mediaeval library

Origenes, ix[2], p. xxiv). The stemma in the preface to G.C.S., *Origenes*, ix[2], p. xxxii,
differs markedly from that in T.U. 47.3, p. 14, and disagrees with Rauer's other statements in the position which it gives to B.

[30] *Codices*, II.128.

[31] *Ibid.*, VI.xviii. For details, see Lindsay, 'The Laon AZ-Type', pp. 15–27.

[32] See above, n. 27. He is followed by Rauer in T.U. 47.3, pp. 16–17, and in G.C.S.,
Origenes, ix[2], p. xxxii.

[33] Becker, *Catalogi*, p. 66. According to Esposito, 'The ancient Bobbio catalogue', the
manuscript from which this catalogue was published (now lost) was a tenth-century
copy of a list drawn up in the second half of the ninth century, probably between 862
and 896.

[34] T.U. 42.1, pp. 137–8, 144, and 153.

[35] He was attacked by Siegmund, *Die Überlieferung*, p. 122, n.1.

catalogues is problematic, because a clear distinction is seldom made between this work and the much commoner homilies on the Song of Songs translated by Jerome. It may indeed be because of the existence of these more popular homilies that the work was less speedily and widely disseminated than most of the other translations of Origen. The late ninth-century Bobbio catalogue includes in its section *de Origenis libris* not only the homilies on Genesis, Exodus, Leviticus, Joshua, Judges and Luke, but also the surprising items *in primo libro regum homelias VI, de epiphania homelias II* and *in canticis canticorum libros II;* and, in the section on books presented by Dúngal, Origen on Genesis, on Romans and *in canticis canticorum librum I*.[36] Baehrens was inclined to regard this Dúngal manuscript as the ancestor of his group A,[37] but the manuscripts presented by Dúngal were not in Irish script, as is apparent from the surviving copy of Origen on Romans with Dúngal's dedication. This need not, however, exclude the possibility that another, earlier, Bobbio manuscript played a role in the transmission. For the possibility of dissemination from Sankt Gallen Baehrens referred for comparison to a branch of the transmission of the homilies on Leviticus descended from Sankt Gallen, Stiftsbibliothek, MS. 87,[38] only to reject such a hypothesis on the grounds that there is evidence that Rufinus's translation of the commentary was unknown there in the latter part of the ninth century. Notker Balbulus in his *Notatio* notes Jerome's praise of the commentary and expresses the desire that a translation should be made,[39] and the Sankt Gallen catalogue of the mid-ninth century does not include the Song of Songs under Origen in its main section. It is not impossible, however, that a lost Insular copy of the work lurks under an anonymous entry in the first section, *libri scottice scripti*, of the same catalogue: 'Expositio in cantica canticorum in quaternionibus II. item in regum quaternio I'.[40] Siegmund, who quoted this entry,[41] argued that in view of the length specified the *expositio* is likely to be the homilies rather than the commentary,[42] but one could get round this objection by suggesting either that the copy of Origen on the Song of Songs was no longer complete when the list was made or that, as in Cassiodorus's list and the Bobbio catalogue, more than one homily on Kings was included in the second item. Of other early mediaeval catalogue references the clearest is that in the fragmentary eleventh-century Corbie catalogue: *Epitalamium Origenis in Cantica Canticorum* (*Epithalamium* is the first word of the prologue to the commentary).[43]

For Rufinus's translation of the commentary on Romans we are fortunate

---

[36] Becker, *Catalogi*, pp. 66, 70.
[37] *T.U.* 42.1, p. 156.
[38] *T.U.* 42.1, p. 144; cf. pp. 52ff.
[39] *Formulae Salomonis*, ed. E. Dümmler (Leipzig, 1857), p. 6.18ff., quoted by Baehrens in the preface to G.C.S., *Origenes*, viii, p. xxvii.
[40] Lehmann, *Mittelalterliche Bibliothekskataloge*, I.76 and 71 (cf. also p. 84).
[41] *Die Überlieferung*, p. 112, n. 4.
[42] In the G.C.S. edition the homily on I Kings occupies pp. 1–25, those on the Song of Songs pp. 26–60, the commentary on the Song of Songs pp. 61–241.
[43] Delisle, *Le Cabinet*, II.105. Cf. also Siegmund, *Die Überlieferung*, pp. 112–15, s. nn.

enough to possess a fifth-century manuscript separated probably by only one intermediate copy from the exemplar in Rufinus's own library.[44] This manuscript, however (Lyons 483),[45] contains only the first five of the ten books of the work and has lost a number of pages at the beginning and the end. It would seem that in the early period the work was copied in two volumes. The surviving manuscripts of the ninth century and earlier either are incomplete or show a change of exemplar during the course of the work. The witnesses to the text may be divided into those descended from Lyons 483 (the vast majority) and those going back independently to the exemplar from which Lyons 483 was copied. Most of the descendants of Lyons 483 derive from a lost Insular manuscript (Φ), which played a key role in the transmission of the work. No complete manuscript survives which is not descended from Φ for some part of the work.

The manuscript Lyons 483 itself was in Verona in the early ninth century (where it was annotated by Pacificus of Verona).[46] The transmission of the translation originates, however, according to a notice reproduced on the title-page of the early ninth-century Saint-Amand manuscript (Copenhagen, Det Kongelige Bibliotek, Gl. Kgl. S. 1338. 4°), from a copy found in Rufinus's library after his death, which took place in Sicily in 411.[47] It would seem likely that disciples of Rufinus took a copy or copies of the work to Campania, where there were monasteries founded by his friends Pinian and Melania, and that Lyons 483 is a copy of such a copy, perhaps written by a north Italian scribe for export to north Italy.[48]

The lines of transmission independent of Lyons 483 may without implausibility be supposed to have branched out from Campania. These are represented by the following manuscripts and groups of manuscripts: (i) Monte Cassino 150 (pp.1–16, in south Italian Uncial script of the late eighth or early ninth century, contain Book I and the first half of Book II only);[49] (ii) Paris, Bibliothèque nationale, MS. nouv. acq. lat. 1629, fos 3–6, consisting of fragments from Books I and VI in seventh-century Italian Uncial script;[50] this manuscript had reached Fleury by the ninth century, and an eleventh-century copy for Books I–VI only survives in Orléans, Bibliothèque municipale, MS. 87; (iii) the lost exemplar from which the ninth-century manuscripts from Weissenburg (Wolfenbüttel, Herzog-August-Bibliothek, MS. Weissenb. 74 of the late eighth or early ninth

---

Gorze, Würzburg, Lobbes (n. 2), S. Riquier (with n. 3), Monte Cassino and Pomposa; also p.118.

[44] For detailed discussion of the transmission, see Hammond, *The Manuscript Tradition*, and, on the early manuscripts only, but with some corrections, Bammel, *Der Römerbrieftext*, pp. 104ff.

[45] Various features of Lyons 483 are described by Bammel, 'Products . . .', I–IV.

[46] Cf. Lowe, *Codices*, VI.779.

[47] Cf. Hammond, 'The Last Ten Years', p. 394, n. 3; p. 401, n. 2.

[48] Cf. Bammel, 'Products . . .', IV, pp. 347–59.

[49] Lowe, *Codices*, III.374b. On this manuscript, see above, p. 7.

[50] Lowe, *Codices*, V.690; Suppl. 1804. Cf. Bammel, 'Products . . .', III, p. 442, n. 1.

century),[51] Reichenau (Karlsruhe, Badische Landesbibliothek, MS. Aug. perg. 126 and 127) and Sankt Gallen (Sankt Gallen, Stiftsbibliothek, MS. 88) are copied or descended for Books VI–X only;[52] (iv) the text of a set of excerpts from Books I–V used by Claudius of Turin and transmitted in the twelfth-century manuscript Ithaca, N.Y., Cornell University Library, MS. B.12; (v) the joint-ancestor, for Books I–V only, of the early ninth-century Dúngal manuscript (Milan, Biblioteca Ambrosiana, MS. A.135 inf., given by Dúngal to the monastery of Bobbio, but copied already during his stay at Saint-Denis before 825)[53] and of a group of later, mostly Italian manuscripts, of which the earliest is Monte Cassino MS. 347 in Beneventan minuscule of the late eleventh century. The same source may be responsible for independent readings in the text of Books I–V in the early ninth-century Saint-Amand manuscript (Copenhagen, G. Kgl. S. 1338 4°). A second contaminated manuscript (London, British Library, MS. Harley 3030, perhaps from Cologne[54]), of the late eleventh century, may be descended from the sister-manuscript of Milan Ambr. A.135 inf. which was also an intermediate ancestor of the Italian group represented by Monte Cassino 347.

Of the witnesses dependent on Lyons 483 some are descended via only one joint intermediate ancestor (Ψ), others via two joint intermediate ancestors (Ψ and Φ). The lost manuscript Ψ was copied from Lyons 483 comparatively carefully, and its own script did not give rise to particular misreadings. We might imagine it to have been a manuscript similar to one of the two surviving sixth-century north Italian Half-uncial copies of Rufinus's translation of the Clementine Recognitions.[55] We have evidence of as many as six copies of Ψ, some for both halves of the work, others for only the first or the second half. The lost Insular manuscript Φ was probably copied direct from Ψ for both halves of the work.[56] A set of excerpts from Books V–VII and IX, transmitted in manuscripts of the late eighth and the ninth century from Saint-Amand and Benediktbeuern, is derived from a copy or descendant of Ψ.[57] For the first half of the work only the

---

[51] Lowe, *Codices*, IX.1390.
[52] It is tempting to see a parallel between this independent branch of the transmission and that of Rufinus's translation of *De principiis*, the leading group of which is represented by ninth-century manuscripts from Weissenburg and Reichenau: see Bammel, *Der Römerbrieftext*, p. 107, n.10, and 'Products . . .', IV, pp. 366–7.
[53] According to Bischoff, *Mittelalterliche Studien*, III. 230–1.
[54] According to Andrew G. Watson, 'An early thirteenth-century low countries booklist', p. 43 and p. 45 n. 31.
[55] Milan, Biblioteca Ambrosiana, MS. C.77 sup. (used for rewriting at Bobbio in the eighth century), and Verona, Biblioteca Capitolare, XXXVII: see Lowe, *Codices*, III. 318, IV.493.
[56] It would be possible to think in terms of more than one intermediate copy (Ψ1 and Ψ2) between Lyons 483 and Φ (if, for example, one found the number and distribution of copies of Ψ posited to be implausible). The second intermediate copy would, however, in this case have been a careful, accurate, and legible one. One might think in terms of a manuscript similar to the recently discovered Insular fragment of Rufinus's continuation of Eusebius's *Ecclesiastical History* (cf. *Mediaeval Studies* 47 [1985] no. 1864).
[57] Vienna, Österreichische Nationalbibliothek, MS. 795 (from Saint-Amand) and Mu-

early ninth-century manuscript Paris, BN, MS. latin 12124 (from Corbie, written *ca* A.D. 800 in a centre in north-east France) and the twelfth-century Admont, Stiftsbibliothek, MS. 112 are descended independently of each other from Ψ. For the second half of the work only the early ninth-century Saint-Amand manuscript and the joint ancestor of the Dungal manuscript and later related manuscripts would seem to have been copied direct from Ψ.

The lost Insular manuscript Φ of the commentary on Romans has left the earliest traces of its existence in north-east France, where two surviving incomplete (probably direct) copies were made at the beginning of the ninth century. The first of these is Paris 12124, which is copied from Φ in Books VI–X and, as has just been mentioned, is descended independently from Ψ in Books I–V. The second is Manchester, John Rylands University Library, MS. lat. 174, from Beauvais, containing only the first six books of the work. Also directly descended from Φ are (i) the text used by Sedulius Scottus for the excerpts in his *Collectanea in epistolas Pauli*; (ii) the exemplar of the early ninth-century Saint-Amand manuscript for Books I–V only (this exemplar included conjectural emendations of which some appear also in the contaminated manuscript London, British Library, MS. Harley 3030); and (iii) a number of later manuscripts including Douai Bibliothèque municipale 204 (of the twelfth century). Other descendants of Φ have an intermediate common ancestor. These include (i) the text used by Rabanus Maurus in his commentary on the Pauline epistles; (ii) a group of French manuscripts whose earliest representatives are Avranches Bibliothèque municipale 32 (of the late ninth or early tenth century, from Saint-Mesmin de Micy near Orléans) and Orléans 87 (from Fleury) for Books VII–X only (this part of the manuscript was written in the ninth century); and (iii) a group of manuscripts led by Karlsruhe, Badische Landesbibliothek, MS. Aug. perg. 126 (written at Reichenau in the second quarter of the ninth century) for Books I–V only, and Sankt Gallen 88 (Books I–VI only, of the late ninth century).

That the lost manuscript Φ was written by an Insular scribe is shown by the fact that its various descendants contain frequent errors caused by the misunderstanding of Insular abbreviations.[58] Thus *enim/autem/is/hoc/haec* are confused, as also are *quam/quod/quia, tantum/tamen* and *ergo/igitur* (and *per* is misread as *post* by the scribe of Paris 12124 and as *is* by the scribe of Rylands 174). Confusion of the letters *u/a, s/p* and *r/p* also occurs. The manuscripts Paris 12124 and Rylands 174 share misspellings probably derived from Φ, including the confusion of *s* and *ss*, of *e* and *i*, of *o* and *u*, of *c* and *qu*, of *b* and *p*, and of *d* and *t*, and addition or omission of the letter *h*. It is clear from the evidence of its descendants that the scribe of Φ used very heavy abbreviation of familiar words (for example, *apōs* = *apostolus* and cases, *mor̄* = both *mortuus* and *mors* and cases) and also in biblical

nich, Bayerische Staatsbibliothek, Clm 14500, perhaps from Niederaltaich: see Bischoff, *Die südostdeutschen Schreibschulen*, II.7, n. 18; p. 116.

58 The evidence summarised in the following paragraph is illustrated fully by Hammond, *The Manuscript Tradition*.

quotations and in lists. These abbreviated forms are often preserved unaltered in the earliest descendants of Φ and have been supplemented, sometimes incorrectly, in later representatives of the group. A further characteristic of Φ was the substitution of the word *usque* for the central part of long biblical quotations. Evidence for direct copying from an Insular exemplar appears not only in the north-east French manuscripts Paris 12124 and Rylands 174, but also in the Reichenau manuscript Karlsruhe Aug. perg. 126, which is separated from Φ by two intermediate copies. It seems likely, therefore, that these two intermediate copies, the first of which was the source of Rabanus's text and the second of which was used at Reichenau, were also Insular manuscripts.

A number of points of interest are worth noting in connexion with the early transmission of the commentary on Romans. First, it would seem clear that copies of the work descended from Φ were already widely diffused in the Carolingian empire before the superior texts represented by the Dúngal manuscript in Books I–V and the Saint-Amand manuscript in Books VI–X became available. Secondly, it is striking that the evidence for late eighth- or early ninth-century interest in the use of a better exemplar and for a thorough collation of one text with another appears only in one closely interconnected group of manuscripts, whose complicated interrelations may be tentatively described as follows. The Saint-Amand manuscript in Books I–V is copied from an exemplar of the group Φ which had incorporated independent readings probably derived from the common exemplar of the Dúngal manuscript and a lost 'sister'-manuscript which was the ancestor of Harley 3030 and of the group of Italian manuscripts led by Monte Cassino 347. The lost 'sister' of the Dúngal manuscript was itself the source of corrections entered in the text of the Saint-Amand manuscript, while its copy (a 'niece' of the Dúngal manuscript), from which Harley 3030 is descended, was corrected from a manuscript of the group Φ similar in text to the exemplar of the Saint-Amand manuscript. In Books VI–X it would seem that both the Saint-Amand manuscript and the common exemplar of the other manuscripts just mentioned were direct copies of Ψ (or of a very accurate copy of Ψ), but, whereas the Saint-Amand manuscript follows Ψ to the end of the work, the common ancestor of the other manuscripts switches to an exemplar from group Φ from near the beginning of Book X onwards. It is tempting to connect the activity reflected in these manuscripts with the group of scholars close to the court of Charles the Great, perhaps also to imagine that one of the lost exemplars was the copy used by Alcuin, who cites the commentary on Romans in his *Adversus haeresim Felicis*[59] and uses the same title for it (*tractatus*, not *explanationes*, *expositio*, or *commentarii*) as appears in the Dúngal manuscript, Harley 3030 and Monte Cassino 347.

A further point of interest is that the main branch of the transmission stretching from Lyons 483 to the early ninth century shows various interconnexions suggesting that the world in which it was carried was a small one. Descendants of

---

[59] Migne, *Patrologia Latina*, CI. 110B–C.

Ψ and Φ meet and form new combinations both in the manuscripts just described and also in Paris 12124, in which Books VI–X are copied from Φ and Books I–V descended from Ψ via an intermediate copy which used the Merovingian symbol for *per* (giving rise to confusion with *pro*).[60] It is difficult to escape the conclusion that the transmission from north Italy to north-east France was mediated by an important and well known centre having links with both areas and also Insular connexions, and that the hypothesis of transmission via Bobbio suggested by Paul Lehmann for the homilies on Luke is in fact correct for the commentary on Romans.

Finally, it may be worth briefly comparing the transmission of the different translations of Origen. It is clear that the transmission of each individual work took a separate course, as was the case even with the early transmission of the two halves of the commentary on Romans. Nonetheless certain parallels do exist, if only because it happened from time to time that a particular scholar or a particular centre (such as Fulda, Saint-Amand or Lorsch) took trouble to form a substantial collection of the writings of Origen. It may be suggested that the subsequent history of the translations made by Rufinus was affected by the time and place of their completion. *De principiis* was translated in south Italy and its transmission derives from Castellum Lucullanum. The homilies on Numbers and probably also the commentary on the Song of Songs (left unfinished) were translated shortly before Rufinus's death in Sicily, and one might suppose that copies were transported by his disciples together with the commentary on Romans via Campania to north Italy, from where Insular scholars later brought them north of the Alps. The transmission of Jerome's translation of the homilies on Luke might well have originated in north Italy too. Other Old Testament homilies, translated by Rufinus before the commentary on Romans, were available already in the south of France by the early seventh century (this is the date of the manuscript Lyons 443 of the homilies on Genesis, Exodus, and Leviticus and of Leningrad, Publichnaja Biblioteka, Q.v.1.2 of those on Leviticus and Joshua).[61] Perhaps this is the reason why there is no evidence for Insular intermediaries in their diffusion within the Carolingian empire.[62]

---

[60] Cf. Bammel, *Der Römerbrieftext*, p. 130.
[61] Cf. Baehrens, G.C.S., *Origenes*, vi (1920), p. xxiv. The early transmission of the Old Testament homilies requires a thorough reinvestigation.
[62] The indirect transmission of the translations of Origen cannot be discussed here. Not every case of citation or use of Origen can be linked to the known manuscript transmission, sometimes because of lack of evidence, sometimes because the branch concerned represented a dead end. Evidence for Insular use inside and outside the British Isles includes the following: the homilies on Genesis by Bede and Alcuin, the homilies on Isaiah and commentary on Romans by Alcuin, the homilies on Leviticus in the (Irish) Penitential of Cummeanus, *De principiis*, and the commentary on Romans by Johannes Scottus. Works of Origen are used in a number of the texts described by Bischoff, 'Wendepunkte' (nos 1, 3, 22, 29, 30, 33). For some further details, see Frede, *Kirchenschriftsteller*, *sub* RUF, ORI and HI; Ogilvy, *Books*, p. 65; Laistner, 'Some early mediaeval commentaries', pp. 27ff.; de Lubac, *Exégèse*, pp. 207ff.; Chatillon, 'Isidore et Origène'.

A French metamorphosis of an English grammatical genre:
declinationes into *terminationes*

VIVIEN LAW

During the seventh and eighth centuries missionaries from the British Isles brought christianity, books and learning to their newly founded monasteries in northern and eastern France and east of the Rhine. In instructing the Germanic peoples of the Continent they naturally continued to rely upon the teaching-aids – grammars, glossaries, and glossed psalters – on which they had been brought up at home in England and Ireland. The basic task, after all, was the same: to introduce a population of Germanic mother-tongue to the language of the Church, Latin. Without Latin there could be no study of christian doctrine, no services and, at the most basic level, no literacy. This problem was one which had been faced before by both Anglo-Saxons and Irishmen. Since the grammar-books of the later Roman empire – the works of Donatus, Priscian, Sergius, and many others – were addressed to native speakers of Latin, they failed to teach what foreigners needed most urgently, the forms of Latin. In the course of the seventh century the first grammars designed for non-native students appear. These elementary foreign-language grammars are characterised by an overriding concern with Latin morphology: the inflecting parts of speech are exhaustively exemplifed, both through paradigms and in lists of examples.[1] A sort of complementary pedagogical aid – scarcely a grammar in the full sense of the word – was devised in parallel, comprising a collection of paradigms and examples with almost no continuous text. Such material – rather similar to the reference-tables included at the end of many modern school-grammars – typically went under the title *Declinationes nominum*.[2] In each declension the author sought to illustrate as

---

[1] On elementary grammars, see Law, *Insular Latin Grammarians*, pp. 53–80.
[2] *Ibid.*, pp. 56–64. Material from versions of the *Declinationes nominum* was incorporated into elementary grammars by two Anglo-Saxon authors working around 700, Boniface and Tatwine, and into Aldhelm's *De pedum regulis*. In addition, the copy of the *Declinationes nominum* in Oxford, Bodleian Library, MS Add. C.144, an eleventh-century manuscript from Italy, shows signs of having been copied from a seventh-century English exemplar.

many sub-categories as he could devise: nouns of each gender, of every possible termination or derivational suffix, of native, Greek, or Hebrew origin. When the first declension was typically represented by five paradigms, each with its own list of examples, the second by eight, and the third by thirty or more, it is clear that the various texts which circulated under the heading of *Declinationes nominum* were more like reference-works or vocabulary-building aids than like modern teaching-grammars.

Transported to the Continent, versions of the *Declinationes nominum* proliferated. Every copyist adapted it to suit his own requirements, rearranging the paradigms, adding examples from other sources, conjoining texts on the declension of pronouns or the conjugation of verbs. It is to these Continental copies of the late eighth and the ninth centuries that we owe our knowledge of the work, for, as is often the case with early Anglo-Latin texts, no copy made in England has come down to us. Even as these Continental copies were being made, however, a new movement was beginning which was to have a rapid and far-reaching effect on grammatical pedagogy. Scholars based at Charlemagne's court did not scorn the humble subject of grammar. On the contrary, three of them – Alcuin, Paulus Diaconus, and Peter of Pisa – themselves wrote grammars. Whereas the grammars by the two Italian scholars look back to Insular models of the eighth century, Alcuin's works on grammar anticipate the new interest in the works of Priscian and herald a different approach to the study of grammar. The contents of grammatical codices of the later ninth century reflect the change that was taking place. The Late Latin works favoured by Insular teachers and their Continental pupils – commentators on Donatus, Consentius, the first book of Isidore's *Etymologiae*, and works on the inflecting parts of speech like Priscian's brief *Institutio de nomine et pronomine et uerbo* and the *Ars Asporii* – are replaced by a new group of texts: the grammars of Phocas and Eutyches (previously used sporadically rather than regularly) and several hitherto neglected works of Priscian's (*Institutiones grammaticae, Partitiones, De accentibus*).[3] Although they deal with the inflecting parts of speech, Eutyches's *Ars de uerbo* and Phocas's *Ars de nomine et uerbo* are organised rather differently from Donatus's grammars or the Insular elementary grammars. Instead of proceeding systematically through each of the five declensions or four conjugations, they are arranged on the principle of the alphabetical index. That is, all possible nominative singular or first-person singular endings are set out in alphabetical order; other features are discussed, where relevant, only under this heading. The usefulness of this arrangement is obvious: faced with a strange noun ending in *-orum*, for example, one might expect it to be a masculine noun of the second declension. But if it seemed to be modified by a feminine adjective, one might wish to find an

---

[3]   Manuscripts of these works can be traced with the assistance of Passalacqua, *I codici di Prisciano*, supplemented by Jeudy, 'Complément'; Ballaira, *Per il catalogo dei codici di Prisciano*; Jeudy, 'Les manuscrits de l'*Ars de uerbo* d'Eutychès', and 'L'*Ars de nomine et uerbo* de Phocas'.

alternative possibility. On turning to the section on nouns in -*us* in Phocas's *Ars de nomine* one would learn that there were a few feminine nouns in -*us* belonging to this class. This alphabetical arrangement also characterises parts of Priscian's *Institutiones grammaticae*, where nouns are listed by termination and assigned to appropriate genders (Book V) and declensions (Book VI) respectively.

Since these alphabetically organised texts were much easier to refer to than works like the *Declinationes nominum*, which could only be used for the identification of forms if their users were prepared to read them from beginning to end, Phocas's grammar and the *Institutiones grammaticae* rapidly replaced the *Declinationes nominum*. After the first quarter of the ninth century the latter work was only rarely included in collections of grammatical texts. Nonetheless, the mass of information it contained was so useful that material from it was often incorporated into other works. One of the sources drawn upon by Usuard of Saint-Germain in his elementary grammar was a collection of lists akin to those found in various versions of the *Declinationes nominum*, along with a few representative paradigms:[4] a copy of this source survives in Clermont-Ferrand, Bibliothèque municipale, MS. 241 (*saec.* x), fos 20r–34v. A second text, the anonymous grammar (attributed, wrongly, to 'Uuolfuinus') in Karlsruhe, Badische Landesbibliothek, MS. Aug. perg. 112 (*saec.* ix *in.*), fos 61v–101v, incorporates chunks of an extant version of the *Declinationes nominum*.[5] A later work, the anonymous *Excerptiones de Prisciano*, on which Ælfric based his Old English grammar of Latin, contains another such text.[6] Sporadic works of the type are found as late as the fourteenth century.[7] However, these survivals of what was fast becoming an outmoded genre need not occupy us further here. Of greater significance in the Carolingian context is an attempt to reorganise the luxuriant but chaotic material of the *Declinationes nominum* into a format more congenial to ninth-century users. Such an attempt is to be found in a text called, by its mediaeval users, *Terminationes nominum*.[8] This text is preserved in three ninth-century manuscripts:[9]

Leiden, Bibliotheek der Rijkuniversiteit, MS. BPL, 122, fos 31r–37v (*saec.* ix *ex.*; Lyon area)

Paris, Bibliothèque nationale, MS. latin 7540, fos 15v–25v (*saec.* ix *ex.*; Lyon-Vienne region)

---

4 Usuard's grammar was edited by Casas Homs, 'Una gramàtica inèdita d'Usuard'.
5 The sources used in this text (apart from the *Declinationes nominum*) are analysed by Holtz, *Donat et la tradition de l'enseignement grammatical*.
6 Translated into Old English by Ælfric (ed. Zupitza, pp. 21,1–83,2).
7 A twelfth-century copy of a text of the type is preserved in Paris, Bibliothèque nationale, MS latin 7492 (French), fos 104ra–108va; a fourteenth-century copy of a different text is to be found in Worcester, Cathedral Library, MS F.61 (Worcester area), fos 186rb–192vb.
8 This title is found in two of the three manuscripts. A space is left for the title in the third, Paris, Bibliothèque nationale, MS latin 7540.
9 Dates and provenances are from Holtz, *Donat*. Holtz mentions the copies of this work in Leiden 122 and BN lat. 7540, but not that in BN lat. 7558.

Paris, Bibliothèque nationale, MS. latin 7558, fos 131r–138v (*saec.* ix[1]; central or southern France)

The homogeneous geographical origin of the manuscripts hints at, but cannot prove, the origin of the text in the same region. This is supported by internal evidence: among the examples of proper names are *Vienna Narbona Tolosa Garonna Sagonna*[10] (Vienne, Narbonne, Toulouse, Garonne, Saône), and *Bachildes Monildes Iunildes*. Both place-names and personal names point to the southern part of France. Other direct evidence as to the place of origin of the text is lacking, and there is no hint of its authorship, as is often the case with early mediaeval grammars.

The scope of *Terminationes nominum* is similar to that of *Declinationes nominum* in that it assigns nouns to formal categories and provides lists of examples. But its approach is quite different. Instead of using declension as the basis of its classification, it indexes different classes of noun by termination. Like its model and chief source, Phocas, *Terminationes nominum* sets out the possible noun-terminations in alphabetical order.[11] Within each entry it indicates what genders are represented and whether the gender-class membership is open-ended or finite; and it names the declension to which nouns of a particular termination and gender belong. The paragraph on nouns in -*ur* is fairly typical:

> Ur finita quattuor inueniuntur masculina, astur turtur uultur satur, quod facit satura femininum. Duo communia, augur et fur. Alia omnia neutra sunt, ut guttur sulphur murmur iecur. Et uniuersa haec tertiae sunt declinationis excepto uno secundae, hic satur.

Terminationes nominum habitually works through the genders in the standard order: masculine, feminine, neuter, common, *omnis generis* (viz adjectives). In this paragraph we are told that there are four masculine nouns in -*ur*, one of which forms a feminine in -*a*, and two common nouns, while all the rest are neuter. This is the structure usually adopted by the compiler of *Terminationes nominum*: after listing the special cases, he formulates a general rule introduced by the words *cetera* (or *alia*) *omnia* . . . *sunt*. This is his practice even when his source formulates the rule differently, as is often the case. In the section on nouns in -*as*, for instance, Phocas begins with the commonest type, feminine nouns,

---

[10] Note the Vulgar form *Sagonna* for the Classical *Arar*.

[11] Several deviations from Phocas's order occur. Between *e* and *o*, *Terminationes nominum* adds *i* and *u*(!). The *i terminata* are not discussed at all by Phocas, but are included in Priscian's *Institutiones grammaticae*. Terminations in -*m* (-*am*, -*im*, -*um*) are placed before those in -*l*. -*t* is placed where it belongs in the alphabetical sequence, between -*us* and -*ax*, rather than following -*ux*, as in Phocas. The miscellaneous material from line 358 on has no parallel in Phocas. The version of Phocas known to the compiler is closer to that of Munich Clm 6281 (Keil's F) than to any other manuscript collated by Keil, but there are enough dissimilarities to show that it was not this manuscript, or a very close relative, which was being used.

and then tells us *pauca inueniuntur masculini generis*.[12] *Terminationes nominum* does the opposite, first listing masculine, neuter and *omnis generis* nouns, and then stating the general rule, *cetera feminina sunt omnia*.[13] The predictability of the structure within sections renders the work easy to use. The reader can normally expect to find the genders dealt with in order; any deviation from this pattern will be signalled at the end of the regular sequence in the form of a generalisation. Following that is a note on the declension (or declensions) associated with this termination. Where appropriate, additional features are taken into consideration: *qualitas* (proper or common), language of origin (Latin, Greek, *barbara*), vowel-length, and special semantic or derivational categories.

However, Phocas's *Ars de nomine* was by no means the only work consulted by the author of *Terminationes nominum*. Priscian's *Institutiones grammaticae* – largely the fifth and sixth books (which the compiler obviously knew well), although details come from other books as well – provided a large amount of supplementary material. Since Priscian had himself taken Phocas as the basis of the relevant sections, he often follows Phocas's order quite closely; thus, when the compiler wanted more detail than Phocas provides, all he had to do was to turn to the corresponding chapter in Priscian to find an updated version of the information. This is well exemplified in the paragraph on nouns in *-is*, where Phocas says *unum tantum feminini est generis, cuspis*;[14] Priscian, however, provides another example (161,11), so that *Terminationes nominum* reports *duo feminina inueniuntur . . . haec cuspis cuspidis, cassis cassidis*.[15] Occasional details are taken from Priscian's *Institutio de nomine* and from the *De accentibus* attributed to him.[16]

The third major source, after Phocas and Priscian's *Institutiones grammaticae*, is a version of the *Declinationes nominum*. This version is of particular interest in that, although no copies of it appear to survive, it seems to be identical with that used by the Anglo-Saxon grammarian Tatwine, active in Mercia in the closing decades of the seventh century. As is typical of Insular elementary grammars, the *Ars Tatuini* incorporates into the noun-section an extended discussion of noun-declension based on a version of *Declinationes nominum*. Rather unusually, Tatwine rearranged most of its numerous lists into alphabetical order, thereby disguising parallels with other versions of the *Declinationes nominum* or texts drawing upon it.[17] To some extent, though, batches from the source used by Tatwine can be traced in *Terminationes nominum*. A particularly clear example is the list of feminine nouns in *-is*: *auis clauis classis turris messis pellis nauis apis auris*

---

12 Prisc. *IG*, V.416, 30.
13 *Terminationes nominum*, 148.
14 Prisc. *IG*, V. 418, 12.
15 *Terminationes nominum*, 180–1.
16 The flicker of interest in prosody betrayed by the borrowings from *De accentibus* is developed in Hrabanus Maurus's *Excerptio de arte grammatica Prisciani*.
17 But it should be noted that a number of the lists in the *Declinationes nominum* itself are in alphabetical order.

cutis sitis uitis uallis.[18] The first seven words come from Phocas,[19] but of the remaining six, *apis* to *uallis*, only one (*cutis*) occurs in Phocas's text. All of them are found in Tatwine's list,[20] which begins *amnis auis apis auris cutis*, and, after some twelve further examples, finishes with *sitis turris uitis uallis*.[21] In other words, the compiler was drawing upon an alphabetically ordered source like Tatwine's, from which he took a few examples from the beginning and the end. The same procedure can be observed in the list of neuters in *-um*, where the first six examples correspond to the first six in Tatwine's list,[22] the next six are chosen at random from that list and the next, and the last three come from the end of the last of Tatwine's three neuter lists, that of diminutives.[23] That the *Ars Tatuini* is not the immediate source is suggested by the fact that *Terminationes nominum* often takes over lists clearly drawn from a version of *Declinationes nominum* but not in alphabetical order.[24] Some lists are closer to those of the *Declinationes nominum* than to Tatwine, suggesting that Tatwine at that point drew upon a different source.[25] Since the version of the *Declinationes nominum* used by the compiler has not yet come to light, points of similarity to various works which draw upon *Declinationes nominum* material have been noted in the apparatus: the grammars of Paulus Diaconus (and his source, a text of *Declinationes nominum* type in BN lat. 7560), Peter of Pisa, Usuard (and his source, in Clermont-Ferrand 241), Boniface, and the *Ars Ambianensis* and the fragment of an elementary grammar in Toledo, Bibl. Cabildo, MS. 99–30. The closest relatives of the

---

18 *Terminationes nominum*, 182–3.
19 Prisc. *IG*, V. 418, 15–16. The compiler frequently omits items from Phocas's lists for reasons which have yet to be identified. In this case he seems to prefer commoner words.
20 Tatw., 37,1179–81.
21 *Auis* and *turris* were omitted because the compiler had already included them in the portion of his list borrowed from Phocas. *Amnis* had been included in an earlier list (177). Other lists which appear to be derived from a source shared with the *Ars Tatuini* are those of neuters in *-a* (40–2, Tatw. 33,1013–15); feminines in *-io* (62–3, Tatw. 34,1049–55); in *-do* and *-go* (73–4, Tatw. 33,1040–4); adjectives in *-is* (186–7, Tatw. 37,1183–90); adjectives in *-ax* (249–50, Tatw. 38,1225–8); masculines in *-ex* (259–60, Tatw. 38,1231–3).
22 Tatw., 31,965ff.
23 The presence of *uexillum* here shows that it was present in Tatwine's source and so definitely belongs to the text of the *Ars Tatuini*: it need not be bracketed (cf. Tatw. 32,987).
24 This is the case, for example, with the list of neuters in *-e* (50–4), where the order of the examples corresponds to that of the *Declinationes nominum*, but some words found only in Tatwine's alphabetical list (*brumale, rationale*) are included.
25 For instance, most of the list of masculine fourth-declension nouns (217–20: *actus . . . cultus*) comes straight from the equivalent list in the *Declinationes nominum*, even retaining the same order, whereas Tatwine has only two of the fifteen items involved. More strikingly, *Terminationes nominum* has three separate lists, of adjectives, participles and nouns in *-us* (225–7, 233–4), which are combined in a single list in all extant versions of the *Declinationes nominum*. This suggests that the compiler – and presumably Tatwine as well – was drawing upon a version of the *Declinationes nominum* more ancient, and more differentiated, than any so far known.

Declinationes nominum material in *Terminationes nominum* remain the Ars *Tatuini* and the version of the *Declinationes nominum* in Munich, Bayerische Staatsbibliothek, Clm 6281, fos 108v–114v, however.

Other sources play only a minor role. The lists of nouns with which the work begins (lines 2–7) come from the Ars *maior* and Ars *minor* of Donatus, where they function as examples of various metrical patterns and as models for paradigms of the five genders.[26] The final sections, a note on the declension of numerals and an extended treatment of the formation of the regular comparative, are of uncertain source; parallels – none of which are likely to be the source – have been noted in the *apparatus fontium* below (pp. 36–42).

Rather unexpectedly, this text of French origin has helped to elucidate the composition of an English work. Although the typological resemblance between the Ars *Tatuini* and other Insular elementary grammars was clear, the material from the *Declinationes nominum* characteristic of the genre was difficult to locate in the Ars *Tatuini* because of Tatwine's habit of alphabetising lists of examples.[27] *Terminationes nominum* provides indirect evidence as to the nature of one of Tatwine's sources. Conversely, the fact that the compiler of *Terminationes nominum*, working in eastern France some time in the first half of the ninth century, had access to a text used by Tatwine in Mercia at the end of the seventh throws light upon the movement of texts. The indebtedness of *Germania* to Insular visitors for pedagogical texts has long been known; that of Carolingian France has only recently begun to be traced. *Terminationes nominum* provides a glimpse of an attempt to fuse the old-fashioned Anglo-Saxon *Declinationes nominum* tradition with the new-found Carolingian interest in *regulae* texts. That its compiler thought it worth making the effort to do so shows that one teacher, at least, found something of value in the old works.

---

[26] Holtz, *Donat*, p. 389, suggests that these lists do not belong to the text of *Terminationes nominum* proper. Although I share his reservations, I have preferred to treat them as part of the text since they are so treated in the manuscripts. With most works of this kind it is not possible to reconstruct a primitive version free from all interpolations. Often such texts are clearly compilatory in nature in any case; and scarcely a single copy is likely to have been made without liberties of some kind being taken. This is well exemplified by the three extant manuscripts of *Terminationes nominum* itself: B frequently drops arbitrarily chosen examples from lists, while P, especially towards the end of the text, revises and corrects it. All three scribes attempted to find it appropriate company: L combined it with a text on the *coniugationes uerborum*, while the parent of BP incorporated it into a parsing grammar.

[27] Cf. Law, *Insular Latin Grammarians*, p. 65, n. 60.

[1]INCIPIUNT TERMINATIONES NOMINUM[1]

Fuga aestas parens moeta macula Aeneas Eratho Menalus carina insulae Achates [2]natura auicula[2] oratores propinquitas cantilena Saloninus armipotens Diomedes Iunonius legitimus colonia Menedemus celeritas sacerdotes conditores
5   Demostenes Fescenninus. Fax pix nux res dos spes moeta Creta nepos leges bonus malus Tullius Hostilius Catullus[3] Metellus latebrae tenebrae Cethegus perosus Athenae Micenae. Magister musa scamnum sacerdos felix.

Monosyllaba nomina generis masculini: as dens grex flos fons las[4] mons mos mus mas pres Mars pons lar pes ros rex sal sol uir uas uadis. Ex his unum inuenitur
10   secundae declinationis, id est uir. Cetera tertiae sunt declinationis.

Item feminini generis: arx ars calx crux cos dos frons[5] gens falx fax[6] fex lux lex lis[7] glis[8] lens grans uel grandis glans lanx mors merx mens nux nix nex nox pix ops prex pars res spes sors scrobs[9] stips stirps trabs uis[10] grus urbs uox nar naris. Ex his duo[11] sunt quintae declinationis contra regulam, [12]spes et res[12]. Cetera tertiae
15   sunt declinationis.

Item neutri generis: aes crus cor fas git pus far yr[13] ius mel ós oris os ossis [14]<pus par tus fel lac rus uer uas uasis>[14]. Ex his tria in plurali numero deficiunt, fel lac uer. Sex in plurali numero tres tantum casus habent, nominatiuum accusatiuum et uocatiuum: aes far ius mel tus rus. Quattuor minime declinantur: fas git pus ir.

20   Masculina nomina septem litteris finiuntur, a o l n r s x, ut scriba Cicero sol flamen Cesar bonus rex. Sed et feminina eisdem, ut Roma uirgo Tanaquil siren mater ciuitas pax. Neutra nomina xii litteris finiuntur, a e i u l m n r s c t d, ut poema mare gummi cornu mel regnum numen tuber sidus lac caput aliquod.

A finita, si sint uirorum propria, masculina sunt, ut Sylla Seneca Catilina
25   Cotta Agrippa Niceta Galba. Si feminarum, feminina sunt, ut Iulia Martia Matuta Laurentina Flora. Aliarum uero rerum, siue sint propria siue[15] appellatiua, similiter feminini sunt generis: propria, ut Roma Uienna Narbona Tolosa Garonna Sagonna; appellatiua, ut fortuna sella terra arena. Similiter sapientia prudentia iustitia scientia, uirtutum nomina saepe in plurali numero deficientia;

SIGLA

B   Paris, Bibliothèque nationale, MS. lat. 7540, fos 15v–24r
L   Leiden, Bibliotheek der Rijksuniversiteit, MS. BPL 122, fos 31r–37v
P   Paris, Bibliothèque nationale, MS. lat. 7558, fos 131r–138v

1   Om. B, sed duo lineae titulo vacuae relic-
    tae sunt.
2   Trsp. BP
3   Om. BP
4   Om. L
5   Om. BP
6   Om. B
7   Add. L

8   Post fex trsp. P
9   Om. P
10 ius P
11 duae BP
12 Om. B
13 fas far git yr P
14 Om. BLP, supplevi ex Phoca
15 seu BP

30 insipientia inprudentia iniustitia inscientia nomina uitiorum; et artium nomina,
ut grammatica rethorica dialectica aritmetica[16] geometrica musica astronomia,
quae et propria dici possunt et appellatiua. Duo inueniuntur masculina nomina
animalium, talpa et damma. Quae autem ad officia uirorum pertinent masculina
sunt, ut lixa scriba lanista scurra sophista propheta leuita psalmista tympanista[17]
35 citarista poeta. Ex his deriuata feminina sunt, ut a sophista sophistria, a propheta
prophetissa, a [18]tympanista tympanistria[18], a citarista citaristria, a poeta poetria.
Quae utrique sexui conueniunt communia sunt, ut agricola rurigena aduena
parricida collega conuiua. Et [19]haec uniuersa[19] primae sunt declinationis. Nomina
litterarum indeclinabilia sunt tam apud graecos quam apud latinos, ut alfa beta
40 gamma[20] a k h. Graeca uero et neutra sunt et tertiae declinationis, ut poema
pascha schema emblema epigramma dogma paradigma chrisma anathema fantas-
ma baptisma celeuma plasma idioma diadema gramma enigma. Pascha tamen
sicut et manna frequentius primae inuenitur declinationis. [21]Numerorum nomina[21] in a desinens intra decem unum inuenitur, tria, et est neutri generis et tertiae
45 declinationis. Intra centum septem: triginta quadraginta quinquaginta sexaginta
septuaginta octoginta nonaginta, quae sunt omnis generis et eandem terminationem per omnes casus seruant. Intra mille octo: ducenta trecenta quadringenta
quingenta sexcenta septingenta octingenta nongenta[22], quae sunt neutra et secundae declinationis. Milia quoque neutri generis est et tertiae declinationis.
50 [23]E finita neutri generis sunt omnia et tertiae declinationis[23], ut hoc sedile
munile mantile altare luminare superliminare[24] [25]antemurale omne uolatile ar-
gentile conflatile tornatile cubile hastile[25] ouile cocleare brumale rationale rep-
tile[26] sculptile superhumerale amictile placabile suspicabile amabile rationabile
desiderabile irascibile.
55 In i neutra duo, gummi senapi. Omnis generis, frugi nihili mancipi huiuscemodi.
In u neutra sunt omnia et quartae declinationis, ut cornu genu[27] gelu ueru
specu.
O finita precedente e masculina sunt et nominatiuum tantum ac uocatiuum
60 habent, ut hic aleo ganeo labeo. Quae i habent ante o aut propria sunt, ut Scipio
Gerio masculina, Chilio Egio feminina, aut appellatiua t praecedente uel s uel x
i[28] feminina, excepto uno masculino, Titio, ut haec cogitatio coniugatio diuisio
electio benedictio iussio enixio. Quaecumque autem alia consonans praecedat i
masculina sunt, ut bibio seni[ci]o stellio unio strio centurio curio[29] mulio gurgulio
65 quaternio. Eiusdem sunt generis etiam illa quae[30] preter d et g quamlibet aliam
consonantem ante o habent, ut hic carbo draco fullo sermo leno[31] mucro tiro

[16] Om. P
[17] timpanistra L
[18] timpanistra tympanistrica L
[19] Trsp. P
[20] gramma P
[21] numeri nominum BLP (nōm P)
[22] Om. B
[23] Add. in marg. B[1]

[24] superluminare BP
[25] Om. BP
[26] Om. B
[27] Om. B
[28] i et P
[29] Om. L
[30] qui B
[31] leo B

pauo turbo preco. Et omnia supradicta o productam habent in penultima genitiui, ut Scipio Scipionis, Chilio Chilionis, Titio Titionis, iussio iussionis, bibio
bibionis, carbo carbonis. Excipiuntur feminina duo, Iuno et caro, quod facit
carnis in genitiuo. Communia duo, latro homo, cuius genitiuum et homonis[32] et
hominis[33] antiqui protulere. Omnis generis unum, octo. Pondo quoque neutrum
est et pluralis numeri tantum. Ambo et duo in masculino et neutro similiter
dicuntur. Si uero d uel g sit ante o feminina sunt[35], ut arundo multitudo altitudo
longitudo fortitudo dulcedo uligo indago compago sartago Cartago[36] testudo. Et
omnia i penultimam[37] in genitiuo habent, ut dulcedo dulcedinis, uligo uliginis.
Excipiuntur ordo cardo predo cudo spado mango margo ligo Cupido (cum est
proprium) masculina; unum commune, uirgo. Et uniuersa haec tertiae sunt declinationis exceptis duo ambo octo[38] pondo. Ex quibus duo et ambo genitiuum in
rum, datiuum et ablatiuum in bus mittunt, octo et pondo eandem terminationem
per omnes casus seruant.

In am unum inuenitur omnis generis, hic et haec et hoc nequam.

In im unum neutrum inuenitur, hoc Cim, indeclinabile[39].

Um syllaba terminata neutri generis sunt omnia et secundae declinationis, ut
hoc templum antrum[40] aratrum aruum bellum baratrum cerebrum tentorium
plaustrum regnum scutum sceptrum uestibulum signaculum uexillum.

Al syllaba finitum unum inuenitur masculinum[41] monosyllabum, hic sal huius
salis, quod et neutro genere dici potest. Et barbara propria masculina sunt, ut hic
Annibal Asdrubal Iempal. Cetera omnia neutra sunt, ut hoc animal uectigal
tribunal lupercal chrismal[42] ceruical. Et uniuersa haec tertiae sunt declinationis.

Il syllaba terminata duo inueniuntur masculina, pugil mugil, quod etiam mugi-
lus dici potest. Unum femininum, Tanaquil. Unum commune, hic et haec uigil.
Et omnia tertiae sunt declinationis.

Ol finitum unum inuenitur[43] masculini generis, hic sol huius solis, nec ullum
amplius.

Ul finita duo sunt masculina, consul praesul. Unum commune, hic et haec
exul. Et sunt tertiae declinationis omnia.

En syllaba finita nouem sunt masculina: lien rien flamen pecten tibicen
fidicen liticen tubicen cornicen. Cetera omnia neutra sunt, ut carmen lumen[44]
nomen culmen crimen limen[45] bitumen. Et omnia haec tertiae sunt declinationis.

Ar finita tria sunt masculina: Cesar lar Nar, [46]cum fluuii nomen est[46]. Unum
femininum, nar, cum sensum corporis significat. Unum omnis generis, par, et ex
eo composita: inpar dispar compar suppar. Cetera omnia neutra sunt, ut hoc

[32] omnis *BP*	[40] *Om. BP*
[33] homonis *P*	[41] *Corr. ex* masculini generis *L*
[35] *Om. BP*	[42] *Om. B*
[36] *Fortasse* cartilago	[43] *Om. P*
[37] penultima *L*	[44] tumen *B*
[38] *Om. B*	[45] lumen *B*
[39] declinabile *B*	[46] confluuium + *ras. iv litt. B*

Apparatus fontium at pp. 36–42

torcular lucar lacunar puluinar laquear. Et uniuersa haec tertiae sunt declina-
05 tionis.

Er finita duo sunt feminina, mater mulier. Undecim neutra: suber tuber pa-
pauer cadauer laser siler iter cicer uer piper ruder. Tria communia: pauper uber
celer. Alia omnia masculina sunt, ut pulcher ater niger pater frater passer anser
puer gener socer liber auster. Sed huius terminationis nomina feminina quidem et
10 neutra et communia tertiae sunt declinationis omnia, masculina uero[47] uel secundae uel tertiae. Secundae illa sunt quae aut in femininum transeunt genus, ut
pulcher pulchra, [48]liber libera, ater atra, niger nigra, ruber rubra, aper apra, caper
capra[48], piger pigra, asper aspera, macer macra, creber crebra, [49]aut ast[49] ante er
habent, ut oleaster apiaster falcaster parasitaster catulaster surdaster, quamuis
15 inueniuntur[50] pauca huius formae nomina etiam tertiae declinationis, ut paluster
campester equester pedester siluester (cum appellatiuum est). Sed huiuscemodi
nomina e semper uel u habent ante ster, ut campester paluster, illa uero quae
secundi[51] sunt ordinis a uel i, ut falcaster magister, excepto auster et Siluester
cum proprium est. Et illa quidem[52] feminina in is faciunt, ut campester [53]campes-
20 tris, paluster palustris, haec uero in a, ut magister magistra[53], surdaster surdastra,
catulaster catulastra. Unum inuenitur est[54] ante er habens quod et femininum in
a facit et est tam secundae quam tertiae declinationis, [55]sequester, cuius femininum est sequestra[55]. Dicimus enim et[56] hic sequester huius sequestri et hic sequester sequestris. Septem inueniuntur secundae declinationis quae neque in
25 femininum transeunt genus neque st[57] ante er habent, ut puer gener socer faber
cancer culter liber libri. Cetera omnia quae nihil horum habent tertiae sunt
declinationis, ut pater patris, frater fratris, passer passeris, anser anseris.

Ir finita duo sunt masculina, treuir uir, et ex eo composita: leuir duumuir
triumuir septemuir decemuir. Neutra duo, ir gradir. [58]Et omnia secundae sunt
30 declinationis excepto ir, quod minime declinatur, et gradir[58], quod est tertiae
declinationis.

Or finita tria sunt feminina, soror uxor arbor. Septem neutra, ador marmor
equor ebor robor femor cor. Duo communia, auctor memor et ex eo compositum
immemor. Similiter et a colore composita communia sunt, ut discolor concolor
35 bicolor tricolor multicolor ignicolor. Eiusdem sunt generis omnia[59] etiam com-
paratiua, ut doctior melior peior[60] fortior beatior excellentior sublimior. Excipitur
unum comparatiuum [61]tantum masculini[61] generis, hic senior. Cetera omnia siue
sint propria siue[62] appellatiua similiter [63]masculina sunt[63]: propria, ut Ector

[47] Om. P
[48] Om. B
[49] aut st B auster P
[50] inueniunt B inueniantur L
[51] secund(a)e BP
[52] Om. BP
[53] Om. P
[54] st BP
[55] Om. BP

[56] ut L
[57] est L
[58] Om. P
[59] Om. BP
[60] Om. B
[61] Trsp. P
[62] seu P
[63] masculini sunt generis B sunt generis P

Antenor Nicanor; appellatiua, ut orator furor doctor. Et uniuersa haec tertiae
140   sunt declinationis.

Ur finita quattuor inueniuntur masculina, astur turtur uultur satur, quod facit
satura femininum. Duo communia, augur et fur. Alia omnia neutra sunt, ut guttur
sulphur murmur iecur. Et uniuersa haec tertiae sunt declinationis [64]excepto uno[64]
secundae, hic satur.

145   As finita, si sint uirorum propria, masculina [65]sunt et primae declinationis, ut
Eneas Lisias Andreas. Appellatiua uero tria inueniuntur masculina[65,66], as [67]mas
uas[67], cuius genitiuus uadis[68]. Duo neutra, uas, cuius genitiuus uasis[69], fas et ex eo
compositum nefas. Unum omnis generis, nugas. Cetera feminina sunt omnia, ut
haec dignitas pietas facultas ciuitas potestas. Et uniuersa haec tertiae sunt decli-
150   nationis exceptis fas nefas nugas, [70]quae minime declinantur[70].

Es finita, si sint uirorum propria, masculina sunt, ut Hercules Ulixes Anchises
Demostenes Mitridates Orontes; si feminarum, feminina sunt, ut Bachildes
Munildes Iunildes. Masculina et feminina tertiae sunt declinationis propria. Si
sint uero patronomica, id est a patrum nominibus deriuata, primae, ut a Priamo
155   Priamides, ab Atreo Atrides, a Peleo Pelides, ab Anchisa Anchisiades. I ante es
habentia tria inueniuntur[71] generis masculini, paries [72]aries meridies[72]. Cetera
omnia i ante es habentia feminina sunt, ut facies acies abies macies glaties quies.
Eiusdem generis habentur etiam illa quorum nominatiuus et genitiuus pares
habent syllabas, ut haec nubes nubis, cedes cedis, sedes[73] sedis, [74]lues luis[75], strues
160   struis, proles prolis, pubes pubis[74]. Que autem crescunt una syllaba in genitiuo,
consonante precedente es in nominatiuo, feminina haec tantum sunt, fides spes
res Ceres merces seges teges. Cetera omnia, si ad utrumque sexum referuntur,
communia sunt, i uel e correptam in penultima genitiui[76] habentia, ut hic et haec
comes comitis, diues diuitis, [77]hospes hospitis[77], cocles coclitis, sospes sospitis,
165   miles militis, [78]hebes hebetis[78], teres teretis, interpres interpretis, praeses
praesidis, obses obsidis, deses desidis, reses residis, ales alitis, alipes alipedis,
cornipes cornipedis, bipes bipedis, tripes tripedis, quadrupes quadrupedis, semipes
semipedis. Excipiuntur duo e productam in penultima genitiui habentia, heres
heredis, locuples locupletis. Si uero sint rerum insensibilium uocabula, masculina
170   sunt omnia, ut limes limitis, fomes fomitis, gurges gurgitis, stipes stipitis, lebes
lebetis, pes pedis. Et omnia haec i correptam habent in penultima genitiui excepto lebes, quod e productam seruat[79]. Sed i ante es habentia omnia quintae sunt
declinationis, exceptis [80]paries abies aries quies[80], quae sunt tertiae declinationis.

---

[64] exceptis unum *P*
[65] *Om. P*
[66] masc;n *add. L*
[67] *Trsp. L*
[68] est uadis *B*
[69] est uasis *B*
[70] *Om. P*
[71] inuenitur *P* sunt *B*
[72] habies aries *P*

[73] *Om. P*
[74] luis pubis proles prolis strues struis
       pubes *P*
[75] *Corr. ex* lues *L*
[76] *Om. P*
[77] aspes ospitis *P*
[78] *Corr. ex* habes habetis *B*
[79] *post* seruat *add.* in genitiuo *P*
[80] *Trsp. P*

Quaecumque[81] uero alia uocali uel consonante praecedente es[82] tertiae sunt
exceptis spes fides res, quae sunt quintae declinationis.

In is desinentia, si n uel c ante is habent, masculina sunt, ut panis funis [83]finis
ignis[83] amnis splenis renis piscis fascis. Unum [84]inuenitur femininum[84] n ante is[85]
habens, haec bipennis. Unum commune, hic et haec canis. Similiter quae una
syllaba crescunt in genitiuo masculina sunt, ut hic puluis huius pulueris, cinis
cineris, sanguis sanguinis, lapis lapidis. Duo feminina inueniuntur is terminata
una syllaba in genitiuo[86] crescentia, haec cuspis cuspidis, cassis cassidis. Quae in
genitiuo non crescunt, [87]nisi sint adiectiua[87], feminina sunt, ut haec auis clauis
classis turris messis[88] pellis nauis apis auris cutis sitis uitis uallis. Inueniuntur
pauca[89] huiuscemodi masculina, hic fustis ensis postis anguis unguis[90] collis follis
corbis uectis mensis torquis axis orbis. Si uero sint adiectiua uel hominum uel
aliarum rerum, communia sunt, ut hic et haec fortis amabilis affabilis laudabilis
fragilis gracilis humilis dulcis suauis. Et omnia huius formae nomina[91] in e faciunt
neutrum et declinantur ita[92], hic et haec fortis et hoc forte, dulcis dulce, amabilis
amabile. Et uniuersa haec tertiae sunt declinationis.

In os tria sunt feminina, cos dos glos. Duo neutra, ós oris, os ossis. Quinque
communia, custos sacerdos bos compos impos. Alia omnia masculina sunt, ut
mos ros flos nepos lepos. Et omnia tertiae sunt declinationis.

In us propria masculina sunt, ut Uirgilius Mercurius Terentius Laurentius
Uincentius Marcus Saturnus Paulus, et sunt secundae declinationis omnia.
Unum inuenitur femininum proprium, Uenus, et est tertiae declinationis. Tria
inueniuntur neutra secundae declinationis, uulgus uirus pelagus. Cetera autem
neutra us finita tertiae sunt declinationis, ut ius rus tus pondus pectus. Et omnia
monosyllaba us finita neutra sunt excepto uno masculino, mus, et duobus com-
munibus, grus sus, quae tamen et ipsa[93] tertiae sunt declinationis. Similiter neutra
sunt omnia e uel o correptam[94] in penultima geniuiui habentia, ut munus
muneris, pondus ponderis, funus funeris, pectus pectoris, corpus corporis, pignus
[95]pignoris uel pigneris, fenus fenoris uel feneris, foedus foederis[95]. Excipitur unum
masculinum, lepus leporis. Unum omnis generis, [96]hic et haec et hoc[96] uetus
ueteris. U productam in penultima genitiui habentia feminina sunt et tertiae
declinationis, ut haec tellus telluris, uirtus uirtutis, salus salutis, palus paludis.
Ligus autem commune est et tertiae declinationis, u correptam in penultima
genitiui habens. Nomina arborum us finita feminina sunt et secundae declinationis, ut pirus prunus malus cyparissus cedrus laurus mirtus. Quinque ex his[97] tam

81 quacumque *P*
82 s *L om. P*
83 funis *P*
84 *Trsp. P*
85 his *L*
86 genitiuo non *P*
87 *Om. P*
88 mensis *B*
89 *Om. B*

90 *Om. B*
91 nominatiua *B*
92 ita ut *L*
93 ipse *B*
94 correptas *P*
95 pignoris fẹdus fẹderis uel fenoris fedus
   federis *B*
96 *Om. B*
97 eis *B*

secundae quam quartae [98]declinationis inueniuntur[98], ut quercus laurus pinus[99]
210   cornus ficus (quod et masculinum est cum uitium corporis significat). Eiusdem
sunt generis ac declinationis quaedam etiam[100] ciuitatum insularum et siderum
nomina uel prouinciarum, ut Tyrus Cyprus Naxus Arctus[101] Aegyptus; sic et
abissus. Octo tantum sunt feminina et quarte declinationis, haec anus manus
acus porticus tribus domus [102]nurus socrus[102]. Quae deriuantur a uerbis nec trans-
215   eunt in femininum masculina sunt et quartae declinationis, ut hic fluctus [103]a
fluo, questus a quaero, rictus a ringo[103], a uideo uisus, a gusto gustus[104], ab audio
auditus, a curro cursus, a fleo fletus, a uerto uersus, a sto status, ab ago actus, a
gradior gressus, ab introeo[105] introitus, ab exeo exitus, a gemo gemitus, a fremo
fremitus, a mugio mugitus, a rugio rugitus, a uagio uagitus, a sono sonitus, ab
220   ambio ambitus, ab exerceo exercitus, ab arceo arcus[106], a salio saltus, a colo
cultus, a uolo uultus[107], a metuo metus, a rideo risus. A lego lectus [108]excipitur
quod est secundae declinationis[108]. Eiusdem sunt regulae etiam illa quae a nominibus deriuantur nec transeunt in femininum, ut a duce ducatus, a consule
consulatus, a tribuno tribunatus, [109]magistratus a magistro[109], a principe principa-
225   tus. Quae uero[110] in femininum transeunt genus secundae sunt declinationis, ut
mustus musta, agnus agna, ceruus cerua, seruus serua, equus equa, mulus mula,
ferus fera, [111]firmus firma, iustus iusta[111], ursus ursa; emptus empta, pictus picta,
doctus docta, unctus uncta, quae sunt a uerbis emo pingo doceo ungo deriuata,
sed quia [112]mobilia sunt[112] secundi[113] ordinis regulam sortiuntur. [114]Similiter ab
230   auro auratus aurata, ab aere aeratus aerata, a lorica[115] loricatus loricata[116], quia
faciunt ex se femininum secundi ordinis habentur, licet ab aliis deriuentur[114].
Eiusdem sunt regulae omnia etiam illa quae neque a uerbis deriuantur neque ab
aliis nominibus ueniunt neque in femininum transeunt genus, ut somnus cibus
nidus[117] lucus culmus botrus oculus stilus armus[118] remus[119] girus gibbus, exceptis
235   colus aluus humus, quae sunt secundae[120] declinationis sed generis feminini.
Aluus autem etiam masculino genere dici potest. Excipiuntur etiam[121] sexus lacus
quartae declinationis. Penus quoque et specus tam masculini quam feminini et
neutri generis habentur. Quando desinunt in us masculina dici possunt et femi-
na et possunt esse tam secundae quam tertiae et quartae declinationis. Dicimus
240   enim et hic specus et [122]haec specus et hic penus et haec penus et huius speci
specoris uel specus et[122] huius peni penoris uel penus. Neutri uero generis tunc

98 *Trsp. P*
99 *Om. B*
100 *Om. B*
101 arcus *P* aurctus *B*
102 a uerbis nec transeunt *P*
103 *Om. P*
104 *Om. P*
105 intro *B*
106 artus *L*
107 uultis *P* uolatus *L*
108 *Om. B*
109 *Trsp. L¹*
110 uo *P om. B*

111 *Om. B*
112 *Trsp. P*
113 secundae *B*
114 *om. P*
115 lorico *B*
116 loricata et similiter *B*
117 nidus campus *P*
118 *Om. P*
119 *Om. B*
120 eiusdem *P*
121 enim *L*
122 *Om. P*

sunt cum in um desinunt uel in u, ut hoc specum uel[123] specu, hoc penum uel[123] penu[124]. [125]Sed quando in um desinunt secundae, quando uero[126] in u quartae sunt declinationis, ut hoc specum huius speci, hoc penum huius peni[125]; itemque hoc specu huius specu, hoc penu huius penu.

T[127] littera terminatum unum inuenitur neutri generis et tertiae declinationis, hoc caput huius capitis[128], et ex eo composita, sinciput occiput.

Ax syllaba terminata omnis generis sunt uniuersa et tertiae declinationis, ut hic et haec et hoc audax[129] rapax fallax loquax pertinax procax peruicax[130] efficax capax dicax edax emax tenax[131] mendax uerax[132] furax sagax[133]. [134]Excipitur unum proprium generis masculini, hic Agax[134], unum femininum, haec fornax, quae et ipsa[135] tertiae sunt[136] declinationis.

Ex finita septem inueniuntur feminina, lex ilex carex fex prex nex pelex. Duo incerti generis inter masculinum et femininum, cortex silex. Et quae utrique sexui conueniunt omnis generis sunt[137], ut hic et haec et hoc simplex duplex[138] artifex opifex aurifex. Eiusdem sunt generis etiam illa quae a multum aduerbio et duo uel tria nominibus et sub uel se uel con praepositionibus conposita sunt, ut multiplex duplex triplex supplex segrex congrex complex. Cetera omnia masculina sunt, ut hic rex[139] grex[140] apex uertex pollex murex pumex pulex[141] pontifex latex codex culex cimex uerbex, quod e productam seruat in genetiuo. Et omnia haec tertiae sunt declinationis.

Ix fininta, si sint a nominibus in tor desinentibus deriuata, feminina sunt omnia, ut ab eo quod est orator oratrix, [142]uictor uictrix[142], genitor genetrix, nutritor nutrix, doctor doctrix, inuentor inuentrix, lector lectrix, peccator peccatrix. Quae utrique[143] sexui conueniunt omnis generis sunt, ut felix pernix. Cetera omnia masculina sunt, ut hic calix fornix perdix[144] uarix bernix lodix natrix. Excipiuntur pauca feminina haec tantum, salix[145] radix ceruix cornix meretrix cicatrix. Et uniuersa haec tertiae sunt declinationis.

Ox finita, si utrique sexui[146] conueniunt, omnis generis sunt, ut hic et haec et hoc ferox atrox uelox pernox. Tria feminina inueniuntur, uox[147] nox celox. Et omnia tertiae sunt declinationis.

Ux finita quattuor[148] inueniuntur feminina, lux nux crux [149]frux (cum fructum

[123] huius B bis
[124] penui B
[125] Add. in marg. L[1]
[126] Om. BL[1]
[127] Om. P
[128] Om. B
[129] Om. P
[130] Om. B
[131] tepax B
[132] Om. B
[133] Om. P
[134] Reliqua omnia siue sint propria seu appellatiua masculini sunt generis ut hic Agax sagax P

[135] ips(a)e BP
[136] est P
[137] sunt uniuersa B
[138] Om. B
[139] Om. B
[140] grex rex P
[141] pulex post codex trsp. BP
[142] Om. B
[143] Om. B
[144] Om. P
[145] salix filex B
[146] Om. P
[147] uelox B
[148] tria P
[149] Om. P

terrae significat[149]). Duo[150] omnis[151] generis, trux [152]frux (cum sobrium significat[152]). Unum proprium masculinum, Pollux, quod u productam seruat in geni-
275   tiuo. [153]Unum commune[153] quod n habet ante x, ut hic et haec coniunx[154]. Et
omnia[155] tertiae sunt declinationis.

Monosyllaba nomina in duas desinentia consonantes quinque inueniuntur
masculina, mons fons pons dens Mars. Cetera omnia feminina sunt, ut ars fors
calxs puls falx glans lanx daps traps arx[156]. Pollisyllaba uero, si utrique sexui
280   conueniunt, omnis generis sunt uniuersa, ut hic et haec et hoc expers prudens
inops celebs princeps. Duo inueniuntur propria generis masculini, Mauors Ar-
runs. Unum appellatiuum eiusdem generis, hic adeps. Duo feminina, cohors
hiems. Et omnia tertiae sunt declinationis.

Aus syllaba finita duo inueniuntur generis feminini et tertiae[157] declinationis,
285   laus laudis, fraus fraudis.

Aes finitum unum inuenitur masculinum[158], praes praedis. Unum neutrum,
aes aeris.

Unus una unum pronominis declinationem[159] sequitur, sed non deficit in
uocatiuo. A quattuor usque ad centum numerorum nomina omnis generis sunt et
290   eandem terminationem per omnes casus seruant. A ducentis usque ad mille per
tria genera mouentur, ut ducenti ducentae ducenta, trecenti[160] trecentae trecenta, quadringenti quadringentae quadringenta, quorum masculinum et neutrum
secundae, femininum uero[161] primae est declinationis. Mille uero [162]omnis generis
est[162] et eandem terminationem per omnes casus seruat[163].

295   Propria nomina aut angelorum sunt aut [164]demonum aut deorum[164] aut hominum aut prouinciarum aut ciuitatum aut montium aut fluminum aut unius dei, ut
Micahel Gabrihel, Asmodeus Apollion Saturnus Iuppiter, Iulius Cornelius Iulia
Cornelia, Asia Africa Europa, Roma Alexandria Antiochia, Olimpus Parnasus
Liceus, Rodanus Nilus Renus, Deus Conditor Creator. Quaecumque ergo huius-
300   cemodi[165] inuenta fuerint minime comparantur. Sola enim appellatiua comparari
possunt, et desinunt uel in a ut docta[166], uel in e ut amabile, uel in er ut pulcher,
uel in es ut diues, uel in is ut dulcis, uel in us ut sanctus, uel in ans ut prestans, uel
in ens ut excellens, uel in ers ut iners, uel in eps ut praeceps, uel in ax ut audax,
uel in ex ut simplex, uel in ix ut felix, uel in ox ut ferox, uel in ux ut trux, uel in
305   um ut[167] iustum. Sunt igitur terminationes positiui quae[168] transeunt in comparatiuum sedecim[169]. In a illa comparantur quae ueniunt a nominatiuo uel in us
desinente, ut doctus docta. Facit enim doctior doctissima. Uel in er, ut pulcher

150 onum P
151 omnis sunt P
152 Om. P
153 duo communia dux coniunx P
154 coniux B
155 communia P
156 Om. B
157 tertiae sunt L
158 masculini L
159 declinationis L

160 Om. P
161 Om. P
162 bm̄is P omnis est generis B
163 seruant BL et corr. L
164 deorum aut demonum B
165 huiusmodi BP
166 indocta L
167 Om. L
168 gradus quae B
169 fere xvi BP

pulchra. Facit enim pulchrior pulcherrima. In e quae ueniunt a nominatiuo is terminato[170] generis communis, ut hic et haec dulcis. Facit enim dulce dulcius dulcissimum. In er quae significant qualitatem, siue sint secundae siue[171] tertiae declinationis, ut pulcher pulchrior pulcherrimus, niger nigrior nigerrimus, acer acrior acerrimus, celer celerior celerrimus. In es quae sunt tertiae declinationis et utrique sexui conueniunt, ut diues uir, diues mulier. Facit enim diues[172] [173]diuitior diuitissimus[173]. In is quae utrique sexui conueniunt et in e faciunt neutrum, ut dulcis uir[174] et mulier. Facit enim dulce uinum, et comparatur ita: dulcior[175] dulcissimum[176] uel dulcissima[177]. In us quae sunt secundae declinationis et femininum in a faciunt, ut sanctus sancta. Facit enim sanctus sanctior sanctissimus, nisi sint superlatiua. In ans quaecumque sunt omnis generis, ut praestans praestantior praestantissimus. In ens similiter, ut prudens prudentior prudentissimus. In ers similiter, ut iners inertior inertissimus. In eps unum inuenitur, preceps precipitior praecipitissimus. In ax quecumque sunt omnis generis, ut audax audatior audacissimus. In ex similiter, ut simplex simplicior simplicissimus, praeter senex, quod est tantum generis masculini et facit senior comparatiuum, in superlatiuo uero deficit. In ix similiter, ut felix felicior felicissimus. In ox similiter, ut ferox ferocior ferocissimus, excepto pernox, quod a nocte compositum minime comparatur. In ux similiter, ut trux trucior trucissimus. In um quae a nominatiuo in us desinente ueniunt medio feminino a finito, ut iustus iusta [178]iustum. Facit enim iustum iustius[178] iustissimum. Omnis comparatiuus masculini feminini communis atque omnis[179] generis or finitur[180] et conuersa or in us neutri generis comparatiuum facit, ut doctus doctior et docta doctior, hic et haec dulcis dulcior, hic et haec et hoc audax audatior, quorum neutra sunt doctius dulcius audacius. Neutri uero nominis comparatiuus tantum us finitur, ut dulce dulcius[181], iustum iustius[182]. Omnis comparatiuus or finitus communis est generis semper, uel a nominatiuo [183]mobili per tria genera uel a communi aut ab omnis generis nominatiuo[183] uenit, ut hic sanctus sancta sanctum, [184]hic et haec[184] sanctior, hic et haec [185]suauis, hic et haec suauior, hic et haec[185] et hoc uelox, hic et haec uelocior. Excipitur senior, quod quia a masculino nascitur nominatiuo, masculini tantum generis habetur. Dicimus enim hic senex, similiter[186] hic senior. Superlatiuus masculini generis us finitur ut sanctissimus, feminini a ut sanctissima, neutri um ut sanctissimum semper.[187]

---

[170] terminata L
[171] seu BP
[172] Om. P
[173] corr. in ditior ditissimus L, sed lectio difficilior retinenda est
[174] et uir P
[175] Om. B
[176] dulcissimum BP
[177] dulcissime P
[178] Om. BP
[179] omnis est B
[180] finitus B
[181] dulcius dulcissimum B
[182] iustius iustissimum B
[183] Om. P
[184] Om. BP
[185] Om. P
[186] et B
[187] semper. ECPLICIT L

THE EDITION

B and P share many errors – particularly omissions – which show that they are descended from a common ancestor. L, on the other hand, is independent. Therefore, the agreement of L with either or both of B and P signifies the agreement of these two branches of the tradition, and such readings have normally been adopted both for the orthography and for major variants. Where the choice seemed arbitrary, L has usually been followed since it tends to be more accurate than BP. (This principle has been broken in the case of numbers: I have followed BP in writing them out rather than adopting L's Roman numerals; and for the spelling of the word *cetera*, where L habitually uses *e caudata*.) That the immediate common ancestor of BLP was not the autograph is suggested by the omission by all three manuscripts of *pus . . . uasis* (16–7) and the wrong reading *numeri nominum* for *numerorum nomina* (43). It follows from this that the individual variants of B and of P are of no significance in establishing the original version of the text. However, since the interest of a grammar lies as much in the use that was made of it as in its composition, the original version is only part of its story. For this reason, the apparatus includes many readings from B and P which have some intrinsic interest: they show the scribes trying to put lists into alphabetical order (for example, P at lines 11–12 and 16), adding examples (B 267; P 233) or phrases of clarification (P 172), correcting the text (B 98–9, 156, 184(!); P 250–2, 273–5), making minor stylistic improvements (B 305, 329; P 137, 235). Omissions of examples and of significant portions of the text (but not normally of *et, ut, sunt, hic haec hoc*) have been reported for all three manuscripts.[28]

FONTES ET LOCI PARALLELI

Amb.	Amiens, Bibliothèque municipale MS 426, fos 48r–71v
Aug. Reg.	pseudo-Augustine, *Regulae*, GL V 496–524
Beatus	*Beatus quid est*: London, British Library, Harley 3271, fos 93r–113v
BN lat. 7560	Paris, Bibliothèque Nationale lat. 7560, fos 43r–45r
Bon.	*Ars Bonifatii*, ed. G.J. Gebauer and B. Löfstedt, CCSL 133B
CCSL	*Corpus Christianorum Series Latina*
Cl. F.	Clermont Ferrand, Bibliothèque municipale MS 241, fos 20r–34v
Decl. nom.	*Declinationes nominum*: Munich, Bayerische Staatsbibliothek Clm 6281, fos 108v–114v

[28] I am grateful to the staff of the libraries concerned for preparing microfilms of the manuscripts cited. Special thanks are due to Dr Obbema and his staff at the Leiden University Library for their hospitality during a visit in December 1976 in the course of which this text was transcribed.

De dubiis nom.	*De dubiis nominibus*, ed. F. Glorie, CCSL 133A, 743–820
Donatus	*Ars minor* and *Ars maior*, ed. L. Holtz, *Donat et la tradition de l'enseignement grammatical* pp. 585–674
Dos.	*Ars Dosithei*, GL VII 376–436
Exc. Char.	*Ex Charisii arte grammatica excerpta*, GL I 533–65
GL	*Grammatici Latini*, ed. H.Keil
P. Diac.	*Ars Donati quam Paulus Diaconus exposuit*, ed. A.Amelli (Monte Cassino 1899)
Ph.	Phocas, *Ars de nomine et uerbo*, GL V 410–39
P. Pis.	*Ars Petri Pisani*: St Gall, Stiftsbibliothek 876, pp. 34–85
Prisc. *De accent.*	Priscian, *De accentibus*, GL III 519–28
Prisc. *De fig. num.*	Priscian, *De figuris numerorum*, GL III 406–17
Prisc. *IG*	Priscian, *Institutiones grammaticae*, ed. M. Hertz, GL II–III
Prisc. *Inst. de nom.*	Priscian, *Institutio de nomine et pronomine et uerbo*, GL III 443–56
Prisc. *Part.*	Priscian, *Partitiones*, GL III 459–515
Scaurus	*Ars Scauri*: Munich, Bayerische Staatsbibliothek Clm 6281, fos 52r–62v
Tatw.	*Ars Tatuini*, ed. M. De Marco, CCSL 133, pp. 1–93
Tol. 99–30	Toledo, Biblioteca del Cabildo 99–30, fos 33v–34v
Usuard	*Usuardi Grammatica*, ed. J.M.Casas Homs, *Miscel·lània Anselm M. Albareda* (= *Analecta Montserratensia* 10), pp. 85–129

APPARATUS FONTIUM

line		
	2	fuga – 5 Fescenninus *e Don. mai. lib. I c. iv* (607,9–608,20) *excerpta*
	5	fax – 7 Micenae *e Don. mai. lib. I c. v* (609,11–610,7) *excerpta*
	7	magister – felix *e Don. min. c. ii* (586,19–587, 24) *excerpta*
	8–10	– uir Ph. 411,32–412,1
		las Ph. Clm 6281 fo. 92v
	10	cf. Ph. 411,30–2
	11–14	– res Ph. 412,1–5
	14–5	cf. Ph. 411,30–2
	16–7	Ph. 412,5–6
	17	tria–deficiunt Ph. 412,7
		lac Prisc. IG VI 213,1
		uer Aug. Reg. 500,1
	18	tres–habent Ph. 412,7
	19	aes far ius rus Ph. 412,7–8
		mel Prisc. IG VII 310,16
	19	Ph. 412,6–7
	20–2	Prisc. IG V 142,19–22
	22–3	Prisc. IG V 142,27–143,1
	24–5	– Agrippa Ph. 412,18–19
		Niceta Galba BN lat. 7560 fo. 43r (P. Diac. 4,35–6); Niceta Cl. F. 241 fo. 20r (Usuard 88,4); Galba Amb. fo. 49r; Tol. 99–30 f. 34r
	27–8	cf. BN lat. 7560 fo. 43r (P. Diac. 5,10); P. Pis. p. 41; Cl. F. 241 fo. 20r (Usuard 89,17)
	28	Ph. 412,25
	28–9	sapientia – scientia cf. Decl. nom. fo.108v; BN lat. 7560 fo. 43r (P. Diac. 5,8–9)
	29–32	saepe – 41 appellatiua cf. BN lat. 7560 fo. 43r (P. Diac. 5,8)
	32–3	Ph. 412,20, cf. Prisc. IG V 144,11–145,1
	33–4	quae-scriba Prisc. IG V 143,20–144,1
	34–5	lixa-scurra + poeta Ph. 412,20–1
	34	scurra–36 poetria BN lat. 7560 fo. 43r (P. Diac. 4,33–5,2)
	37–8	agricola–conuiua Prisc. IG V 144,5
		rurigena Ph. 412,24
		collega Ph. 412,20
	38–40	Amb. fo. 49r; Prisc. IG V 145,3–5
	40–2	cf. Tatw. 33,1009–15; Amb. fo. 52r; al.
	42–3	cf. Amb. fo. 48v; BN lat. 7560 fo. 43r (P. Diac. 5,11–13);[29] P. Pis. p. 42; Cl. F. 241 fo. 20r (Usuard 89,21); al.

[29] Amelli's text should be corrected to read, with the manuscript: 'Similiter declinatur manna et si qua repperiuntur similia.'

Apparatus fontium to pp. 24–33

| ne | 43–9 | cf. Prisc. IG V 145,5–10; De fig. num. 412,20–413,2 |

ne 43–9 cf. Prisc. IG V 145,5–10; De fig. num. 412,20–413,2
50–1 E–munile Ph. 413,1–2
50–4 sedile–tornatile + amictile–irascibile Decl. nom. fo.112r; cubile–superhumerale Tatw. 33,1021–3
55–6 Prisc. IG V 145,13–15
        senapi IG VI 205,1
57–8 Prisc. IG V 146,15 (cornu–gelu); Ph. 414,11–13
59–61 Ph. 413,4–7
62–3 cogitatio–enixio cf. Tatw. 34,1050–2
        coniugatio Prisc. IG V 145,18
64–5 senio–quaternio Ph. 413,8
        bibio cf. Prisc. IG V 146,2 (bubo, bibo MSS)
65–6 cf. Ph. 413,14–15 + 18–19
66–7 Ph. 413,15–16; Decl. nom. fo.110v; cf. Tatw. 33,1033–4
67–8 Ph. 413,8–9; cf. Tatw. 33,1035 (Scipio)
69–70 Ph. 413,16–18
70–1 Prisc. IG V 146,8 (homo latro) + IG VI 206,22 (homonis)
71 octo cf. Amb. fo. 52v
71–2 pondo Ph. 413,24–7
72–3 ambo duo Amb. fo. 52v
73 Ph. 413,18–19
73–4 Ph. 413,20–1; Prisc. IG IV 122,5–6; Tatw. 33,1041–3 + 34,1056–62; cf. Amb. fo. 52rv
74–5 cf. Ph. 413,21–2; Prisc. IG V 145,19–21
76 Ph. 413,22–4; Prisc. IG V 145,21–2 (Cupido) + 24 (margo)
77 cf. Ph. 413,3
78–9 cf. Ph. 414,8–9
79–80 Ph. 413,26–7
81 Prisc. IG VI 215,11–12
82 Prisc. IG VI 215,13
83 Ph. 414,27
84–5 Tatw. 31,965–9 + 972–3 + 32,980 (tentorium < territorium) + 986–7
86–7 Ph. 414,17–18; Prisc. IG V 147,6–7; cf. Amb. fo. 52v
87–8 Ph. 414,18–19; Prisc. IG V 147,7–8
88–9 animal – lupercal Ph. 414,17
        ceruical Prisc. IG V 147,1; VI 214,10; Tatw. 34, 1078
        ceruical chrismal Decl. nom. fo.112r; Amb. fo. 52v; al.
89 cf. Ph. 414,16
90–2 Ph. 414,19–22
        mugilus cf. Clm 6281 fo. 94r
93–4 Ph. 414,22–3
95–6 Ph. 414,23–5
97–100 – carmen Ph. 414,30–415,5
98–9 Tatw. 35,1092–8; Decl. nom. fo. 112r; al.

line   101 Prisc. IG V 149,10–11
    101–2 cum fluuii–significat Prisc. IG VI 222,11–12
    102–3 Prisc. IG V 150,6–8
    103–5 Ph. 415,8–9 + 10–11
    106–7 Er – cicer Ph. 415,14–16
      107 uer Ph. 412,6
           piper Prisc. IG VI 205,9
           ruder Amb. fo. 53v
           pauper Prisc. IG V 152,8; Ph. 415,33
           uber Prisc. IG V 152,13; Ph. 415,34
           celer Prisc. IG V 152,1
      108 alia – sunt Ph. 415,17
           pulcher–niger Ph. 415,20
           pater–anser Ph. 415,23–4
      109 puer–auster Ph. 415,29–30
  109–11 Ph. 415,17–18
  111–2 Secundae–nigra Ph. 415,19–21
  112–3 cf. Cl. F. 241 fo. 20v (Usuard 90,32–3)
113–24 cf. Prisc. IG IV 127,8–15; VI 223,17–24; Prisc. Inst. de nom. 444,
         12–15
  124–6 Prisc. Inst. de nom. 444,17–19; cf. Ph. 415,29–32
  126–7 Ph. 415,22–4
      128 Prisc. Inst. de nom. 444,19–21
  128–9 Ph. 416,3
129–31 Prisc. Inst. de nom. 444,21–3
  132–3 Ph. 416,7–12
           cor Ph. 412,5; Prisc. IG V 154,19
  133–5 Prisc. IG V 154,20–1
  135–6 – melior Ph. 416,17–19
  137–9 Prisc. IG V 154,8–9
  138–9 Ector Ph. 416,16 Antenor Hector cf. Cl. F. 241 fo. 23r (Usuard 94,99)
139–40 Ph. 416,6
  141–2 Prisc. IG V 154,24–155,3
           satur–femininum Ph. 416,22–3
  142–3 Ph. 416,24–6
  143–4 excepto – satur Ph. 416,22
      146 Eneas Prisc. Inst. de nom. 443,12; al.
           Lysias Prisc. Inst. de nom. 443,25
           Lysias Andreas BN lat. 7560 fo. 43v (P. Diac. 5,30–1)
  146–7 Prisc. IG V 155,22–156,1
  148–9 Ph. 416,28–9
149–50 cf. Ph. 416,28 + 412,13–14
      151 es–Ulixes Prisc. IG V 159,8–9
           Anchises Prisc. IG VI 245,12; Inst. de nom. 443,12; al.

ine   152 Demostenes Prisc. IG VI 246,17
              Mithridates Prisc. IG VI 246,11
              Orontes Prisc. IG VI 245,14
      153–5 Don. mai. 616,3–4
              Priamides Prisc. IG II 66,14
              Atrides Don. mai. 616,3
              Pelides Prisc. IG II 66,3
              Anchisiades Prisc. IG II 66,9
      155–6 Ph. 417,33–418,1
         156 meridies Ph. 417,31
      156–7 Ph. 417,27–9
              abies Ph. 418,2
              quies Ph. 417,33
              macies glaties cf. Tatw. 41,1312; al.
   158–60 eiusdem–cedis, proles pubes Ph. 417,5–8
              strues lues Prisc. IG V 159,13–14
              sedes cf. Tatw. 37,1173; al.
      160–2 que–merces Ph. 417,8–11
              seges teges Ph. 417,22
      162–3 cf. Prisc. IG V 156,10–14
      164–5 comes–teres Prisc. IG V 156,14–22; cf. Ph. 417,23–4
              cocles Ph. 417,12
         165 interpres Prisc. IG VI 241,7
      165–6 praeses–residis Ph. 417,26–7
         166 ales cf. Tatw. 37,1173; al.
      166–7 alipes bipes–quadrupes Ph. 417,14–15
              semipes cf. Ph. 417,15 (sonipes)
      168–9 Prisc. De accent. 524,16–17
   169–70 – stipes Prisc. IG V 158,4–6
         171 pes cf. Prisc. IG VI 243,7
      171–2 cf. Prisc. De accent. 524,26–8
      172–3 Ph. 417,33–418,2
      174–5 cf. Ph. 417,8–9
      176–7 Ph. 418,4–6
              splenis renis cf. Tatw. 37,1177; al.
      177–8 Ph. 418,6–7
   178–80 Ph. 418,8–10
      180–1 Prisc. IG V 161,11; cf. Ph. 418,11–12
      181–3 quae–nauis Ph. 418,12–16
         183 apis–uallis Tatw. 37,1179 + 1181
      183–5 Ph. 418,25–6 + 28–30
      185–7 si–fortis, dulcis suauis Ph. 418,17–18 + 20–2
              amabilis–humilis Tatw. 37,1183–7
      187–9 Ph. 418,18–21

line   190 Prisc. IG V 161,22–3
                Prisc. IG V 161,24
     190–1 Prisc. IG V 161,23–4
     191–2 Prisc. IG V 161,24–5
      192 Ph. 419,5–7
    193–4 Ph. 419,24–6
           Virgilius cf. Prisc. IG VI 258,21 + VII 301,18; Amb. fo. 50v;
           Bon. 22,212 + 28,360; Usuard 91,63; BN lat. 7560 fo. 43v; al.
           Mercurius Prisc. IG VII 301,20; cf. Bon. 28,359
           Terrentius Ph. 419,26; Prisc. IG VII 303,11; Bon. 22,212 + 28,360;
               Usuard 91,64
           Laurentius Bon. 28,360; Cl. F. 241 fo. 21v (Usuard 61,65 + 68)
           Vincentius Cl. F. 241 fo. 21v (Usuard 91,68)
           Marcus Ph. 419,27; Amb. fo. 50v; Cl. F. 241 fo. 21r (Usuard 90,56)
           Saturnus cf. Prisc. Part. 511,14
           Paulus Amb. 50v; Cl. F. 241 fo. 21r (Usuard 90,56)
    194–5 Prisc. IG VI 269,21–2
    195–6 Ph. 420,18–20
    196–9 cf. Prisc. IG V 163,19 + 23–164,1; Inst. de nom. 445,25–6
199–202   Prisc. IG VI 273,12–274,1; Inst. de nom. 445,24–6; Tatw. 38,1206–11
    202–3 Prisc. IG V 163,20–1
    203–5 Prisc. Inst. de nom. 445,37–9; cf. Ph. 420,11–12
    205–6 cf. Prisc. Inst. de nom. 445,29–30; IG V 163,19–20; VI 264,8; De
               accent. 525,21–2
    207–8 Nomina–prunus Ph. 420,8–9
           cyparissus laurus mirtus IG V 162,1–2; Cl. F. 241 fo. 21v (Usuard
               91,70–1)
           malus Tatw. 31,959; Bon. 22,221; Cl. F. 241 fo. 21v (Usuard 91,71)
           cedrus Cl. F. 241 fo. 21v (Usuard 91,71); BN lat. 7560 fo. 43v (P. Diac.
               6,28)
    208–9 Prisc. Inst. de nom. 445,18–20
      210 Prisc. IG VI 261,9
    210–12 cf. P. Pis. p. 44; Bern. 105,7–8
           Tyrus Cyprus Arctus Prisc. Inst. de nom. 445,17–18
           Aegyptus P. Diac. 6,35; Amb. fo. 50v; Cl. F. 241 fo. 21v (Usuard
               91,72); Decl. nom. fo. 109r; P. Pis. p. 44; al.
           abissus Amb. fo. 50v; Cl. F. 241 fo. 21v (Usuard 91,70); Decl.
               nom. fo. 109r; al.
    212–14 Ph. 420,13–16
           acus Prisc. IG V 162,10
           tribus Prisc. IG V 163,8
    214–16 quae–rictus cf. Prisc. Inst. de nom. 444,33–5
    216–17 uisus–uersus cf. BN lat. 7560 fo. 44v (P. Diac. 9,34–9)
      217 status Ph. 419,32

ine 217–20 actus–cultus Decl. nom. fos 112v–113r
      220 a uolo uultus Prisc. Inst. de nom. 445,3
      221 lectus Prisc. Inst. de nom. 444,36; cf. IG VI 257,4–5
           Ph. 419,30–420,1
     224–7 Decl. nom. fo. 109r
           mustus Prisc. Inst. de nom. 444,36
     231–3 Eiusdem–lucus Ph. 419,24–8
           cibus Prisc. IG VI 258,22
     233–4 culmus–gibbus Decl. nom. fo. 109r
     234–5 exceptis–feminini Ph. 420,6–8
     235–6 Prisc. IG VI 268,16–7
      236 sexus cf. Prisc. IG VI 256,5
           lacus cf. Prisc. IG VI 259,18; Inst. de nom. 445,3
    236–45 Prisc. Inst. de nom. 445,10–15
     246–7 Ph. 421,28–9
     248–9 –peruicax Ph. 420,24–6
    249–50 efficax–sagax Tatw. 38,1225–8
     250–2 Ph. 420,23–4
      253 lex fex prex nex Ph. 412,1–3
           ilex carex Ph. 420,31
           pelex carex Prisc. IG V 164,20
     253–4 IG V 167,6–7
     254–6 Ph. 421,1–3
     256–8 cf. Tatw. 38,1234–6; Amb. fo. 55r; Cl. F. 241 fo. 24v (Usuard
                96,229–30); Prisc. IG VII 340,3–11
     258–9 Ph. 420,28
      259 rex grex Prisc. IG V 164,8; Ph. 411,33–4
    259–60 apex–murex codex culex Ph. 420,29–30; Prisc. IG V 164,23–4
           uerbex Ph. 421,5; Prisc. IG V 165,5
           rex grex apex pollex pumex pontifex latex Tatw. 38,1231–3; cf. Decl.
                nom. fo.112v; Amb. fo. 55r; al.
      260 uerbex–genetiuo Ph. 421,4–5
     260–1 cf. Ph. 420,28 + 421,2
     262–3 –genetrix Ph. 421,12–15
      264 nutritor nutrix Prisc. IG IV 140,16–18 et alibi
     263–4 uictrix–peccatrix Tatw. 39,1240–2
      265 Ph. 421,9–10
      266 calix fornix uarix Ph. 421,6
           bernix (berfix < beruix) lodix Tatw. 39,1237–8
           natrix Ph. 421,16
      267 salix–cornix Ph. 421,7–8
     267–8 meretrix cicatrix Ph. 421,17
      268 Ph. 421,18
    269–70 –uelox Ph. 421,18–20

line   270 pernox Prisc. IG V 166,10
               uox nox Ph. 412,3–4; Prisc. IG V 166,12
               celox Ph. 421,22; Prisc. IG V 166,11
         271–2 cf. Ph. 421,20–1
         272 –crux Ph. 421,25
         273 trux Ph. 412,9
               frux cf. De dubiis nom. 775,294
         274 Unum–Pollux Ph. 421,23–4
         274–5 u–genitiuo Prisc. De accent. 526,4
         275 Prisc. IG V 166,14–15
         277–9 cf. Ph. 411,32–412,3
               fors Prisc. IG V 168,6
               puls IG VII 320,12
               daps IG VII 321,6
         279–80 Ph. 422,1–2
         280–1 expers–inops Prisc. IG V 167,11
               celebs Ph. 422,4
               princeps Prisc. IG V 167,13
         281–3 Ph. 422,6–9
         283 Ph. 422,2–3
         284–5 Prisc. IG VII 319,5–6
         286–7 Prisc. IG V 169,4–5; VII 318,20–1
         288–94 cf. Amb. fo. 57r; Prisc. De fig. num. 412,22–413,2
         288–9 cf. Prisc. IG V 188,21–189,1
         293–4 Prisc. IG V 145,9–10
         295–9 cf. Dos. 390,3–7; Scaurus fos 53v–54r; Exc. Char. 533,12–15
         299–340 cf. Beatus fo. 93rv; Aug Reg. 504,3–505,25

A Breton pilgrim in England
in the reign of King Æthelstan

CAROLINE BRETT

INTRODUCTION

In one of the partly burned manuscripts of the Cottonian collection (London, British Library, MS. Cotton Tiberius A.xv),[1] there is an isolated anonymous letter which may shed a ray of light on the relations between England and Brittany in the tenth century. It was printed, together with other letters from the same manuscript, by William Stubbs,[2] but with a few errors and silent emendations; it has never received a translation or separate comment. It seems to be worth re-editing it and setting what meaning may be elicited from its awkward Latin and fire-damaged lines in the context of a body of evidence for the religious and cultural links which must have accompanied King Æthelstan's political aid to an exiled Breton noble family in the 930s.[3] The discussion of the letter's date and place of origin necessitates a close examination of the manuscript; as the bulk of the manuscript consists of a collection of letters by Alcuin, this study may incidentally illuminate the textual transmission of that author also.

THE LETTER

The letter introduces a warrior (*miles*) of Brittany who has become an anchorite and, at a time of peace, has travelled to England, sought the help of Æthelstan and been installed by him as a religious at a place called *Cen*. He now wishes to make another pilgrimage, and the writer of the letter asks 'all observers of the Catholic faith' to assist him on his travels. The writer, like the anchorite, is

---

[1] In 1731 the manuscript-collection of Sir Robert Cotton, then kept at Westminster, was partly destroyed in a fire: see Planta, *Catalogue of the Manuscripts in the Cottonian Library*, pp. xii–xiv.
[2] *Memorials*, pp. 381–2: editorially entitled *Epistola Commendatoria*.
[3] Existing treatments of this theme include Robinson, *The Times*; Keynes, 'King Athelstan's books'; Chédeville and Guillotel, *La Bretagne*, pp. 309–402; Dumville, *Wessex and England*, ch. 4.

anonymous. The letter may once have ended with his name, but unfortunately the last twenty or so characters are completely illegible. From the way in which he contrasts *Britannia citra marina* with *uestram . . . Anglo-Saxonum Britanniam*, it seems clear that the writer was from the Continent.[4] He would seem to have been a religious superior or spiritual director of the anchorite, although it is hard to divine his exact position at the time of writing. If he was still on the Continent, would he have been asked to write on behalf of a religious who had long been in England, and what weight would his recommendation have carried? To dispose of these difficulties one may best picture him as a Continental who had gained some ecclesiastical office in England (probably in Wessex), or as head of a Continental religious establishment which had formed links with the English Church. More will be said on these possibilities below.

The only internal dating evidence in the letter is the reference to Æthelstan: 'by permission of the most Christian King Æthelstan, having become an anchorite, he led his life religiously . . . for no few days. By his [Æthelstan's] advice and permission he comes on this pilgrimage also . . .'. The writing of the letter may thus be placed within the reign of Æthelstan, 924 x 939, and the content must be related to the historical background of that time.[5]

Brittany was politically troubled for the entire period. The annalist Flodoard of Rheims recounts for 919 that Scandinavian invaders seized Brittany, 'having captured, sold or else thrown out all the Bretons'.[6] From 919 to 936 the region seems from the scanty evidence to have been under Scandinavian overlordship, interrupted by scattered 'revolts' and Frankish pressure on Nantes and the lower Loire. The mid-eleventh-century Chronicle of Nantes[7] states that a Breton ruler, Matuedoi, count of Poher, son-in-law of King Alan 'the Great', spent this time in exile at the court of Æthelstan with his son, Alan, and a large number of Bretons. This probably did not leave Brittany void of any native political initiative: a shadowy figure 'Berenger' appears as a count in a few late sources, *Translatio Sancti Maglorii* and the *Historia Moderna* of Hugh of Fleury.[8] However, Flodoard saw the return of the Bretons from Æthelstan's protection in 936 as a decisive event: 'The Bretons, coming back from overseas with the support of King *Alstanus*, regained their land'. The Chronicle of Nantes states that Alan, son of Matuedoi, was their leader; this finds some support in a charter in the eleventh-century Cartulary of Landévennec,[9] in which *Alanus dux Britonum*

---

[4]   This is the earliest known use of the compound form *Anglo-Saxones*, other than in royal charters, in which it had been used since the reign of Alfred: see Keynes, 'King Athelstan's books', p. 158, nn. 77–8.

[5]   For the context, see Dumville, *England and the Celtic World*.

[6]   *Les annales de Flodoard*, ed. Lauer.

[7]   *La chronique de Nantes*, ed. Merlet (§ 27).

[8]   *Translatio Sancti Maglorii*, *apud* Bollandus *et al.*, *Acta Sanctorum*, October, vol. X, pp. 791–3; *Liber modernorum regum Francorum*, ed. Waitz, *apud* Pertz, *Monumenta Germaniae Historica*, *Scriptores*, IX.337–95. For comment, see Merlet, 'Les origines du monastère'; Chédeville and Guillotel, *La Bretagne*, pp. 390–5.

[9]   *Le Cartulaire*, edd. Le Men and Ernault, pp. 562–3, no. 25. Because of its importance

grants land to the abbot of Landévennec, John, 'because he [John] had called him [Alan] and invited him to this side of the sea' (*quia uocauit illum infra mare atque inuitatuit*). The charter refers further, though obscurely, to John's diplomatic activities. For 937 Flodoard stated that the re-established Bretons fought a number of campaigns against the Scandinavians; for 939 he reported a Breton victory involving the capture of some castles.

The warfare of the period is implicitly referred to in our letter-writer's statement that his protégé crossed the sea *adhuc quiete temporis et pacis*; but the interval of peace which he meant is impossible to pin-point in Flodoard's account. Unless the anchorite really came to England before 919, in the reign of Æthelstan's father, Edward the Elder (899–924), whom we also know to have cultivated relations with Breton churchmen,[10] the 'peace' of the letter must refer to some temporary local period of peace within Brittany during the period 924–939, and warns us against taking Flodoard's notices to represent the total picture. The point of the letter-writer's using the phrase, however, seems to have been to stress that the anchorite came to England for religious purposes, as a bona fide pilgrim, and not as a refugee using religious status to gain preferential treatment. We may picture a fairly constant drift of pilgrims in either direction across the English Channel and the Irish Sea in the early middle ages – compare, for example, the incident in the Anglo-Saxon Chronicle of the three Irishmen who arrived at King Alfred's court.[11] However, the letter implies that their numbers were increasing as a result of the political circumstances.

Æthelstan's political support of exiled Bretons[12] was complemented by interest in and aid to Breton clergy uprooted by viking attacks. Other sources than our letter give explicit evidence of this, notably a letter to Æthelstan from Radbod, prior of the community of St Samson of Dol, preserved in William of Malmesbury's *De gestis pontificum Anglorum*.[13] Like ours, this letter is datable only by its reference to Æthelstan. Radbod, calling himself the *praepositus* of the *summus pontifex* Samson, reminded Æthelstan that the latter's father had commended himself to the community's prayers, assured him of their continued intercession,

---

and ambiguity on the subject of Anglo-Breton relations, I reproduce the charter from Le Men and Ernault's edition in Appendix 1 below, with a translation. For comment, see Guillotel, 'Le premier siècle', p. 71.

[10] The community of Dol: see below on this page.

[11] *s.a.* 891.

[12] Some doubt is thrown on this support by the Welsh poem *Armes Prydein Vawr*, conventionally dates to the 930s, which prophesied that Bretons would join in a Welsh-led war against the English. David Dumville has raised the possibility that this might indicate that there was a faction of Bretons who aligned themselves with vikings against Æthelstan and his protégés, but has rejected the suggestion as unproven, since the mythical elements in the poem make it seem likely that the poet was referring to an ancient tradition rather than to immediate political circumstances: see Dumville, 'Brittany and "Armes Prydein Vawr" '.

[13] William of Malmesbury, *De Gestis Pontificum*, § 249 (ed. Hamilton, pp. 399–400).

sent him a gift of the relics of SS. Senator, Paternus, and Scubilio, and asked for his help, since 'for our just deserts and sins we dwell in exile and captivity in Francia'. The letter, states William of Malmesbury, was stored in a shrine of relics at the monastery of *Medeltun*, which Æthelstan had founded, endowing it with relics of St Samson. It thus seems that Æthelstan acquired relics of Samson also, although it is not clear whether he responded to the Dol canons' request for help. In William's own day the shrine was at Middleton: it bore the inscription 'King Æthelstan, emperor of all Britain and of many peoples round about, ordered this [shrine], which deserved to receive these relics from lands across the sea, to be made in honour of St Paternus'.

That Æthelstan was the recipient of relics from Brittany is further evidenced by a note in the abbey-register of Middleton (unfortunately of unknown date, since the manuscript is now lost)[14] on the relics given by *rex Adelstanus*: 'an arm and many bones of St Samson the archbishop . . . again an arm of St Branwalatr, bishop . . .'. William of Malmesbury gives similar information: Æthelstan 'deposited [in Middleton] many saints' relics bought from Britain across the sea, among which the bones of the most blessed Samson, once most holy archbishop of Dol, stand out pre-eminently . . .'.[15] Equally explicit is the evidence of an Old English list of relics added about the year 1100 to a Breton gospel-book then at Exeter (Oxford, Bodleian Library, MS. Auct.D.2.16 [S.C. 2719]) and repeated, with some differences, in Latin in Oxford, Bodleian Library, MS. Bodley 579 (S.C. 2675) (the 'Leofric Missal'), given to Exeter Cathedral by Bishop Leofric (1050–1072).[16] This records how Æthelstan founded the monastery of SS. Mary and Peter at Exeter and enriched it with the greater part of the relics listed; the Old English version refers to his systematically sending messengers to foreign lands to buy relics.[17] The list includes parts of the bodies of the Breton saints Winwaloe, Wennal, Conocan, Melanius, Withenoc, Machutus (Malo), Tudwal, and Wigenoc;[18] also of St Ipotemius (or Hypothemius), bishop of Angers, whose body had been translated to Redon in Brittany between 832 and 842.[19] The gospel-book itself is evidence for links with Brittany, as it shows signs of having

---

[14] Dugdale, *Monasticon Anglicanum*, II.349–50; Davis, *Medieval Cartularies*, p. 75, no. 668. The manuscript was kept in the King's Remembrancer's Office at the time when the extracts printed by Dugdale were made, and contained material relating to the tenth to fourteenth centuries.

[15] *Gesta Pontificum*, § 85 (ed. Hamilton, p. 186).

[16] *The Leofric Missal*, ed. Warren, p. xix. See now Conner, *Anglo-Saxon Exeter*.

[17] Apparently not all English relic-collectors were legitimate buyers: in eleventh-century hagiographical texts written on the Continent it became a topos for Englishmen to attempt to steal relics; see Geary, *Furta Sacra*, pp. 60–3.

[18] For summary details and bibliography on the lives of these saints, see Duine, 'Mémento', nos 7, 6, 56, 13, 211, 11, 208; Lapidge and Sharpe, *A Bibliography*, nos 827, 919–20, 938–40, 930–1, 825, 955–7.

[19] *The Monks of Redon*, ed. Brett, pp. 7, 170–4; *Cartulaire*, ed. de Courson, pp. 164–5, no. 214.

been written at Landévennec, St Winwaloe's principal monastery, destroyed by vikings in 913.[20]

Æthelstan gave the initial impetus to a flood of Breton relic-imports and liturgical influence in south-west England, the result of which we see in the more plentiful sources of the late tenth and the eleventh centuries. A selection of Breton saints – Malo/Machutus, Winnoc, Samson, Winwaloe, Iudos, Branwalatr, Iwi – came to be widely honoured with feast-days in surviving calendars,[21] and many abbeys boasted possession of the relics of one or more. An Old English tract from ca 1030 on 'the resting-places of the saints'[22] mentions Samson and Branwalatr at Middleton, Iwi at Wilton, Iudoc in New Minster, Winchester, and Melor at Amesbury; William of Malmesbury, in Gesta pontificum, mentions Melor also.[23] Winchester especially was a centre of 'Bretonism': St Machutus was 'adopted' as a bishop of Winchester, and an Old English Life of him was adapted according to this theory.[24] London, British Library, MS Cotton Galba A.xiv, a prayer-book of the first half of the eleventh century from Nunnaminster in the diocese of Winchester, founded in 963, contains a litany with a string of Breton names (some illegible) and a hymn to St Machutus. Three eleventh-century Winchester kalendars – those in London, British Library, MSS. Arundel 60, Arundel 155, and Cotton Vitellius E.xviii – are particularly rich in feasts of Breton saints.[25] Of course not all this activity was caused directly by Æthelstan and his imports of Breton relics. It would seem that the cult of St Iudoc arrived at the beginning of the tenth century, according to a note in version F of the Anglo-Saxon Chronicle (from Canterbury) placing 'St Iudoc's arrival' in 903, together with the consecration of the New Minster, Winchester.[26] The link with Landévennec and St Winwaloe may not have begun until St Dunstan stayed from 955 to 957 in Blandinium (Ghent), which claimed to possess the saint's relics.[27] However, the years between 919 and 939 undoubtedly saw a greater concentration of Breton influence in England than ever before. It could be said to have borne fruit in the Benedictine reform of the 970s. The first models for

[20] Lapidge and Sharpe, A Bibliography, no. 965; Calendar of Landévennec, ed. Deuffic, 'Calendrier', p. 21.

[21] For the texts, see Wormald, English Kalendars; for additional comment on Breton saints in the English liturgy, see Wormald, 'The English saints'; Gasquet and Bishop, The Bosworth Psalter; Gougaud, 'Mentions anglaises'; Warren, 'Un monument' (on litanies from Salisbury, Cathedral Library, MS. 180); Bishop, Liturgica Historica, p. 389 (hymn to St Machutus from London, British Library, MS. Cotton Galba A.xiv); Dewick and Frere, The Leofric Collectar, II.618–26 (litany from the same manuscript).

[22] Die Heiligen Englands, ed. Liebermann; discussed by Rollason, 'Lists'.

[23] Gesta Pontificum, § 87 (ed. Hamilton, p. 188).

[24] Gasquet and Bishop, The Bosworth Psalter, p. 56; Ker, A Catalogue, pp. 218–19, no. 168; London, British Library, MSS. Cotton Otho A.viii, fos 7–34, and Cotton Otho B.x, fo 66.

[25] On Cotton Galba A.xiv, see Ker, Catalogue, no. 157 (p. 198); on the calendars, see Gasquet and Bishop, The Bosworth Psalter, p. 56.

[26] Trier, Der heilige Jodocus, pp. 152–3.

[27] Doble, St Winwaloe, p. 46; Whitelock, 'The appointment', p. 233.

the new Anglo-Caroline script which had been developed in connexion with the reform included Breton manuscripts.[28] But that the Breton influence was not universally appreciated is evident in an Old English poem, 'Seasons of Fasting', written perhaps in the circle of Wulfstan, bishop of London, bishop of Worcester and archbishop of York, between 980 and 1020: the poem refers to the differences in the dating of the Ember fasts in England and on the Continent and contains the warning: 'If Bretons or Franks, having come from the south, should then say to you that you should hold any forbidding here on earth of what Moses once spoke to men, not at all should you ever become receivers of it'.[29]

This makes it plain that Breton personnel, and not just books and relics, had come into the English Church; part of the value of the letter in Cotton Tiberius A.xv is that it is a specific piece of evidence for this less tangible import.

Unfortunately the attempt to trace the author and the subject of the letter further gives no certain results. Cen, where the anchorite is said to have lived, cannot be identified with any known Anglo-Saxon ecclesiastical site. Stubbs rejected an identification with Cerne, the Anglo-Saxon name of which was not Cen but Cernel.[30] There are two places called Kenn – Kenn in Somerset, ten miles north-west of Congresbury near the Severn estuary, and Kenn in Devon, between Exeter and Dawlish – but neither is referred to in any pre-Conquest source, and neither has or had a church dedicated to a Breton saint or any other distinctive sign. To look for a modern-day Kenn may be pointless, since, as Stubbs suggested, the place in question might have changed its name to that of the saint who lived there. It is also possible that the text of the letter is corrupt here, as it fails to make sense at some other points. However, the name Kenn comes from a Celtic river-name cognate with Welsh Caint;[31] each of the surviving places named Kenn is so called because it is sited on a stream of the same name. Our Cen, therefore, was most probably near one of these two rivers too. Whether the anchorite is more likely to have lived on the Somerset Kenn, in a remote region, possibly still with a British strain, where St Congar, probably a local British saint, was venerated nearby at a monastery which had been active in Alfred's time,[32] or near Exeter closer to a known centre of Æthelstan's activity, or at some third Cen, as yet unidentified, it is impossible to guess.

---

[28] Examples: Oxford, Bodleian Library, MS. Hatton 42 was written on the Continent and glossed in Breton in the second half of the ninth century, except the first seven folios, which were added later in an Anglo-Caroline hand; Oxford, St John's College, MS. 194 is a gospel-book written probably in Brittany, to which was added a colour-wash drawing of St Matthew in the style of the early Benedictine reform in England. For these and other examples of Breton manuscripts brought to England in the tenth century, see Bullough, 'The educational tradition', p. 475; Alexander, 'The Benedictional', p. 173; An Early Breton Gospel Book, edd. Wormald and Alexander. For the context, see Bullough, 'The Continental background', especially p. 27.

[29] Sisam, Studies, pp. 45–60. I am indebted to Mr Paul Bibire for the translation.

[30] Stubbs, Memorials, p. 382.

[31] Ekwall, English Place-Names, p. 271.

[32] Doble, 'St Congar'; Asser, § 81 (ed. Stevenson, p. 68).

Equally impossible to trace are his movements afterwards. The implied addressing of the letter to christians of England suggests that his intended pilgrimage would have been within England. The reference to the apostles and martyrs hints that pilgrimage to Rome was in the author's mind, but he seems to introduce it as a pious reflection rather than as having any relevance to the particular case.

The author is no more readily identifiable than the anchorite, but, as was remarked above, he is likely to have belonged to a Continental religious house with which King Æthelstan was in contact, or to have been of Continental origin and holding ecclesiastical office in England. In the former category, we know of Æthelstan's correspondence with the community of Dol and the monastery of Saint-Bertin;[33] it is likely that the diplomatic marriages of his relatives to Continental rulers resulted in more such links, as when Ælfthryth, daughter of King Alfred, had married Count Baldwin II of Flanders in 893 x 899 and granted an English estate, Lewisham, to the abbey of *Blandinium* in 918.[34] If the Exeter account of Æthelstan's relic-collecting is true, however, the number of Continental churches with which he had contacts may have been far greater than we know. We have to include all western Francia in the reckoning as well as Brittany itself: in the tenth century Breton clergy fleeing the vikings formed a diaspora all over this area, the monks of Redon, for instance, moving to Poitou, those of Landévennec to Montreuil-sur-Mer (whence they influenced other Flemish monasteries) and those of Lehon and Saint-Malo to Paris and Orléans.[35] The anchorite of our letter might have paused at any of these places before moving to England, and equally his superior might have been writing on his behalf from anywhere in this area.

The desirability of having one's patron close at hand makes it seem inherently more likely that the anchorite would if at all possible have asked for a reference from a bishop or abbot who lived near his retreat. Unfortunately we know of no Bretons who held ecclesiastical posts within England under Æthelstan. All known sees and abbacies are accounted for. Yet some important foreign ecclesiastics may have made stays at his court without leaving their names on record, as perhaps had the Irish churchmen Bishop Dubinsi and Abbot Maelbrigte mac Tornáin, whose names have chanced to survive, linked with Æthelstan's, in notes in gospel-books,[36] and the *Iohannes* who appears with Æthelstan in an acrostic poem in a manuscript of Bury St Edmunds provenance.[37] Michael Lapidge has suggested that the Iohannes of this poem was John the Old Saxon,

---

[33] See above, pp. 45–6; Stenton, *Anglo-Saxon England*, p. 355.

[34] The evidence is a charter of King Edgar, issued in 964 and preserved in the fourteenth-century register of Bishop Hamo of Rochester, in which Ælfthryth's grant was confirmed: see Sawyer, *Anglo-Saxon Charters*, no. 728; *Registrum*, ed. Johnson, I. 32–3.

[35] Lot, 'La date de l'exode', and references.

[36] Robinson, *The Times*, pp. 55–9, 69–71; Dumville, 'Mael Brigte mac Tornáin'; Keynes, 'King Athelstan's books', pp. 153–9.

[37] Lapidge, 'Some Latin poems', pp. 72–83.

mentioned in Asser's Life of King Alfred (§94), and that the poem was composed in Alfred's reign, when Æthelstan was a small child. However, it is perhaps conceivable as an alternative that Iohannes was the diplomat and abbot of Landévennec referred to in the charter cited above;[38] this Iohannes is also a possible candidate for the authorship of our letter, given that he may have had some standing at the Anglo-Saxon court. The charter tells us that he 'served the cause of reparation [satisfactione deseruiuit] among the barbarians and among very many peoples of the Saxons and the Northmen and announced what was needful, and peace, many times constantly beyond and on this side of the sea . . .'. But Iohannes was made abbot only after Alan's restoration in 937; his status before that, even whether he was a cleric, is unknown. There is no evidence, then, that Iohannes of Landévennec wrote either poem or letter. Nevertheless, named or unnamed, the abbot or bishop and the anchorite of the Cotton letter may represent a considerable number of Breton immigrants into the English Church.

Generally, the letter provides supporting evidence for well known features of Æthelstan's reign: the busy diplomatic intercourse of his court and his personal interest in a variety of religious enterprises. It also raises the possibility that various as yet unsuspected forms of religious life flourished in England in the early tenth century. It has sometimes been implied that minsters served by groups of secular clergy, and a few rather fragile monastic foundations, were the only infra-diocesan religious institutions of Wessex between the First Viking-Age and the Benedictine reform of Edgar's reign.[39] Here, however, we see a man living as an anchorite – presumably leading a solitary ascetic life, whether or not attached to a larger community. His case may be paralleled by those of the various single 'religious women' or 'handmaids of Christ' to whom Æthelstan made two grants of land in 939; and his successors Edmund (939–946) and Eadred (946–955) made others.[40] We also find from the letter that pilgrimage within England was a possibility, with a system of references and support for pilgrims on their way.

THE MANUSCRIPT

London, British Library, MS. Cotton Tiberius A.xv was one of the manuscripts damaged in the Cottonian library fire of 1731. The outer leaves were charred and much of the ink washed off all the pages, so that, in Stubbs's words, 'many whole pages can only be read by catching the light on the hollows in which the ink has once been'.[41] The manuscript has since been rebound with the separate leaves mounted on strong paper.

[38] See pp. 44–5 and Appendix 1.
[39] See, for example, Stenton, Anglo-Saxon England, pp. 440–5.
[40] Dumville, The Historia Brittonum, III.14.
[41] Stubbs, Memorials, p. liv.

It is in fact a codex composed of several units, originally distinct manuscripts, probably brought together by Robert Cotton. They are as follows.[42]

1. fos 1–173	*saec.* xi[1]	Collection of letters, mainly by Alcuin
2. fo 174r	*saec.* x	Conclusion of the Gospel of St John in Latin
3. fo 174v	*saec.* xii	Part of a charter of William II, duke of Normandy, for the chapel of Notre-Dame, Cherbourg, datable to 1063 x 1066
4. fos 175–80	*saec.* viii	Iunilius, *De pastibus diuinae legis*, II.13–17
5. fos 181–94	*saec.* xiv/xv	Works by Richard Rolle: *Apocalipsis Iesus Christi; Officium de sancto Richardo heremita; Super mulierem fortem*

Only the first unit directly concerns the purpose of this article. Its contents may be presented in more detail:

fo 1	Letter of Alcuin to Abbot Hygbald of Lindisfarne, so burned as to be almost entirely illegible; out of order
2–66	Collection of Alcuin's letters, nos 1–51
67	Contents-list to following collection, nos 52–103
68r–144v	Second collection of Alcuin's letters, nos 52–125
144v–145v	Letter of Lantfred to community of St Peter's, Winchester (Stubbs, *Memorials*, no. IX)
145v–146v	Letter of Odbert, abbot of Saint-Bertin, to Archbishop Sigeric (Stubbs XXII)
146v–154r	Letter of St Augustine to Consentius (Migne, *Patrologia Latina*, XXXIII.942–9; Dekkers, *Clavis Patrum Latinorum*, no. 262)
154v–155r	Letter to Archbishop Dunstan (Stubbs X)
155r–156v	Letter of Halitgar, bishop of Cambrai, to Ebbo, archbishop of Rheims (Migne, *Patrologia Latina*, CV. 653–4)
156v–157r	Letter of Wido to Dunstan (Stubbs XVII)
157r–158r	Letter in recommendation of a pilgrim (edited below) (Stubbs XVIII)
158r/v	Letter to Dunstan (Stubbs XI)
158v–159v	Letter of the community of Saint-Ouen to King Edgar (Stubbs VI)
159v–160v	Letter of Arnulf to Dunstan (Stubbs IV)
160v	Anonymous letter, assuring the recipient that the writer is employed in study (Stubbs XXIX)
160v–161r	Letter to Dunstan (Stubbs XII)

[42] For references to the various portions of the manuscript, see Sickel, 'Alcuinstudien', pp. 506–9, 517–27; *Epistolae Karolini Aevi*, ed. Dümmler, II.9–11; Chase, *Two Alcuin Letter-books*, pp.10–12; Lindsay, *Notae Latinae*, p. 461; Lowe, *Codices*, II, no. 189; *Richard Rolle*, ed. Marzac, pp. 89, 181–9.

161v–162v	Letter of Odbert to Archbishop Æthelgar (Stubbs XX)
162v–164r	Letter of B. to Æthelgar (Stubbs XXI)
164r/v	Letter to Bishop [sic] Sigeric (Stubbs XXVII)
164v–166r	Letter to Dunstan (Stubbs XIII)
166r	Letter to Archbishop Wulfhelm (Stubbs I)
166r–167r	Letter of Archbishop Ebbo of Rheims to Bishop Halitgar (Migne, *Patrologia Latina*, CV. 651–2; cf. fos 155r–156v above)
167r–168r	Letter of the community of Sainte-Geneviève, Paris, to King Edgar (Stubbs VIII)
168r/v	Letter to Dunstan (Stubbs XIV)
168v	Poem (Stubbs XV)
169r/v	Anonymous letter to N. (Stubbs XXIII)
169v–170r	Letter of Pope John XV to Ealdorman Ælfric of Hampshire (Stubbs XXV)
170r–172v	Letter of Ælfweard, abbot of Glastonbury, to Archbishop Sigeric (Stubbs XXVIII)
172v–173r	Letter of Pope John XV to the English (Stubbs XXVI)
173v	blank

The manuscript, then, is a collection of letters of theological, literary and historical interest, chiefly by Alcuin, with a small amount of correspondence addressed to the archbishops of Canterbury of the late tenth century, two papal letters on English affairs, a letter of St Augustine on the nature of the Resurrection, and the exchange of letters between Ebbo of Rheims (816–835) and Halitgar of Cambrai which prefaced the latter's work *De uitiis et uirtutibus*.[43] Fos 1–173 are a unit, written by a single scribe.

Something of the history of the manuscript can be traced. Before entering the library of Robert Cotton, it was owned by the antiquary Laurence Nowell (*ob.* 1576) and used by John Joscelyn (*ob.* 1603), secretary to Archbishop Parker. It contains notes in Joscelyn's hand, and Joscelyn's notebook, London, British Library, MS. Cotton Vitellius D.vii, contains on fo 143 citations from the two papal letters in Cotton Tiberius A.xv with the note 'Haec . . . ex libro epistolarum Alcuini . . . et liber est in manibus m^ri Nowell'.[44] Prior to this the manuscript had been used by John Leland (*ob.* 1552), who annotated it and included extracts from it, among them a few lines of the letter under discussion, in his *Collectanea* – unfortunately without any indication of where he found it.[45] Robin Flower suggested as a sequence of events that Leland gave the book to Nowell, who passed some books to William Lambarde (1536–1601), who in turn bequeathed some – apparently including this one – to Sir Robert Cotton.[46] Sub-

---

[43] Migne, *Patrologia Latina*, CV.649–730.
[44] Flower, 'Laurence Nowell', pp. 50–1; Gale, 'John Joscelyn's Notebook', pp. 254–5.
[45] Leland, *Collectanea*, II.392–404; IV.157.
[46] Flower, 'Laurence Nowell', pp. 51–2.

sequently the Alcuin letters in it were transcribed by Thomas Gale (*ob.* 1702) in Cambridge, Trinity College, MS. 0.10.16 (1468).

The earlier history of the manuscript and its date and place of origin are harder to discern. The ultimate origin of the letter-collection and the origin of the manuscript itself are formally two different questions, and analysis of the contents[47] suggests that the compilation of the letter-collection took place in several stages, further multiplying the question of origins. Some of the sub-groups may have been collected in Alcuin's lifetime by his followers, as Sickel suggests, others at various times in the interim. The final ordering, however, cannot have long preceded the writing of the manuscript. The latest letter in the manuscript, to Archbishop Sigeric, dates from 990 x 994, providing a *terminus post quem* for the collection. For the script – a neat Caroline minuscule with a thick-set, square appearance given by straight, heavily shaded upright strokes, round bowls and blunt wedges on the ascenders – the closest parallels which I have found are in manuscripts of a series which T. A. M. Bishop considered to have been produced at Christ Church, Canterbury, in the opening years of the eleventh century;[48] particularly similar is the script of the scribe of quire N of Cambridge, Trinity College, MS. B.4.27 (141). In the 1010s and 1020s a radically different style of script was introduced at Christ Church by Eadwig Basan, this providing a tentative *terminus ante quem* for the writing of Cotton Tiberius A.xv.

The script seems to assign the manuscript to Christ Church, Canterbury; the content, too, mostly points towards Christ Church as the place where the final arranging of the letters took place. Cotton Tiberius A.xv may be separated by comparison with other Alcuin manuscripts into three sequences of letters,[49] of which the last, letters nos 104–151, reveals a predominant interest in Canterbury both in its twenty-two Alcuin letters and in the twenty-six tenth-century letters which follow them. At least five, perhaps ten, of the Alcuin letters and thirteen of the others are addressed to archbishops of Canterbury; no other recipient is associated with more than two letters. It seems, then, that Christ Church, Canterbury played at least a part in the 'pre-production' of Cotton Tiberius A.xv. However, two of the tenth-century letters show local interests other than in Canterbury, and no clear literary or religious interest. These are a letter of Pope John XV to Ælfric (ealdorman of Hampshire *ca* 982–1016) on behalf of Glastonbury Abbey, and the letter edited in this article. Our letter's provenance is uncertain, but the presence of the Glastonbury letter introduces a small possibility that the final copying was done at Glastonbury. The script does not preclude this. There are too few known specimens of late tenth- and early eleventh-century Glastonbury script to provide a secure basis for comparison between it and the well evidenced script of Christ Church, Canterbury, but such examples as there are reveal the links between the two places. The type of

---

[47] For more detail on this, see below, Appendix 2.
[48] Bishop, 'Notes on Cambridge manuscripts', VII.
[49] Sickel, 'Alcuinstudien', p. 517; Thomson, 'William of Malmesbury', p. 149.

Anglo-Caroline script christened 'Style II' by Bishop was probably created at Glastonbury in the mid-tenth century, and in the last quarter of the tenth century began to be written at St Augustine's (and then at Christ Church), Canterbury, gradually evolving its own character in each of the houses. Two Glastonbury calendars, from ca 970–980 and from 1023 or after, show a little-changed, small, flowing Style II script quite unlike the writing of Cotton Tiberius A.xv,[50] but a script more like the developed Canterbury variety could in theory have been written in the same scriptorium. The difficulty of making a rigid distinction between Christ Church and Glastonbury becomes clear when one considers that three of the archbishops of Canterbury who feature in the correspondence in Cotton Tiberius A.xv (Dunstan 960–988, Æthelgar 988–990, Sigeric 990–994) were former monks of Glastonbury, if the information on the latter two in De antiquitate Glastonie can be trusted.[51] However, one may perhaps more easily imagine a copy of the papal letter to Ælfric being sent to Canterbury and there copied (perhaps together with the letter from Abbot Ælfweard of Glastonbury which immediately follows it in Cotton Tiberius A.xv) than large amounts of Canterbury correspondence being collected at Glastonbury.

On balance, the less uneconomical hypothesis is that the letters were both gathered and copied at Christ Church, and this is what scholars have tended to assume.[52] Rodney Thomson has claimed, moreover, that there is independent evidence for the existence of a manuscript of one of the 'parent' collections of Cotton Tiberius A.xv, the 'Canterbury' collection, comprising letters 104–151.[53] He has argued that the quotations from this series of letters in William of Malmesbury's Gesta regum and Gesta pontificum (published in 1125) contain – unlike William's quotations from the first two groups of Alcuin letters in Cotton Tiberius A.xv – some readings which seem to come from an older, better text than that of Cotton Tiberius A.xv, although no other manuscript of them now exists; and he has suggested that William, who certainly used the archives of Christ Church for his research, made a copy of Alcuin's letters there using Cotton Tiberius A.xv for the first two sections and this lost exemplar for the third. This means that three copies of our letter-collection may once have existed, of which now only one, Cotton Tiberius A.xv, remains, the archetype and William's copy having been lost.

This hypothesis too lacks economy, however, and the small number of variants which Thomson adduced in its support[54] could be explained as independent

---

50 Bishop, English Caroline Minuscule, pp. xxii–xxiii and nos 1–3; see also Bishop, 'An early example'.
51 John Scott says of this chapter of the De antiquitate: 'The source ... was probably an eleventh-century necrology ... There are, however, reasons for suspecting an interpolator has been at work ... It cannot be determined what William's original contribution consisted of': The Early History, pp. 136–7 §67, and p. 206, n. 133. The evidence for interpolation does not directly affect the entries on Æthelgar and Sigeric, however.
52 Gneuss, 'A preliminary list', p. 25, no. 368; Hohler, 'Some service-books', p. 74.
53 'William of Malmesbury and the letters', pp. 148–50.
54 ibid., p. 148; p. 149, n. 19; p. 150, n. 27.

corrections of the text of Cotton Tiberius A.xv by William. Thomson further argued that the excerpts from Alcuin's letters in Leland's *Collectanea* must have been taken from William's hypothetical copy, not from Cotton Tiberius A.xv itself, since they agree in a small number of readings with those of William against Cotton Tiberius A.xv. But the nature of these variants is even less conclusive, and Thomson did not take into account the appearance of Leland's handwriting in Cotton Tiberius A.xv, which, if correctly identified, must undermine his argument. If Leland's excerpts are from Cotton Tiberius A.xv, this may give us a clue to the manuscript's sixteenth-century provenance. Leland did not state the whereabouts of the *uetus codex* from which he took his excerpts,[55] but elsewhere in the *Collectanea* he mentions having seen a book of letters by Alcuin, *epistolae Albini*, at Malmesbury Abbey. If this were the same as the *uetus codex* – as Thomson suggested – it could also be identified with Cotton Tiberius A.xv, although Thomson considered it to have been a lost copy by William of Malmesbury. If Cotton Tiberius A.xv was at Malmesbury in the sixteenth century, this may be a small point in favour of its having been written at Glastonbury rather than at Canterbury. However, it might have been brought from either place by William of Malmesbury. We know that he visited both the Canterbury houses to gather material – he used, for instance, the E-version of the Anglo-Saxon Chronicle,[56] which was at St Augustine's by the mid-eleventh century, and the Canterbury version of the *Liber Pontificalis* from the early twelfth century[57] – but he also used Glastonbury manuscripts, particularly in the compilation of his next work, *De antiquitate Glastonie ecclesie*.

A tangential problem is the relationship of Cotton Tiberius A.xv with another letter-collection in London, British Library, MS. Cotton Vespasian A.xiv.[58] This also is a manuscript of the early eleventh century, containing letters and ecclesiastical legislation, copied for Wulfstan, bishop of London and Worcester and archbishop of York (996–1023): it contains a dedicatory poem to him and some samples of what Neil Ker identified as his handwriting.[59] It gives a selection of Alcuin's letters which is a subset of that in Cotton Tiberius A.xv and shows some correspondence with it in order; it also contains six of the tenth-century letters found in Cotton Tiberius A.xv (Stubbs IX, XVII, XIX, XX, XXI, and XXII). These and many of the Alcuin letters are found in no manuscripts other than these two. The two are clearly related, and if the origins of Cotton Vespasian A.xiv were clear they might throw some light on those of Cotton Tiberius A.xv. In a way they do (as I have set out more fully in Apppendix 2 below) but it is not of a sort which would distinguish between a Canterbury and a Glastonbury origin

---

55 Leland, *Collectanea*, II.392–404; IV.157.
56 On the E-Chronicle, see Dumville, 'Some aspects of annalistic writing'.
57 Thomson, 'The reading'; see also Thomson, 'Identifiable books'.
58 For references to this manuscript, see Stubbs, *Memorials*, pp. liv–lv; Sickel, 'Alcuinstudien', p. 519; Chase, *Two Alcuin Letter-books*, pp. 8–9; Ker, *Catalogue*, pp. 267–8, no. 204.
59 Ker, 'The handwriting'.

for Cotton Tiberius A.xv. The relative order of letters in Cotton Tiberius A.xv and Cotton Vespasian A.xiv suggests that the two were compiled in a parallel process, Vespasian showing some of Tiberius's letters out of order and others arranged in their finished sequences. Archbishop Wulfstan or his copyists would seem to have been in touch with the compilers of Cotton Tiberius A.xv. Among his known contacts was Archbishop Ælfric of Canterbury (995–1005), of whose will he was an executor[60] – and who thereby becomes a candidate for the compiler of Cotton Tiberius A.xv –; but Ælfric may have been a former abbot of Glastonbury;[61] and doubtless, also, Wulfstan as a principal royal adviser had connexions with this and other monasteries.[62]

A third manuscript of Alcuin letters may enter into the argument: London, British Library, MS Harley 208, a ninth-century Continental manuscript which contains an Anglo-Saxon scribble from *ca* 1000 and a fifteenth-century inscription *Ebor*, which shows that it was by then at York.[63] Comparing Harley 208 with Cotton Vespasian A.xiv, one finds that both select letters addressed to English, especially Northumbrian, recipients, but that only two letters are common to the two collections – nos 128 and 209 in Dümmler's edition – and, of these, no. 128's presence in Harley 208 is disguised because its opening is missing. Dorothy Whitelock pointed this out[64] and argued that Harley 208 was already at York in Wulfstan's time and that the letters in Cotton Vespasian A.xiv were selected to complement the Harley collection, hence that Cotton Vespasian A.xiv, too, was written at or for York. (It contains no evidence in favour of its having been written at Worcester, Wulfstan's other main centre of scholarly activity.) But how one regards this argument depends on how one views the relationship between Cotton Vespasian A.xiv and Cotton Tiberius A.xv, which Whitelock did not consider. If Cotton Vespasian A.xiv were a copy of random parts of the sources of Cotton Tiberius A.xv, then the fact that it contained hardly any overlap with Harley 208 could be seen as coincidence, not selection: out of its 125 Alcuin-letters, Cotton Tiberius A.xv contains only eight which are also in Harley 208. This may, on the other hand, suggest that the compilers of Cotton Tiberius A.xv, too, were aware of the contents of Harley 208. A York origin for Cotton Vespasian A.xiv remains possible but doubtful, and the place of origin of Cotton Tiberius A.xv is no further elucidated.

This whole discussion was begun in the hope that it would shed some light on the place of origin of the letter edited in this article; it has to end by saying that if the latter were known it might help significantly in deciding the place of origin of the manuscript! It is a distinctly local document, but from an unknown locality, and so enough unknown space surrounds it for it to fit easily, though too

---

60 Whitelock, 'Wulfstan at York', p. 219.
61 Knowles *et al.*, *The Heads*, p. 50.
62 For some of Wulfstan's contacts with other churches, see Wulfstan, *Sermo Lupi ad Anglos* (ed. Whitelock, pp. 7–14).
63 Ker, *Catalogue*, p. 304, no. 229.
64 'Wulfstan at York', pp. 218–19.

loosely for satisfaction, into either hypothesis: that Cotton Tiberius A.xv was written at Christ Church, Canterbury, or at Glastonbury. The anchorite may have begun his pilgrimage in the South-west, but he may have ended it any-where, bringing the letter with him. Likewise, the author of the letter may have kept, deposited, or forgotten a reference-copy at any religious house. What is surprising is the lucky accident by which this piece of administrative debris slipped into the pile of unrelated, much later letters which went to compose the archetype of the final section of Cotton Tiberius A.xv between 990 and *ca* 1010. It survived, with unintended appropriateness, between works of Alcuin and letters to the luminaries of the Benedictine reform, a witness to a less glittering but perhaps equally interesting phase of intercourse between France and England.

THE TEXT

7r [1]Omnigenis catholice fidei cultoribus in caritate radicatis et fundatis gratiam et pacem tandem a domino consolatore omnium qui digne lugent omniumque remuneratore[2] qui recte desudant in cultu uineae. Quoniam apostolo teste non sunt condigne pasiones huius temporis ad futuram gloriam que reuelabitur in nobis;[3] et dominus, beati qui lugent nunc, inquid, quoniam[4] ipsi consolabuntur:[5] hic[6] monachus, olim militarem indutus[7] clamidem, conuersus iam elegit abiectus esse in domo domini[8] quam ambulare[9] in tabernaculis [ ][10] breui curriculo suspe[ ][11] fatigatus miserque paucis lugere contemptus ut [ ][12] securus quiescat consolatusque beatitudinem sine fine percipiat. Nos autem haec scripsimus illi in caritate Dei ut haec pagina dignantibus eam tractare loquatur pro ipso idiota et elingui. Accipite[13] ergo hunc [14]optime psalmidicum[14] in Brittania citra[14a] marina

7v (marginal)

---

1 Stubbs provided heading: *Epistola Commendatoria*.
2 Stubbs silently added *eorum* after this word.
3 Romans viii.18
4 MS.; *quia* Stubbs
5 Matthew v.5
6 Leland's extract begins with this word.
7 MS. and Leland; *induens* Stubbs
8 MS. and Stubbs; *Dei* Leland. Leland's extract breaks off with this word.
9 MS.; *habitare* Stubbs
10 Approximately 28 characters illegible. Stubbs silently supplied the word *peccatorum*.
11 5–6 characters illegible
12 About 2 characters illegible
13 Leland's extract resumes with this word.
14...14 MS., Stubbs; omitted by Leland
14a MS., Leland; *circa* Stubbs

clare editum, adhuc quietae[14b] temporis et pacis ultro exilium trans freta subisse in uestram fideli Anglosaxonum[14c] Britanniam, ubi consulto christianissimi regis Ethelstani anachoreta factus religiose ac laudabiliter apud Cen[15] non paucis diebus conuersatus.[16] Cuius consilio ac licentia in hanc quoque peregrinationem pro[17] amore Christi[17] uenit,[18] non quod Deum, qui ubique est, iter agendo localiter querat, sed dum plus laborat plus mercedis accipiat. Ubi enim durior pugna ibi[18a] gloriosior corona. Hinc est quod perfecti etiam uiri de suis actibus non confidentes a[d] sanctorum martyrum protectionem currunt [ ][19] omnia[20] corpora fletibus adsilum promereri ibi[21] fruendum[22] ubi deliquerant eis intercedentibus credunt[ ][23] iuxta quod ibi de infirmioribus dicit non habentes uelamen amplexantur lapides,[24] id est apostolos ceterosque sanctos. Sed hoc[ ][25] ne scientes agrauentur prolixitate. Vos uero[ ][26] scientibus erga hunc uestrum exercete[ ][27] fraternitatis participes sanctitatis illius isque[ ][28] de mamona iniquitatis recepturi aeterna tabernacula. Quod/ mihi uobiscum fieri precor[ ][29]

158r

[14b] MS.; *quiete* Leland, Stubbs
[14c] The manuscript had *angelosaxonum*, with the *e* deleted.
[15] Leland added *cern* above this word.
[16] MS.; *conuersatus est* Leland; *conuersus est* Stubbs
[17...17] MS., Stubbs; *Christi amore* Leland
[18] Leland's extract ends with this word.
[18a] *ubi* altered to *ibi*, MS.
[19] The parchment has split to obliterate about 12 characters.
[20] Doubtful; omitted by Stubbs
[21] Doubtful, omitted by Stubbs
[22] Stubbs mistakenly indicated an illegible passage after this word.
[23] Possibly 2 illegible characters
[24] Job xxiv.8
[25] About 6 characters illegible in the MS.; *heu* Stubbs
[26] About 5 characters illegible
[27] About 5 characters illegible
[28] About 10 characters illegible; gap not indicated by Stubbs
[29] About 20 characters illegible; gap not indicated by Stubbs

TRANSLATION

A literal translation is aimed at, and the clumsiness and occasional obscurity reflect the original.

To all sorts of keepers of the catholic faith, rooted and founded in charity, grace and peace[1] from the Lord, consoler of all who fitly mourn and rewarder of all who righteously labour in the tending of the vine. Since, as the apostle bears witness, the sufferings of this time are not comparable to the future glory which will be revealed in us, and the Lord says, 'Blessed are those who mourn now for they shall be comforted': this monk, once having worn[2] the military cloak, now converted, has chosen to be cast down in the house of the Lord rather than to walk in the tents[3] [3–6 words missing] [in] a brief career [1–2 words missing] wearied and unhappy, to mourn, despised, in a few things so that he may rest safely[4] and, consoled, receive bliss without end. We, indeed, have written this for him in the charity of God so that this page may speak for him, simple and inarticulate [as he is], to those who deign to run through it. Understand, then, most excellent [reader],[5] that this psalm-singer, nobly born in Britain on this side of the sea [Brittany], underwent exile across the straits voluntarily, still in the

---

[1]   The text adds *tandem*, which I have left untranslated.

[2]   *indutus* This is a solecism: a passive form of the verb cannot take a direct object. The phrase could be corrected either to *militarem induens clamidem*, as by Stubbs, or (less well) to *militare indutus clamide*. It is impossible to say whether the mistake is authorial or scribal.

[3]   *ambulare in tabernaculis . . .*   *Ambulare* is clearly the manuscript's reading, but Stubbs's alteration to *habitare* makes the phrase more clearly a reference to Psalm lxxxiii.11, as does his conjectural addition of the word *peccatorum*. He could not have read *peccatorum*: the last word on fo 157r is clearly *tabernaculis*, and at the top of the verso the parchment has actually been destroyed for the space of about twenty-eight characters. His conjecture is almost certainly correct, but to fill in the rest of the gap with any certainty is impossible. The part-word *suspe. . .* could be a part of *suspectus* ('esteem' as a noun) or of the verb *suspicio* ('respect' or 'mistrust') or *suspendo* in the sense of 'break off', 'interrupt'. With *breui curriculo* the sense could be a reference to the interruption of the anchorite's military career, a contrast of the brief esteem of his military life with the life of humility which is next described, or a reference to a brief period of disrespect which he must undergo to earn eternal life, with the same meaning as the phrases which follow. In any case the drift of the letter is not seriously interrupted.

[4]   There is a very short illegible space, the width of about two letters, between the words *ut* and *securus*. The passage seems to make sense as it stands: possibly the scribe himself deleted a couple of letters.

[5]   *Accipite ergo hunc optime psalmidicum . . .*   This phrase is problematic. *Accipite* (2nd plural imperative) must have the meaning 'understand', 'believe', rather than 'receive', since it governs an accusative-and-infinitive construction for the rest of the sentence; I have therefore taken *optime* as a vocative, 'most excellent reader', but this disagrees with the plural verb. It is perhaps more likely, given its position in the sentence, that *optime* is a mistake for *optimum*: 'understand that this excellent psalm-singer . . .'.

time of quiet and peace,[6] to your Britain of the Anglo-Saxon faithful,[7] where, by permission[8] of the most christian King Æthelstan, having become an anchorite, he led his life[9] religiously and in a praiseworthy fashion at Cen for no few days. By his [Æthelstan's] advice and permission he comes on this pilgrimage also for the love of Christ, not because he seeks God, who is everywhere, in any one place by travelling, but [because] when he labours more he receives a greater reward: for where the fight is harder, there the crown is more glorious. It is hence that even perfect men, not trusting in their own deeds, run to the protection of the holy martyrs [2–3 words missing][10] [watering] all their bodies with tears, they hope by their [the martyrs'] intercessions to earn a refuge to enjoy there where they [the pilgrims] have offended,[11] according to what Scripture says there of the weaker – not having a shelter they cling to rocks, that is, [they embrace] the apostles and the other saints. But this [1 word missing][12] lest the wise be oppressed by prolixity. You, however, [1 word missing][13] exert your [1 word missing] [love] of fraternity towards this man, partakers of his sanctity, and [may] he [2–3 words missing],[14] to receive [viz the addressees], out of the mammon of unrighteousness, eternal dwelling-places. Which I pray will happen to me together with you . . .

[6] *quietae temporis et pacis* There is no such word as *quietae*. Leland's and Stubbs's emendation to *quiete* is obvious orthographically but gives a reading – 'in quiet of time and of peace' – which makes no sense grammatically. Following a suggestion by Dr Neil Wright, I emend the phrase to *quietis tempore et pacis* in translation. How either author or scribe could have arrived at the existing reading is far from clear, however.

[7] *fideli* There is no way of fitting this dative or ablative singular adjective into the sentence. I propose to emend it to *fidelium* (genitive plural); the scribe might have arrived at *fideli* by misreading and failing to expand a suspension. *Fidelis* or *fidelem* is perhaps equally likely to have been the original reading.

[8] *consulto* Could be translated as 'by decree'.

[9] *Est* has to be understood after *conuersatus*. Its omission is not necessarily a scribal error but may be ellipsis by the author.

[10] *currunt . . . omnia corpora* Part of what is missing is probably a verb of which *corpora* is the object and *fletibus* the instrument: *irrigantes* or the like. *Corpora* could mean either the bodies of the pilgrims or those of the saints.

[11] There is an illegible space of two characters' width between the words *credunt* and *iuxta*. As in the case discussed in 4 above, there may be no actual material missing.

[12] *sed hoc . . . ne scientes* I cannot see the reason for Stubbs's suggestion of *heu*, 'alas', to fill this gap. Possibly the missing word is something like *satis*, 'enough'.

[13] *exercete . . . fraternitatis* The missing word must be *amorem* or something similar.

[14] *isque . . . de mamona* It is difficult to fill this gap: the space seems too small for a whole clause of which *is* (the anchorite) could be the subject. Perhaps *isque* should read *hisque* and the missing word be *donatis* or an equivalent; in this case the translation should read 'these things having been granted, [you are] to receive eternal dwelling-places out of the mammon of unrighteousness'.

Appendix 1

A Charter of Alain Barbetorte to Landévennec Abbey

The text is from the Cartulary of Landévennec, no. 25 (edd. Le Men and Ernault, pp. 562–4).

DE BAHT VVE<N>RANN[1]

Or In nomine sanctae Trinitatis et unicae Deitatis. Diuina concedente clementia, Alanus, dux Britonum, uidens sanctum corpus Uuingualoei exul a patria peregri-naturumque in aliena hostium crudelium perturbationis causa, et reminiscens
Ov Iohannis euangelistae uerba: 'Quicunque uiderit fratrem suum neces/sitatem habere, et clauserit uiscera sua ab eo, quomodo caritas Dei manet in eo?'[2] uer-baque sancti euangelii: 'Quod uni ex minimis meis fecistis, mihi fecistis';[3] et, 'Qui uos spernit, me contempnit';[4] et, 'Qui dat pauperi, feneratur Deo, tribuensque paruum in hoc seculo comparat regnum aeternum in futuro';[5] his et aliis uerbis mente timente, solidaque in Deo perscrutans omni intentione dispensatione regis superni suique miseratione: et idcirco Alanus, nutu Dei dux, qui, cuncta despi-ciens terrena, modis omnibus cupiens adipisci caelestia, tradidit de sua propria hereditate Sancto Uuingualoeo eiusque abbati Iohanni, quia uocauit illum infra
1r mare atque inuitauit. Et iusiurandum iurauerunt eius fideles illi, / antequam uenisset: hi sunt Amalgod atque Uuethenoc, super altare sancti Petri apostoli. Et iste Iohannes satisfactione deseruiuit inter barbaros plurimaque inter genera Sax-onum atque Normanorum et necessariam multis uicibus assiduis pacemque trans mare atque infra mare ad gaudium nostrum nuntiauit. Et ideo propria iussit eum ordinare ad abbaticium supradicti sancti. Addidit quoque Sancto Uuingualoeo de sua propria hereditate, sicut supra diximus, specialiter sibi a cunctis parentibus inclitis, id est monasterium sancti Medardi eiusque terram, quatuor miliaria in longitudine, in latitudine duo miliaria, cum siluis et aquis et pratis, terrisque
v cultis et incultis et omnibus ei apendiciis; / et aecclesiam Sanctae Crucis intus urbe cum omnibus eius apendiciis, atque aecclesiam Sancti Cyrici extra ciuita-tem; eiusdemque sancti aecclesiam, omnemque insulam, quae nominatur Bath[6] Uuenran, cum omnibus ei apendiciis et dimidium unius uicariae, quae nominatur

---

1 VVECRANN, MS.
2 I John, iii.17
3 Matthew xxv.40
4 Luke x.16
5 Non-Vulgate quotation, unidentified by the editors
6 *Baz* is added in a seventeenth-century hand in the margin.

Sulse, sita in pago Namnetensium, quinque miliario[7] distans ab urbe; eiusque aecclesiae dimidium cum omnibus ei apendiciis, ita etiam decimas uini sui et duas partes decimarum piscium et xx modios salis de teloneo uel censu suo;[8] atque modios xx tritici, decimasque numorum assidue, et teloneum uel censum[9] salis lib[ere],[10] unoquoque anno, prefato Sancto Uuingualoeo eiusque abbati Iohanni in dicumbitione atque in hereditate perpetua pro stabilitate regni / et

152r   pro redemptione animae suae siue pro longeuitate filiorum suorum atque pro animabus parentum suorum siue uiuorum atque defunctorum. Ista misericordia facta, meditans more sapientis uentura, iussit hanc priuilegionem facere, ut, si aliqui uenturi sint, quod minime credimus, qui hanc scriptionem uoluerint frangere aut uiolare, sciant alienos se fore a cunctis liminibus sanctae Dei aecclesiae, et sit pars eorum cum Dathan et Abiron, quos terra deglutiuit, nec [non][11] cum Iuda et Pilato qui Dominum crucifixerunt. Terra sancta eos cymiterii non recipiat et filii eorum orfani et uxores eorum uiduae. Hi sunt testes, qui audierunt et uiderunt haec omnia: Alan, dux; Iudhaeel, comes; Iuthouen, archiepiscopus;

152v   Hedrenn, episcopus; Blenliuett, episcopus; Houuel, comes; Vuerec, / Nuuenoe, Saluator, episcopus; Iestin, uicecomes; Diles, uicecomes; Pritient, Uuethenoc, Amalgod, Amhedr, Chenmarchoc, Nut, Huon, Moysen, et alii plurimi fideles, qui uiderunt et audierunt testimonium, sicut scriptum est. Et qui frangere aut minuere uoluerit, ira Dei incurrat super eum et anathema sit. Amen.

Post obitum Alani, ego Tetbaldus, nutu Dei comes, hoc idem affirmo, sicut supra dictum est.

[E]go[12] Ioseph, toronensia urbe pastor, hoc affirmo.

Ego Fulcun, gratia Dei comes, ita etiam hoc affirmo, in tantum ut michi pertinet, sicut supra scriptum est.

153r   Alanus dux iussit Hedrenno, episcopo, construere hanc cartam, / et dedit Sancto Uuingualoeo eiusque abbati Iohanni sicut supra diximus in dicumbitione aeterna. Et qui hoc frangere presumpserit, ira Dei et sanctorum offensa incurrat super eum in presenti seculo, et insuper in futuro ante tribunal Christi rationem reddat. Amen.

TRANSLATION

In the name of the holy Trinity and sole Deity: divine clemency allowing, Alan, *dux* of the Bretons, seeing the holy body of Winwaloe an exile from his

---

[7] *sic*. Read *miliaria*?
[8] *uel censu suo* above the line
[9] *uel censum* above the line
[10] Square brackets as in the edition (indicating that these letters have been supplied by the editors?)
[11] As n. 10
[12] As n. 10

country and about to set off wandering in foreign lands because of the harass-
ment of fierce enemies, and remembering the words of John the evangelist, 'If
anyone sees his brother in need, and shuts his heart against him, how will the
love of God remain in him?', and the words of the holy Gospel, 'What you have
done to one of the least of mine, you have done to me' and 'He who despises you,
despises me' and 'He who gives to the poor, gains credit with God, and granting a
little in this world he gains an eternal kingdom in the world to come'; awed in
mind by these and other words, examining all the things which are fixed in God
with all attention and by the dispensation of the most high King and by his
mercy – therefore Alan, *dux* by God's concession, who, despising all earthly
things, desiring to strive for heavenly things by every means, gave from his own
inheritance to St Winwaloe and to his abbot John, because he had called him
and invited him to this side of the sea. And his followers swore an oath to him
before he came: these are Amalgod and Uuethenoc, on the altar of the holy
apostle Peter. And this John served the cause of reparation among the barbarians
and among many peoples of the Saxons and Northmen and announced what was
necessary, and peace, many attentive times across and on this side of the sea, to
our joy. And therefore by his own [will][1] he ordered him to be ordained to the
abbacy of the aforesaid saint. He added moreover to St Winwaloe out of his own
inheritance, as we said above, [what belonged] to him in particular from all his
noble ancestors, viz the monastery of St Médard and its land, four miles in
length, two miles in breadth, with woods and waters and meadows, and cultivated and uncultivated land and all appendages [belonging] to it; and the church
of the Holy Cross within the city with all things [belonging] to it, and the church
of St Cyricus outside the town; and the church of the same [saint] and all the
island which is called Bath Uuenran, with all the appendages to it; and half of
one *uicaria* which is called Sulsae situated in the *pagus* of Nantes, five miles away
from the city, and half of its church with all the appendages to it; likewise also
the tithes of its wine and two parts of the tithes of fish and twenty *modii* of salt
from its toll or levy, and twenty *modii* of wheat, and the tithes of money without
fail, and the toll or levy of salt freely each year, to the aforesaid St Winwaloe and
his abbot John in *dicumbitio* and in permanent inheritance for the stability of the
kingdom and for the redemption of his soul and for the long life of his sons and
for the souls of his relations living or dead. Having done this [act of] mercy,
meditating in the manner of the wise on [times] to come, he ordered this charter
to be drawn up so that if any should come, which we do not in the least believe,
who may wish to break or violate this writing, they may know that they will be
outcasts from all doors of the holy Church of God, and may their lot be with
Dathan and Abiron, whom the earth swallowed up, and with Judas and Pilate,
who crucified the Lord. May the holy ground of the cemetery not receive them

---

[1] Either some such word as *uoluntate* must be supplied or one must assume that the word
propria was copied by mistake, the scribe perhaps anticipating its actual occurrence in
the next sentence. I am grateful to Dr Neil Wright for the former suggestion.

and their children [be] orphans and their wives widows. These are the witnesses who heard and saw all this: Alan, *dux*; Iudhaeel, *comes*; Iuthouen, archbishop; Hedrenn, bishop; Blenliuett, bishop; Houuel, *comes*; Vuerec; Nuuenoe; Saluator, bishop; Iestin, *uicecomes*; Diles, *uicecomes*; Pritient, Uuethenoc, Amalgod, Amhedr, Chenmarchoc, Nut, Huon, Moysen, and very many other faithful men, who saw and heard the testimony as it is written. And anyone who wishes to break or diminish it, may the wrath of God fall on him and let him be anathema. Amen.

After the death of Alan, I, Tetbaldus, *comes* by grant of God, confirm the same thing, as it is said above.

I, Joseph, pastor in the city of Tours, confirm this.

I, Fulcun, *comes* by grace of God, also confirm this, insofar as it belongs to me, as it is written above.

Dux Alan ordered Bishop Hedrenn to draw up this charter, and gave St Winwaloe and his abbot John what we have said above in eternal inheritance. And anyone who presumes to break it, may the wrath of God and the offence of the saints fall upon him in the present world, and let him also answer for it in the [world] to come before the tribunal of Christ. Amen.

Appendix 2

The relationship between Cotton Tiberius A.xv and Cotton Vespasian A.xiv

As I have stated above, MS. Cotton Vespasian A.xiv throws no direct light on the place of origin of Cotton Tiberius A.xv or of the letter edited in this article. However, to clarify the relationship between the two manuscripts may shed some light on how both were compiled. This is a question which was touched upon by Colin Chase in *Two Alcuin Letter-books*,[1] in which he edited two sequences of letters from the Vespasian manuscript; he presented a table of the letters in the two manuscripts with their numberings in Dümmler's edition, which is convenient but contains a few mistakes and raises more questions than could be discussed in his introduction.

Sickel, followed by Dümmler,[2] pointed out that the Alcuin-letters in Cotton Tiberius A.xv fall into three distinct sequences. Sickel omitted the tenth-century letters from his discussion, but Thomson showed that there was reason to reckon them as part of the third series.[3] The sequences are as follows.

1. Letters 1–51, fos 1–66 (Series 1)
2. Letters 52–103, with contents-list, fos 67–122 (Series 2)
3. Letters 104–125 (Alcuin) and 126–151 (*saec.* x, etc.), fos 123–173 (Series 3)

Series 3 stands out by its Canterbury bias; series 2 is almost identical with the collection of Alcuin's letters found in two manuscripts – London, British Library, MS. Royal 8.E.xv (*saec.* ix, provenance Saint-Omer, in England by the sixteenth century) and Sankt Gallen, Stiftsbibliothek, MS. 271 (*saec.* ix) – and Dümmler considered that it had been taken from their exemplar. Thus Series 2 probably had a single source, but series 1 and 3 may have been put together from various shorter collections and even single letters. Sickel identified such subdivisions in Series 1: most of the letters 18–31 of Cotton Tiberius A.xv can be found in various combinations in the two manuscripts just cited and in the manuscripts Vienna, Österreichische Nationalbibliothek, MS. 808, fos 101–162 (*saec.* ix in., written for Bishop Arno of Salzburg) and Troyes, Bibliothèque municipale, MS. 1165 (*saec.* x ex.), but nowhere as fully as in Cotton Tiberius A.xv, and Sickel considered this to have been a collection which was made and sent to Canterbury by Alcuin's circle in his lifetime; letters 1–17 of Cotton Tiberius A.xv, he

---

[1] Pp. 8–11.
[2] Sickel, 'Alcuinstudien', p. 517; *Epistolae Karolini Aevi*, ed. Dümmler, II.11.
[3] 'William of Malmesbury and the letters', p. 149.

thought, had been collected by Alcuin's disciple Dodo.[4] Sickel did not, however, use a detailed comparison of Cotton Tiberius A.xv with Cotton Vespasian A.xiv as part of his argument for separating out these sources, but merely observed, 'Wir ersehen . . . dass V [Vespasian A.xiv] und A [Tiberius A.xv] auf dieselben Sammlungen zurückzuführen sind, dass diese Sammlungen aber dem Schreiber von V und dem von A nicht in gleicher Reihenfolge vorlagen und dass sie von den Schreibern in verschiedenem Grade ausgebeutet worden sind'.[5] Can this hypothesis be refined?

The common contents of Cotton Vespasian A.xiv and Cotton Tiberius A.xv, with the numbering of their letters by Dümmler and in Stubbs's *Memorials of Saint Dunstan*, are set out in Table I (after Dümmler and Chase, with corrections).

As may be seen, the letters in Cotton Vespasian A.xiv switch between the 'series' of Cotton Tiberius A.xv in what seems an arbitrary manner, and the order of quire 6 is particularly jumbled. Does anything point to the 'series' having been arranged as in Cotton Tiberius A.xv in Cotton Vespasian A.xiv's exemplar(s), and what are the principles of selection in Cotton Vespasian A.xiv?

The first group of letters in Cotton Vespasian A.xiv, filling quires 1–5, written in a single hand, consists of ten letters addressed to English, mostly Northumbrian, recipients. Many of them refer to viking attacks, and all stress the need for moral reform: Archbishop Wulfstan's interests are easy to detect. All these letters are from the first series in Cotton Tiberius A.xv, except the last, which is the first of Cotton Tiberius A.xv's Series 2. They occur in the same order as in Cotton Tiberius A.xv. It seems reasonable to deduce that the scribe of this section of Cotton Vespasian A.xiv used a ready-arranged manuscript of Series 1 as his exemplar, perhaps already joined to Series 2. Many letters of Series 1 are omitted, including some to English recipients (for example Cotton Tiberius A.xv nos 41, 45, 46 = Dümmler 44, 24, 21), but these are letters which deal with practical concerns and have little or no homiletic content: the omissions can be explained by the compiler's interests.

There follows, in Cotton Vespasian A.xiv, a quire (Quire 6) of ten leaves (all the other quires in the manuscript have eight), in a different hand, which begins with seven letters from Series 3 of Tiberius A.xv: two by Alcuin, then five of the tenth-century letters found at the end of the Tiberius manuscript.[6] After this, the quire contains four more letters from Cotton Tiberius A.xv's Series 1. One of these (Cotton Tiberius A.xv, no. 39; Cotton Vespasian A.xiv, no. 20) is from

4   'Alcuinstudien', pp. 521–6.
5   *ibid.*, p. 520.
6   Chase's table is at fault here: it states, as does his note on pp. 8–9, that there are only four tenth-century letters at this point in Cotton Vespasian A.xiv and that Cotton Tiberius A.xv omits them and the other tenth-century letter in quire 7. In the table, I have numbered the letter which Chase omits 16a, in order to avoid confusion when collating with his table.

Pope Paul I to Eadberht, king of Northumbria 737–758;[7] the other three are Alcuinian. In this quire as a whole there is no thematic unity: the first two Alcuin-letters are both to Æthelheard, archbishop of Canterbury (793–805), four of the tenth-century ones are to archbishops of Canterbury also, but the fifth is Lantfred's epistolary preface to his *Vita et miracula Sancti Swithuni*, addressed to the monks of St Peter's, Winchester, and of the remaining Alcuin-letters one is to a Continental, two to English recipients, on very diverse subjects. In addition to this the order of the letters is jumbled as compared with that of Cotton Tiberius A.xv.

The last group of Alcuin's letters in Cotton Vespasian A.xiv, which occupies quire 7, is seen to stand somewhere between the first two when compared with the three sequences of Cotton Tiberius A.xv. It is written by a third scribe and begins with six of the first eight letters of Series 1, continuing with nos 117–124 from Series 3. There is then one more tenth-century letter, no.131 in Series 3, and – squeezed in in another hand again, supposed to be Wulfstan's own – Cotton Tiberius A.xv's letter 100, from Series 2. The principle of selection in this quire is less strong than that in quires 1–5: Chase called these items 'letters for daily correspondence'. The first six are to named recipients and shed some light on Alcuin's private life; the next eight, to anonymous correspondents, are shorter and more obviously reproduced as patterns for certain formal types of letter. This difference gives a clue to the reason for the selection from two different series, but the reason for the addition of the last two letters in the quire – both on trivial personal matters – is unclear.

The fact that the latter two groups of letters in Cotton Vespasian A.xiv, those in quires 6 and 7, are by different scribes from the first and selected on different principles (if any), may mean that they were collected at different times and for different reasons. The third group (quire 7) seems, like the first, to have been taken from an exemplar which was in much the same state of arrangement as Cotton Tiberius A.xv: the letters, like those of quires 1–5, are in sequences in the same order, except for the final letter (Cotton Tiberius A.xv, no.100, added by a different writer), a common text found in three Continental manuscripts, which may have been taken from a different manuscript or perhaps even from a single sheet. Compared with this, the confusion of quire 6 demands explanation. The fact that it begins with seven letters from Cotton Tiberius A.xv's Series 3 – two Alcuinian, five tenth-century – in a jumbled order, neither corresponding to that of Cotton Tiberius A.xv nor with any chronological or thematic principle of its own – might suggest that Series 3 was a loose pile of letters when the scribe of quire 6 came to copy it. However, he then subjoined four letters from Series 1 which are equally out of order. In this he may, if he was working after the scribes of quires 1–5 and 7, have been trying to fill in some of their omissions from Series 1, but if so it was a languid effort and the omission of others from the same series remains unexplained.

[7]   *Councils*, edd. Haddan and Stubbs, III.394–6.

TABLE I

Dümmler/Stubbs	Vespasian A.xiv			SERIES	Tiberius A.xv		Dümmler/Stubbs
					fos		
D18	1 fos	114r–118v	QUIRES 1–5 (fos 114–153) Hand 1	SERIES 1	25	21v–26r	D18
D19	2	118v–123r			26	26r–30r	D19
D20	3	123r–125v			27	30r–32v	D20
D16	4	125v–129v			29	34r–37r	D16
D30	5	129v–130r			30	37r/v	D30
D43	6	130r–133r			31	37v–40r	D43
— (letter of anchorite Alchfrith to Higlac)	7	133r–136r			37	48v–50v	—
D114	8	136r–142r		SERIES 2	40	53v–57v	D114
D116	9	142r/v			50	63v–64r	D116
D17	10	142v–148v			52	68r–72r	D17
—	10a	148v Poem on Wulfstan	Hand 2		—		—
—	10b	149r–153v Synod of 816			—		—
D311	11	154r–155v	QUIRE 6 (fos 154–163) Hand 3	SERIES 3	104	122v–125r	D311
D128	12	155v–157r			107	127r–129r	D128
S20	13	157r–158r			139	161v–162v	S20
S21	14	158r/v			140	162v–164r	S21
S9	15	158v–159r			126	144v–145v	S9
S19	16	159r/v			138	161r/v	S19
S22	16a	160r (omitted by Chase)			127	145v–146r	S22
D209	17	160v–162v		SERIES 1	36	44v–48v	D209
D273	18	162v–163r			35	44r/v	D273

Right-hand sequence:

	fos		Series
39	52r–53v	—	
12	13r–14r	D70	
1	2r–3v	D65	SERIES 1
2	3v–4v	D66	
3	4v–6r	D67	
4	6r–7r	D7	
5	7r–8r	D8	
8	9r/v	D10	
117	139v–140r	D45	SERIES 3
118	140r/v	D46	
119	140v	D256	
120	140v–141r	D274	
121	141r/v	D235	
122	141v	D292	
123	142r/v	D293	
124	142v–143r	D103	
131	156v–157r	S17	
100	121r/v	D96	SERIES 2

Left-hand sequence:

	fos			
19	162v–163r	— (letter of Pope Paul to Eadberht)		
20	163v	D70		
21	164r–5r	D65	QUIRE 7	Hand 4
22	165r/v	D66		
23	165v–166v	D67		
24	166v–167v	D7		
25	167v–168r	D8		
26	168r/v	D10		
27	168v–169r	D45		
28	169r	D46		
29	169r/v	D256		
30	169v	D274		
31	169v–170r	D235		
32	170r	D292		
33	170r–171r	D293		
34	171r	D103		
34a	171r/v (Chase: Uuido)	S17		
34b	171v (Chase: Alcuin)	D96		Hand 5

Scribes were not bound to rationality in choosing material from their exemplars, and the possible reasons for the 'disorder' of quire 6 are infinite in number, but one explanation may perhaps be suggested. It is that Archbishop Wulfstan (for whom Cotton Vespasian A.xiv was apparently written) and his scribes were in touch with the compilers of Cotton Tiberius A.xv as they worked and made selections from their letter-collection at different stages in its compilation. That the two manuscripts both date from the early eleventh century may support this. In this case, quire 6 would have been the first to be copied. It consists of letters from Series 1 and 3 in Cotton Tiberius A.xv, with none from the well defined Series 2, the source of which was probably a single manuscript. Many of the letters of Series 1 and 3 are found only in Cotton Tiberius A.xv and Cotton Vespasian A.xiv; this supports the idea that before incorporation into these collections they existed only singly, scattered in other manuscripts or even on loose sheets. Quire 6 of Cotton Vespasian A.xiv might represent the first scraping together of what would later be augmented and separated into Series 1 and 3: in other words, a first workbook or sampler offered to Wulfstan. Quires 1–5 and 7 would have been copied later by scribes sent to make deliberate selections from the work once it was complete, or nearing completion. The shortage of letters from Series 2 in Cotton Vespasian A.xiv might imply that the exemplar of this section was one of the last sources to be discovered and 'fed into' Cotton Tiberius A.xv. One might even envisage an exchange of sources, with Wulfstan bringing single letters or small collections preserved, say, at York down to the compilers at Canterbury or Glastonbury in exchange for the chance to copy some of the letters which they had gathered.

Of course this is no more than a hypothesis which could be borne out – or disproved – only by an exhaustive examination and comparison of Cotton Tiberius A.xv and Cotton Vespasian A.xiv. However, few would deny that much evidence for scholarly methods and interchange of this kind may be waiting to be extracted from these manuscripts and others and that the text-history of Alcuin's letters as we know it is far from complete.

The place of Henry of Huntingdon's *Epistola ad Warinum* in the text-history of Geoffrey of Monmouth's *Historia regum Britannie*: a preliminary investigation

NEIL WRIGHT

Geoffrey of Monmouth's *Historia regum Britannie*, one of the most influential literary products of the twelfth century, is transmitted in over 210 manuscripts.[1] The number of surviving manuscripts has up to now impeded their systematic examination, with the result that the text-history of the *Historia* remains largely unknown.[2] For this reason, Henry of Huntingdon's *Epistola ad Warinum*, which is the earliest known witness to Geoffrey's *magnum opus* and can be dated securely to the year after the probable publication of the *Historia* (in 1138),[3] has received special attention from Galfridian scholars. However, the fact that the *Epistola ad Warinum* is not a complete copy of the *Historia*, but is instead a drastic abbreviation, has left the question of the exact relationship of the *Epistola* to its exemplar, and indeed the nature of the contents of that exemplar itself, unresolved. Moreover, speculation, sometimes ill founded, about the *Epistola* and certain extant early manuscripts of the *Historia* has further complicated an already uncertain issue. Critical investigation of the *Epistola ad Warinum* is therefore long overdue. The present paper attempts to reconsider the problems raised by the *Epistola*, to re-examine its relationship to the *Historia*, and to reassess its place in the textual history of Geoffrey's *œuvre*.

Henry of Huntingdon was a historian, a *littérateur*, and, by virtue of his posi-

---

[1] *Historia regum Britannie*, ed. Wright, I. For the manuscripts, see Crick, *Historia regum Britannie*, III.

[2] Cf. Dumville, 'An early text'; *Historia regum Britannie*, ed. Wright, I.xlvi–lii; Crick, *Historia regum Britannie*, III. Two forthcoming studies, by Julia Crick and Michael Reeve, begin the systematic study of the textual history of *Historia regum Britannie*.

[3] The dating of Geoffrey's opus is discussed in *Historia regum Britannie*, ed. Wright, I.xii–xvi.

tion as archdeacon of the diocese of Lincoln, a man of affairs.[4] In this latter role, Henry in January 1139 accompanied Theobald, archbishop of Canterbury, to Rome.[5] During their journey they stayed at the monastery of Le Bec in Normandy, where Theobald had been abbot. There Henry met with Robert of Torigni, the future abbot of Mont-Saint-Michel (1154–1186), who was at that time a monk at Le Bec.[6] There must have been much to discuss, since the two men shared an interest in history and both were actively involved in writing. Robert was engaged in producing a version of William of Jumièges's *Gesta Normannorum ducum* with interpolations and a continuation down to 1135.[7] Henry, the first edition of whose *Historia Anglorum* (down to 1129) was begun in the 1120s, may perhaps have brought with him a copy of the subsequent edition (to 1135) to present to Robert, who undoubtedly knew Henry's *Historia* in this form.[8] Certainly, the *Historia Anglorum* was discussed, and in this connexion Robert showed Henry a copy of Geoffrey of Monmouth's *Historia regum Britannie*.[9] This latter work, which modern scholars regard as a pseudo-history of great imaginative power, presented a revolutionary new, and largely coherent, account of the British people from their founder Brutus down to the seventh century A.D.[10] Henry, who had been entirely ignorant of the existence of such a book, was amazed and immediately made excerpts from it.[11]

The details of this discovery, and an account of the narrative of the *Historia regum Britannie* based on these excerpts, form the contents of Henry's *Epistola ad Warinum*. This letter was written to answer Warinus's enquiry as to why Henry's *Historia Anglorum* gave no account of the long period between the reign of Brutus (allegedly a contemporary of the high priest Eli) and the invasions of Julius

---

4   For details of Henry's life see *Henrici Archidiaconi Huntendunensis Historia Anglorum*, ed. Arnold, pp. xxxi–iv; Gransden, *Historical Writing*, pp. 193–201, especially pp. 193–4.
5   On the background of this trip, see Saltman, *Theobald*, pp. 14–15.
6   Robert of Torigni's life and works are described in *Chronique de Robert de Torigni*, ed. Delisle, II.i–xix.
7   Gransden, *Historical Writing*, pp. 199–200; but see also Chibnall, 'Orderic Vitalis and Robert of Toringi', pp. 133–9.
8   The dates of the various editions of the *Historia Anglorum* are discussed in *Henrici archidiaconi Huntendunensis Historia Anglorum*, ed. Arnold, pp. xi–vi, Gransden, *Historical Writing*, p. 194, and now Greenway, 'Henry of Huntingdon'; Robert of Torigni states that he used the 1135 edition (viz, down to the death of Henry I) in the preface of his extended version of the world-chronicle of Sigibert of Gembloux (*Chronique*, ed. Delisle, I.94, n. 1, and 97).
9   As is confirmed by Robert himself: see below, n. 26.
10 *Historia regum Britannie*, ed. Wright, I.xvi–ix; Brooke, *The Church and the Welsh Border*, pp. 95–100.
11 Since Henry was a colleague of Geoffrey of Monmouth's close associate Walter of Oxford and had moreover dedicated his *Historia Anglorum* to Alexander, bishop of Lincoln, who was also the addressee of Geoffrey's *Prophetie Merlini*, it is somewhat surprising that, despite these connexions, he was left to 'happen on' the *Historia* at Le Bec. Christopher Brooke's attractive suggestion (*The Church and the Welsh Border*, p. 43 and n. 103) that Henry was the victim of a plot to float Geoffrey's audacious pseudo-history must, however, remain speculative.

Opening capital of *Epistola ad Warinum* from a copy of Robert of Torigni's Chronicle in Avranches MS. 159 (fo 174). Although the iconography is not entirely certain, the illumination appears to show Robert discussing Henry of Huntingdon's *Historia Anglorum* with its author, and, below, presenting the 'amazed' Henry with Geoffrey of Monmouth's *Historia regum Britannie*.

Caesar – viz the same question which Robert of Torigni presumably asked Henry at Le Bec before showing him Geoffrey's *Historia*. Henry replies that he could find no records of that period and recounts his discovery at Le Bec; since he states that this occurred *hoc anno*, the *Epistola* may be dated with certainty to the year of Henry's stay at Le Bec (1139), possibly being composed shortly after his return. The body of the *Epistola* comprised the *excerpta* – to which it is the sole witness – made from Geoffrey's *Historia*, and the letter closed with the advice that Warinus should attempt to secure a copy of the *liber grandis Galfridi Arturi*[12] if he wishes for further details.

Of Warinus Brito, the addressee of the letter, nothing is known save that he was of Celtic origin. The by-name 'Brito' ('a Briton') might at this date mean either a Welshman, a Cornishman, or a Breton.[13] In fact, Henry affirms within the *Epistola* that the Breton hope of King Arthur's return was entertained by Warinus's *parentes*, which argues strongly that Warinus was of Breton descent.[14] Further, Henry's reference to Britain as *patria nostra*[15] may imply that Warinus was resident in Britain rather than on the Continent, but we cannot be certain of this.[16]

We owe the survival of Henry's *Epistola* to its inclusion in two larger historical works. The first of these is his own *Historia Anglorum*.[17] As we have seen, Henry of Huntingdon published the *Historia Anglorum* in a number of editions.[18] In the edition which extended the narrative down to 1147, Henry added three books to the seven which the work originally comprised. Only one of these new books (Book X) in fact continued the narrative. The other two books contained other compositions which Henry included in the *Historia* largely, it appears, in order to enhance his literary standing in the eyes of posterity. Of these books, the second (Book IX), *De miraculis*, dealt with English saints. The first (Book VIII), entitled

---

12 On Geoffrey's by-name Arturus, see *Historia regum Britannie*, ed. Wright, I.x; and, for other contemporary references to Geoffrey in this manner, see Tatlock, *The Legendary History*, pp. 438–9.

13 *Historia regum Britannie*, ed. Wright, I.ix.

14 *Epistola*, § 9. All chapter references are to the interim edition of the *Epistola* printed below, pp. 92–113.

15 *ibid.*, § 1.

16 Tatlock, *The Legendary History*, p. 433, n. 2, suggested that the recipient of Henry's letter might be Warinus, prior of Le Bec about 1130, or any of five monks of that name in the monastery in the early eleventh century; if that were indeed so, it might further be surmised that Warinus's (lost) enquiry about early British history was part of the plan to foist Geoffrey's *Historia* on Henry (see above, n. 11). However, Tatlock's proposed identifications are highly unlikely since Henry would hardly have sent a précis of Geoffrey's opus (along with instructions to seek out a complete copy) to a correspondent whom he knew to have access to the very library where those excerpts were made.

17 Arnold's text (see above, n. 4), which is deficient in many ways (see below, n. 20), will be superseded by the re-edition (to appear in the series Oxford Medieval Texts) currently being undertaken by Diana Greenway of the Institute of Historical Research, University of London.

18 See above, n. 8.

De summitatibus, consisted of three letters: the first, addressed to Henry I, concerned the succession of the rulers of various kingdoms of the world; the second was the *Epistola ad Warinum* itself, which thus formed a species of appendix to the *Historia* proper, filling in the narrative gap before the Roman conquest and offering an alternative account of British history down to the seventh century; the third letter, to one Walter (possibly an archdeacon of Leicester), was devoted to one of Henry's favourite themes, *contemptus mundi*.[19] This new division into ten books was retained in the final edition of the *Historia Anglorum* (down to 1154), and henceforth the *Epistola ad Warinum* was transmitted as part of Henry's historical *œuvre*.[20]

Robert of Torigni, who introduced Henry to the *Historia regum Britannie*, also played a part in the survival of the *Epistola ad Warinum*. Between 1147 and 1150 Robert compiled an extended and supplemented version of the world-chronicle of Sigibert of Gembloux (of which further recensions were made in 1162 and 1182).[21] In this Chronicle, Robert included the *Epistola ad Warinum* from the 1147 edition of Henry's *Historia*, which was (in addition to the earlier 1135 version) certainly known to him.[22] Robert's stated intention in thus incorporating the *Epistola* wholesale was to avoid excessive interpolation of its Galfridian material throughout the earlier part of the Chronicle, which rested on the venerable authority of Eusebius and Jerome.[23] A similar motive probably lay behind Henry's decision to append the *Epistola* to his own *Historia* rather than to attempt considerably to recast the latter in the light of the contents of the *Historia regum Britannie*. However, it is also possible that both writers, Robert in particular, may have entertained doubts about the veracity of Geoffrey's *Historia* and hence have welcomed the opportunity of relegating its contents to a subsidiary role within their own works.[24]

Of the two versions of the *Epistola ad Warinum*, only that in Robert of Torigni's Chronicle has ever been printed.[25] While this version is for the most part in agreement with that included in Henry's *Historia*, it differs in some minor additions and editorial changes introduced by Robert. In order therefore that the *Epistola* may more readily be consulted in the form in which Henry himself intended, an interim edition (and translation) of the text found in the *Historia Anglorum* has been appended to the present study.[26]

---

19 See further Partner, *Serious Entertainments*, pp. 11–48.
20 Nevertheless the *Epistola* is not printed in Arnold's edition, where Books VIII and IX are omitted, and Book X is numbered as VIII.
21 Edited by Delisle, *Chronique* (see above, n. 6); on the dating of the various recensions, see Dumville, 'An early text', pp. 30–3.
22 *Chronique*, ed. Delisle, I.117–19; and Dumville, 'An early text', p. 32.
23 *Chronique*, ed. Delisle, I.95–6.
24 Cf. the remarks of Leckie, *The Passage of Dominion*, pp. 46–9 (Robert of Torigni) and 76–8 (Henry of Huntingdon).
25 *Chronique*, ed. Delisle, I.97–111; there is also an edition in *Chronicles*, ed. Howlett, IV.65–75.
26 See below, pp. 92–113. The text printed there has been collated with Delisle's edition

The central problem raised by the *Epistola ad Warinum* – that of its value as a witness to the copy of the *Historia regum Britannie* excerpted by Henry of Huntingdon at Le Bec – was first addressed by H. D. L. Ward, who asserted that 'from Huntingdons's abstract, one ought to be able to form some idea of Geoffrey's work as it existed in January 1139'.[27] Ward listed a number of discrepancies between the *Epistola* and Geoffrey's *Historia* and advanced two possible explanations for them: first, that these peculiarities were found in the Le Bec manuscript itself and were faithfully reported by Henry; secondly, that they are due to Henry, who not only abbreviated Geoffrey's text, but also modified it as he saw fit. Ward drew no firm conclusion, although he may have favoured the first position. The discrepancies noted by Ward, in addition to further examples (all of which will be discussed below), were reconsidered by R. H. Fletcher, who rejected Ward's first proposition and maintained that Henry was entirely responsible for these peculiarities.[28] Edmond Faral and J. S. P. Tatlock, both of whom dealt with the *Epistola* only in passing,[29] also subscribed to Fletcher's view. However, the arguments advanced by these three scholars, which depend only on certain aspects of the text rather than on its entirety, cannot be regarded as completely convincing or satisfactory. As the most recent critic to consider this issue has commented 'it is not completely certain in what form Henry found the *Historia Regum Britanniae* at Bec'.[30]

Such knowledge as we do possess of the early text-history of Geoffrey's *Historia* does not preclude prima facie the possibility that Henry saw a variant text at Le Bec. We know of at least two major variant versions of the *Historia*; the first of these was already in existence by 1155 (although it is not the work of Geoffrey himself),[31] and the second can be dated on the evidence of manuscripts to the latter half of the twelfth century, if not earlier.[32] The vulgate text is itself found with four different dedications (three of which are probably attributable to

and the latter's divergences reported in the apparatus (with the siglum R). The most important of Torigni's additions (in so far as these can be distinguished from manuscript variants) occur in § 1 (below, p. 93), where Robert explicitly dates Henry's visit to Le Bec to 1139 and describes in more detail the circumstances under which he showed him Geoffrey's *Historia* (see above, p. 72). In the preface of the Chronicle (*Chronique*, ed. Delisle, I.96), Robert also confirms that Henry's excerpts were made at Le Bec (rather than, as might be held, from another copy of the *Historia* secured on Henry's return to England).

[27] Ward, *Catalogue*, I.210.
[28] Fletcher, 'Two notes', pp. 461–3, and *The Arthurian Material*, pp. 119–21.
[29] Faral, *La Légende arthurienne*, II.20–3, especially p. 22, n. 3; Tatlock, *The Legendary History*, p. 433, n. 3.
[30] Leckie, *The Passage*, p. 134, n. 5.
[31] The date and authorship of this text are discussed in detail in my edition, *The Historia Regum Britannie of Geoffrey of Monmouth*, II.xi–lxxviii.
[32] Jacob Hammer was engaged on an edition of the Second Variant version at the time of his death; on its characteristics, see Emanuel, 'Geoffrey of Monmouth's *Historia Regum Britanniae*'.

Geoffrey himself).[33] Some manuscripts contain further minor variations,[34] and more such manuscripts doubtless remain to be discovered. However, it must be stressed at the outset that the peculiarities found in the *Epistola ad Warinum* cannot adequately be accounted for by any of the known variant versions, none of which can therefore be identified with the source used by Henry at Le Bec. If the Le Bec manuscript did indeed diverge from the vulgate in any way, then the *Epistola ad Warinum* is at present the sole known witness to its special peculiarities. It is thus of the utmost importance to reconsider the relationship of the *Epistola ad Warinum* to the vulgate text of Geoffrey's *Historia* and to re-examine the conflicting views about the genesis of the discrepancies found in Henry's abbreviated version.

Careful comparison of the two texts in question[35] reveals three types of divergence: first, episodes (or characters) present in the *Historia* but absent from the *Epistola*; secondly, material found only in the *Epistola*; and, finally (the largest category) episodes which are treated differently in each text. We must examine these three categories more closely to determine if they can provide any indication whether any (or all) of these differences are due to Henry or are attributable directly to the manuscript which he consulted at Le Bec.

Let us begin with the material which is absent from the *Epistola*. Since Henry refers to the Le Bec copy of Geoffrey's *Historia* as a *liber grandis*,[36] it is unlikely that his exemplar was itself markedly less complete than the vulgate text. The general lack of detail and the narrative compression characteristic of the much shorter *Epistola* must therefore chiefly be due to the *excerpta* on which is was based – which may have been no more than the briefest of notes. It is, however, possible that certain important episodes were omitted because they contained elements of the supernatural or the monstrous. They are as follows: all reference to Corineus,[37] including his wrestling-bout with the giant Gogmagog;[38] the *Prophetie Merlini*[39] and, indeed, all reference to Merlin; the miraculous circumstances attendant on Arthur's conception[40] and his battle with the giant of Tumba Helene;[41] all reference to Brianus, who at one point cuts flesh from his own thigh to feed his king.[42] The problem arises of whether these omissions are Henry's doing or had already been made in his exemplar, which could arguably have represented a revised, more sober version of Geoffrey's *Historia*.

---

[33] *Historia regum Britannie*, ed. Wright, I.xii–xvi.
[34] J. Hammer, 'Some additional manuscripts', pp. 236–8; Dumville, 'The manuscripts', p. 128, and 'An early text', pp. 16–19.
[35] The texts employed were that appended below and *Historia regum Britannie*, ed. Wright, I (disregarding the minor peculiarities of Bern 568, discussed *ibid.*, pp. liv–ix).
[36] *Epistola*, § 10.
[37] *Historia regum Britannie*, §§ 17–24.
[38] *ibid.*, § 21.
[39] *ibid.*, §§ 109–18.
[40] *ibid.*, §§ 137–9.
[41] *ibid.*, § 165.
[42] *ibid.*, § 193.

Some light is shed on this problem by two further episodes absent from the *Epistola* but containing no miraculous elements. The first of these is the so-called 'night of the long knives', when British leaders were treacherously massacred by Hengist and the English.[43] It is not easy to see why this important incident should have been omitted from the Le Bec manuscript of the *Historia*, since it forms an integral part of the narrative. Geoffrey derived this episode from one of his prime sources, the pseudo-Nennian *Historia Brittonum*[44] – a text also familiar to Henry of Huntingdon, who made considerable use of it in the first two books of the *Historia Anglorum*.[45] It is significant that the 'night of the long knives' was not one of the passages on which Henry drew, probably because he reacted against the anti-English tone of the stress laid on Hengist's perfidy.[46] The likelihood that Henry for the same reason omitted this episode from the *Epistola* therefore far outweighs the possibility that it may have been absent from his Le Bec exemplar.

The second episode not found in the *Epistola* is the account of Brutus's early career in Greece,[47] where he acquired the Trojan followers necessary to populate Britain, and the wife Innogen by whom he would father the first dynasty of British kings. Since this episode plays so important a role in explaining the origin of the British people, it is hardly conceivable that it was not present in Henry's exemplar of the *Historia*. But there are no objections to the proposition that it was omitted from the *Epistola* by Henry. Geoffrey's account of Brutus is again partially derived from the *Historia Brittonum*,[48] but there is in that text no mention of the events in Greece. Henry had, moreover, followed the pseudo-Nennian version of Brutus's (or Bruto's) career in his own *Historia Anglorum*.[49] Hence it appears that Henry suppressed the lengthy Grecian episode in the *Epistola* so that the latter should broadly agree with the existing account in the *Historia Anglorum*, and also perhaps in order to reach the main narrative dealing with Britain proper more quickly. If the responsibility for these two omissions can plausibly be attributed to Henry, we may also suspect that he was the author of the rest, motivated not only by the need to abbreviate Geoffrey's *Historia*, but possibly also by the desire to eliminate some of its preternatural elements.[50]

[43] *ibid.*, §§ 104–105.
[44] *Nennius et l'Historia Brittonum*, ed. Lot, § 46. A comprehensive re-edition of the *Historia Brittonum* is being prepared by David N. Dumville, but only one volume, *The Historia Brittonum, 3: the 'Vatican' Recension*, has as yet appeared.
[45] Henry's borrowings from the *Historia Brittonum* are noted *ad loc.* in Arnold's edition (see also *ibid.*, p. lii).
[46] The incident is omitted from Henry's narrative in *Historia Anglorum*, II.2, despite the fact that Henry there relies heavily on the *Historia Brittonum*.
[47] *Historia regum Britannie*, §§ 7–15.
[48] § 10.
[49] *Historia Anglorum*, I.9.
[50] However, the *Epistola* retains references to Bladud's magic flight (§ 2), a three day rain of blood (§ 3), and a monster from the underworld (§ 6).

The second category of divergence consists of material unique to the *Epistola*. Of this material, the introductory description of the discovery at Le Bec[51] and a paragraph marking the transition from the pre-Roman period with Caesar's invasion,[52] which are external to the narrative of the *Historia* proper, are obviously the work of Henry himself. The remaining matter in question comprises smaller details, some of which are also manifestly due to Henry. In § 9 of the *Epistola* there is a reference to the Breton hope of Arthur's return, which is nowhere explicitly mentioned in Geoffrey's *Historia*;[53] since in this passage the Bretons are termed *parentes tui* (viz, of Warinus), it is clear that this detail was included by Henry because of its special relevance to his Breton addressee. Henry must also have been responsible for cross-references to his own account of Caesar's invasions,[54] and of the arrival of christianity in the reign of Lucius and the construction of the Severan *uallum*[55] Other material unique to the *Epistola* is fully in accord with Henry's known literary preoccupations and habits. In § 5 he laments that the deeds of many British kings have been forgotten because of a dearth of historical records:[56]

> Tot uero regum predictorum bella et fortitudines et magnificentie, nonne hec uel scripta sunt in libris innotissimis uel penitus a memoria deleta? Det igitur michi Deus et meis tam nichili pendere laudes hominum quam nichili sunt.

Such emphasis on the transience of human existence and the consequent importance of contempt for worldly things is a leitmotiv of Henry's historiography.[57] Compare, for example, with the passage quoted above the similar sentiments expressed in *Historia Anglorum*:[58]

---

[51] *Epistola*, § 1.

[52] *ibid.*, § 7.

[53] In *Historia regum Britannie*, § 178, Arthur's fate is ambiguously treated: although mortally wounded ('letaliter uulneratus'), he is conveyed to Avallon to have his wounds cured ('ad sananda uulnera sua').

[54] *Historia Anglorum*, I.12–14; cf. *Epistola*, § 6.

[55] *Historia Anglorum*, I.28 and 31; cf. *Epistola*, § 8.

[56] Translated on p. 110 below.

[57] Above, n. 19.

[58] *Historia Anglorum*, II.1. 'The forty-five emperors who ruled both Britain and the rest of the world have been set out above. If any of them enjoy glory in heaven, that is all they have; for they have none on earth. To talk of them has become cheap and further discussion of their deeds seems a bitter cause of distaste and rancour. Therefore let us, in comparison with those for whose power and majesty the whole world was scarcely enough, consider the worthlessness of our glory, power, and pride, which cause us to toil, sweat, and rave.' Compare also the closing verse of the prologue of the *Historia Anglorum* (Arnold, p. 4), 'Aspice *quam nichili sit* honor, lux, gloria mundi' (and, indeed, Henry's opening remarks in *Epistola ad Warinum*, § 1, 'Tanta pernicies oblivionis mortalium gloriam successu diuturnitatis obumbrat et extinguit.'). See also nn. 67 and 98 below.

Tractatum est in superioribus de .xlv. imperatoribus qui tam Britanniam quam ceteras mundi partes rexerunt: quorum si aliqui gloria potiuntur in celis, illam tantum habent, quia iam hic nullam habent. Uiluit enim sermocinatio de eis et prolixior confabulatio de actibus eorum uidetur amara, tedii scilicet et odii generatrix. Quapropter excogitemus ex eorum comparatione, quorum potentie et maiestati uix sufficiebat uniuersus mundus, quam nichil sit gloria nostra, potentia nostra, tumor noster, quorum de causa laboramus, sudamus, insanimus.

The presence in the *Epistola* of this note of *contemptus mundi*, a concept which is totally alien to Geoffrey's *Historia*, clearly betrays, then, another of Henry's additions to his source.[59]

In two further passages of the *Epistola* are found *sententiae* absent from the *Historia*: 'moderate dicta semper sunt apprecianda';[60] and 'sed sepe letis interueniunt mesta'.[61] The inclusion of such sayings is paralleled elsewhere in Henry's writings. In particular, with the second of the examples quoted above compare the similarly banal sentiment cited in *Historia Anglorum*: 'sed uulgo dicitur, "uento pluuia et risus dolore miscetur" '.[62] It is most likely, therefore, that these *sententiae* too were added to the *Epistola* by Henry. Once these additions have been eliminated, only two elements unique to the *Epistola* cannot immediately be accounted for by reference to Henry's other works.[63] In § 5, the musical British king Blagabred is compared to Orpheus and Nero. But the use of such classical *exempla*, one in this case mythological, the other historical, is exactly what might be expected from a *littérateur* such as Henry.[64] In the same chapter, a sea-monster which devours the cruel king Morvid is described as being 'sent, as they say, from hell' ('ab inferis, ut aiunt, missa'); however, this emotive detail runs closely parallel to the *sententiae* already discussed. In short, there is every reason to suppose that all the material unique to the *Epistola* is attributable to Henry.

The third category, that of narrative differences between the *Epistola* and Geoffrey's *Historia*, is both the largest and the most problematical. Three episodes in particular have attracted scholarly attention. In the *Epistola*, some of the giants who were the first inhabitants of Britain are destroyed after wading out beyond their depth to attack Brutus's ships; this incident has no parallel in

---

[59] Henry's moralising can also be detected in the non-Galfridian statement that Aganippus of Gaul was inspired to seek Cordeilla's hand by 'Deus ... qui eruditis interest cogitationibus' (*Epistola*, § 3). See further n. 98 below.

[60] *Epistola*, § 3.

[61] ibid., § 4.

[62] *Historia Anglorum*, I.10. 'But as is commonly said, "rain is mixed with wind and laughter with pain".' None of the above sayings is recorded in Walther, *Proverbia*, although there is some similarity between *Epistola*, § 4, 'sed sepe letis interveniunt mesta' and Ovid's *Fasti* VI.463, 'scilicet interdum miscentur tristia laetis'.

[63] There is also, however, a non-Galfridian allusion (in *Epistola*, § 8) to the foundation of Chester (*Cestria*) by King Marius for which there is no obvious explanation.

[64] And see further below, p. 86.

Geoffrey's *Historia*.[65] In the *Epistola*, the replies of Lear's elder daughters are somewhat different from those found in the corresponding passage of the *Historia*.[66] And – perhaps the most striking example – the final confrontation between Arthur and his rebellious nephew Mordred is quite differently treated from the account of the full-pitched battle of Camlan in *Historia regum Britannie* where the two do not meet in single combat; in the *Epistola*, Arthur chances dramatically on Mordred in Cornwall, hacks his way through to him, and, grasping his helmet (presumably by the nasal), severs his head with one stroke.[67] It is very difficult to determine whether the different handling of these three passages, as well as some other details,[68] is due to Henry or was present in the Le

---

[65] *Epistola*, § 2. This episode may perhaps have been inspired (although the parallel is far from exact) by *Aeneid*, III.662–91, where the blinded giant Polyphemus, having waded out into the sea, is unable to pursue Aeneas's ships beyond his depth (especially line 671, *Nec potis Ionios fluctus aequare sequendo*). If so, it is possible, given Henry's fondness for Latin poetry (see below, p. 86), that this non-Galfridian element too may be attributable to him.

[66] *Epistola*, § 3; cf. *Historia regum Britannie*, § 31.

[67] *Epistola*, § 9; cf. *Historia regum Britannie*, § 178. This duel between Arthur and Mordred may draw on an earlier dramatic single combat between Eldol and Hengist (*Historia regum Britannie*, § 124), where Hengist is caught *per nasale cassidis* (although he is then captured rather than killed). There are also some interesting parallels between the *Epistola* and Henry's later account of the battle of Lincoln (in 1141), when King Stephen was taken in a similar manner: with 'gladio per aciem uiam sibi parans in medio suorum Modredum galea arripuit' (*Epistola*, § 9), compare *Historia Anglorum*, X [Arnold's VIII].14, 'gladio michi uiam per hostes parabo' (also X.15, 'gladiis uiam paretis') and X.18, 'eum galea arripiens'. The latter passages must of course post-date the *Epistola*, but the close verbal similarities certainly suggest that the letter's diction (and hence its peculiarities) is that of Henry rather than of his Le Bec exemplar. Indeed, there are several other occasions on which the phrasing of *Epistola ad Warinum* closely parallels that of Henry's *Historia*: compare *Epistola ad Warinum*, § 2, 'discurrens per aera cecidit super Trinouantum uolatu infausto *et fractis ceruicibus expirauit*' and *Historia Anglorum*, IV.17, 'discurrebant per aera', and VII.40, 'cecidit rex nouus et fractis ceruicibus expirauit'; *Epistola ad Warinum*, § 3, 'Parua fuit medii mora temporis' and *Historia Anglorum*, X.34, 'Paruum fuit medii spatium temporis', and X.38, 'Nec longa fuit medii mora temporis' (see also n. 99 below); *Epistola ad Warinum*, § 5, 'Tot uero regum . . . bella et fortitudines, . . . nonne hec vel scripta sunt in libris innotissimis' and *Historia Anglorum*, VI.12, 'De bellis vero regis Edmundi, et de fortitudine eius, nonne hec scripta sunt in historiis veterum'(see also n. 98 below); *Epistola ad Warinum*, § 6, 'Hoc discordie seminario et odii fomite', and X.31, 'incentiuum fomesque odii fuit et discordie'; *Epistola ad Warinum*, § 9, 'Successu uero temporis' and *Historia Anglorum*, X.1, 'Successu uero temporis'; *Epistola ad Warinum*, § 9, 'Inter eundum . . . tot uulnera recepit' (again in the description of Arthur's duel with Mordred) and *Historia Anglorum*, IV.26, 'inter eundum captus est'; and finally *Epistola ad Warinum*, § 10, 'quo non erat alter forma pulchrior, affatu dulcior' (also § 2, 'qua non erat forma uenustior') and *Historia Anglorum*, VII.3, 'quo non erat alter forma uenustior, mente serenior, affatu dulcior'. See also n. 98 below.

[68] In *Epistola*, § 8, for instance, Vortigern has the monk Constans crowned and carried round his old monastery on spears, a pagan Germanic ceremony (cf. the remarks of Wallace-Hadrill, *The Long-haired Kings*, p. 158, on shield-raising) which heightens the irregularity of this coronation *sine episcopis* (cf. *Historia regum Britannie*, § 94). Also, in

Bec manuscript. Henry's free adaptation of his source (as witnessed by his omissions and additions) could certainly have extended to these narrative changes, but his other works provide no strong parallels which might demonstrate that this was indeed the case. Similarly, there is no intrinsic reason why these episodes could not have been so handled in his Le Bec exemplar, although Henry's other changes might seem to argue against the latter hypothesis. The question appears to be deadlocked.

However, consideration of some other narrative discrepancies may help to solve this problem. Some minor divergences, for instance, can be shown with certainty to be due to mistakes made by Henry. In Geoffrey's *Historia*, Brennius's Norwegian bride is lost when a Danish prince tows away her ship in a naval battle ('cepit forte nauem in qua erat predicta puella et illatis uncis illam inter consocios attraxit').[69] In the *Epistola*, it is the princess herself, not the boat, which is dragged off ('maxime intendens naui in qua puella residebat unco puellam extraxit');[70] this grotesque variation can only have arisen because Henry, who presumably excerpted the Le Bec manuscript at speed, erroneously understood *illam* (in the sentence quoted) to refer not to *nauis* but to *puella*. There are other similar confusions. In the *Epistola*, Fulgentius, who is in the *Historia* a British leader allied to the Picts, is carelessly termed *dux Pictorum*.[71] Also, in the *Epistola*, Utherpendragon is referred to as the son, rather than the brother (as in the *Historia*), of Aurelius Ambrosius.[72] So major a divergence, which would involve serious disruption of the narrative of the *Historia*, is most unlikely to have been found in Henry's exemplar; but it is easily explained as a slip on Henry's part, made because Uther succeeded Ambrosius as king. In the same chapter, Vortigern, *consul Gewisseorum* in the *Historia*[73] is wrongly called *dux Cornubie*. Finally, in the *Epistola*, the English utterly destroy not Bath (which, after ravaging the Severn area, they besiege in the corresponding passage in the *Historia*), but *Urbs Legionum*;[74] this is nonsensical, since Arthur later holds an elaborate crown-wearing in that place[75] – an episode most unlikely to have been omitted from the Le Bec manuscript.[76]

Epistola, § 9, Arthur's two Continental expeditions (*Historia regum Britannie*, §§ 155 and 164–76) are telescoped into one.

69 *Historia regum Britannie*, § 36. 'By chance he took the ship in which the girl was, fixed grappling hooks, and dragged it amongst his allies.'

70 *Epistola*, § 4; translated below, p. 109.

71 *Epistola*, § 8; cf. *Historia regum Britannie*, § 74.

72 *Epistola*, § 8.

73 § 94.

74 *Epistola*, § 9; cf. *Historia regum Britannie*, §§ 145–146.

75 *Historia regum Britannie*, §§ 156–157.

76 Another confusion occurs in *Epistola*, § 4, where the manuscripts are divided (see below, p. 99) as to whether Belinus was buried at Trinouantum or at his own foundation of *Urbs Legionum*, while in § 5, it is stated that his son Gurguitbartruc was buried in the same place as his father. Since Geoffrey claims that Belinus was buried at Trinouantum (*Historia regum Britannie*, § 44) and his son Gurguint at *Urbs Legionum* (§ 46), one of Henry's assertions must be in error, although which remains unclear. Also,

Even more important for the question of the discrepancies in Henry's letter is a group of related passages in which the narrative of the *Epistola*, while it diverges from that of Geoffrey's *Historia*, is found to be in agreement with other historical sources. A case in point is the treatment in the *Epistola* of the royal brothers Belinus and Brennius (as Geoffrey calls him), whose complicated story is told in the *Historia regum Britannie*.[77] In Geoffrey's version, Brennius is driven from Britain by Belinus and becomes leader of a Gallic people, the Allobroges. On his return to Britain, civil war is narrowly averted and the two brothers join forces to attack and take Rome. It has long been recognised that this part of the *Historia* is loosely based on the sack of Rome by the Gallic chieftain Brennus in 394 B.C., an event which was well known to mediaeval readers from Orosius or Jerome's version of Eusebius's Chronicle.[78] Although the account of the reign of Belinus and Brennius in the *Epistola*[79] agrees in outline with that of the *Historia*, there are a number of important points of difference. Brennius is in the *Epistola* called Brennus, as was the historical Gallic leader; similarly, the Gallic tribe over whom he exercised power are not the Allobroges, but the Senones – again, the historically correct name of the tribe who sacked Rome;[80] moreover, Belinus does not in the *Epistola* accompany his brother to Italy (as he does in the *Historia*) so that the omission of the former by Continental sources no longer constitutes a contradiction. In effect, Geoffrey's Brennius has in the *Epistola* been more clearly identified as the Brennus of history and a number of necessary modifications accordingly made.[81] A parallel example is provided by the British ruler Maximianus, who became emperor of Rome.[82] This Maximianus corresponds to the historical Spanish usurper Magnus Maximus, although Geoffrey follows the anonymous *Historia Brittonum*[83] in naming him Maximianus. In the *Epistola* this evident inaccuracy is eliminated and the historically correct name Maximus is restored.[84]

The question immediately arises as to whether these corrections were made by Henry or may have been a feature of the Le Bec manuscript itself. With this problem in mind, we must examine some further passages in which the *Epistola*

---

in *Epistola*, § 2, Henry erroneously states that Maddan was eaten by wolves, an end which Geoffrey ascribes to Maddan's son Mempricius (*Historia regum Britannie*, § 26).

77 §§ 35–44.

78 *Pauli Orosii historiae*, ed. Zangemeister, II.19; and Migne, *Patrologia Latina*, XXVII.464, respectively.

79 § 4.

80 Indeed, at one point (*Historia regum Britannie*, § 43), Geoffrey himself nods and refers to Brennius's troops (supposedly the Allobroges) as *Senones Gallos*; cf. Tatlock, *The Legendary History*, pp. 100–1.

81 There is, however, no obvious source for the claim (*Epistola*, § 4) that Brennus subsequently occupied Greece and Asia; possibly this constitutes a vague recollection of Gallic depredations in Greece (under another Brennus; see Justinus, *Epitoma*, ed. Seel, XXIV.6–8) and the foundation of Galatia in Asia Minor in the third century B.C.

82 *Historia regum Britannie*, §§ 81–88.

83 §§ 27 and 29.

84 *Epistola*, § 8.

agrees with other sources against the vulgate *Historia regum Britannie*. The first of these passages occurs, once again, in the early career of Brutus. In the *Historia* Brutus is exiled from Italy to Greece.[85] On leaving Greece, he lands at the island of Loegetia and there consults an oracle of Diana. Then, after a long Mediterranean voyage, he arrives on the Atlantic coast of Gaul (in Aquitania), founds Tours, and finally reaches Britain. In the *Epistola* the narrative is much compressed and, as we have seen, the episode in Greece entirely omitted.[86] After his exile from Italy, Brutus visits 'various lands' (*diuerse terre*, which are not specified) and builds Tours in Gaul. Only then does he consult Diana (whose oracle is vaguely situated in *terra longinqua*) and proceeds directly to Britain. As has been noted, Henry was aware that Geoffrey's account of Brutus was loosely based on *Historia Brittonum*, which Henry himself had used in *Historia Anglorum*.[87] In both the latter texts, Brutus goes directly from Italy to Gaul, where Tours is founded, and thence to Britain (no mention of Diana being made).[88] The narrative sequence of the *Epistola*, which places the foundation of Tours before the consultation of Diana (as opposed to after it, as in Geoffrey's *Historia*), therefore corresponds more closely to that of the *Historia Brittonum* and Henry's *Historia Anglorum*; it thus seems certain that this correspondence is due to Henry's manipulation – whether conscious or unconscious – of his Le Bec exemplar in the light of other sources known to him.

We may point to other similar modifications. In the *Epistola*, the usurper Vortigern summons to Britain the English who will eventually betray him (*adscitis Anglis*).[89] The view that Vortigern sent to the Continent for the English (which derives ultimately from Gildas) was sanctioned by Bede[90] and hence became the accepted orthodoxy, being found, for instance, in Henry's own *Historia Anglorum*.[91] Geoffrey, however, offered an alternative account, again based on the anonymous *Historia Brittonum*, in which the English were exiled from Germany and arrived in Britain purely by chance.[92] The presence in the *Epistola* of an allusion to the Bedan version affords a further example of Henry's attempts to align the *Epistola* with his own historical tenets (and with his *Historia Anglorum*).[93] A further instance of such reinterpretation of Geoffrey's narrative occurs in *Epistola*, § 8, where the reigns of Carausius, Allectus, and Asclepiodotus are

---

[85] *Historia regum Britannie*, §§ 6–21.
[86] *Epistola*, § 2. See above, p. 78.
[87] *Historia Anglorum*, I.9; cf. *Historia Brittonum*, § 10.
[88] Henry does, however, add that Brutus reached Britain by way of Armorica, doubtless because of the claim that the British originated from the *tractus Armoricanus* made in Bede's *Historia ecclesiastica gentis Anglorum* (edd. Colgrave and Mynors, I.1).
[89] *Epistola*, § 8.
[90] *Historia ecclesiastica gentis Anglorum*, I.14–15.
[91] *Historia Anglorum*, II.1.
[92] *Historia regum Britannie*, § 98.
[93] It is extremely unlikely that Henry is referring merely to the summons issued by Vortigern to the English after their landing (*Historia regum Britannie*, § 98), as there would then be no explanation for the *aduentus Saxonum* in the *Epistola*.

described. According to Geoffrey,[94] Allectus was sent by the Roman senate to Britain to kill the usurper Carausius, but, having achieved that end, was himself killed by Asclepiodotus, *dux Cornubie* (and hence by implication a Briton). Yet in the *Epistola* Allectus is depicted as Carausius's 'companion' (*socius*) and Asclepiodotus as a 'prefect' (*prefectus*). Both these epithets reflect the narrative of Bede's *Historia ecclesiastica gentis Anglorum* (closely based on Orosius's *Historia aduersum paganos*), where Allectus is termed Carausius's *socius* and Asclepiodotus a *prefectus pretorio* or 'guards' commander' (there is no suggestion that he might be of British birth).[95] Since Bede's account is copied verbatim in Henry's *Historia Anglorum*,[96] it seems certain that the presence of these non-Galfridian elements in the *Epistola* is once again directly attributable to Henry. Henry's evident responsibility for these modifications, therefore, constitutes a powerful argument that he was in fact the author of all the 'historical' corrections found in the *Epistola*.

Another point of difference between the *Epistola* and the vulgate *Historia regum Britannie* is the presence in the former of literary allusions not found in the latter. In the *Epistola*, for example, Lear's rejection of his youngest daughter is couched in the following words: 'Rex igitur iratus auertit faciem suam ab ea.'[97] This expression, which is not paralleled at the same point in Geoffrey's *Historia* is modelled on a phrase found in Psalm xxi.25: 'nec *auertit faciem suam a me*'.[98] Moreover, the description of Aeneas as 'Romani generis auctor' constitutes an echo of a line of Vergil: '*generis nec Dardanus auctor*'.[99] Similarly, King Blagabred is compared to Orpheus and Nero in the following phrase: 'nec magis Traces

---

[94] *Historia regum Britannie*, § 76.

[95] *Historia ecclesiastica gentis Anglorum* (edd. Colgrave and Mynors, I.6); cf. Orosius, *Historia adversum paganos*, VII.25–26.

[96] *Historia Anglorum*, I. 36.

[97] *Epistola*, § 3.

[98] Also II *Paralipomenon* xxx.9: 'non *auertet faciem suam a uobis*'. There are numerous other biblical borrowings in the *Epistola*: compare *Epistola ad Warinum*, § 2 'inhabitavit igitur terram et divisit eam *funiculis distributionis*' and Psalm lxxvii.54 '*divisit eis terram in funiculo distributionis*'; *Epistola ad Warinum*, § 2 'et *fractis cervicibus* expirauit' and I Samuel iv.18 '*et fractis cervicibus* mortuus est'; *Epistola ad Warinum*, § 3 'Deus qui *eruditis interest cogitationibus*' and Proverbs viii.12 'ego sapientia ... *eruditis intersum cogitationibus*'; *Epistola ad Warinum*, § 5 'Tot uero predictorum bela et *fortitudines et magnificentie*, nonne hec uel *scripta sunt in libris* innotissimis' and (*inter al.*) III Kings xv.23 'universae *fortitudines* eius ... nonne haec scripta sunt in libro uerborum dierum'; *Epistola ad Warinum*, § 6 'Hoc discordie *seminario et odii fomite*' and Genesis xxxvii.5 'maicris *odii seminarium*' and xxxvii.8 '*odii fomitem*'. Compare also *Epistola ad Warinum*, § 3 'Preciosior est cunctis opibus et omnia que desiderantur huic non valent comparari', with its biblical source, Proverbs iii.15 (which is quoted verbatim). It is significant that Henry repeated this citation of proverbs almost exactly in *De contemptu mundi*, § 7 (Arnold, p. 306), 'Illa namque pretiosior est cunctis opibus terre; et omnia que in mundo desiderantur huic non valent comparari'; for further verbal similarities between the *Epistola ad Warinum* and Henry's other works, see n. 67 above.

[99] *Epistola*, § 2; cf. *Aeneid*, VI.365. Compare also *Epistola ad Warinum*, § 3 'Parua fuit medii mora temporis' and Ovid, *Metamorphoses* IX.134 'Longa fuit medii mora temporis'.

Orpheum nec Romani Neronem obstupuere canentes quam Britanni regem predictum'.[100] The words *obstupuere canentes* by their rhythm immediately suggest hexameter poetry.[101] In fact, a very similar verbal collocation is found in Statius's *Thebaid*, to which the *Epistola* probably alludes:[102]

> casus terraeque marisque *canentem*
> *Obstupuere* duces.

Reminiscences such as these are found in the works of almost all twelfth-century historians. Geoffrey of Monmouth himself borrows from the Bible and from Classical poets (including Vergil and Statius);[103] but similar echoes are also very much part of Henry of Huntingdon's style.[104] Once again we must ask whether Henry or his Le Bec source was responsible for these literary allusions found uniquely in the *Epistola*.

In this connexion, it is important to consider another literary echo in the *Epistola*. In § 6 Lud's rebuilding activities in London are recorded as follows:[105]

> Luid, filius regis predicti, considerans Trinouantum tam bellorum copia quam uetustate decidisse, reedificauit Lundoniam edificiis uenustissimis murorum, turrium, portarum, serarum, pontium, regiarum.

The piling-up of architectural nouns in this sentence owes its inspiration ultimately to Gildas's *De excidio Britanniae*, which gives an elaborate description of Britain, including the following details of its fortifications:[106]

---

[100] *ibid.*, § 5; translated below, p. 110.

[101] The words form the last three feet of a hexameter, *obstŭpŭerĕ cănentēs*. Note too that the phrase linking two passages of elegiac couplets in *Epistola*, § 2 constitutes the first half of a hexameter line, *Cūi deă rĕspōndīt*.

[102] *Thebaid*, III.519–20. 'The leaders were amazed by my singing of their exploits on land and sea'. The more correct form *obstipuere* is printed by modern editors, but the variant *obstupuere* is found in several manuscripts: see *P. Papini Stati Thebais*, edd. Klotz and Klinnert, p. 102.

[103] See Hammer, 'Geoffrey of Monmouth's use of the Bible'; Tausendfreund, *Vergil und Gottfried von Monmouth*; Faral, *La Légende*, II.134 (Statius).

[104] He quotes Matthew xxvi.52 ('Qui gladio percusserit, gladio peribit') in *Historia Anglorum*, II.34, for example; and the phrase 'omnes ore gladii deuorati sunt' (*Historia Anglorum*, II.10) combines two biblical models: '*gladius deuorabit uos*' (Isaiah i.20) and 'percutio in *ore gladii*' (Joshua vi.21, *inter alia*). Of the Classical poets, Henry quotes Vergil (*Historia Anglorum*, V.4), Horace (*ibid.*, *prologus*), Ovid (VII.43), Lucan (II.33), and Juvenal (I.1), while verses cited at II.33 (which are most likely by Henry himself) also echo Vergil and Statius; compare line 2, 'Molle pecus, nec pro meritis, mactatque uoratque' with *Aeneid*, IX.340–1, 'manditque trahitque / *Molle pecus*'; and line 4, 'latus undique sanguine manat' with *Thebaid*, X.311–12, '*undique manant / Sanguine* permixti latices' (the parallel with Lucan, VII.560, '*gladios qui toti sanguine manant*', being less close).

[105] Translated below, p. 110.

[106] *De excidio Britannie*, § 3 (ed. Winterbottom, *Gildas*): 'it is ornamented with twenty-eight towns and a number of castles, well equipped with defences consisting of walls, towers, bolted gates and houses'.

... bis denis bisque quaternis ciuitatibus ac nonnullis castellis *murorum, turrium, seratarum portarum,* domorum ... munitionibus non improbabiliter instructis decorata.

However, this passage was imitated by Bede, who, in a similar sketch of the British Isles, adapts it as follows:[107]

Erat et ciuitatibus quondam .xx. et .viii. nobilissimis insignita, preter castella innumera que et ipsa *muris, turribus, portis ac seris* erant instructa firmissimis.

At first sight it might appear that the *Epistola* has strong affinities with the passage in the *De excidio Britanniae*, since, in both, the nouns connected by asyndeton appear in the genitive; but the *Epistola's* relationship to Bede's reworking is much closer, since both texts share the change from the participle *seratus* ('bolted') to the noun *sera* ('bolt') and the repositioning of that noun after *porta*.[108] Bede, then, unquestionably influenced the diction of the *Epistola* at this point. Although Geoffrey knew Bede's *Historia ecclesiastica* well,[109] the passage quoted above is nowhere echoed in the *Historia regum Britannie*; but Henry most certainly used this passage. In *Historia Anglorum*, it is reproduced almost verbatim:[110]

Erat autem et ciuitatibus quondam uiginti octo nobilissimis insignita, preter castella innumera, que et ipsa *muris, turribus, portis ac seris* erant instructa firmissimis.

The natural inference is that Henry himself introduced this verbal reminiscence of Bede from the *Historia Anglorum* into his summary of Geoffrey's *Historia*. And, if he was responsible for improving his original on one occasion, the remaining independent literary echoes found in the *Epistola ad Warinum* can also readily be attributed to him.

Henry is also likely to be the author of an element of *paronomasia*, or wordplay, found uniquely in the *Epistola*.[111] In that passage, it is prophesied before Brutus's birth that he will kill both his father and his mother. This prophecy is fulfilled when Brutus kills his mother in childbirth (*nascens*) and his father with an arrow unintentionally (*nesciens*): 'matrem namque *nascens* enecauit; postea uero iuuenis sagitta ludens patrem *nesciens* percussit'.[112] A very similar verbal

---

[107] *Historia ecclesiastica gentis Anglorum,* I.1. 'Formerly it was notable for twenty-eight very distinguished towns in addition to innumerable castles, themselves equipped with the most secure walls, towers, gates and bolts'.

[108] In fact it was probably the recognition that Gildas was echoing I Maccabees xiii.33, '*muniens* ea *turribus* excelsis et *muris* magnis et *portis* et *seris*' (cf. II *Paralipomenon* xiv.17) which led Bede to substitute the more biblical *portis ac seris* for *seratarum portarum*.

[109] Wright, 'Geoffrey of Monmouth and Bede'.

[110] *Historia Anglorum,* I.3.

[111] § 2.

[112] Translated below, p. 107.

conceit (this time based on *nequeo* and *nescio*) is found in *Historia Anglorum*, I.13: '[probitas] tot in periculis toties probata crescere *nequit*, decrescere *nescit*'.[113] This parallel with the *Historia Anglorum* again argues that Henry introduced the similar word-play on *nascor* and *nescio* into the *Epistola*.

Thorough comparison of the *Epistola ad Warinum* with the vulgate *Historia regum Britannie*, then, allows us to draw the following conclusions. There is no evidence to suggest that material omitted from or added to the *Epistola* was similarly treated in the Le Bec manuscript consulted by Henry; all such omissions and additions can easily be explained by Henry's need to abbreviate, by comparison with Henry's known literary methods and habits, or by a desire on Henry's part to ensure that the *Epistola* agreed in some measure with his own *Historia Anglorum*. While we cannot entirely rule out the possibility that some passages – particularly the annihilation of the British giants, the replies of Lear's daughters, and Arthur's death[114] – might have been handled differently from the vulgate in Henry's exemplar, other changes in the *Epistola*, demonstrably made by Henry to modify the narrative in the light of other historical sources or to improve the text by the introduction of literary echoes, argue very firmly indeed against this hypothesis. Unless, therefore, a manuscript which substantially agrees with Henry's *Epistola* should be found, there is no reason to suppose that the Le Bec manuscript on which it was based differed in any significant way from the vulgate text of Geoffrey's *Historia*.

In that case, the possibility arises of identifying the copy of the *Historia regum Britannie* which Robert of Torigni showed to Henry of Huntingdon with vulgate manuscripts of known Le Bec provenance or connexions. Two candidates merit consideration. The first of these is the archetype (now apparently lost) of three surviving manuscripts (London, British Library, MS. Arundel 237; Bern, Burgerbibliothek, MS. 568; and Rouen, MS. U.74 [1177]), which included among its characteristics a double dedication, to King Stephen and Robert of Gloucester.[115] On the strength of this dedication to the king, David Dumville has recently suggested that the archetype of these manuscripts may have passed into the possession of Philippe de Harcourt, who was chancellor of England (from June 1139 to March 1140) and had links with Le Bec.[116] Could Philippe, then, be responsible for the presence of Geoffrey's *Historia* at Le Bec in 1139, and could Henry's exemplar have been the ancestor of the Arundel, Bern, and Rouen manuscripts? Certainly, on his death (February 1164), Philippe (by then bishop of Bayeux) bequeathed a copy of Geoffrey's *Historia* to Le Bec.[117] However,

---

[113] '[Your worth] which, proven so often in so many battles, is unable to increase, yet does not know how to decrease'.

[114] *Epistola*, §§ 2, 3, and 9.

[115] Dumville, 'An early text', especially pp. 16–17; the Stephen-Robert dedication (which now survives only in Bern MS. 568) is printed in *Historia regum Britannie*, ed. Wright, I.1–2 (see also pp. xiii–xiv, with the Robert of Gloucester and Robert-Waleran dedications).

[116] 'An early text', pp. 24–6.

[117] *ibid.*, p. 24.

although this book may have been the archetype of the three manuscripts in question, it is hardly likely to have been at Le Bec as early as January 1139. Moreover, since Philippe became chancellor only in June 1139, it is difficult to see how he could be responsible for a text with the dedication to King Stephen being at Le Bec as early as January of that year. In fact, a common characteristic of the texts of the *Historia regum Britannie* transmitted by the Arundel, Bern, and Rouen manuscripts is the omission (through a saut-du-même-au-même) of the pentameter line 'Insula in occeano est undique clausa mari' in a passage of elegiac couplets.[118] The most likely explanation for the omission of this line from all three manuscripts is its similar absence in their common ancestor. If so, this ancestor cannot have been Henry's exemplar, since the *Epistola ad Warinum* does not omit the line in question.[119]

The second candidate for identification with Henry's source is the well known Leiden, Bibliotheek der Rijksuniversiteit, MS. BPL 20. This book comprises two manuscripts, the second of which contains Geoffrey's *Historia*.[120] The contents table on fo 1v agrees almost verbatim with an entry in a Le Bec library catalogue of the 1150s, so that the united volume must have been at Le Bec no later than that decade.[121] In fact the codex has been assigned to the Le Bec scriptorium on the grounds of its script.[122] It is, then, hardly surprising that Edmond Faral and others have maintained that Leiden BPL 20 was the very manuscript which Henry of Huntingdon consulted at Le Bec.[123] However, David Dumville has argued that the contents of Leiden BPL 20 (including the *Historia regum Britannie*) show signs of revision (perhaps by Robert of Torigni himself).[124] If Geoffrey's *Historia* appeared only in 1138, Robert must have acquired the work for Le Bec [125] and had it revised and copied with remarkable speed in order to show this Le Bec copy (rather than its original) to Henry in January 1139. And, in fact, the script and decoration of the Leiden manuscript argue in favour of its production slightly later than that date.[126] It is, therefore, most unlikely that Henry's source was the Leiden manuscript itself. However, we should not entirely discount the possibility that the exemplar on which Leiden BPL 20 was based was the manuscript seen by Henry, although future examination of the Leiden manuscript may

---

[118] *Historia regum Britannie*, § 16. See *Historia regum Britannie*, I.liv–vi.
[119] See *Epistola*, § 2.
[120] Fos 60r–101v.
[121] Dumville, 'An early text', pp. 2–4 (and 23).
[122] *ibid.*, p. 4, n. 15.
[123] *La Légende*, II.20–3; also Tatlock, *The Legendary History*, pp. 311–13 (and 433, n. 3).
[124] 'An early text', pp. 4–6.
[125] The presence of a copy of the *Historia* at Le Bec so soon after its probable publication led Tatlock (*The Legendary History*, p. 444, n. 36) to speculate that Geoffrey, despite his close connexions with Oxford, may have written (or completed) his work at that monastery; but there is no evidence to support his hypothesis. Robert's swift acquisition of the *Historia* might just as easily be accounted for by the position of Waleran of Meulan, one of the addressees of the double-dedication of that work, as sometime patron or lay protector of Le Bec (Dumville, 'An early text', p. 23).
[126] Dumville, *ibid.*

preclude this too.[127] But it is equally possibly that Henry excerpted yet another (lost or untraced) manuscript at Le Bec; it is, therefore, wise to conclude provisionally that such evidence as we possess at present does not permit the firm identification of Henry's source with any extant codex.

In the past, then, somewhat exaggerated claims have been made for the *Epistola ad Warinum*. The status of Henry of Huntingdon's abbreviation as the earliest known witness to the *Historia regum Britannie* led not only to the assertion that it preserved elements of an early non-standard version of the Galfridian text, but also to ill-directed efforts to identify Henry's Le Bec exemplar with surviving manuscripts and so to enhance the stature of the latter by carrying their history back to 1139. In fact, the divergences found in the *Epistola* are most readily explicable in terms of changes made by Henry himself; and there is no reason to postulate that the manuscript which he excerpted at Le Bec did not largely resemble the vulgate text as it is known today. Since we cannot with certainty demonstrate that any extant manuscript is identical with or related to Henry's exemplar, any further assessment of the place of the *Epistola* in the text-history of Geoffrey's work must be postponed until the bulk of surviving manuscripts of the *Historia* have been studied and the transmission of the latter text is better understood.

However, the *Epistola* remains a work of the utmost importance in revealing the reaction of one twelfth-century historian to Geoffrey's pseudo-history. Critics have not in this respect been kind to Henry: Christopher Brooke has, as we have seen, suggested that Henry may have been selected as a suitably credulous victim on whom Geoffrey's audacious construct might be foisted;[128] Leckie more charitably contrasts Henry's initially uncritical acceptance (in the *Epistola*) of the newly published *Historia* with his later more guarded policy of appending the letter to his *Historia Anglorum* rather than attempting to reconcile Geoffrey's narrative with his own.[129] Both views have some justification, but neither is entirely fair. Certainly Henry's excerpting of the *Historia* at Le Bec betrays enthusiasm for a startling new discovery, and certainly Henry never explicitly addressed the major contradictions between Geoffrey's *Historia* and his own; yet the modifications which Henry introduced into the *Epistola* demonstrate that his approach was not entirely unthinking. At a number of points he omitted, added, or altered material in order to bring Geoffrey's version of events more closely into line with the *Historia Brittonum*, Bede's *Historia ecclesiastica*, and his own *Historia Anglorum*. Since we cannot be sure how extensive were the excerpts made at Le Bec, it is possible that some of these changes were effected not on the spot, but on Henry's return to England; he may have consulted the works in question while recasting the *excerpta* for inclusion in the *Epistola ad Warinum* – at the same

---

127 Leiden BPL 20 was one of the manuscripts used by Faral in preparing his edition of the *Historia* (*La Légende*, III.63–303), but, as Faral's apparatus is notoriously unreliable (see *Historia regum Britannie*, ed. Wright, I.xlix, n. 90), re-edition is much needed.
128 See above, n. 11.
129 See above, n. 22.

time, that is, as he presumably introduced literary echoes of the Bible, of Classical poets, and of Bede. The *Epistola*, then, is not simply a précis; Henry's modifications, however tentative, deserve to be recognised as a first, faint adumbration of the misgivings with which some mediaeval historians (most notably William of Newburgh) received Geoffrey's *Historia*, and which were in time to lead to its downfall in the sixteenth and seventeenth centuries.[130]

---

[130] On the mediaeval reception of Geoffrey's opus, see Leckie, *The Passage*, pp. 73–119; and for the later period, see Kendrick, *British Antiquity*, pp. 65–133. I am indebted to Dr J. A. Seeley and Dr Diana Greenway for reading a draft of this paper and for a number of helpful comments.

Appendix

Epistola ad Warinum: an interim edition

SIGLA

A   London, British Library, MS. Add. 24061, fos 57v–60r
C   Cambridge, Corpus Christi College, MS. 280, fos 151r–157r
E   London, British Library, MS. Egerton 3668, fos 123v–128r
L   London, Lambeth Palace, MS. 327, fos 133r–138r
R   Robert of Torigni, *Chronicon* (ed. Delisle, *Chronique*, I.97–111)

PREFACE

The present interim edition is based on four manuscripts. Three of these represent the earliest texts of the *Epistola ad Warinum*, being those in which the letter occurs together with the historical narrative down to 1138. They are: British Library, MS. Egerton 3668 (*olim* Phillipps 25151), a twelfth-century manuscript from Durham Cathedral priory, in which the text to 1138 was later amended (to bring it closer to conformity with the 1147 edition) and continued 1139–47;[1] Cambridge, Corpus Christi College, MS. 280, a twelfth-century manuscript with continuation 1139–54;[2] British Library, MS. Additional 24061, a fourteenth-century manuscript from the Augustinian priory of Llanthony in Gloucestershire,[3] with a continuation to 1202.[4] The text of the *Epistola* transmitted by these three manuscripts is largely in agreement. The fourth manuscript used is London, Lambeth Palace, MS. 327, a twelfth- or thirteenth-century manuscript from the Augustinian abbey of Bourne in Lincolnshire,[5] which breaks off in 1148.[6] This manuscript offers a slightly different text which, as the apparatus of the present edition demonstrates, was very similar to that on which Robert of Torigni drew in his *Chronicon* (here collated from Delisle's edition). However, any speculation about the relationship of Lambeth 327 to the other three manuscripts and also to Paris, BN, MS. lat. 6042, which may be a descendant of Robert's exemplar of the

---

[1]   *The British Library, Catalogue of Additions to the Manuscripts 1946–1950* (3 vols, London 1979), I.352–3.
[2]   James, *A Descriptive Catalogue of the Manuscripts in the Library of Corpus Christi College Cambridge*, II.44–5; Arnold's assertion (p. xxxvi, n. 2) of provenance from St Augustine's, Canterbury was denied by N. R. Ker, *Medieval Libraries, p.* 338.
[3]   *Catalogue of Additions to the Manuscripts in the British Museum in the years MDCCCLIV–MDCCCLXXV* (3 vols, London 1875–80), II.2; Ker, *Medieval Libraries*, p. 108.
[4]   Arnold, p. xl, n. 3.
[5]   *A Catalogue of the Archiepiscopal Manuscripts in the Library at Lambeth Palace* (London 1812), p. 43; Ker, *Medieval Libraries*, p. 11.
[6]   Arnold, p. xxxviii, n. 4.

Historia Anglorum,[7] must be suspended until the appearance of Diana Greenway's comprehensive re-edition of Henry's *oeuvre*.[8]

Editorial corrections have here been kept to a minimum. I have not employed Classical orthography but have followed the spelling of the manuscripts (except in the case of *e-caudata* which is found only in Lambeth 327 and which, for the sake of simplicity, I have treated as *e* throughout). In collating Robert of Torigni's *Chronicon* I have generally ignored Delisle's Classical forms, but have noted all variant spellings of proper names. To aid the reader, modern punctuation has been introduced; and, for ease of reference, the letter has been divided into ten chapters which closely reflect the paragraphing of the manuscripts.

[7] Delisle, *Chronique*, I.lv–lxi.
[8] I am extremely grateful to Dr Greenway for advice on selecting the manuscripts edited here, for information about their contents, and above all for the kind loan of microfilms.

\<Epistola ad Warinum\>

[1]Exemplar autem secunde epistole de serie Britonum hoc est[1]

§ 1   Queris a me, Warine[1] Brito, uir comis et facete, cur patrie nostre gesta narrans a temporibus Iulii Cesaris inceperim et florentissima regna que a Bruto usque ad Iulium fuerunt omiserim. Respondeo igitur tibi quod nec uoce nec scripto horum temporum [2]noticiam sepissime[2] querens inuenire potui. Tanta pernicies obliuionis mortalium gloriam successu diuturnitatis obumbrat et extinguit. Hoc tamen anno,[3] cum Romam proficiscerer,[4] apud [5]Beccensem abbaciam[6] [5] scripta rerum predictarum stupens inueni.[7] Quorum excerpta,[8] ut in epistola decet, breuissime scilicet, tibi, dilectissime, mitto.

Rubric
[1...1] ACEL; *Incipit epistola Henrici archidiaconi ad Warinum de regibus Britonum* R

§ 1
[1]   AELR; *Waurine* C
[2...2] ACEL; *sepissime noticiam* R
[3]   ACEL; *anno qui est ab incarnatione Domini .mcxxx. nonus* R
[4]   ACEL; *proficiscerer cum Theobaldo Cantuariensi archiepiscopo* R
[5...5] ACEL; *Beccum ubi idem archiepiscopus abbas fuerat* R
[6]   CL; *abbatiam* AE (altered from *abatiam* in E)
[7]   ACEL; *inueni. Siquidem Robertum de Torinneio eiusdem loci monachum, uirum tam diuinorum quam secularium librorum inquisitorem et coaceruatorem studiosissimum, ibidem conueni. Qui cum de ordine hystorie de regibus Anglorum a me edite me interrogaret et id quod a me querebat libens audisset, obtulit michi librum ad legendum de regibus Britonum qui ante Anglos nostram insulam tenuerunt.* R
[8]   CELR; *excepta* A

§ 2   Eneas igitur Romani generis auctor[1] genuit Ascanium, Ascanius genuit[2] Siluium,[3] Siluius[4] Brutum. De quo cum magus predixisset quia interfecturus esset patrem et matrem, id casu euenit; matrem namque nascens[5] enecauit, postea iuuenis sagitta ludens patrem nesciens percussit. Exulatus igitur ex Italia diuersas terras adiit; edificauit autem urbem Turonis in Gallia. Tandem in [6]terram longinquam[6] proficiscens oblato sacrificio responsum peciit[7] a Diana[8] his uerbis:

> 'Diua potens nemorum, terror siluestribus apris,
> Dic michi quas terras nos habitare uelis.'

Cui [9]dea respondit:[9]

> 'Brute, sub occasu solis,[10] trans Gallica[11] regna,
> Insula in occeano est undique clausa mari.
> Hanc pete: namque tibi sedes erit ista perhennis;
> Hic[12] fiet natis altera[13] Troia tuis.'

Hoc igitur Brutus responso fretus hanc insulam adiit, cui nomen Albion[14] erat nec habitabatur nisi a gigantibus. Illi autem stature mirabilis[15] et uigoris inenarrabilis erant, sed stolidissime mentis. Cucurrerunt ergo[16] contra naues Bruti in mare et, cum in tantam profunditatem peruenissent quod nec in Brutum progredi nec facile regredi potuissent, sagittis et balistis occisi sunt. Obrutis autem [17]eis et pulsis[17] ceteros gigantes qui non affuerunt noctibus et insidiis tam balistis quam aliis artificiis[18] deleuit. Inhabitauit igitur terram et diuisit eam suis funiculis[19] distributionis;[20] et uocauit terram ex nomine suo Britanniam.[21] Edificauit proinde Trinouantum in memoriale sempiternum, id est Troiam nouam, quam nunc[22]

---

§ 2
1   ACEL; *actor* R
2   ACEL; *uero* R
3   ACELR (altered from *Siluinum* in E?)
4   ACELR (altered from *Siluinus* in E?)
5   ACELR (first s suprascript in E)
6...6   CELR; *terra longinqua* A
7   ACL; *petiit* ER
8   CELR; *Diano* A
9...9   AELR; *respondit dea* C
10   AELR; *solis* bis (second occurrence deleted) C
11   AER; *Gallia,* altered to *Gallica* CL
12   ACE; *Hec* LR
13   ACELR (altered from *atera* in L)
14   ACEL (altered from *Albio* in L); *Albio* R
15   ACELR (altered from *miribiles* in E?)
16   ACE; *igitur* LR
17...17   CELR; *et expulsis* A
18   ACELR (altered from *artificis* in L)
19   ACEL; *funiculo* R
20   ELR; *distribucionis* AC
21   AER; *Brittanniam* CL
22   ACER; *nunc* suprascript in L

Lundoniam[23] uocamus. Urbs igitur magna Trinouantum tempore Eli[24] sacerdotis et Siluii[25] Enee stabilita est. Brutus autem feliciter regnans et gloriose decedens[26] Lucrino primogenito suo Britannie[27] regnum reliquit. Quem, cum decem[28] annis potentissime regnasset, uxor sua Gondolouea [29]occidit in[30] bello sagitta, quia eam dimiserat. Puniuit igitur Gondolouea[29] crimen adulterii in uiro suo quod perpetrauerat in ancilla ipsius Gondolouee, qua non erat forma uenustior, uisu delectabilior: unde in reginam promota est expulsa domina[31] sua. Gondolouea[32] post interfectionem[33] uiri[34] sui regnauit .xv. annis tempore Samuelis[35] et Homeri.[36] Post quam regnauit Maddan filius eius, uir ferinus et crudelis, et[37] deuoratus est a lupis. Proinde regnauit Menpricius[38] filius predicti regis [39].xx. annis[39] tempore Saul[40] regis.[41] Deinde Ebraucus filius Menpricii[42] .lx. annis tempore Dauid regis et Siluii[43] Latini. Hic Eboracum fecit et Castellum Puellarum construxit. Ebraucus etiam rex genuit .xx.[44] filios et totidem filias; ex quorum numero Brutus cognomine Uiride Scutum regnauit post patrem miles inuictissimus .xii. annis. [45]Exinde regnauit Leir[46] filius Bruti .xxv. annis;[45] hic construxit Carloil[47] tempore Salomonis[48] et Roboam regis.[49] Et tunc Siluius Epitus patri Albe successit in Italia. Postea regnauit filius eius Rudbudibras, uir fortissimus, .xxxix. annis; hic edificauit Cantuariam et Wintoniam, quam tunc uocauit Uuente,[50] tempore Capi[51] filii Epiti et Aggei et Iohel[52] et Amos prophetarum. Post quem Bladud filius eius .xx.[53] annis; hic construxit urbem Bade et balnea et ibi posuit ignem

23   ACEL; *Londoniam* R
24   AE; *Heli* CR; *Hely* L
25   CLR; *Silui*.m A; *Silui* E
26   ACELR (over an erasure in L?)
27   AER; *Brittannie* CL
28   ACER; *.x.* L
29...29   ACER; om. (from text), but added at foot of page in L
30   LR (in suprascript in L); om. ACE
31   ACELR (corrected from *dominina* in C)
32   ACE; *Gandolouea* L; *Gondolouea igitur* R
33   ACEL; *mortem* R
34   AELR; *domini* C
35   ACEL; *Samuhelis* R
36   ACEL; *Homeri poete* R
37   ACER; om. (but space left) L
38   AELR; *Mempricius* C
39...39   AELR; *annis .xx.* C
40   AELR; *Saulis* C
41   ACEL; *regis Iudeorum* R
42   AELR; *Mempricii* C
43   CELR; *Saluii* A
44   ACEL; *uiginti* R
45...45   ACEL; om. R
46   AC; *Lier* EL
47   ACE; *Carleil* LR
48   CELR; *Salamonis* A
49   ACEL; *regum* R
50   AELR (altered from *Uente* in L); *Wente* C
51   ACER; *Campi* L (?)
52   ACEL; *Ioel* R
53   ACEL; *uiginti* R

perpetuum[54] in domo Minerue. Erat quippe omni genere scientiarum eruditissimus, sed arte nigromantica perfectissimus. Arte nimirum nigromantica discurrens per aera cecidit super[55] Trinouantum uolatu infausto et fractis ceruicibus expirauit.[56]

§ 3   Lier[1] filius eius regnauit pro eo .xl. annis; hic construxit Leicestriam[2] super fluuium Sore. Tandem masculina carens prole .iii.[3] filias habuit regni sui heredes posuitque rationem cum eis dixitque primogenite: 'Karissima, quanti[4] est apud te dilectio mei?'[5] Cui primogenita: 'Sub luna que disterminat ab eternis mutabilia nichil inueniri poterit quod esse tanti possit michi.' Tunc rex medie natu: 'Et apud te quanti est amor mei?' Respondit illa: 'Preciosior[6] est cunctis opibus et omnia que desiderantur huic non ualent comparari.' Deinde rex iuniori dixit: 'Et me, iunior, quantum diligis?' Respondit [7]et dixit:[7] 'Quantum habes, tantum[8] uales tantumque te[9] diligo.' Rex igitur iratus auertit faciem suam ab ea iurauitque nichil eam regni sui participaturam;[10] deditque primogenitam duci magno Britannie[11] cum regni parte australi, alii uero duci mediam natu cum parte boreali.[12] Cordeillam uero[13] iuniorem extorrem fecit sui et [14]amoris et regni.[14] Deus autem qui eruditis interest cogitationibus[15] suscitauit animum Aganippi regis Gallorum, qui eam causa[16] decoris a patre peciit[17] et in matrimonium sibi copulauit. Parua fuit[18] medii mora temporis, cum filie[19] regis in Britannia[20] degentes promouerunt maritos suos ut patrem, quia diutius[21] desiderato uiuebat, regno expellerent. Expulsus[22] ad Cordeillam in Gallias[23] fugiens ad pedes eius prouolutus est cum

---

54   ACELR (altered from *eternum* in C)
55   ACE; *super* suprascript in L; om. R
56   ALR; *exspirauit* CE

§ 3
1   ELR; *Leir* A; *eir* (capital omitted) C
2   CL; *Leircestriam* A; *Leecestriam* ER
3   ACEL; *tres* R
4   AC; *quanta* ELR
5   ACEL; *mea* R
6   CELR; *Pretiosior* A
7...7 ACEL; om. R
8   ACEL; *tantum* repeated suprascript in L
9   CEL; om. AR
10   ACE; *principaturam* LR (with *participaturam* suprascript in L)
11   AER; *Brittannie* CL
12   CLR; *boriali* AE
13   ACER; *uero* suprascript in L
14...14 ACEL; *regni et amoris* R
15   CELR; *cogitacionibus* A
16   CELR; *causam* A
17   AEL; *petiit* CR
18   AELR; *sunt* C
19   AELR; *sue* underpointed after *filie* in C
20   AER; *Brittannia* CL
21   ACER; *diucius* L
22   ACEL; *Expulsus uero* R
23   ACER (altered from *Gallia* in C); *Galliam* L

lacrimis dicens: 'Sorores tue, que de amore mei magnifice locute sunt, regno me crudeles expulerunt. Precor igitur dulcedinem tuam ut, sicut[24] ille [25]magna dicta[25] crudelibus gestis dehonestauerunt, ita tu temperata dicta[26] que de me amando locuta es beneficiis decores[27] et uenustes sempiternumque[28] [29]sit tibi[29] preconium ut, sicut ille [30]bona malis[30] recompensant, sic tu malis bona remutues; uictumque michi saltem uestitumque non abneges.' Cordeilla uero lacrimis commota patris cum uiro suo rege Aganippo Britanniam[31] peciit ducesque sceleratos[32] debellans et interficiens regno patrem triumphose restituit. Hinc igitur[33] tractum[34] est: moderate dicta semper sunt apprecianda.[35] Lier[36] uero senecta demolito regnauit Cordeilla post patrem .v. annis. Sed duo nepotes eius, Marganus et Cunedagius, quasi iniurias patrum uindicaturi fraudulenter eam ceperunt et in carcerem recluserunt; ubi tante mutationi[37] fortune ferociter[38] offensa seipsam uiriliter peremit. Cum igitur nepotes regnum partirentur,[39] Cunedagius interfecit Marganum regnauitque .xxxiii. annis tempore Osee et Ysaie,[40] et tunc Roma facta est. Successit[41] [42]ei Mollo[42] filius eius, in cuius tempore sanguis pluit tribus diebus. Regnauit deinde Gurgucius,[43] successit[44] ei Sisillius; inde Iago; inde[45] Kinemarcus;[46] inde Gabodogo;[47] cuius filius Porrex occidit fratrem suum Ferrex,[48] quem etiam mater eorum occidit; degenerauitque iam regnum Britannie[49] in .v. reges et sedicio[50] pullulabat ubique. Surrexit interea Dummallo[51] et reges[52] .v. solus deleuit; regnauitque igitur .xl. annis splendidissime pacemque peroptimam legesque

[24] ACER; *sicut* suprascript in L
[25]...[25] ACEL (*dicta* suprascript in L); *uerba magniloqua* R
[26] ACEL; *et tamen uera* R
[27] ACELR (corrected from *decoris* in E)
[28] CELR; *sempiternum* A
[29]...[29] ACEL; *tibi sit* R
[30]...[30] ACELR (tampered in L)
[31] AER; *Brittanniam* CL
[32] L; *celeratos* ACE; *soceratos* R
[33] ACEL; *ergo* R
[34] ACELR (altered from *tractatum* in C)
[35] ALR (altered from *apprecienda* in L); *aprecianda* CE (with the e suprascript in C)
[36] ELR; *Leir* AC
[37] CELR; *mutacioni* A
[38] ACEL; om. R
[39] CELR (corrected from *patirentur* in E); *partientur* A
[40] AEL; *Ysaye* C; *Isaie* R
[41] ACEL; *Successit autem* L
[42]...[42] AC; *ei Mallo* E; *Riuallo* (with *ei Mallo* suprascript) L; *ei Riuallo* R
[43] ACL; *Gurgutius* ER
[44] ACEL; *successitque* R
[45] ACEL; *deinde* R
[46] ACER; *Kynemarcus* L
[47] CEL; *Gabobogo* A; *Robodogo uel Gerbodug* R
[48] ACL (altered from *Ferex* in L); *Ferex* ER (over an erasure in E)
[49] AELR; *Brittannie* C
[50] CEL; *seditio* AR
[51] AE; *Dumallo* C; *Dummallo Molmutius* LR
[52] AR; *reges miles* C; *reges milles* (first l erased?) E; *miles* suprascript after *reges* in L

perutiles creauit que Mallonine[53] uocantur, quas Gildas historiographus[54] Britonum magnis laudibus extollit.[55] Duo filii eius Belinus et Brennus post mortem patris compreliati[56] sunt; et erat uterque strenuissimus.

§ 4   Brennus,[1] iunior filius, Norwagiam[2] uictus peciit ducensque filiam regis Norwagie[3] exercitum Norwagensium[4] in Britanniam[5] duxit.[6] Rex autem Dacorum, cum eandem puellam ducere preparasset, uidens se frustratum obuiatus est Brenno[7] in mari;[8] et, dum confligeret, maxime intendens naui in qua puella residebat unco puellam extraxit et abrepta preda naui uelocissime fugiens in fuga uictor extitit.[9] Brennus[10] fugientes persequens et multos perimens pro uicto se habebat. Sed[11] sepe letis interueniunt mesta. Mirabili namque tempestate rex Dacorum appulsus[12] est in Britanniam[13] cum preda sua dilectissima; captus igitur a rege Belino homo eius effectus est et tributarie[14] Daciam recipiens ab eo cum coniuge sua noua in pace reuersus est. Brennus uero eadem tempestate appulsus, amissa coniuge,[15] amissa sociorum multitudine, cum paucis in Belinum uincendus cucurrit;[16] fugiensque in Gallias ad Senonensium regem interuentu sue probitatis et facecie[17] filiam eius duxit; rediensque cum exercitu grandi Senonensium in Britanniam[18] cum fratre maternis lacrimis permotus[19] concordatus est; oblatumque sibi regni dimidium spernens auro sumpto Romam, unde progenies eorum descenderat, peciit. Romam igitur bello primus hominum cepit; que cum tota Italia tamen ei non suffecit, sed omni auro et argento asportato Greciam totam occupauit; Greciam quoque stimulante probitate relinquens in Asia[20] que uoluit sibi regna retinuit, que uoluit suis dedit. Brennus suis temporibus hominum

53 ACEL (with uel Molmutine suprascript in L); Mallonine uel Molmutine R
54 LR; istoriographus AE; hystoriographus C
55 ACEL; attollit R
56 CELR; conpreliati A

§ 4
1   AELR; Brennius C
2   ACER; Nordwagiam L
3   ACER; Nordwagie L
4   ACER; Nordwagensium L
5   AER; Brittanniam CL
6   CELR; conduxit A
7   ACELR (altered from Brennio in CE?)
8   ACELR (altered from mare in C)
9   CLR; exstitit AE
10   ACELR (altered from Brennius in C)
11   CELR; set A
12   ELR (altered from apulsus in E); apulsus AC
13   AER; Brittanniam CL
14   ACELR (altered from tributare in L)
15   ACEL; coniuge et R
16   ACE; occurrit (with uel cucurrit suprascript) L; concurrit R
17   AR; faticie C; facicie E; facetie L
18   AELR; Brittanniam C
19   CELR; promotus A
20   ACER; Asya L

summus, forcium[21] decus, eternum Britannie[22] sydus.[23] Belinus uero frater eius omnibus terris circumiacentibus Britannie subiectis feliciter[24] regnauit; Urbem Legionum construxit [25]in qua sepultus est.[25]

§ 5   Regnauit autem Gurguitbartruc[1] filius Belini pro eo Daciamque, quia nolebat[2] ei reddere tributa que patri reddiderat, bello magno adquisiuit. Hiberniam uero Hispanis[3] petentibus ab eo terram dedit, qui[4] ibi degent usque hodie; et tunc primum inhabitata est Hibernia. Sepultus est ubi pater. Successit[5] ei Kinelinus;[6] cui Sisinnius; cui Kimarus; cui Danius; exinde[7] Moruidus probitate laudabilis et crudelitate detestabilis, qui post multa scelera[8] peracta a fera horribili ab inferis, ut aiunt, missa, dum nimis audacter in eam proruit, absorbetur. Loco eius regnauit Gorbonianus filius eius; successit abhinc Artgallo;[9] huic[10] Elidurus pius, de cuius pietate fama intonuit. Cum enim Peridurus frater eius primogenitus absens esset, sceptra coactus suscepit; post annum uero cum[11] frater eius egenus[12] remearet, cum lacrimis eum suscepit et se sponte regno deponens sceptro et diademate fratrem insigniuit. Peridurus autem natura crudelis erat uexauitque proceres adeo quod[13] eo abiecto Elidurum[14] pium resumpserunt.[15] Elidurus uero fratri regnum malens quam sibi, se ab eo capi et in carcerem poni permisit. Peridurus regnans uindictam[16] in proceres [17]qui eum abiecerant crudeliter[17] exercuit, donec mors eum communis absumpsit. Tunc uero Elidurus pius tercio feliciter[18] omnium communi gaudio usque ad [19]uite finem[19] gloriosus effloruit.

---

21 ACL; *fortium* ER
22 AER; *Brittannie* CL
23 ELR; *sidus* AC
24 ACELR (corrected from *feliter* in L)
25...25 ACE; *sepultusque est in urbe Trinouantum* LR

§ 5
1   ACE (*a* over an erasure in E); Guruitbratruc (altered from *Gurguitbartruc*) L; *Gurguitartruc* R
2   ACELR (altered from *nolebant* in C)
3   AELR; *Hyspanis* C
4   CELR; *quia* (in text) with *qui* in margin A
5   ACEL; *et successit* R
6   A; *Kinelinius* C; *Kinnelimus* E; *Kinelunus* (altered from *Kintelunus*) L; *Kinthelinus* R
7   ACEL; *exinde etiam* R
8   CELR; *celera* A
9   AC; *Artallo* E; *Archgallo* L; *Arthgallo* R
10 ACELR (*c* suprascript in C)
11 AELR; om. C
12 CELR; *egensis* A
13 ACEL; *ut* R
14 ACEL; *Elidurum iterum* R
15 ACEL; *reciperent* R
16 My correction; *uindictam crudeliter* ACELR
17...17 ACEL; om. R
18 ACELR (corrected from *feliter* in L)
19...19 ACER; *finem uite* L

Successit ei Regin[20] filius Gorboniani;[21] postea Marganus filius Artgallonis;[22] post quem Cumanus frater Margani.[23] Et, ne longi<u>s[24] morer, successerunt ex ordine Idwallo, Runo, Gerontius,[25] Catellus, Coillus, Porrex, Cherin; post hunc .iii.[26] filii eius, Fulgenius, Eldradus,[27] Andragius, alter post alterum regnauerunt; deinde Urianus Andragii filius. Regnauerunt ex ordine postea Elius,[28] Clodacus, Clotenus, Gurgincius,[29] Merianus, Bledano, Capoenus, Sisillius. Tunc Blagabred rex facetissimus mira uocis dulcedine prenituit; nec magis Traces Orpheum[30] nec Romani Neronem obstupuere canentes quam Britanni[31] regem predictum. Quo mortuo regnauit Artmai[32] frater eius, uir benignus.[33] Post quos ex ordine Eldol,[34] Redion, Redorchius,[35] Sanuil, Pir, Capoir, Dignellus filius eius;[36] post hos Heli filius proxime dicti. Tot uero regum predictorum bella et fortitudines et magnificentie,[37] nonne hec uel scripta sunt in libris innotissimis uel[38] penitus a memoria deleta? Det igitur michi Deus et meis tam nichili pendere laudes hominum quam nichili[39] sunt.

§ 6   Luid[1] filius Heli regis predicti considerans Trinouantum tam bellorum copia quam uetustate decidisse reedificauit Lundoniam edificiis uenustissimis murorum, turrium, portarum, serarum,[2] pontium,[3] regiarum. Ubi coadunato concilio[4] peciit[5] a suis urbis decorem nouum stupentibus ut ad sui memoriam[6] Carlunden[7] uocaretur et optinuit: unde nunc Lundonia corrupte uocatur.

---

20 CE; *regni* A; *in regnum* LR
21 ACELR (altered from *Goboniani* in L)
22 ACEL; *Arthgallonis* R
23 ACELR (tampered in E)
24 My correction; *longis* ACELR
25 CER; *Geroncius* AL
26 ACEL; *tres* R
27 LR; *Cleradius* AE; *Cleradus* C
28 ELR; *Cliud* A; *Cluid* C
29 ALR; *Gurgintius* CE
30 CLR; *Orfeum* AE
31 AER; *Brittanni* CL
32 ACEL; *Arcinai* R
33 ACEL; *benignissimus* R
34 CELR; *Eidol* A
35 AELR; *Rediorchius* C
36 AELR; *eius* suprascript in C
37 ELR; *munificencie* AC
38 ELR; *idem* AC (?)
39 ACEL; *nichil* R

§ 6
1   AELR; *uid* (capital omitted) C
2   AR; *sarrarum* CE; *serrarum* L
3   AELR; *poncium* C
4   CEL; *consilio* AR
5   ACELR (altered from *pecit* in C)
6   ACLR; *memoriam* suprascript in E
7   ACER; *Kairlunden* (tampered?) L

Superfuerunt [8]ei tres[8] filii, Cassibellanus, Belinus, Androgeus. Quomodo uero Iulius Cesar Cassibellanum et Belinum uicerit, nonne hec scripsi in Historia Anglorum? Audi tamen quid hec dicat historia. Dum Androgeus cum fratribus suis dimicaret contra Cesarem,[9] bis uicti sunt Romani. Pro tanto igitur tripudio sollempnitas splendidissima celebrata est apud Lundoniam; ubi inter ludendum occidit in luctamine filius[10] ducis Androgei filium regis Cassibellani. Unde rex ultra modum iratus minatus est Androgeo[11] mortem nisi redderet ei filium ad occidendum. Hoc discordie seminario et odii fomite[12] misit Androgeus litteras redeundi inuitatorias[13] Iulio[14] Cesari; redeunti Lundoniam tradidit et cum eo in prelio uictor [15]sue gentis exstitit.[15] Cassibellanus tandem Cesari subditus .iii.[16] milia libras argenti Cesari lege tributaria singulis annis persoluit. Sepultus est[17] apud Eboracum.[18]

§ 7   Dictis a Bruto usque Iulium regibus[1] gratum tibi fore puto si ceteros reges Britonum usque ad aduentum Anglorum uel ad tempus Cadwallonis, qui fuit ultimus potentum regum Britonum, distincte prosequar.

§ 8   Temancius,[1] qui Romam cum Cesare perrexit frater Androgei, successit Cassibellano tam in regno quam in tributo; deinde Kinelinus filius eius, quem Augustus armis decorauit. Hic igitur Augusto tributum gratis [2]amans dedit.[2] Cui successit Guidenus [3]filius eius, qui tributum Romanis retinuit.[4] Missus ergo Claudius[3] bello strauit eum et Armigarum[5] fratrem eius regem statuit data ei filia sua; huius auxilio Claudius Orcadas[6] cepit; hic in honore[7] Claudii Gloecestriam[8] fecit. Idem postea Romanis rebellauit sed Uaspasianus eum prius bello, tandem

---

8...8   ACEL; *tres ei* R
9   ACEL; *Iulium Cesarem* R
10   ACER; *filius* suprascript in L
11   ACEL; *Androgeo fratri suo* R
12   AELR; *i* underpointed after *fomite* in C
13   ACER; *in uictatorias* L
14   AELR; *regi* underpointed before *Iulio* in C
15...15   AELR; *extitit sue gentis* C
16   ACEL; *tria* R
17   ACEL; *est enim* R
18   ACEL; *Eboracum dum amplius uiuere non potuit* R

§ 7
1   ACEL; *regibus Britannie* R

§ 8
1   ACL; *Temantius* E; *Themantius* R
2...2   ACEL; *diligenter tradidit* R
3...3   ACER; om. (from text) but added at foot of folio in L
4   ACEL; *renuit* R
5   ACER; *Aruigarum* (tampered?) L
6   AEL; *Horcades* C; *Occades* R
7   ELR; *honorem* AC
8   ACEL; *Cloecestriam* R

amore subiugauit. Successit ei Marius – a quo Westmaria – Romanis seruiens; hic Cestriam edificauit. Post quem regnauit Coillus[9] filius eius; dehinc Lucius, de quo scripsimus quia primus fidem Christi suscepit. Constituit igitur .xxviii. episcopos in Britannia[10] secundum numerum flaminum. Sepultus[11] est rex[12] egregius apud Gloecestriam. Herede caruit[13] ideoque Britones[14] rebellauere Romanis; sed imperator Seuerus bello domuit eos et, cum a Fulgentio[15] duce Pictorum infestaretur, fecit uallum inter Britones et Pictos, de quo prescripsimus.[16] Ab eodem tamen Fulgentio apud Eboracum occiditur et sepelitur. Post quem Bassianus filius eius fratre suo Zeta superato regnum Britannie in proprio tenuit ut pater. Bassianum uero occidit Carausius tirannus.[17] Carausium uero occidit Allectus socius eius. Allectum uero occidit Asclepiodotus[18] prefectus et Gallum[19] [20]socium eius[20] in Lundonia:[21] unde dicitur Walebroc. Asclepiodotum[22] uero occidit Cole dux Colecestrie.[23] Cole uero ducem subiugauit sibi Constancius[24] et post mortem eius regnans decem[25] annis Helenam filiam eius[26] duxit. Quo defuncto apud Eboracum Constantinus[27] filius eius regnauit et postea Romam occupauit. Tunc Octauius dux Wisseorum occidit proconsules Romanos. Constantinus igitur misit Trahern[28] ducem, qui cum Octauio bis confligens prius uictus est et postea uicit; fraude tamen occiditur. Octauius uero dedit filiam et regnum Maximo filio Leonini auunculi Helene. Hic dedit Armoricam Conano nepoti Octauii. Missus est etiam a Maximo Gratianus[29] Municeps in Britanniam[30] ut regnaret sub eo; sed perempto Maximo Gratianus[31] occiditur a Britannis.[32] Cum igitur [33]Picti et Huni[33] asperrime[34] terram[35] destruerent, miserunt Romam. Legio ueniens murum

9   CELR; *Colilus* A
10 AER; *Brittannia* CL
11 ACEL; *sepultusque* R
12 ACEL; *ipse rex* R
13 ACEL; *carens* R
14 AER; *Brittones* CL
15 CER; *Fulgencio* AL
16 ACEL; *alias prescripsimus* R
17 ACE; *tyrannus* LR
18 ALR; *Asclipiodotus* CE
19 ACEL; *Gallium* R
20...20   AELR; suprascript in C
21 CEL; *Londonia* AR
22 ACL; *Asclipiodotum* ER
23 ACER; *Coleceastrie* L
24 LR; *Constans* ACE
25 ACE; .x. LR
26 ACER; *suam* L
27 ACELR (tampered in E?)
28 AELR; *Traern* C
29 AER; *Gracianus* CL
30 AER; *Brittanniam* CL
31 AELR; *Gracianus* C
32 ACER; *Brittannis* L
33...33 AER; *Huni et Picti* C; *Picti et Scoti* (*Scoti* over an erasure) L
34 ACELR (altered from *asperime* in EL)
35 ACELR (altered from *teram* in C)

edificat, sed post destruitur. Mittitur Witelinus Lundoniensis archiepiscopus[36] ad Aldroenum regem Britonum[37] et reducit[38] Constantinum fratrem eius in regem; cuius filii fuerunt Constans monachus et Aurelius Ambrosius. Hos duos nutriit rex Britonum Budicius. Occiso prius Constantino et postea Constante monacho, quem sine episcopis regem creauerat Wortigernus[39] dux Cornubie diadematum et super hastas circa monasterium uectum, idem Wortigernus[40] regnum inuasit; qui adscitis[41] Anglis proditus est ab eis. Britones[42] irati statuerunt Wertimerum[43] filium eius regem; quater uicit Anglos occiso Hors; ueneno[44] periit per nouercam. Wortigernus[45] item rex item proditur; quem Aurelius[46] ut proditorem combussit.[47] Occidit etiam ipse et Eldol dux Gloecestrie[48] Hengistum apud Kinigeburch[49] iudicio quia post concordiam prodicionem fecerat in regem Aurelium. Filio[50] tamen Hengisti Otta[51] nomine concessit uasta trans Eboracum. Interea Uterpendragun, id est 'capud draconis', iuuenis prestantissimus, filius scilicet Aurelii, coream gigantum attulit ab Hibernia;[52] que nunc uocatur Stanhenges.[53] Pascent uero filius Wortigerni fecit uenenari[54] Aurelium. Sed Uter predictus strauit eum bello et regem Hibernie[55] cum eo. Uter etiam cepit Otta[56] et Cosa cognatum eius rebellantes et posuit Lundonie in carcere.[57] Uter quoque Gorloin ducem Cornubie occidit et Igernam sponsam ducis sibi sociauit et genuit Arturum et Annam. Otta[58] et[59] Cosa fugientes a carcere in Germaniam, postea rebellantes, occisi sunt apud Uerolamium; et ibidem rex uenenato fonte periit.

---

[36] ACEL; *episcopus* R
[37] ACER; *Brittonum* L
[38] ACEL; *reduxit* R
[39] CE; *Uortigernus* A; *Wortegirnus* L; *Wortegernus* R
[40] CEL; *Uortigernus* A; *Wortegernus* R
[41] ACEL; *ascitis* R
[42] ACER; *Brittones* L
[43] ACER; *Uortimerum* L
[44] ACEL; *ueneno enim* R
[45] CELR; *Uortigernus* A
[46] AELR; *Aurelius* deleted after *Aurelius* in C
[47] AEL; *conbussit* C; *conbuxit* R
[48] ACER; *Gloeceastrie* L
[49] ER; *Kinegeburh* A; *Kingeburch* C; *Kinigeburh* L
[50] LR; *Filium* ACE
[51] AEL; *Octa* CR
[52] AER; *Hybernia* CL
[53] AELR; *Stanenges* C
[54] CE (altered to *inuenenari* in E); *uenerari* A; *inuenenari* (altered from *inuenerari* in L) LR
[55] ALR; *Hybernie* C; *Hebernie* E
[56] AELR; *Octa* C
[57] AELR; *carcerem* C
[58] AER; *Octa* C; *Ota* L
[59] AELR; *et* suprascript in C

§ 9   Artur ille famosus mortuo patre[1] sceptris[2] insignitur regalibus, licet adolescentior[3] esset, statimque in noua bella exardescens Colgrinum ducem Anglorum
prelio uicit; uictum obsedit in Eboraco sed per aduentum Keldrici[4] desiit.[5] Cum
autem Keldricus[6] obsedisset Lincoliam[7] cum innumera gente Anglorum, uenit
Hoelus filius sororis Arturi et[8] Budicii a minori Britannia[9] et Lincolie[10] obsidio-
nem dissipat per concordiam. Iurauerunt enim hostes quod nunquam[11] amplius in
hanc[12] terram reuerterentur. Spreto autem iuramento circuierunt terram per
maria et peruenerunt ad Urbem Legionum, que super Sibarim sita erat,[13] et eam
nichil cauentem imperpetuum[14] destruxerunt.[15] Post hec fuit apud Bade magnum
prelium in quo Arturus[16] Colgrinum et Baldulfum duces Anglorum occidit et
Cheldricus[17] uix aufugit. Postea tamen occiditur in Tenet.[18] Arturus igitur ualde
confortatus in regno Anglos quotquot remanserunt tributarios fecit;[19] Scotiam[20]
sibi subdidit; omnes circumiacentes terras Britannie[21] in ditionem[22] suam accepit.
Successu uero temporum Romam adquirere studens quia inde progenies eius
descenderat, Modredo nepoti suo reliquit regnum et reginam in custodiam tran-
siensque mare cum mirabili exercitu Romanum exercitum Parisius uicit; Franciam et Burgundiam sibi subdidit. Cum Alpes transiturus[23] esset, dixit ei
nuntius:[24] 'Modredus nepos tuus diadema tuum sibi imposuit[25] auxilio Chelrici[26]
regis Anglorum et sponsam tuam duxit.' Arturus igitur mirabili ebulliens ira
reuersus in Angliam uicit Modredum prelio. [27]Cumque insequeretur eum usque
in Cornubiam, cum paucis incidit super eum inter multos,[27] cumque se non posse

§ 9
1   ACEL; *patre Uter* R
2   AELR; *ceptris* C
3   AER; *adolescencior* C; *adulescentior* (altered from *adolescentior*) L
4   ACE; *Kildrici* L; *Kelderici* R
5   ACE; *periit* LR
6   ACR; *Kceldricus* E; *Kildricus* L
7   CELR; *Lincolniam* A
8   CELR; *con* A (?)
9   AER; *Brittannia* CL
10 CELR; *Lincolnie* A
11 ALR; *numquam* CE
12 ACEL; *illam* R
13 AELR; *est* C
14 AEL; *inperpetuam* C; om. R
15 ACEL; *dextruxerunt* R
16 ACLR; *Arthurus* E
17 ACER; *Childricus* L
18 ACEL; *Teneth* R
19 ACEL; *facit* R
20 AER; *Scociam* CL
21 AER; *Brittannie* CL
22 ALR; *dicionem* CE
23 ACEL; *transsiturus* R
24 CER; *nuncius* AL
25 CELR; *inposuit* A
26 CE; *Celrici* A; *Chilrici* L; *Cheldrici* R
27...27 AELR; om. (from text) but added in margin in C

reuerti uideret, dixit: 'Vendamus, socii, mortes nostras. Ego enim iam caput[28] nepotis et[29] proditoris mei gladio auferam; post quod mori deliciosum est.' Dixit et gladio per aciem uiam sibi parans in medio suorum Modredum galea[30] arripuit et collum loricatum uelut[31] stipulam gladio resecauit. Inter eundum tamen et in ipso actu tot uulnera recepit quod et ipse procubuit. [32]Mortuum tamen fuisse Britones, parentes tui, negant et eum uenturum sollerter[33] expectant.[32] Fuit equidem uir temporibus suis omnium summus milicia, largitate, facecia.

§ 10   Successit ei Constantinus cognatus eius et tercio anno occiditur a Conano et[1] ad Stanheng,[2] ubi Aurelius et Uter,[3] sepultus est. Post hec Aurelius Conanus duobus annis regnauit; Wartiporius uero .iii.[4] annis uicitque Saxones rebellantes; post quem Malgo pulcher, quo non erat[5] alter forma pulchrior,[6] affatu dulcior; deinde Catericus. Cuius tempore Saxones adduxerunt Godmundum Affricanum qui [7]patriam destruxit omnem[7] et Christi cultum. Augustinus uenit.[8] Etdelfridus[9] uicit Brogmail[10] apud Leicestriam,[11] ubi etiam monachi occisi sunt. Postea Caduanus[12] regnans cis[13] Humbram Eadwinum[14] nutriit[15] cum Caddual-lone[16] filio suo.[17] Postea, cum uterque regnaret, uicit Eadwinus[18] et fugauit Cadwallonem in Armoriam. Cadwallo tandem cum magnis copiis reuertens uicit prius Pendan[19] et sibi uniuit. Eadwinus[20] et Osfridus[21] et Osricus occiduntur.

28 CELR; *capud* A
29 CELR; om. A
30 CELR; *gallia* A
31 ELR; *uelud* AC
32...32 ACEL; *licet parentes sui Britones mortuum fore denegant et uenturum adhuc sollenniter expectent* R
33 AE (altered to *sollenniter* in E); *sollert* C; *sollempniter* L

§ 10
1 CELR; om. A
2 AELR; *Staneng* C
3 ACEL; *Uter pater Arturi* R
4 AEL; *quatuor* CR
5 ACLR; suprascript in E
6 AE; *pulcrior* CLR
7...7 ACEL; *omnem destruxit patriam necnon* R
8 ACEL; *uenit a Roma* R
9 AE; *Etelfridus* C; *Edelfridus* L; *et Elfridus* R
10 ACEL; *Broginail* R
11 AL; *Leiecestriam* CE; *Leecestriam* R
12 ELR; *Caduuanus* AC
13 ER (tamp.ered in E); *eis* ACL
14 CLR; *Eaduinum* AE
15 ACER; *nutrit* L
16 AELR; *Cadwallone* C
17 ACER; *suo* bis (first occurrence deleted) L
18 ER; *Eaduinus* A; *Edwinus* CL
19 ACEL; *Pendam* R
20 CELR; *Eaduinus* A
21 ACE; *Offridus* LR

Penda occidit Oswaldum; Oswi[22] occidit Pendan.[23] Chedwallo[24] uero, cum regnasset .xlviii. annis, sepelitur ad portam Lundonie iuxta templum sancti Martini, in imagine enea super equum eneum. Tandem Chedwalladrus[25] regnauit, quem Beda Chedwallam[26] uocat, filius Chedwallonis[27] et sororis Pende. Tunc ueniente peste grauissima fugit in Armoriam ad regem Alanum Salomonis nepotem. Angli uero uenientes a Germania terras peste uacuatas possederunt. Chedwalladrus[28] autem rex Romam iuit non reuersurus. Exinde Britanni[29] et nomen et regnum penitus amiserunt.[30] Hec sunt[31] que[32] tibi[33] breuibus promisi; quorum si prolixitatem desideras, librum grandem Galfridi[34] Arturi, quem apud Beccum[35] inueni, queras,[36] ubi predicta [37]diligenter et prolixe[37] tractata uidebis.[38] Uale.

TRANSLATION

<Letter to Warinus>

This is a copy of the second letter: on the history of the Britons.

§ 1   Warinus Brito, my urbane friend, you ask me why I began my account of the deeds of our nation from the time of Julius Caesar and omitted the dynasties which so flourished from Brutus to Caesar. In reply I tell you that, despite a most diligent search, I was unable to discover a record of that period, either oral or written. Such is the deadly oblivion which with the passing of ages overshadows and snuffs out the glory of mortals. But this year, on my way to Rome, I discovered, to my amazement, a history of the above reigns at the abbey of Le Bec. I forward to you, dear friend, some notes from this, abbreviated as befits inclusion in a letter.

---

[22] CELR; *Osui* A
[23] ACE; *Pendam* LR
[24] CER; *Chedwalo* A; *Cadwallo* L
[25] ER; *Chedwaladrus* AC; *Cedwalladrus* L
[26] ACER; *Cedwallam* L
[27] ACER; *Cedwallonis* L
[28] ACER; *Cedwalladrus* L
[29] AER; *Brittanni* CL
[30] ACEL; *amiserunt. Ex tunc illa Britannia est Anglia nominata* R
[31] ACER; *sunt* suprascript in L
[32] CELR; *qui* A
[33] ACEL; *tibi Warine Brito karissime* R
[34] ACEL; *Gaufridi* R
[35] ACEL; *Beccense cenobium* R
[36] ACEL; *diligenter requiras* R
[37]..[37] ACEL; *satis prolixe et eluculenter* R
[38] ACEL; *reperies* R

§ 2   Aeneas, the forefather of the Roman race, sired Ascanius, Ascanius sired Silvius, and Silvius sired Brutus. A seer prophesied that the latter would kill his father and mother. And so, as chance would have it, he did, killing his mother in childbirth and later, as a youth, unintentionally striking his father with an arrow while playing. For this he was exiled from Italy and, visiting various countries, built the city of Tours in Gaul. Eventually he set off for a far land and sacrificed to Diana, seeking a reply with these words:

> 'Goddess, divinity of the groves, feared by the woodland boars,
>   Tell me what country you wish us to inhabit.'

The goddess answered:

> 'Brutus, beneath the setting sun, beyond the kingdoms of Gaul,
>   Lies an ocean island, girt by the sea.
> Go there: it will be your home forever;
>   Here will be another Troy for your children.'

Armed with that reply, Brutus reached this island, which was called Albion. It was uninhabited, save for giants of amazing size and strength beyond description, but of very limited intelligence. Rushing into the sea against Brutus's ships, they were slaughtered with arrows and crossbows when they reached such a depth that they were prevented from advancing on Brutus or easily retreating. After their death and defeat he destroyed the other giants, who had been absent, with crossbows and other devices in nocturnal ambushes. Then he took possession of the land, divided it with marker-ropes, distributed it to his men, and named it Britain after himself. As an everlasting monument he built Trinovantum, the 'New Troy', which today we call London. This great city was, then, founded in the time of the priest Eli and of Silvius Aeneas. After a prosperous reign Brutus died gloriously and left the kingdom of Britain to his eldest son, Lucrinus. He reigned successfully for ten years until he died by an arrow in battle with his wife Gondolovea. He had abandoned her and she punished her husband for his criminal adultery with one of her own handmaidens; this girl, unrivalled in beauty of form and attractiveness of appearance, had been made queen, while her mistress was driven out. After the killing of her husband, Gondolovea reigned for fifteen years, contemporaneously with Samuel and Homer. She was succeeded by her son Maddan, a man of bestial cruelty, who was eaten by wolves. His son, Menpricius, ruled for twenty years in the time of King Saul; and after him his son, Ebraucus, sixty years in the time of King David and Silvius Latinus. He founded York and Edinburgh. The father of twenty sons and daughters, he was succeeded by one of them, Brutus Green-Shield, an unconquerable soldier, who ruled for twelve years. After him, his son Leir reigned for twenty-five years; he built Carlisle during the reigns of Solomon and Rehoboam, when Silvius Epitus succeeded his father in Italy. Leir's son, Rudbudibras, a man of great bravery, ruled thirty-nine years and built Canterbury and Winchester, which at that time he called Uuente, at the time of Epitus's son, Capys, and the prophets Haggai, Joel, and Amos. After him for twenty years ruled his son, Bladud, the founder of the city of Bath and its bathing-places. There, in the temple of Minerva, he placed an undying flame, since he was skilled in all kinds of knowledge, but most accomplished in the art of sorcery. Using sorcery to make an ill starred flight through the air, he fell when over Trinovantum and died of a broken neck.

§ 3   His son, Lier, who founded Leicester on the river Soar, ruled in his place for forty years. As he was without male issue, he made his three daughters heirs to the kingdom. He discussed the matter with them and said to the eldest: 'My dear, how much do you value your love for me?' The eldest answered: 'Nothing beneath the moon, which divides the changeable from the eternal, can be found which means so much to me.' Then the king addressed the second: 'And what value do you place on your love for me?' She replied: 'It is more precious than any riches; everything that men desire pales in comparison.' Next the king asked the youngest: 'How much do you, my youngest daughter, love me?' In answer she said: 'You are what you have, and that much I love you.' The king turned his face from her in anger and swore that she would have no part of his kingdom. He gave his eldest daughter to a great lord of Britain along with the southern part of his kingdom; and his second to another lord along with the northern part. The youngest, Cordeilla, he disinherited from both his affection and his realm. But God, who partakes in wise thoughts, roused the mind of Aganippus of Gaul, who for the sake of her beauty sought her hand from her father and married her. After some time had elapsed, the daughters who had remained in Britain incited their husbands to exile their father, since he was living too long for them. On being driven out, he fled to Cordeilla in Gaul. Falling at her feet he said, weeping: 'Your sisters, who spoke so finely about their love for me, have cruelly driven me from my kingdom. I beg your sweetness that, as they have cheapened their grand words with cruel deeds, so may you honour and ornament your moderate words about your love for me with acts of kindness. May you win eternal praise if, as they repaid good with bad, you return good for evil. At least do not deny me food and clothing.' Moved by her father's tears, Cordeilla set out for Britain with her husband, King Aganippus, and, having defeated and killed the wicked lords, triumphantly restored her father to power: hence the saying 'restrained words should always be valued'. When Lier died of old age, Cordeilla ruled after her father for five years. But his two grandsons, Marganus and Cunedagius, intending to revenge the wrongs inflicted on their fathers, captured her by trickery and shut her in prison. There, savagely mortified by so complete a reversal of fortune, with a man's courage she took her own life. When the grandsons divided the kingdom, Cunedagius killed Marganus. He ruled thirty-three years at the time of Hosea and Isaiah and of the foundation of Rome; he was succeeded by his son, Mollo, in whose reign there was a shower of blood for three days. Next reigned Gurgucius, followed by Sisillius, Iago, Kinemarcus, and Gabodogo, whose son Porrex killed his brother Ferrex, only to be killed in his turn by their mother. Then the realm of Britain declined, becoming five kingdoms with rebellion rife everywhere. Meanwhile Dummalo rose up and unaided destroyed the five kings. He reigned for forty years with great splendour, bestowing the blessings of peace and practical laws, called Mallonine, which Gildas, the historian of the Britons, extols with great praise. After his death his two sons Belinus and Brennus, both very active men, fought each other.

§ 4   Brennus, the younger son, was defeated and made for Norway. There he married the daughter of the king and led an army of Norwegians to Britain. However, the king of the Danes had hoped to marry the same girl and, realising that he had been pre-empted, confronted Brennus at sea. In the battle he kept a special watch on the ship in which the girl sat and dragged her off with a grappling-iron. His ship sped sway with the spoil and the victor fled. Although he pursued the fugitives and killed many, Brennus counted himself as beaten. But joy is often interrupted by sorrow. A huge storm drove the Danish king and his beloved spoil to Britain, where he was captured by Belinus. Doing him homage, he received Denmark under tribute and returned in peace with his new wife. Brennus, having lost his wife and many of his men, was driven before the same storm. With a few companions he rushed into a futile attack on Belinus. He fled to the king of the Senones in Gaul, where by virtue of his fine character and charm he married the king's daughter. On his return to Britain with a large army of Senones, his mother's tears moved him to a reconciliation with his brother. But he rejected the offer of half of the kingdom in favour of gold and, setting out for Rome, the ultimate origin of his people, became the first man to capture it. However, neither it nor the whole of Italy was enough for him; instead he stripped it of all its gold and silver and took Greece. This too his bravery drove him to abandon, and in Asia he kept kingdoms for himself or gave them to his followers, as he pleased. He was the best man of his day, a jewel of bravery, an undying star of Britain. His brother, Belinus, subjugated all the lands surrounding Britain, ruled happily, and built *Urbs Legionum*, where he was buried.

§ 5   His successor was his son, Gurguitbartruc, who conquered Denmark in a major battle, since it would not pay him the tribute customary under his father. At the request of some Spaniards for land, he granted them Ireland, and they live there to this day: they were Ireland's first inhabitants. Gurguitbartruc was buried in the same place as his father. Next reigned Kinelinus, then Sisinnius, Kimarus, Danius, and Morvidus, a man of praiseworthy character but vile savagery. After many crimes he was swallowed by a terrible beast, sent it is said from hell, when he rushed on it too boldly. His place was taken by his son, Gorbonianus. After him ruled Artgallo, followed by Elidurus the Good, whose loyalty was loudly acclaimed by fame. He was compelled to assume power in the absence of his elder brother, Peridurus, but, when the latter returned penniless after a year, Elidurus received him with tears, readily abdicated and gave him the insignia of sceptre and crown. But Peridurus was of a vindictive bent and so irritated the nobles that they deposed him and took back Elidurus the Good. He, however, wishing his brother to reign rather than himself, allowed himself to be captured and imprisoned by him. Restored to power, Peridurus exacted a cruel revenge on the nobles who had deposed him, until death, the common enemy, removed him. Then, happily and to the universal joy of all, Elidurus flourished in glory for the third time. He ruled until his death and was succeeded by Regin, the son of Gorbonianus; next came Marganus, the son of Artgallo; then Marganus's brother, Cumanus. To be brief, there followed in order, Idwallo, Runo, Gerontius, Catellus, Coillus, Porrex, and Cherin; after whom his three sons, Fulgentius, Eldradus, and Andragius, ruled one after the other. Urianus succeeded his father, Andragius; and after him ruled successively Eliud, Clodacus, Clotenus, Gurgincius, Merianus, Bledano, Capoenus, Sisillius, and Blagabred, a most cultivated monarch, famous for the miraculous sweetness of his voice. The British were as amazed by his singing as were the Thracians by that of Orpheus or the Romans by that of Nero. On his death he was succeeded by his brother, the kindly Artmai, followed successively by Eldol, Redion, Redorchius, Sanuil, Pir, Capoir, his son Dignellus, and then his son Heli. But all the wars, bravery and pomp of these kings were either recorded in unknown books or completely lost to memory; God grant that I and my people understand the true worthlessness of mortal praise.

§ 6   Luid, the son of the above-mentioned King Heli, noting the detrimental effect of frequent wars and the passage of time on Trinovantum, restored London with most handsome buildings – walls, towers, gates, bolts, bridges, and courts. There he held a council and successfully requested his subjects, who were amazed by the new-found beauty of the city, that it should be called Carlunden as a memorial to himself: today the name has been corrupted to London. Luid left three children, Cassibellanus, Belinus, and Androgeus. Though I have given an account of the defeat of Cassibellanus and Belinus by Julius Caesar in my *Historia Anglorum*, hear the version given by this text. In the struggle against Caesar, Androgeus and his brothers three times overcame the Romans. So great was their elation that a splendid festival was held at London. During the games Androgeus's son killed Cassibellanus's in a wrestling-match. The king could not control his anger and demanded on pain of death that Androgeus surrender his son for execution. This proved the seed-bed of strife and spark of hatred. Androgeus by letter invited Caesar to return, surrendered London to him on his arrival, and, joining him in battle, became the conqueror of his own people. Eventually Cassibellanus submitted to Caesar and paid a yearly tribute of three thousand pounds of silver. He was buried at York.

§ 7   Now that I have enumerated the rulers from Brutus to Caesar, I think you will be pleased by a clear account of the remaining British kings up to the arrival of the English or the time of Cadwallon, the last powerful king of the Britons.

§ 8   Temancius, Androgeus's brother, who accompanied Caesar to Rome, inherited both Cassibellanus's kingdom and his tribute. He was succeeded by his son, Kinelinus, who had been knighted by Augustus and therefore paid the tribute freely out of affection for him. His son and successor, Guidenus, refused the Romans their tribute. Accordingly Claudius was despatched and defeated him in battle. He made Guidenus's brother, Armigarus, king, giving him his daughter in marriage. Armigarus helped Claudius to conquer the Orkneys and built Gloucester in his honour. Later he rebelled against the Romans; but Vespasian overcame him, first in battle and eventually by his charm. Marius was the next ruler, after whom Westmoreland is named. Loyal to the Romans, he built Chester and was succeeded by his son, Coillus. Next came Lucius, whom I have described because he was the first to accept christianity; he established twenty-eight bishops in Britain, following the number of pagan priests. This exceptional king was buried at Gloucester. As he died without issue, the Britons rebelled against the Romans but were overcome by the emperor Severus. On being harassed by Fulgentius, the leader of the Picts, he built the rampart between the British and the Picts, which I have dealt with previously. However, he was killed by Fulgentius at York and buried in the same place. His son, Bassianus, like his father, ruled Britain as his own after he had defeated his brother, Zeta. Bassianus was killed by the usurper Carausius, who in his turn was killed by his companion, Allectus. He too with his companion, Gallus, was killed by the prefect Asclepiodotus in London: hence the name Walabroc. Asclepiodotus was killed by Cole, duke of Colchester. Constancius overcame him and, marrying his daughter Helena, ruled for ten years after his death. On Constancius's demise at York, his son, Constantine, succeeded, who later took Rome. Then Octavius, duke of Gwent, killed the Roman proconsuls. Trahern was despatched as commander by Constantine to engage him; but, after a defeat and later a victory, he was killed by trickery. Octavius bestowed his daughter and his kingdom on Maximus, the son of Leoninus, Helena's uncle. Maximus gave Brittany to Conanus, Octavius's nephew, and sent Gratianus Municeps to rule as his subordinate in Britain. But, when Maximus was killed, Gratianus was murdered by the British. The country was then terribly devastated by the Picts and Huns; the British sent to Rome for help. A legion arrived which built a wall, but this was later destroyed. Witelinus, the archbishop of London, was sent to Aldroenus, king of Brittany, and returned with Constantinus, his brother, as king. His sons, the monk Constans and Aurelius Ambrosius, were brought up by Budicius, king of Brittany. After the killings of first Constantinus and then the monk Constans – whom Vortigern, duke of Cornwall, had consecrated king without bishops by having him crowned and carried round his monastery on spears – this same Vortigern usurped the kingdom. The Britons, angry because he called in the English only to be betrayed by them, made his son, Wertimerus, king. He beat the English four times, killing Hors, but was poisoned by his stepmother. Vortigern again became king, was again betrayed, and was burned as a traitor by Aurelius. The latter, together with Eldol, duke of Gloucester, executed Hengist at Kinigeburch after trying him for betraying his alliance with Aurelius. To Hengist's son, Otta, Aurelius granted deserted land beyond York. Meanwhile Aurelius's son, Uterpendragon (or 'dragon's head'), an outstanding youth, transported from Ireland the giants' ring, which is now known as Stonehenge. Pascent, Vortigern's son, had Aurelius poisoned but was defeated along with the king of Ireland by Uter. Uter also captured Otta and his brother Cosa, who had revolted, and imprisoned them at London. Further he killed Gorlois, duke of Cornwall, and married his wife, Igerna, who bore him Arthur and Anna. Otta and Cosa escaped from prison to Germany. Later these rebels were killed at Verulamium, where Uter died after drinking from a poisoned spring.

§ 9   On his death, his son, the famous Arthur, was, despite his comparative youth, endowed with the royal insignia. His enthusiasm for new wars was immediate. He defeated Colgrinus, the leader of the English, and besieged him in York, but desisted on the arrival of Keldricus. The latter was besieging Lincoln with countless English, when Hoel, the son of Budicius and Arthur's sister, arrived from Brittany. The siege ended with the sworn agreement that the enemy should never again return to this land. But, disdaining this oath, the English circumvented the island by sea; *Urbs Legionum* on the Severn was taken unawares by their arrival and destroyed forever. Then there was a great battle at Bath; Colgrinus and Baldulfus died at Arthur's hands, while Keldricus with difficulty escaped, only to be killed later at Thanet. This greatly increased Arthur's power, and he made the remnants of the English tributary. After overcoming Ireland and gaining control of all the lands surrounding Britain, he came in the course of time to contemplate the conquest of Rome, the ultimate origin of his people. Entrusting his nephew, Mordred, with the protection of his queen and kingdom, he crossed the sea with a vast army. Roman forces were beaten at Paris, and France and Burgundy conquered. But, as he prepared to cross the Alps, a messenger announced to him: 'With the help of Chelricus, king of the English, your nephew, Mordred, has usurped your crown and married your wife.' Seething with unbelievable anger, Arthur returned to England and defeated Mordred in battle. In the course of a pursuit as far as Cornwall, with a few men he chanced on Mordred with a large following. Seeing that retreat was impossible, he declared: 'Companions, let us sell our lives dearly. Once I have cut off the head of my treacherous nephew with my sword, death will be sweet.' With these words he carved a path through the enemy with his sword and, seizing Mordred by the helmet, in the midst of his men severed his armoured neck at a stroke, like a blade of corn. But, as he advanced and as he struck, he received so many wounds that he too fell. All the same, the Bretons, your fathers, Warinus, do not accept his death and eagerly await his coming. Certainly he was the finest man of his times in warfare, generosity, and courtesy.

§ 10   After him his cousin, Constantinus, ruled until he was killed by Conanus in the third year of his reign and buried, like Aurelius and Uter, at

Stonehenge. Aurelius Conanus ruled for two years and Wartiporius, who defeated an English revolt, for four. Next succeeded Malgo the handsome, who was unsurpassed in physical beauty and sweetness of speech. In the time of his successor, Catericus, the English summoned the African Godmund, who destroyed the whole country and its christianity. After the arrival of Augustine, Etdelfridus defeated Brogmail at Leicester in a battle where even monks were among the casualties. Later Caduanus, who ruled south of the Humber, brought up Eadwinus with his own son, Cadwallon. After each had succeeded to his kingdom, Cadwallon was beaten by Eadwinus and fled to Brittany. Eventually he returned with large forces, defeated Penda, and secured his allegiance. Eadwinus, Osfridus, and Osricus were slain; Penda killed Oswald but died by Oswi's hand. Cadwallon, however, reigned for forty-eight years and was buried at the gate of London by the church of St Martin, placed in a bronze statue on a bronze horse. Last came the reign of Cadwaladr, whom Bede calls Chedwalla; he was the son of Cadwallon by Penda's sister. The advent of a severe plague caused him to flee to king Alanus, grandson of Solomon, in Brittany. The English came from Germany and occupied the island, which had been emptied by the plague. Cadwaladr journeyed to Rome, never to return. From that point the British entirely relinquished their name and kingdom. This is the sum of the notes which I promised you. If you require a fuller version, seek out the large volume by Geoffrey Arthur, which I discovered at Le Bec; in it you will find a careful and detailed account of the above. Farewell.

King Arthur and
the growth of French nationalism

ROSEMARY MORRIS

The idea that early mediaeval literature, including Arthurian literature, can have a political significance is not new. The *Historia regum Britanniae* of 1138 has been claimed as an English counter-blow to French monarchic propaganda.[1] More recently, Beate Schmolke-Hasselmann has suggested that many, if not all, Arthurian romances in verse are propaganda for English dynastic claims of the thirteenth century.[2] My contention is that some thirteenth-century Arthurian prose romances are, in part, a subtle expression of *French* national feeling. However, as many people are reluctant to admit that such feeling even existed in mediaeval France,[3] I shall first attempt briefly to show that it did.

Manifestations of national feeling can be broadly divided into three categories: dynastic, racial, and geographical. All three must exist before a true sense of nationhood develops, but they may be analysed separately.

The dynastic convictions of the French Capetian kings are undeniable.[4] From its foundation in 987, the Capetian house preserved a remarkable continuity, thanks to its fortunate capacity for producing male heirs, and to its shrewd policy of co-opting them as kings during their father's lifetime. Such continuity, in a chaotic world, ensured that seekers after a political identity would readily look to the monarchy. Of course, the Capetian monarchs of the tenth and eleventh centuries controlled only a tiny part of what is now France. But they claimed sovereignty over nearly all of it, never forgetting that their imperial predecessor, Charlemagne, had *effectively* ruled all of it. A surprisingly large number of 'French' barons, many of whom were far more powerful than the early Capetians, acknowledged their suzerainty and rendered feudal services. Most importantly, they rendered host-service, allowing the king to raise a far larger army than his

---

[1]   Gerould, 'King Arthur and politics'; *Historia regum Britannie*, I, ed. Wright.
[2]   Schmolke-Hasselmann, *Der arthurische Versroman*, especially pp. 237–47.
[3]   'L'ancienne France a-t-elle connu le sentiment que nous appelons . . . patriotisme? On se refuse généralement à l'admettre' (Grosjean, *Le Sentiment national*, p. 5). Historians have progressed since then; literati, on the whole, have not.
[4]   Historical details drawn from Fawtier, *The Capetian Kings*; Petit-Dutaillis, *The Feudal Monarchy*; Hallam, *Capetian France*; Dunbabin, *France in the Making*.

own domain could provide. Rebellions there were in plenty, but never enough to tip the balance against the monarchy. The kings also enjoyed (with interruptions) the support of the only other body which retained a stable and pervasive authority, the Church.

The Capetians' great aim in life was to regain actual control over the ancient kingdom. It took four centuries to achieve, but in the fourteenth century it made France into the most powerful and cohesive nation in Europe.[5] The hardest struggle of all was against the English kings, in their role as dukes of Normandy and, later, Angevin 'emperors'. It was through self-contrast with this perennial enemy that the French monarchy became fully conscious of its Frenchness. Important contemporary texts show how devotion to the monarchy was coupled with assertive 'Frenchness'.

First comes the life of Louis VI (reigned 1108–1137) written by his first minister, Archbishop Suger.[6] Both were men of vigour and vision. Louis strove to safeguard and extend the royal domain; Suger foresaw how these strivings would succeed, to the glory of God. When the young Louis is menaced by William Rufus, Suger comments: 'uerum, quia nec fas nec naturale est Francos Anglis, immo Anglos Francis subici, spem repulsiuam rei delisit euentus'.[7] Note the immediate identification of the second-generation Norman king as 'English'; the assumption of racial superiority and racial mission; the divine mission to subjugate others. And this at a time when the king was fighting desperately to subdue the castellans in his own domain! Describing these struggles, Suger always designates Louis's supporters as not only *regales* but also *Franci*. His power is local and limited, but on the ideological plane the idea of France as a unified monarchy is clear. In 1105 another great Norman, Robert Guiscard, visits France in the hope of marrying Louis's sister: 'tanta etenim et regni Francorum et domini Ludouici preconabatur strenuitas, ut ipsi et iam Saraceni huius terrore copule terrerentur'.[8] Here, already, we see France as the defender of christianity, through the crusades. From the time of St Louis, this notion was to culminate in the notion of France herself as the sacred nation whose defence was the most imperative christian task.[9]

It is in describing a grave threat of invasion that Suger shows most clearly the nationalistic fervour which Louis VI could inspire. In 1124, the Emperor Henry joins with Henry I of England to attack territories which Louis claimed as his.[10] Immediately, the great nobles drop their grudges against the king and rally round him, crying:[11]

---

5   Under St Louis: see Strayer, 'The Holy Land'.
6   *Vie de Louis le Gros*, ed. Wauquet.
7   *Ibid.*, p. 10.
8   *Ibid.*, p. 48.
9   Strayer, 'The Holy Land', pp. 306–8. Expressed by Joinville, *Vie de Saint Louis* (ed. Corbett, pp. 236–7).
10 *Vie de Louis le Gros*, ed. Wauquet, pp. 218–30.
11 *Ibid.*, p. 222.

Transeamus audacter ad eos, ne redeuntes impune ferant quod in *terrarum dominam Franciam* superbe presumpserunt. Senciant contumaciae sue meritum, non in nostra sed in terra sua, que iure regio Francorum Francis sepe perdomita subiacet, ut, quod ipsi furtim in nos machinabantur atemptare, nos in eos coram retorqueamus.

This nationalistic reaction did not outlast the immediate danger. The Capetian monarchy still had a long way to go. However, even if Suger exaggerated the account, it does show that national feeling existed in the early twelfth century: it needed only to be fostered, not created.

If we accept its traditional dating,[12] the greatest of all mediaeval French works can be cited as evidence for national feeling around Suger's time. The *Chanson de Roland* lays enormous emphasis on the imperial destiny of *douce France* and its emblematic monarch, Charlemagne. The love and loyalty of the peers is riveted on both. France stretches from the Pyrenees to Aix-la-Chapelle. The cosmic lamentation for Roland's death is felt from Mont-Saint-Michel to Saintes, from Ushant to Besançon (lines 1427–1429). This kingdom, geographically roughly coterminous with modern France, is ideologically coterminous with Christendom, God's kingdom upon earth entrusted to his holy viceregent. This exalted notion does not, of course, pervade the entire genre of the *chanson de geste*, but any later work which draws on *Roland* (as most do) must feel its influence.

The reign of Philip Augustus (1180–1223) spanned the most productive period for Arthurian romance. It also saw the definitive establishment of the French monarchy as an unchallengeable institution. Philip still had to struggle against his own barons, the Angevins and the emperor, but his victories were durable. He undoubtedly aspired to be the new Charlemagne, and under him chroniclers set up a veritable industry for the glorification of France, which they identified with Philip as *Roland* had identified her with Charlemagne. As one example among many, I shall take the *Philippiad* of Philip's chaplain and literary champion Guillaume le Breton.[13] Guillaume begins by linking king and people: he proudly describes first the national origin of the Franks, and then that of the royal unction, which was a key-element in French sacro-monarchic propaganda.[14] He insists on the Franks' innate love of independence:[15]

>   empta sibi sanguine Franci
> libertate suo, dicunt se corde feroci
> malle pati exilium, patriaque exedere tota,
> quam Romae subici sub dura lege tributi   (140–4)

---

[12] Challenged by Keller, 'The Song of Roland'. If his views are correct, which I doubt, *Roland* would still be a nationalistic work, but almost contemporary with the first Arthurian romances – which would tend to bolster my argument.

[13] Ed. H. F. Delaborde, Société de l'Histoire de France (Paris, 1885).

[14] *Ibid.*, I.1–356. See Bloch, *Les Rois thaumaturges*, pp. 186–204.

[15] Guillaume le Breton, *Philippiad*, ed. Delaborde lines.

Philip will defend this integrity, but under him the French, far from leaving their *patria*, will cleave to it as never before. Menaced above all by the English (not Angevins but *Angli*), who *naturaliter oderunt* (267–8) them, the *inuicti Francigenae* prove themselves worthy of their title. French identity is also asserted in the south, when Simon de Montfort, leading them to victory over the Aragonese, reminds the *Francigenae* that they are the heirs of the Trojans, of Charlemagne, Roland, and Ogier.[16] The most overwhelming victory of Guillaume's *Carolides* is Bouvines (1214), at which the French routed a formidable Anglo-German coalition.[17] Guillaume devotes two and a half books (X–XII) to this magnificent theme. He draws an explicit parallel between Philip and Charlemagne, both conquerors of the Germans.[18] The battle begins with both sides in a fervour of racial and national enthusiasm. The French 'laeti clamore paratos/ se pugnare ferunt pro regni et Regis honore'.[19] *Alemannia rabies* collapses utterly under *Francorum uirtus*.[20] As for the English contingent, it flees precipitately, as those 'quod crapula donaque Bacchi/dulcius alliciunt quam duri munia Martis'.[21]

At the end of this epic, Philip dies in an odour of sanctity (!), leaving the author to exhort the next heir to subdue England once and for all, starting with her Continental possessions:[22]

> Cumque tibi fuerit Aquitania subdita tota,
> cum nihil in regno possederit aduena nostra . . .

Then France will at last fully occupy the 'garden'[23] within her natural boundaries. The noisy chauvinists of the 1840 *querelle du Rhin* were no more fervent than Guillaume in 1223.

If *Roland* can be linked with national sentiment in the early twelfth century, Jean Bodel's *Chanson des Saisnes*[24] can be taken to express similar feelings around 1200. Bodel had no obvious reason to flatter Philip, and his homeland, Artois, had no tradition of loyalty to the French Crown.[25] And yet the preface of the *Chanson* proclaims the imperial destiny of France:[26]

> La corone de France doit estre mis avant
> Qar tuit autre roi doivent estre a lui apandant
> De la loi crestiene qui an Deu sont creant.
> Le premier roi de France fist Dex par son commant

---

16 *Ibid.*, VII.632–8.
17 On Bouvines see, for example, Hutton, *Philip Augustus*, pp. 95–110.
18 *Ibid.*, X.698–703.
19 *Ibid.*, X.791–2.
20 *Ibid.*, XI.401–2.
21 *Ibid.*, XI.560–1.
22 *Ibid.*, XII.852–3.
23 *Ibid.*, XII.862.
24 Ed. F. Michel (Paris, 1839).
25 Hallam, *Capetian France*, p. 50.
26 Bodel, *Chanson* (ed. Michel, p. 2).

Coroner a ses angeles dignemant an chantant,
Puis le comanda estre an terre son sergant.

The *Chanson* itself clearly echoes Philip's struggle with the Angevins (disguised as Charlemagne's rebellious vassals, the Hurepois) and with the Germans (the *Saisnes*). Charlemagne – like Philip – also has trouble with his closest vassals, but insofar as he represents France his triumph is assured.

It will be clear, from what precedes, that the 'racial' aspect of early nationalism is closely connected with the 'dynastic' aspect. Indeed, the king's race itself was vital: French writers of the thirteenth century frequently congratulated their country on never having had to endure a foreign ruler.[27] However, the 'racial' theme had a strong independent existence. The Franks–French, like other peoples who emerged from the chaos of the post-Roman period, felt the need to establish creditable roots.[28] The French decided that they, like the Romans, had Trojan origins, being descended from Francio, son of Hector. They prided themselves on their heroic resistance to Roman domination. Their very name spelled 'freedom'. This racial pride is vigorously expressed in chronicles.[29] More surprisingly, it features in many *chansons de geste*, even those relating to areas not generally thought to have been under strong 'French' political influence in the twelfth century. This is strikingly true of the Guillaume cycle.[30] The family dwells in the south, round Narbonne, Nîmes and Orange. The primary loyalty of its members is to the family. Paris and the king are far away. Nevertheless they consider themselves as 'de tote France la flor et la bonté'.[31] More even than the (unworthy) king, Guillaume is the defender of a France coterminous with christendom: 'Car douce France doi jo por droit garder, / Et en bataille l'oriflambe porter.'[32] He strives unremittingly to increase the prestige of the French imperial throne.

Racial pride is always accompanied by contempt for other races. Mediaeval Frenchmen despised the Lombards (so cowardly that they were even afraid of snails),[33] the Germans, and, especially, the English: they had tails; they brooded eggs (!);[34] they could be silly and womanish. But the typical Englishmen, in mediaeval French eyes, is a jovial, beer-swilling, lumbering fool, easily outwitted by the nimble-minded French.[35] The perfect example is the count of Gloucester in *Jehan et Blonde* (early thirteenth century).[36] He is, of course, a Norman, but no

---

[27] See, for example, Kampf, 'Pierre Dubois', p. 98. Kampf adduces much excellent material on French nationalism, and imperialism, in the thirteenth century.
[28] Hanning, *The Vision of History*, pp. 96–101.
[29] Kampf, 'Pierre Dubois'; Strayer, 'The Holy Land', p. 311; Guillaume le Breton, *Philippiad*, ed. Delaborde, I.1–128.
[30] On which see Frappier, *Les Chansons de geste*, especially II.57–78.
[31] *Aliscans*, ed. Wienbeck *et al.*, lines 805e–f.
[32] *Ibid.*, lines 2555–7.
[33] Randall, 'The snail'. pp. 358–67.
[34] Långfors, 'L'Anglais qui couve'.
[35] For more details and nuances, see Rickard, *Britain*, pp. 163–87.
[36] *Jehan et Blonde*, ed. Lécuyer.

less English for that: the distinction is drawn by the Channel. He blunders through the narrative, cursing other men for fools in his abominable French, and sublimely unconscious of his own stupidity, while Jehan, the nonpareil of Dammartin, not only runs off with the count's daughter but also tricks him into giving them their passage-money back to France!

French political poems from the thirteenth century show the same attitude. In the *Chanson de la paix d'Angleterre*, written after Henry III's humiliation in 1264,[37] the 'English' Simon de Montfort reproaches his countrymen for their fatuous over-confidence:[38]

> Laissiez or cesti chos, Francois n'est mie anel.
> Se vous aler seur leus, il se voudra dafandre.
> Mult sarra maubali qui le Francois puet prandre.

(Note the customarily abominable French.) On the eve of the Hundred Years' War, another poem sums up two centuries of resentment:[39]

> Englois onc Francois n'ama,
> male dragié entre' eulz y a:
> hui sont en pais, demain en guerre.
> De tel matire est Engleterre . . .
> ne puet avoir ferme pensee.

Harder to describe is the twelfth- and thirteenth-century perception of 'France' as a geographical unit. The average peasant in Burgundy, Anjou, or Artois probably did not think of himself as 'French', but this would still have been true centuries later: such thoughts were beyond his horizon. Educated men of the world, nobles, and politicians seem to have had a dual vision. On the one hand, 'France' was the equivalent of Roman Gaul, and of Charlemagne's Romance-speaking territories. This usage was vehemently advocated by monarchic propagandists from the reign of Philip Augustus onwards. On the other, 'France' in casual parlance very often meant the royal domain, the Ile de France. When, in *Le moniage Guillaume* (late twelfth century), King Louis calls upon 'Franchois et Angevin, /Normans, Bretons et Borgignons et Fris, / et Avalois et Flamens les hardis', he is making a typical set of distinctions. Equally typical, however, is his denotation of his army *en bloc* as 'cil de France, le signori pais'. It is a difference of perspective, not a contradiction. Similarly, in our own day a Welshman or Scot may consent to be called 'British', or even 'English', when abroad, but will insist on the narrower distinction when at home. Conon de Béthune was furious when the *François* at court mocked his Artois accent, but on crusade he would undoutedly have thought of himself as French, as his fellow-ambassador, Villehardouin, did – and both prided themselves on their skill in

---

[37] In Wright, *The Political Songs*, pp. 63–8; cf. Rickard, p. 170.
[38] *Chanson de la paix d'Angleterre* (ed. Wright, *Political Songs*, p. 68).
[39] 'Le dit de la rebellion d'Engleterre et de Flandres', in Jubinal, *Nouveau Recueil*, I.75.

speaking, in good French.[40] Of course, in the twelfth century, and through the Albigensian crusades, many inhabitants of Provence undoubtedly considered 'France' as a distant region of detestably uncouth and interfering people.[41] On such regions the sense of nationhood was imposed from above: 'The thirteenth-century Capetians had to invent the France which they claimed to rule'.[42] This they did. Philip Augustus incorporated (or, as he would have said, re-incorporated) Normandy and Aquitaine; Louis IX annexed Provence and tidied up the Pyrenean border. The eastern border remained unsettled, but as this remained the case until 1945 we can scarcely accuse the Capetians of neglect. It is true that many of the incorporated provinces were reluctant, and fell away when the chaos of the Hundred Years' War weakened the central authority. Throughout Froissart's account of that war, barons great and small se tournent François or se tournent Anglois with perfect equanimity, as self-interest dictates. It is equally true, however, that hostility to, and alienation from, the central authority persists in France to this day: indeed, it seems resurgent, and manifest in every sphere of existence. So long as the integrity of France is preserved as an ideal by those loyal to the central authority, French nationhood remains a fact, as it was in the twelfth and thirteenth centuries.

I hope that this brief survey has convinced the reader that it is worthwhile at least to look for traces of French national feeling in certain Arthurian romances. It can certainly be shown that the figure of Arthur could constitute a political irritant. Geoffrey of Monmouth established this potential by making the conquest of France Arthur's most important early exploit. According to Geoffrey's political thought, which was enthusiastically adopted by English propagandists, such a conquest established a permanent right of the conquering nation to dominate the conquered.[43] The Arthur of Chrétien's Cligès, who is a clear reflexion of the successful Angevin Henry II,[44] adds a further provocation. Reaction and counter-reaction to such provocation are demonstrated in the late twelfth-century Roman des Franceis by 'André'.[45] The French, says André, tell an insulting lie about Arthur: that he was killed by the monster Chapalu, who reigned in Britain after him. (We have no reason to doubt the existence of this extraordinary legend, which is abundantly, though peculiarly, attested elsewhere.)[46] The

---

40 Le Moniage Guillaume, ed. Cloetta, I.3711–13, 4551. On the frequent use of Francia to refer to the whole kingdom, see Dunbabin, France, pp. 374–9. Conon de Béthune, Chansons, ed. Wallensköld, p. 5; Villehardouin, Conquête de Constantinople, ed. Pauphilet, in Historiens, especially chs 29 and 46.

41 See, for example, Belperron, La Croisade, pp. 58–70. Unlike many Provençal scholars, Belperron does not share his subjects' views on the north, where he discerns and praises 'un sentiment de solidarité nationale, s'élevant au-dessus des classes' (ibid., p. 64).

42 Strayer, 'The Holy Land', p. 203. A better word would be 're-invent'.

43 Ullmann, 'On the influence', pp. 257–76.

44 Noble, 'Chrétien's Arthur', p. 226.

45 In Jubinal, Nouveau Recueil, II.1–17.

46 Freymond, Artus' Kampf.

truth, continues André, is otherwise. Arthur came from a long line of kings, all of whom had conquered France: 'Bien' [Brennius], 'Belin', 'Maximien', 'Constantine' (all from the *Historia*). Arthur invaded France *o ses Engleis*,[47] and offered single combat to the French king, Frollo. The reluctant Frollo rose late on the day of combat and had himself dressed lying down, 'as is customary with the French'. He fainted with fright three times whilst he was being made ready, but recovered sufficiently to give his people some parting instructions:[48]

> Cruel seiez a desmesure,
> cruel, fei-menti, parjure . . .
> De l'autrui prenez a dreiture,
> Haez ceus qui vos ferunt bien,
> plus ordement vivez que chien.

The French have faithfully followed these instructions ever since. Frollo was easily and shamefully overcome in the combat, and the victorious Arthur reduced the French to slavery, 'where they still are'.[49]

Faced with such inflammatory stuff as that, the French, I believe, retaliated in a subtler way, through a gradual perversion of the Arthurian universe established by Geoffrey of Monmouth and Chrétien. Their tool was an element in that universe which was already potentially subversive: the figure of Lancelot. Chrétien never finished Lancelot's story, probably because its ending could only be disastrous. Either Lancelot would return to Arthur's court and make him a perennial cuckold, or Arthur would accuse him and the subsequent strife would rend Arthurian society. This menace suited anti-Arthur writers very well. Lancelot could remain at court, a canker eating away the Arthurian system; at any desired point, the intrigue could be brought into the open, and the whole, apparently glorious, edifice of the *roi de Bretagne* would come crashing down. What the pro-French writers needed to do was to annexe Lancelot. The process begins with the first words of the prose *Lancelot*:[50]

> En la marche de Gaule et de la petite Bertaigne avoit deus rois anchienement . . . Bans de Benoich et Bohours de Gaunes . . . Li rois Bans avoit .i. sien voisin qui marchisoit a lui par devers Berri, qui lors estoit apelee la Terre Deserte.

We are, in fact, in France, or at least in territory which the contemporary French king would claim. Claudas, Ban's *voisin*, is in fact a vassal of 'le roi de

[47] *Ibid.*, p. 4.
[48] *Ibid.*, p. 7.
[49] *Ibid.*, p. 9.
[50] Ed. A. Micha, 9 vols, Textes Littéraires Français (Geneva, 1978–83), VII.1. Portions of text were published in an irritatingly illogical sequence. Another edition of the early *Lancelot* was published by E. Kennedy, 2 vols (Oxford, 1980). For place-names, see Carman, *A Study of the Pseudo-Map Cycle*, pp. 1–16 (with reservations).

Gaule *qui ore est apelee Franche*'.[51] Bohort and Ban are sub-vassals of Uther Pendragon, Arthur's father. Arthur inherits Uther's seigneurial obligation towards them, and his failure to save them, and Ban's son, Lancelot, from the ravages of Claudas redounds to his discredit through the whole colossal work. Thus a 'French connexion' with Lancelot is established. It is tenuous at first; one could even argue that the villain, Claudas, is the most obviously French character at this early stage. This, however, is the thin end of the wedge. Arthur's prestige, at the beginning of the *Lancelot*, is high. But constant reminders of his failure to punish Claudas, together with allusions to his illegitimate birth, erode this prestige.[52] Meanwhile, Lancelot, during his secret upbringing by the Lady of the Lake, is joined by Hector and Lionel, sons of his uncle, Bohort.[53] This meeting is momentous, for the three boys form the nucleus of a clan or faction which is always to be loyal to itself, not to Arthur. It resembles the fiercely cohesive Guillaume clan in the *chanson de geste*, with one vital difference: Guillaume is the king's vassal, and supports him however unworthy; because of Arthur's failure to redeem Lancelot's lands from Claudas, Lancelot does not become his vassal and feels no obligation towards him. He feels no emotional attraction towards him, either. He goes to Arthur's court not because of Arthur, but because 'l'en dist que tout li preudomme sont en la maison le roi Artu'.[54] As soon as he reaches the court he meets Guinevere. Significantly, the first thing Guinevere learns about him is that he is *del pais de Gaule*.[55] Queen and Frenchman fall in love immediately, and one of the first, fatal results of that love is that Lancelot refuses to let Arthur complete the knighting ceremony 'car il n'atent pas a estre chevaliers de la main le roi, mais d'un autre dont il quide plus amender'[56] – that is, Guinevere.[57] To rob Arthur of his traditional function of making knights is almost to rob him of existence; certainly this curious incident ensures that Lancelot has no ties with the king.

Adulterous love, however courtly, still bears a risk of discredit to the lovers, especially if the deceived husband is a worthy man (as in some early versions of *Tristan*). To prevent this discredit falling on Lancelot, the author now systematically downgrades Arthur. He is forced to do humiliating penance for his neglect of Ban.[58] He proves himself an unfaithful husband, in a singularly stupid and damaging intrigue.[59] The chief instrument of his humiliation, however, is King Galehot of Sorelois, who defeats him in war and snatches from him the flower of

51 *Ibid.*, VII.2.
52 See Kennedy, 'King Arthur', pp.186–92. (Dr Kennedy's interpretation of Arthur's presentation here differs from mine.)
53 *Lancelot*, ed. Micha, VII.121–3.
54 *Ibid.*, VII.247.
55 *Ibid.*, VII.274.
56 *Ibid.*, VII.286.
57 *Ibid.*, VII.298.
58 *Ibid.*, VIII.15–16.
59 *Ibid.*, VII.411ff.

kingship.[60] Now, Galehot is passionately in love with Lancelot and obeys his lightest word. For Guinevere's sake, Lancelot persuades Galehot to surrender to Arthur.[61] Arthur is restored, but his position now depends entirely on Lancelot's love for his wife. For Arthur's downfall to be completed, all that is necessary is for him to become estranged from his wife – and that is exactly what happens, in the episode of the False Guinevere.[62] Arthur abandons his true wife, who flees with Lancelot to Sorelois, and Arthur's kingdom crumbles.

The manuscript tradition of *Lancelot* is very confused at this point. There are several versions of the False Guinevere story, some of which paint Arthur blacker than others. If, as Elspeth Kennedy thinks, the original *Lancelot* ended immediately afterwards, then it could well be sub-titled 'the fall of King Arthur'. In the rest of the 'cyclic' *Lancelot*, the attack on Arthur is remitted; but it is not forgotten. Arthur still depends on Lancelot for his prestige, and still owes him vengeance. Eventually, hundreds of pages (and many years) later, Arthur does at last attack Claudas, the unworthy lord of 'Gaule, qui or est apelee la Novele France'.[63] It is now, in fact, a question of restoring Lancelot to the kingship of *all* France. In the course of a complicated war, Arthur defeats both Claudas and Frollo, here called a count of Germany.[64] Note that in neither case does Arthur overcome a true king of France!

In the outcome, Lancelot and his clan refuse to accept the kingdoms offered by Arthur, as they wish to continue the practice of chivalry.[65] This is in accord with the ethos of *Lancelot*, but it has an ominous political consequence: the French clan avoids coming under Arthur's suzerainty. This prepares the tragedy of the *Mort Artu*.[66]

Arthur is not attacked on a nationalistic basis in the *Queste*, though much is said about the unworthiness of his kingdom, now to be abandoned by the hallowing Grail. In the *Mort*, however, the key-factor in Arthur's downfall, more even than Mordred's hatred and the discovery of Guinevere's adultery, is the secession from his court of Lancelot's clan, the French faction without which he has few worthy knights, and against which he cannot prevail. The clan eventually withdraws to its French possessions,[67] and while Arthur pursues a useless war against it Mordred seizes his kingdom. Without the French knights, Arthur can barely overcome Mordred, and Arthur perishes. It is Lancelot who returns to exterminate Mordred's sons and set the realm in order.[68] In the original *Historia* this was

---

60   *Ibid.*, VIII.1–28.
61   *Ibid.*, VIII.88–93.
62   This is a much disputed episode. See A. Micha, in *Romania*, 76 (1955), 334–41; 293–318, 478–517; 86 (1965), 330–59; 87 (1966), 194–233, and in *Mélanges Delbouille*, II.495–507, versus E. Kennedy in *Romania*, 77 (1956), 94–104.
63   *Lancelot*, ed. Micha, VI.42.
64   *Ibid.*, VI.30–170.
65   *Ibid.*, VI.169–70.
66   Ed. J. Frappier, TLF, 3rd edn (Paris 1964).
67   *Ibid.*, line 163.
68   *Ibid.*, lines 252–60.

done by Constantine, Arthur's heir, who ruled after him:[69] a measure of the shift in the balance of Arthurian power.

Another disastrous development (for Arthur) in the *Mort* is the fact that Lancelot's clan is opposed, through a developing blood-feud, to another clan, led by Gawain and consisting of Arthur's kindred. Now, as the *Lancelot* took over Chrétien's hero to turn him against Arthur, so the *Mort's* Gawain-faction is taken over, for the same purpose, by the second great Arthurian cycle, the so-called 'post-Vulgate'.[70] Within Arthurian 'society', Gawain is a natural rival to Lancelot. He was the original nonpareil; he remains so in the verse romances (which may well have a pro-English bias), and he re-emerges triumphantly in English Arthurian literature.[71] In the post-Vulgate, Gawain is a thug and a murderer from first to last, and the rest of his family (which, of course, includes Mordred) takes after him. Arthur is neither thug nor murderer, but as a member of the *lineage* he is, by legal extension, guilty of Gawain's crimes.[72] Throughout the narrative, 'le lineage le roi Artu' is opposed in jealous hatred to 'le lineage le roi Ban': the court is split long before the final scandal. Arthur is in an impossible position. Bound by blood-loyalty to the former clan, he depends politically on the latter. He must flatter and cajole them. Arthur himself explains the position to his illegitimate son: 'and if peradventure you slew one of them, and they slew you, I should punish [them] to avenge you. But I could not do that without harm to myself, because they are wonderfully good knights'.[73] Eventually, in the post-Vulgate *Mort*, the precarious balance is shattered. The Gawain-clan, in its hatred for Lancelot, denounces his love for the queen. Arthur is then bound to declare for his own clan, though he knows that the Lancelot-clan is 'exalted by God above all other lineages . . . in the number of their supporters and in the power of their lords'.[74] The author's predilection for Lancelot's lineage invades even the final battle between Arthur and Mordred. Mordred is slain not by Arthur (as in the tremendous corresponding scene from the earlier Vulgate *Mort*), but by Blioberis, an obscure character whose only merit is that he is of Ban's lineage.[75] Lancelot returns, as in the Vulgate *Mort*, to settle the realm, and the author insists that, were it not for their wholesale retirement into hermitages, Ban's lineage 'would have conquered all the territory of Logres very easily'.[76] There was probably a particular edge to this remark in its original French. In 1215, Prince Louis of France profited from King John's quarrel with his barons to invade England, and

[69] *Historia*, § 132.
[70] On which see Bogdanow, *Romance*.
[71] Busby, *Gawain*; Schmolke-Hasselmann, *Versroman*, p. 244.
[72] See Bloch, *Medieval French Literature and Law*, pp. 63–4 and 77–81.
[73] Translated from the Spanish *Demanda del Sancto Grial*, in *Libros de Cabellerías*, ed. Bonilla y San Martin, I.235. The French original does not survive. For textual relationships, see Bogdanow, *Romance*, pp. 88–120.
[74] *Demanda*, ed. Bonilla y San Martin, I.321.
[75] *Ibid.*, I.326.
[76] *Ibid.*, I.334.

was dislodged only with difficulty, amidst an explosion of anti-French feeling.[77] The post-Vulgate Lancelot may well be a successful avatar of Louis.

Poor Arthur has not yet completed his Calvary. The prose *Tristan*, which owes much to both the *Lancelot* and the post-Vulgate,[78] brings a third character into the fray: King Mark, a degraded character whom Arthur, through Lancelot's adultery, is made to resemble. Tristan himself, a model of chivalry because of his education *at the court of France*,[79] sees in Lancelot's cause the portraiture of his, and consequently earns the love of the Lancelot, and the hatred of the Gawain, clan. The worst consequences of this situation occur at the end of the vast romance. After Arthur's passing, Mark invades Logres, confident of victory: 'puis que cil du paranté le roy Ban sont mort; et mesmement la mort de celui seul [Lancelot] me la [Logres] donne'.[80] In fact, enough Bans survive to bring Mark to an unpleasant end, but not before he has obliterated almost every mark and memorial of Arthur's reign, beginning with the Round Table.[81] If the most despicable character in the Arthurian world can thus obliterate Arthur's achievement, what was its value in the first place?

Mark's *razzia* was evidently not as thorough as he believed. Sporadically through the prose *Tristan* there emerges a theme connected with the notion of Arthurian monuments, the most overtly nationalistic theme of all.[82] There is a scattering of references to a triumphant tour of Logres made, years later, by Charlemagne and the Twelve Peers. Charlemagne is of Ban's lineage – clear proof that the latter were thought of as Frenchmen.[83] At every Arthurian site Charlemagne, or the author, makes some remark which shows that the French worthy was superior to the British one. Charlemagne opines that Arthur must have been *de tres pauvre sen*,[84] for with four such knights as Galahad, Lancelot, Tristan, and Perceval he, Charlemagne, would have conquered the world. Arthur himself dreams that Logres will one day be conquered by a descendant of Ban who will be a better and holier knight than he.[85] Charlemagne rebuilds a symbolic tower which Arthur could not maintain, and records the knights' adventures in a great book.[86] If the Arthur of Geoffrey of Monmouth, who began the whole development, was a challenge to Charlemagne, then in the prose *Tristan* Charlemagne answers the challenge with a vengeance.

The nationalistic theme is only one of many threads in the vast interweave of

[77] The invasion is described with patriotic indignation in *Histoire de Guillaume le Maré-chal*, ed. Meyer, II.14490–17870.
[78] Baumgartner, *Le Tristan*, pp. 42–52 and 118–32. The textual relationships are complex.
[79] *Le Roman de Tristan en prose*, ed. Curtis, I.137–47.
[80] Fragment given by Bogdanow, *Romance*, p. 266. Bogdanow sees it as part of the post-Vulgate, but it clearly belongs to the Tristan theme.
[81] *Ibid.*, pp. 267–8.
[82] Noted by Muir, 'King Arthur, style Louis XVI'. Detailed summary of the later *Tristan* is given by Löseth, *Tristan*.
[83] *Ibid.*, p. 371.
[84] *Ibid.*, p. 3
[85] *Ibid.*, p. 37
[86] *Ibid.*, pp. 302 and 3

Postulated interrelationships of the major French Arthurian texts in prose (dates between *ca* 1200 and *ca* 1250)

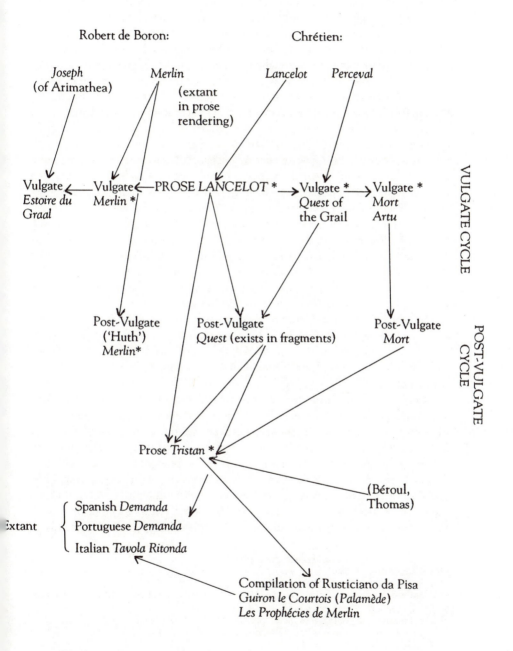

Robert de Boron:

Chrétien:

Joseph (of Arimathea)

Merlin (extant in prose rendering)

Lancelot

Perceval

Vulgate *Estoire du Graal*

Vulgate *Merlin* *

PROSE LANCELOT *

Vulgate * *Quest* of the Grail

Vulgate * *Mort Artu*

VULGATE CYCLE

Post-Vulgate ('Huth') *Merlin**

Post-Vulgate *Quest* (exists in fragments)

Post-Vulgate *Mort*

POST-VULGATE CYCLE

Prose *Tristan* *

(Béroul, Thomas)

Spanish *Demanda*

Portuguese *Demanda*

Italian *Tavola Ritonda*

Extant

Compilation of Rusticiano da Pisa *Guiron le Courtois* (*Palamède*) *Les Prophécies de Merlin*

* Used by Malory.

these prose romances. It is often lost as innumerable deeds of chivalry are re-counted; Arthur is often mentioned with great praise. But the theme is persist-ent, and often prominent, particularly in accounts of Arthur's end, so that memory of it lingers when one's reading of the text is over. And these texts were hugely popular, and spawned others, such as the *Palamède*, the *Prophécies de Merlin*, and Rusticiano's compilation,[87] which inherited their ideology. The strongest evidence of their nationalistic impact, however, is given in their recep-tion by late mediaeval British authors, as shown by the ways in which the French texts were adapted. There is, in fact, a dual reaction: that of the Scots and that of the English. The Scots loathed Arthur as a symbol of English domination, as can be seen in their radical re-writing of the *Historia* to show Mordred, the north-erner, as rightful king of England and Arthur as a bastard and usurper.[88] The fifteenth-century Scots romance *Lancelot of the Laik*[89] selects from the early prose *Lancelot* the episodes in which Arthur is humiliated by Galehot and castigated fro his neglect of Ban. Earlier still, it was in Edinburgh that the fourteenth-century English knight Thomas Gray found a copy of the rare post-Vulgate cycle, parts of which he adapted into his *Scalachronica*.[90] Gray represents the second, purely English, reaction. As a good Englishman, he eliminates the elements which are discreditable to Arthur and minimises Lancelot's importance, filling the gaps with borrowings from Geoffrey's *Historia*. In the last battle Mordred is killed not by Blioberis, but by Yvain, a relative of Arthur. After Arthur's passing it is Constantine, not Lancelot, who reorganises the kingdom.

Gray knew what the French authors were up to. So did other writers and readers south of the Border. It is, I am sure, no coincidence that there is no complete English translation of the *Lancelot*, the prose *Tristan*, or the post-Vulgate, whereas the Vulgate *Merlin*, which is not anti-Arthur, was englished at least three times.[91]

Deeply significant, from our point of view, is the attitude of Malory. He had access to an extensive Arthurian library, mainly of French origin,[92] and he made his selections carefully. He draws extensively on the early parts of the post-Vulgate cycle, which are not hostile to Arthur; indeed, they present him as an impressive tragic figure.[93] He makes no use of the post-Vulgate *Queste* or *Mort*. The early part of the prose *Lancelot*, in which Lancelot's Frenchness is established and Arthur is humiliated, is replaced by the English alliterative *Mort*, in which Lancelot is scarcely mentioned and Arthur is exalted, crushing France on his way to conquer Rome. Galehot, Arthur's superior rival king, is mentioned only in

87 Pickford, 'Miscellaneous French prose romances'.
88 Göller, 'König Arthur'.
89 *Lancelot of the Laik*, ed. Skeat.
90 Cambridge, Corpus Christi College, MS. 133. Excerpts have been inaccurately edited by Meneghetti, *I fatti*, pp. 49–51 and 67–71.
91 Ackerman 'The English romances', pp. 485–8.
92 Probably that of Sir Anthony Woodville, looted from the French royal family: see Griffith, 'The authorship', p. 172.
93 Bogdanow, *Romance*, pp. 200–21.

passing, among the innumerable minor knights at tournaments. The prose *Tristan* is used, but references hostile to Arthur are filtered out, and his likeness to Mark is carefully neutralised.[94] Some (not all) of Gawain's unpleasantness is removed. Most impressive, however, is the treatment of Lancelot. Malory does not sully him as the French writers sully Gawain. He emerges nobler and more generous than ever before, as Arthur's friend, admirer, and most reluctant betrayer. When, at the end, he returns to England, it is not to make war and tidy up Arthur's kingdom, because Arthur's victory over Mordred was complete. Constantine has no difficulty with his inheritance, *and worshipfully he rulyd this royaume.*[95] Lancelot comes only to repent and renounce the world, in a series of unbearably moving scenes. In rescuing Arthur, greatest of English heroes, from his humiliation in the French romances, Malory shows himself superior to their authors not only in literary art, but in magnanimity.

Enough has, I hope, been said to show that French nationalism existed before the fourteenth century, and that it is reflected in the Arthurian prose romances. If it is sad to think of Arthur being a pawn in an age-old enmity, it is also uplifting to know that national passion contributed to a series of literary creations of enduring value.

[94] Kennedy, 'Malory's King Mark'.
[95] Malory, *Works*, ed. Vinaver, p. 725.

The thirteenth-century French
Dit d'avarice and the
Disputatio corporis et animae tradition

KATHARINA BRETT

INTRODUCTION

The Old French *Dit d'avarice* is a moral poem of fourteen strophes, each of six octosyallabic lines. It survives in two late thirteenth-century manuscripts: Paris, Bibliothèque de l'Arsenal, MS. 3142, fo 286r (A), and Paris, Bibliothèque nationale, MS. fr. 12467, fo 55v (B).[1]

DESCRIPTION OF MANUSCRIPTS USED

CONTENTS

From the published descriptions of the manuscripts it is apparent that their contents are very similar: all twenty-seven texts in B appear among the forty-five in A, though not in the same order. For ease of comparison, a table of incipits and folio-numbers follows.

---

[1] For description of the manuscripts, see Martin, *Catalogue des manuscrits de la Bibliothèque de l'Arsenal*, III.256–60; Omont, *Bibliothèque nationale. Ancien supplément français*, II.534ff. On the *Dit d'avarice*, see *Rutebeuf: Oeuvres complètes*, ed. Jubinal (referred to in the critical apparatus as J), 12n.; Långfors, *Les incipit*, p. 179; Naetebus, *Die nicht-lyrischen Strophenformen*, pp. 103–4; *Jean Bodel: La Chanson des Saxons*, ed. Michel, I.lxix; *Oeuvres complètes de Rutebeuf*, edd. Faral and Bastin (hereafter F&B), I.384n.

MS. B			MS. A	
No.	fo	Incipit	No.	fo
1	1r	Bien doit chascuns son afaire arreer	2	73r
2	49r	Quant Diex fist le monde premiers	13	280r
3	50v	Par un sien saintisme poete	14	281v
4	53v	Cest l jus c'on dit es prés	15	284v
5	54v	Ave, en cui sans nul nombre a	29a	300v
6	54v	Diex te saut, estoile de mer	16	285r
7	55r	Diex te saut, tres douce Marie	*	285v
8	55v	Je ne sai dou monde que dire	17	286r
9	55v	Par maintes fois oy retraire	29c	302r
10	57v	Cil n'ont soing que je monte en pris	29b	301r
11	58v	Douce dame, sainte Marie	18	286v
12	59r	Pour ce que je ne vueil mentir	19	287r
13	59v	Pour ce que trop ai jut en mue	29d	304r
14	61r	Qui de bons est si mete entente	29e	305r
15	62v	En dist k'en taisir gist grant sens	29f	306v
16	63r	Pour tous les bons sont fait mi conte	29g	307r
17	63v	Ce dist uns clerc plante folie	21	291v
18	64v	Seignour, cis siecles ne vaut rien	22	292r
19	65v	Selong le siecle qui est ore	29h	307v
20	67r	Au saint Espir commant m'entente	20	287v
21	71r	Droite racine de savoir	23	293r
22	74r	Royne e pitié, Marie	24	296r
23	74v	Ave, sainte Marie, de grant misericorde	25	296v
24	75v	Encor ne soit loenge de pecheor pas bele	26	297v
25	77v	Ave dame des angres, de paradis royne	27	299v
26	78r	Dame resplendissans, royne glorieuse	28	300r
27	78v	A l'issue d'avrill, un tans dous et joli	3	120v

* Previous editors of these manuscripts, with the exception of Francisque Michel,[2] have overlooked the fact that the poem *Diex te saut, tres douce Marie* occurs in MS. A as well as in MS. B. Henry Martin does not list it as a separate piece in his catalogue, and it also escaped the attention of Artur Långfors.[3] The reason for this seems to be that the rubric in A (fo 285v, col. 2) does not stand out from the Latin portions of the two poems, which are also written in red ink. Also, there is no miniature at the start of this poem in A, whereas there is one in the corresponding position in B. The fact that both poems begin with the words 'Diex te saut' may also have disguised their separate identities.

2   *La Chanson des Saxons*, ed. Michel, I.lxviii–lxix (nos 16 and 17).
3   Långfors, 'Une paraphrase anonyme', p. 119.

The poems contained in MS. A only, with their positions in the manuscript, are as follows;

MS. A

No.	fo	
1	1r	En non de Dieu le creatour
4	141r	Cil qui en soi a point de sens
5	166r	Uns homs fu d'estragne pays
6	179r	Ce fu ou tans d'esté, si comme ou mois de mai
7	203r	Miserere mei, deus
8	216v	Dire me plaist et bien doit plaire
9	227r	Pitiez ou ma matere puise
10	229r	Qui d'oyr et d'entendre a loisir ne talant
11	256r	Cil qui sevent de lettréure
12	273r	Frans cuers, vostre manaie
29i	309v	Ja ne mesisse contredit
29j	311v	Selonc la matere vous conte
29k	312r	Cil qui trouva dou gardecors
29l	313r	Ki veut k'en amour adroit maigne
29m	314v	Amours qui maint amant la prent
29n	316v	L'autr'an ainsi com apres mai
29o	319r	Sor toute rien d'une merveille
30	320r	Noirons fist morir Seneke son maistre a poi d'ochoison . . .

DATE AND PROVENANCE

Both manuscripts are clearly *de luxe* copies, made of good-quality vellum, although B has occasional holes around which the scribe has written. They have generous margins and fine decorations and miniatures. In A especially, large quantities of gold-leaf are used to provide the backgrounds of the miniatures and the body of the decorated initials. MS. A also contains a significant number of blank columns and even whole blank folios which have been left in place rather than being excised for use elsewhere.

I should like to add the following details to the information already published concerning these manuscripts. In both manuscripts, the standard number of lines per page is forty-four. The fluctuation between the use of two and three columns per page is entirely due to the metres of the poems to be copied: alexandrines or decasyllabics require two wide columns, whereas octosyllabic verse permits the use of three narrower ones. Occasionally this produces inhteresting details where the preparation of the parchment is concerned: for example, in the tenth gathering of MS. B, where there are abandoned prick-marks and even some rulings (fos 75r, 80v) put in for three-column use, but where pricking and ruling were subsequently added for the two-column division needed for the alexandrines.

In both manuscripts the collation is very regular. In MS. B, gatherings I–XII have eight leaves each, and gathering XIII consists of two written leaves, a stub and a blank folio. At the end of each gathering except VI (the end of a poem) and XIII (the end of the volume), there are catchwords in the same hand as the texts, which all correspond to the lines which follow them. MS. A likewise consists almost entirely of regular eight-leaf gatherings. The exceptions are as follows: XV (seven leaves, 113–19, with a stub after fo 119, probably cut out because it was blank – the poem ends on fo 119v); XVI (a stub followed by three leaves, the new text beginning on 120v; 120r is blank); XXXIII (probably six leaves originally, but there is a stub at the centre right of the gathering, where either a leaf has been removed or a singleton (153) has been used; fos 154 and 155 are completely blank); LXI, the final gathering, is preceded by two stubs, though the words on the first leaf (fo 312r) correspond to the catchwords at the end of the previous gathering. These stubs are therefore probably the ends of two singletons (fos 320–1) which were all that was needed to complete the volume. There are two parchment flyleaves (not mentioned in Martin's description) and three modern paper flyleaves at the end of the volume, which correspond to three modern paper flyleaves, an old paper flyleaf and a parchment flyleaf at the beginning, the last two mentioned being bound in by means of paper tabs at present. Like MS. B, MS. A has catchwords in the same hand as the texts at the end of the gatherings, except in cases where (i) a poem ends – IX (72v), XV (119v), XXIII (178v), XXVI (202v), XXIX (226v), XXXIII (255v), XXXVI (279v) (in all these positions, sections of the manuscript could have been bound in or removed); (ii) a rhyme carries over on to the next folio – XIX (146v), XX (154v), XXXVIII (195v); or (iii) XXXVII (187v). Occasionally the catchwords have been damaged by subsequent trimming of the pages: for example, fos 218v, 234v. MS A also contains some quire-numbers apparently contemporaneous with the text. Quires I–IX are marked i–ix at the bottom of the last page, and quires X–XIV are numbered i–v. There are no more numbers visible after this, however; this could possibly mark a change of scribe.

Appreciable blank spaces are found in the manuscripts as follows. B: 47v (part col. 2), 48r, 48v, 98v (part col. 1 and all col. 2); A: 72r (col. 3), 72v, 119v (part col. 2), 120r, 140v (part col. 1 and all col. 2), 178v (col. 3), 201v (except first two lines), 202r, 202v, 226v (part col. 2 and all col. 3), 229r (part col. 1), 254r, 254v, 255r, 255v, 278v (part col. 2 and all col. 3), 279r (except insertion in modern hand), 279v.

Scholars seem to agree that the two manuscripts date from the end of the thirteenth century, probably from the final decade.[4] The orthography and the style of decoration indicate that they were made in the Ile-de-France, most probably in Paris itself.[5] Indeed, it seems almost certain from the similarity in script, layout and decoration, even to the details of the miniatures, that they

---

[4]   See most recently *Adenet le Roi: Berte as grans piés* ed. Henry (hereafter *Berte*), pp. 1–2.
[5]   *Les oeuvres d'Adenet le Roi*, ed. Henry, I.95–101; *Berte*, pp. 1–2.

were both produced in the same scriptorium, possibly, in part, even by the same scribe.[6]

MS. B seems to me to be the work of one scribe, who might be identified with the scribe of the opening of MS. A. His hand is a small and regular gothic, with ample space between the words and lines. MS. A, however, appears to contain at least three hands. The first is found from fo 1 up to the end of col. 1 of fo 166r. In col. 2 of this page, at the beginning of the paraphrase of the Book of Job (*Uns homs fu d'estrange pays*), the script changes to a much squarer-looking compressed hand, reminiscent of later gothic textura rather than the more cursive hand of Scribe 1. Only this one text is written in this hand, however, though it is just possible, since the piece ends at the end of a quire, that more pieces copied by the same scribe were not bound in. At fo 179, the next gathering, a third scribe takes over. His hand is in most respects very similar to that of Scribe 1, but has more hairlines, especially vertical ones at the ends of words and long ones on letters such as *y* and *h*, and is characterised by a vertical hairline descending from the cross-stroke of the letter *t*, where Scribe 1 has an oblique hairline to the right of the bottom of the shank of the *t*. Urban T. Holmes in his edition provides useful plates of the opening of *Berte* from MSS. A and B, though he, it must be pointed out, is arguing that both are the work of one scribe.[7] It has been suggested by A. G. van Hamel that the portion of the manuscript beginning at fo 280 originally constituted a separate volume, because it is only from this point on that the titles of pieces are given as rubrics, but since Scribe 3's hand is discernible right to the end of the volume it seems more likely that the rubrics were necessitated by the shorter poems contained in this part of the manuscript.[8]

Abbreviations are used more frequently by Scribe A3 than by Scribe B. The Tironian note for *et* is found in both manuscripts; Scribe A3 also uses abbreviations for *per*, *grant*, *qui/que*. There is no punctuation in either manuscript.

The initial capital of each line is separate from the main body of the line in both manuscripts. At the beginning of stanzas there are often decorated initials two lines high, in which blue and pink alternately dominate. Usually, there is no decoration in the margins, but occasionally an initial spreads up or down, for example in both manuscripts at the beginning of *Berte*, or at the beginning of the *Dit d'avarice* in MS. A.

The miniatures of MSS. A and B still await thorough study by art-historians. It has been suggested, most recently by E. G. Millar,[9] that both sets were produced in the workshop of Honoré of Paris, who is attested from 1288 but seems to have died before 1318. However, Ellen V. Kosmer[10] points out the uncertainty surrounding such attributions. The *Dit d'avarice* is preceded by a miniature in both A and B, and these differ from one another in more respects than many of

6   *Les Oeuvres d'Adenet le Roi*, ed. Henry, I.100–1; *Berte*, p. 2; Holmes, p. 13.
7   Holmes, *Adenet le Roi's Berte*, pp. 14–15.
8   *Li Romans de Carité et Miserere*, ed. Van Hamel, p. xxi.
9   Millar, *The Parisian Miniaturist Honoré*, ed. Van Hamel, p. xxi.
10   Kosmer, 'Master Honoré', pp. 63–8.

the others in the volumes. That in MS. A is seven lines high and shows a white-haired, beardless man in a red-brown tunic sitting on a chair with his head propped on his left hand. Before him, some way away, is a strong-box on which are two heavy goblets and two piles of coins. Three garments, grey, blue, and orange, hang from rails above him. The whole composition, like the other miniatures in A, has a gold background and a border consisting of an outer rim of gold and a pink and blue inner frame decorated with white. The miniature in MS. B is ten lines tall, and represents a man with short, curly grey hair and a short, grey beard, wearing a simple purple robe and brown sandals, seated on a chair next to a strong-box. On this are three bags, one of which he is picking up; he is holding another bag in his lap. The background is dark blue, with a superimposed trellis-pattern of black lines forming squares and white lines forming lozenges. The border has a gold outer rim and a pink inner frame with decoration in white. In the miniatures of MS. B the positions of the pink and blue alternate: that is, the next miniature has a pink background and blue frame, and so on.

There is some similarity between the miniatures at the head of the *Dit d'avarice* in MSS. A and B and that depicting avarice personified in a thirteenth-century manuscript of the *Somme le Roi* (London, British Library, MS. Add. 54180 (M), fo 136v). This is interesting in that MS. M previously belonged to Millar, who attributed it, along with A and B, to the workshop of Honoré.[11] The frames of the miniatures in M are like those of B, but the background is gold paint rather than coloured. As in AB, there is no architectural background. The miser is bare-headed, as in AB; and his worried expression, short beard and curly grey hair bear a striking resemblance to those in B, as do his hands and sandals. The miniatures of the miser in MSS. B and M could thus be quite closely related, and if this is indeed the case, the fact that Kosmer classifies the iconography of M as Parisian would further support the generally accepted opinion that MS. B originates from the Paris area.

On the other hand, M differs from A and B in general appearance, being of smaller dimensions and written on thinner vellum. There are red and blue paragraph-marks in the prose, and the decorated initials are much more elaborate. The hand of M does not appear in A or B. As far as the miniature of the miser is concerned, the principal difference between AB and M is the presence of a devil in M. The miser's treasure in the *Somme* depiction consists entirely of coins, whereas in the *Dit* miniatures, bags or precious artefacts are shown, and in M, unlike AB, the miser wears patched clothes.

In her dissertation Kosmer discusses the illuminations in M in great detail, and attributes them and those in the Breviary of Philippe le Bel (Paris, Bibliothèque nationale, MS. latin 1023) to an anonymous Parisian artist, the 'Somme Master'. She further associates the style of these works with that of the Martyro-

---

[11]   An illustration of this folio may be found in Millar, *The Parisian Miniaturist Honoré*, pl. 8.

logy of Saint-Germain des Prés, (Paris, Bibliothèque nationale, MS. latin 12834) and in the light of this suggests new approximate datings for all three manuscripts as follows: Martyrology, 1278; Somme (M), 1285; Breviary, 1290.[12] It is interesting that Kosmer also gives slightly earlier dates than are usually assumed for MSS. BN fr. 12467 ('c. 1280') and Arsenal 3142 ('c. 1280–1290'), although she does not discuss the style or attribution of these manuscripts.[13] Her datings would be consistent with an attribution of A and/or B to the 'Somme Master'. The differences between the manuscripts, however, suggest a more complicated state of affairs.[14] Bearing in mind Millar's attribution of M, A, and B to one and the same workshop, the subject deserves further specialist investigation.

RELATIONSHIPS BETWEEN THE MANUSCRIPTS

As well as the physical similarities between the two manuscripts, there is a striking unanimity in their textual readings, which has been noted by the editors of several poems contained in them.[15] Långfors, Holmes, and Mustanoja all suggest that the two manuscripts were copied from the same exemplar. There seems to be little to choose between the two manuscripts as regards accuracy of the text. A. Henry, after detailed deliberation, expresses a slight preference for A,[16] and Långfors chooses this manuscript (his 'P1') as his base in editing the ABC *Plantefolie*.[17] On the other hand, Holmes, takes MS. B as his base, assuming that it is 'a more independent and perhaps earlier copy', since it sometimes shows variants against all six other manuscripts of *Berte*.[18] Mustanoja suggests that MS. B (his 'E'), is 'a little more reliable' than MS. A (his 'I'), but takes another manuscript as his base.[19]

After examining the *Dit d'avarice* and some other pieces which have not yet been edited from both manuscripts (*C'est la jus*: A, fo 284v; B, fo 53v; Jean de Douai, *Dit de la vigne*: A, fo 293r, B, fo 71r; Baudouin de Condé, *Ave Maria*: A, fo 300v, B fo 54v; Baudouin de Condé, *Dis dou preudome*: A fo 306v; B fo 62v), as

---

[12] Kosmer, 'Style and Iconography', I.258–62.

[13] *Ibid.*, III.v–vi.

[14] A further complication is that MS. A, while very close to B in many respects, may show some northern French influence in the style of its decoration, which resembles that of another thirteenth-century *Somme*-manuscript – London, British Library, MS. Add. 28162 (L) – where a miser appears on fo 9v. The similarities are in the colouring (pink, blue, and gold) of the frame of the miniature, the use of these colours in large initials, the gold background, and the fact that the miser has no beard. However, unlike A, B, or M, MS. L shows the miser wearing a hood; it differs from them also in having architectural backgrounds in its miniatures, and the hand is again different.

[15] See Holmes, *Adenet le Roi's Berte*, p. 13; Långfors, loc. cit.; *Les Oeuvres d'Adenet le Roi*, ed. Henry, I.100–1, 177–8, 204, 222–9; *Berte*, pp. 1–3; *Les Neuf Joies Nostre Dame*, ed. Mustanoja, pp. 22–9.

[16] *Les Oeuvres d'Adenet le Roi*, ed. Henry I.229; see also *Berte*, p. 3.

[17] Romania 41, 1912, p. 238.

[18] Homes, *Adenet le Roi's Berte*, p. 13.

[19] *Les Neuf Joies*, ed. Mustanoja, pp. 22–9.

well as such published editions as do exist, I am inclined to share the view that it is more likely that the two manuscripts were produced in the same environment from common originals than that one of them was copied directly from the other.

EDITORIAL PRINCIPLES

As has already been mentioned, MSS. A and B are closely related. I have chosen A as my base because it offers a clearer meaning at line 32 than B, this being the only significant variant. The other variants are purely orthographic and give no indication of possible regionalisms on the part of either author or scribe. Almost all the variants fall into one of four categories: *our/or*, *y/i*, *pooir/povoir*, use or omission of *-s* ending in the nominative case. I follow modern editorial conventions as set out by J. Vielliard in matters such as the use of *e* acute and the printing of consonantal *u* as *v*.[20] The capital letters at the beginning of each line follow the manuscript, but all other punctuation is mine. With the exceptions just mentioned, I follow the orthography of A throughout, expanding the few abbreviations as necessary, and indicating the variants in B in the apparatus. In the translation, square brackets indicate words supplied by the editor.

[20] Vieilliard, 'Conseils'.

TEXT OF *DIT D'AVARICE*

Ci commence d'avarice

I   Je ne sai dou monde que dire:
        Hui est mauvais et demain pire.
        Tous iours va il en enpirant,
        Et cil qui sont dou monde sire
5   Si ont fait dou roiaume empire,
        Et li iuge sont li tirant.

II   Nus n'a cure de povreté:
        Povre sont arriere bouté
        Et li riche si sont trop sage.
10   Li povre si sont sot clamé
        Et li riche si sont amé:
        Ci a dolor et grant outrage.

III   Chascuns hom couvoite l'avoir,

Title: Cest uns dis d'avarice B;   Cest uns dis d'avarisce J.   3 tousiours B.   13 convoite B.

Et qui plus a plus veut avoir,
Ne nus biens torp ne li abonde.
15 Nous poons bien apercevoir
Que chascuns hom met son savoir
A aquerre les biens dou monde.

IV   Aquis sont trop a grant labour,
20   Et gardez a trop grant paour,
Et laissié a trop grant tristece.
Hom avers est tous iors en plor:
Pensis est et a grant dolor;
Un seul bon iour n'a en leece.

V   Avarice de mal racine
25   Es cuers humains si s'enracine
C'on ne la puet desraciner.
Et li cuers humains si s'encline
A avoir qui si tost termine,
30   Dont on pert l'ame sans finer.

VI   N'est pas sages qui trop amasse
Et qui por avoir trop se lasse:
Tresor fait et ne set a cui.
Pour avoir qui si tost trespasse
35   En enfer met s'ame la lasse;
Lors li poise c'onques nasqui.

VII   Quant hom per son pechié perit
Li dyables a l'esperit,
Et l'avoir au monde remaint,
40   Et li ver si ont leur delit
Dou cors qui en terre lit.
Per pechié sont il dampné maint.

VIII   Avers vit tous iors en doutance:
Li mndes li a fait creance
45   De ses biens; or les veut ravoir.
Lors ont dyable lor baance,
Et li ver ont lor soustenance,
Et li mondes ra son avoir.

IX   Chascuns des trois ne donroit mie
50   Pour les .ij. sa seule partie:
Chascuns sa partie miex aime.
Li cors si a vie fenie,
Et la charoigne est tost porrie,
Et l'ame en enfer se reclaime.

16 pouons B.   22 hons avers est tous iors en plour B.   23 dolour B.   26 sen racine A; senracine B.   32 et que pour avoir si se lasse B.   38 diables B.   43 iours B.

X 55   Iluec sans finer finera:
        Tous iours en morant vis sera.
        Dyaable auront sor lui pooir:
        Tous iours sans mengier mengera,
        Bevra tous iours et soif aura,
   60   Et tous iours verra sans veoir.

XI   Pour avoir qui si petit dure
        Pert on a veoir la figure
        De dieu et de sa conpaignie.
        S'ame met en la grant ordure
   65   D'enfer, et en la porreture:
        Ilueques trueve il dure vie.

XII   Il n'est nus qui ne vueille tendre
        A richece qui n'est que cendre.
        Avoir et aver porrira.
   70   Chascuns achate sans riens vendre,
        Et chascuns veut sans donner prendre:
        Au dyable ainsi tout ira.

XIII   Chascuns a son donnet perdu:
        Li menestrel sont esperdu
   75   Car nus ne lor veut riens donner.
        De don ont esté soustenu;
        Maintenant sont souz pié tenu:
        Or voisent aillors sermonner.

XIV   D'avarice plus ne dirai,
   80   Mais mon dit ici finerai;
        Chascuns set bien que c'est grant visce.
        Le roy de gloire si com sai
        En finant mon dit proierai
        Qu'il nous gart tous d'avarice.

   85   Amen. Amen. Amen.

---

57 povoir B. **62** aveoir A (but *v* rather than *u* indicates new word); a veoir B. **65** pourreture B. **69** avers pourrira B. **72** diable B. **76** soutenu (Jubinal, *Rutebeuf*, nouvelle édition, 1874; J has soustenu). **81** vice B. **82** roi B. **85** om. B.

TRANSLATION

Here begins [a poem] about avarice

I   I do not know what to say about the world:
it is bad one day and worse the next.
Every day it goes on deteriorating,
and those who are the masters of the world
5   have got the kingdom into a proper state,
and the judges are the executioners.

II   Nobody cares about poverty:
poor men are pushed into the background
and the rich are [considered] exceedingly wise.
10   The poor, indeed, are called fools
and the rich are well-liked:
in this there is pain and great injustice.

III   Every man desires wealth,
and whoever has most desires to have more,
15   and he can never have too much of any commodity.
We are well able to observe
that every man applies his mind
to acquiring worldly goods.

IV   They are acquired too laboriously,
20   and kept too fearfully,
and left behind too sadly.
An avaricious man is always weeping:
he is preoccupied [with worries] and suffers great pain;
he does not have a single good day [spent] in happiness.

V 25   Avarice, the root of evil,
takes root in human hearts in such a way
that one cannot uproot it.
And thus the human heart is attracted
to wealth, which comes to an end so quickly,
30   [and] because of this the soul is lost eternally.

VI   A man is not wise if he amasses too much
and wears himself out too much for the sake of wealth:
he is piling up treasure and does not know for whom.
For the sake of wealth which passes away so swiftly
35   he consigns his unhappy soul to hell;
then he regrets ever having been born.

VII   When a man perishes as a result of his sin
the devil gets his spirit,
and the wealth stays in the world,
40   and the worms too get their enjoyment
from the body which has its resting-place in the earth.
Because of sin, many are damned.

VIII   A miser lives in constant fear:
         the world has given him credit
   45   on its goods; now it wants to have them back.
         Then the devils achieve their aims,
         and the worms have their food,
         and the world has its wealth back.

IX   None of the three would ever give up
   50   its own single share for the [other] two:
         each likes its own share best.
         The body has thus completed its life,
         and the carcase quickly decays,
         and the soul laments in hell.

X 55   There it will expire endlessly:
         always dying, it will stay alive.
         Devils will have power over it:
         it will always eat without eating,
         it will always drink and yet be thirsty,
   60   and it will always see without seeing.

XI   For the sake of wealth which lasts so short a time
         one loses [the privilege of] seeing the person
         of God and of his followers.
         One consigns one's soul to the great filth
   65   and decay of hell:
         there it finds a harsh life.

XII   There is no one who does not wish to strive
         for riches, which are but ashes.
         Wealth and the miser will decay.
   70   Everyone buys without selling anything
         and everyone wants to take without giving:
         thus everything will go to the devil.

XIII   Everyone has lost his Donatus:
         the minstrels are scattered
   75   for nobody is prepared to give them anything.
         They used to be supported by gifts;
         now they are trampled underfoot:
         let them go now and preach elsewhere.

XIV   I shall say no more about avarice,
   80   but end my verse here;
         everyone is well aware that it is a serious vice.
         I shall pray to the King of Glory as well as I know how
         as I finish my verse,
         that he may protect us all from avarice.

   85   Amen. Amen. Amen.

LANGUAGE AND FORM

There are no traces of regional dialect in either manuscript which might help locate the author or scribe. The language used is, in a very pure form, that of the Ile-de-France which was becoming accepted as the literary language of the whole of France in the latter part of the thirteenth century.

In its form, the *Dit d'avarice* is relatively unusual. The great majority of moral poems in Old French are in octosyllabic couplets: for instance, most of the *Dits* of Baudouin de Condé and Watriquet de Couvin, Robert de Blois's *Enseignement des Princes* and the *Bibles* of Guiot de Provins and Hugo de Berzé. Some, like Thibaut de Marly's *Vers* and the *Sermon* of Guischard de Beaulieu, are in long *laisses* on a single rhyme. Naetebus lists (Form XXIX) only twenty pieces in the metre of the *Dit d'avarice*, of which seven occur in manuscripts of the late thirteenth century. Three of these are on moral themes (2–Mesdisans, 10–Orguillos, 13–Avrice), and three basically religious (5–Saints, 6–Mary, 12–Pater Noster), the seventh (XXIX, 15) being a secular love-poem. Another seven can be accurately dated from internal evidence as having been composed in the years 1324–1326.[21] The remaining six are assigned to various dates in the fourteenth and early fifteenth centuries.[22]

Mölk and Wolfzettel add only five more poems which share the strophic form of the *Dit d'avarice* to Naetebus's list.[23] The first two of these[24] are bilingual hymns, with the *a*-lines in Latin and the *b*-lines in Old French, from a thirteenth-century manuscript (Paris, Bibliothèque nationale, MS. latin 15131). Another (no. 436), *Cil ki por nos prist char humaine*, is also on a religious theme, though entirely in Old French.[25] It is a lengthy exhortation to love God, and was probably written into Laon, Bibliothèque municipale, MS. 470 in the mid-thirteenth century.[26] Nos 435 and 437 are among the interpolations in the *Roman de Fauvel* in Paris, Bibliothèque nationale, MS. fr. 146, which are ascribed to Chaillou de Pestain, a contemporary and friend of Gervais du Bus, who wrote *Fauvel* between 1310 and 1314; both are laments, one by Yglise on the corrupt practices of the Knights Templar, and the other by an unhappy lover.[27]

---

[21] These seven (XXIX. 1, 3, 4, 14, 16, 17, 18) are found in two Metz manuscripts relating to the war of 1324–1326; there are five polemics, a poem celebrating the return of peace, and a panegyric of the bishop of Metz who brought it about. Two of them follow the 'ABC'-form, while the others are built around religious texts.

[22] Of these remaining poems, three are addressed to the Virgin Mary (8, 9, 11) and three are fables (two under 19, the other referred to in a postscript); there are also a poem on a comet (7), and verse sections of a moralising tract on the 'Memento mori' (20).

[23] Mölk & Wolfzettel, *Répertoire métrique*, items 433–7.

[24] *Universa creatura* (Mölk & Wolfzettel, *Répertoire métrique*, no. 433) celebrates the Nativity of Christ, and *Christicola, recordare* (ibid., no. 434; fo 183v) the Passion and Resurrection.

[25] See Långfors, p. 67.

[26] See Meyer, 'Poésie pieuse', p. 44.

[27] *Nourri les ay et alleitiez* (Mölk & Wolfzettel, *Répertoire métrique*, no. 43) occurs on fo 8v. It is not really a *chanson de croisade*, as Mö and Wolfzettel suggest, but an extra stanza

The total number of known Old French poems in this strophic form is thus about twenty-five, and therefore it may be considered a slight exaggeration on the part of Meyer to assert that 'de nombreux exemples' exist, though he is right in pointing out the preponderance of religious poems.[28] Indeed, it seems that the author of the *Dit d'avarice* may have deliberately chosen a metre with religious connotations to underline the message of his poem.

There exist a number of Latin poems, especially hymns and moralising works, which use strophic forms very similar to that of the *Dit d'avarice*, though the question of date raises considerable problems and it is impossible to produce a complete list here.[29] Hans Spanke touches on the problem, referring *inter alia* to the *Stabat Mater*. and several troubadours.[30] Full lists of Provençal poems in the form may be found in the standard metrical indices.[31] The related form *aabccb* is also used by the troubadours;[32] both forms are attested from the days of the early troubadours onwards and occur almost exclusively in the *sirventes* genre.

There is alsy a twelve-line octosyllabic form closely related to that of the *Dit d'avarice* which is quite commonly used in Old French moral poetry, but is apparently absent from Provençal and Latin, with the rhyme-scheme *aab aab bba bba*. It is often referred to as the 'Helinandstrophe', as it first occurs in Hélinant's *Vers de la mort* (1194 × 1197). It appears in the *Roman de Charité* and *Miserere* of the Renclus de Moiliens, which were probably written in the 1220s,[33] and then seems to have become very popular, being found in several of Rutebeuf's poems,[34] as well as in some twenty-three others listed by Raynaud,[35] and in another eleven mentioned by Van Hamel.[36] Naetebus XXXVI gives sixty-four occurrences, about

---

inserted into a lament by Yglise on the corrupt practices of the knights Templar (ed. Långfors 945–1028; this stanza comes between line 950 and line 951 in BN MS. fr. 146 only). This lament and the longer passage surrounding it (lines 843–1130) *Die nicht-lynischen Strophenformen*, basically follow the rhyme scheme *aab ccb*, (found also in Naetebus, XXIX, 12 above and in fables from the early fourteenth-century *Isopet de Chartres* (ed. Bastin, I.xxiv), though there is one other stanza (lines 957–62) of *aab aab*, and a case where the *c*-rhyme of one stanza becomes the next *a*-rhyme (lines 978–83). *Hau diex, de tout le monde sire* (Mölk & Wolfenzettel, *Répertoire métrique* no 433) in BN MS. fr. 146, fo. 26v, but it is not printed in *Fauvel*, ed. Långfors; see instead the edition by Hoepffner. Mölk & Wolfzettel call it a hymn, but it is in fact a lover's lament on his lady's cruel lack of interest in him, which he rhetorically addresses to God, without however asking for divine intervention or expressing any pious thoughts.

28 Meyer, 'Poésie pieuse', p. 44.
29 See *Analecta hymnica medii aevi*, ed. Dreves, XXI.95, 211, 234; XXIX.279, 254.
30 Spanke, *Beziehungen*, pp. 11 and 161–2.
31 Maus, *Peire Cardenals Strophenbau*, pp. 99, 84 and 87; Frank, *Répertoire métrique*, I, no. 99.
32 See Maus, *Peire Cardenals Strophenbau*, pp. 102, 181; Frank, *Répertoire métrique*, I, no. 193.
33 See *Les Vers de la mort*, edd. Wulff and Walberg, pp. xxvii–xxxi.
34 F&B, nos XI, XX, XXIV, XXXVIII, XXXIX, XL.
35 Raynaud, 'Les congés de Jean Bodel', pp. 231–2.
36 *Li Romans de Carité et Miserere*, ed. Van Hamel, pp. xciii–xciv.

twenty-five of which are not in either of the earlier works; Mölk and Wolfzettel do not mention the Helinandstrophe at all, which would suggest that its use was completely confined to non-lyric poetry.

STYLE AND CONTENT

The style of the *Dit d'avarice* is fairly typical of the French moral poetry of its day.[37] Three rhetorical devices in particular are used to give some shape to the piece: word-plays (*anominatio*), repetition, and parallel constructions. There are two categories of word-play: the purely decorative, as in lines 25–7 (*racine, s'enracine, desraciner*), and the pun, which at this time was not merely frivolous, but was held to reveal certain truths about the order of the world.[38] This second category includes the popular word-play on *empire* ('empire' and 'deteriorate'), found here in line 5, which I have attempted to echo in the translation;[39] the expansion of temporal power has done nothing for moral values. A similar use of language occurs in lines 61–2 (*avoir . . . a veoir*), where the word-play underlines the contrast between the choice open to man: wealth on earth or the beatific vision. Another interesting instance is *donnet* (line 73) which, as well as picking up the sound of *sans donner* (line 71), plays on the grammar of Donatus, widely circulated in the Middle Ages, and 'a small gift': the 'tool' of the composer-poet and the payment he works for are so closely interdependent that the one is lost without the other.[40] Repetition is used particularly effectively in lines 56–60, where *tous iours* stresses the eternal nature of the soul's punishment and, in additon, the figure of paradox underlines the soul's utter helplessness.[41] The rhetorical repetition of *trop grant* in lines 19–21 hammers home the poet's message in a similar way, and it is further strengthened by the enumeration at the ends of the lines of the troubles involved in getting and keeping wealth: *labour, paour, tristece*. These lines are also an example of parallel construction adding

[37] See, for example Rutebeuf (F&B, no. XVI); Baudouin de Condé, *Dits*, ed. Scheler, and *Le Dit des Médisants*, and *Dit des sept Vices et des sept Vertus* (ed. Bastin, 'Trois dits', pp. 467–507).

[38] See Mann, 'Satiric subject', especially pp. 66–73.

[39] Compare Rutebeuf (F&B, no. XXV); Baudouin de Condé (ed. Scheler, I.17–18); *Le Dit des Médisants* (ed. Bastin, 'Trois dits', pp. 198–9). Tobler, *Vermischte Beiträge*, II.198–9, lists a number of similar plays on words, including *La roe de Fortune*, 29–30, ed. Jubinal, *Jongleurs et trouvères*, pp. 177–81.

[40] See F&B, I.388n. An early instance of this usage may be found in Marcabru's *Pois l'inverns d'ogan es anatz* (ed. Dejeanne, XXXIX.43) and it continued at least until the sixteenth century: see Le Roux de Lince, *Le Livre des Proverbes*. II.36 (*Donat est mort et Restaurat dort*). Lehmann, *Die Parodie*, p. 49, quotes a fourteenth-century Latin manuscript in which the grammarian's name, though not actually used in word-play, appears in the loaded context of a satire on Rome concerning the *accusativus* and *dativus*.

[41] For a similar use of the *vis morans* paradox, see *Le Poème moral*, ed. Bayot, line 3708.

emphasis to the ideas expressed, such as is found again in lines 70–1, where it adds weight to the accusation of selfishness.

The main theme of the *Dit d'avarice* is that of the transience of life and all that is worldly: the *memento mori*, in the particular context of the desire to amass material possessions. The poem opens, however, with another motif which pervades European literature of this period, the decline of the world.[42] In common with a number of other writers, the poet says that it is the rulers and judges who are to blame for this decline.[43] He does not, however, dwell on the effects of the vices, including avarice, on society as a whole, but after one stanza implying injustice and venality in the unequal treatment of rich and poor men (stanza II),[44] he moves on to observations on the behaviour of individual misers.

We first see the miser's insatiability, a characteristic which has been noted at least since Ecclesiastes v.9, and which is often mentioned in mediaeval literature.[45] People devote excessive efforts to acquiring and keeping wealth (stanzas IV and VI), and are possessed by avarice (stanza V). The lack of *leece* mentioned in line 24 suggests that the miser is not acceptable in courtly society, where this virtue is highly regarded.[46] During the course of these three stanzas, the emphasis gradually shifts from the unsatisfactory nature of the miser's lifestyle and the worries associated with wealth[47] to the principal theme of the *Dit*: namely, that riches quickly fade (lines 29, 34; taken up again in lines 61, 68) but

---

42 See Colin Muset (ed. Bédier, XX.1); Guiot de Provins, *Bible*, 583 (ed. Orr); Rutebeuf (F&B XI, 8); *Li Vers de la mort*, ed. Windahl, stansza 80, line 9; Robert de Blois *Enseignement des Princes*, line 8 (ed. Ulrich, *Durmart le Gallois*, ed. Gildea, line 15973), to name but a few.

43 Compare, for example, Marcabru, ed. Dejeanne, XI, 41–8; Baudouin de Condé, ed. Scheler, I.42–3; *Li Vers de la mort*, ed. Windahl, stanza 310, line 9.

44 For the popularity of the rich man while the poor man is ignored, see: Rutebeuf (F&B VIII, 115ff.; XIV, 653–56); Colin Muset, ed. Bédier, XVII *passim* (on women's venality); *Carmina Burana*, ed. Hilka and Schumann, no. 42 (Walter of Chatillon, *Utar contra vitia*), stanza 12, and no. 44 (the Gospel of the Silver Mark) *passim*; Bertran Carbonel (ed. Bartsch, *Denkmäler*, pp. 5–26; or Jeanroy, pp.137–88); coblas 13, 19, 34, 35, 57, 68 Peire Cardenal, ed. Lavaud, XLIX.13–21; Guilhem Anelier, ed. Gisi, I.23–4.

45 For the insatiability of avarice, cf. Maurice de Sully, ed. Robson, Sermon 39, 14–18 (covetousness is like hydropsy). *Le Poème moral*, ed Bayot, line 1853–4; Guiot de Provins, Bible, ed. Orr, 520; Hugo de Berzé Bible (ed. Lecoy, 76–7); Hue de Rotelande, *Ipomedon* (edd. Kölbing & Köschwitz, lines 8411–12); *Li Vers de la mort*, ed. Windahl, stanzas 96, 122, 218, 2219, 283. *Chil qui ces vers fist et trova*, a thirteenth-century *dit* in Paris, Bibliothèque nationale, Moreau 1727, fos 356r–365r, which I intend to publish soon, refers to the insatiability of avarice in lines 649–50: 'Car con plus ont, plus sont en songne / Et del aquerre et del garder.' This list could be continued almost indefinitely.

46 Compare the *Roman de la Rose*, ed. Lecoy, lines 195–234, 588, 775–862, where gloomy Avarice is excluded from the garden where Deduit dances with Leece and Cortoisie with the poet.

47 For the worries of the miser, cf. Le Poème moral, ed. Bayot, lines 1849–64; Hugo de Berzé Bible, ed. Lecoy, pp. 381–4; *Li Vers de la mort*, ed. Windahl, stanzas 188, 282, 283, 284; *Le Mireour du monde*, ed. Chavannes, p. 152; English homily on *Estote prudentes* . . . from Cambridge, Trinity College, MS. B.14.52 (ed. Morris, II.195); Peire Cardenal,

can cause the damnation of man's eternal soul (lines 30, 35). The first signal that
the poem is going to launch into religious argumentation comes in line 25, with
the words *avarice de mal racine*, the famous dictum from I Timothy vi.10.[48] Lines
32–3 are almost certainly taken from Psalm XXXIX. where we read: '. . . frustra
conturbatur, thesaurizat et ignorat cui congregabit'.[49]

Stanzas VII–IX concentrate on the separation of the body, the soul, and the
wealth of the miser at the time of his death. Though the individual components
are commonplaces, the treatment of them as an explicit threesome is relatively
uncommon.[50] By means of this device, the poet suggests that the miser's wealth is
no mere external accoutrement, but that it has become an intrinsic part of his
being: its fate concerns him at least as much as that of his body and soul. In this
poem, the wealth reverts to *le monde*, the *saeculum* which the dead man served,
whose goods he acquired, and which the poet condemned as evil at the outset of
his poem. It is pictured as a usurer (lines 44–5), a figure regarded with extreme
suspicion by the Church even at this late date, and understandably feared by the
general public.[51] In other, similar pieces, a more personal element is brought into
play: namely, the indifference of the heirs, who, far from wishing their deceased
relative were still alive, do not even spend any of the inheritance on praying for
his soul.[52] The body, on the other hand, is eaten by worms, a symbol of transience

ed. Lavaud, LIV, stanza 3; Bertran del Pojet, ed. de Lollis, no. I, 5, 13–14, 17–24; Hugo
of St Victor, *loc. cit.*; Innocent III, *ed. cit.*, Lib. I, xv; Lib. II, xvi.

[48] See Schapiro, 'From Mozarabic to Romanesque', p. 326; Little, 'Pride goes before
Avarice', for the importance of avarice on the scale of evil. Avarice appears as the root
of all evil in one of the twelfth-century homilies in Oxford, Bodleian Library, MS.
Bodley 343 (ed. Belfour, no. XIII) and in the *De octo vitiis & de duodecim abusivis, loc. cit.*
See also *Le Poème moral*, ed. Bayot, line 1856; *Le Mireour du monde*, ed. Chavannies,
pp. 136–7; Peire d'Alvernha, ed. del Monte, VI.17–18, and for a similar image,
Marcabru, ed. Dejeanne, especially line 24.

[49] It is interesting to note that in the Breviary of Philippe le Bel, Paris, Bibl. Nat., MS.
latin 1023, which dates from about the same time as the manuscripts of the *Dit
d'avarice*, this verse of the psalm (fo 21r) is accompanied by a miniature not unlike
those found at the head of our poem.

[50] Compare *Le Mireour du monde*, ed. Chavannes, p. 155: 'Le Déable emporte l'âme, les
vers la charoigne, les parens l'avoir . . . et si n'y a nul de ces trois compaignons qui sa
part donnast pour les deux autres.' A similar passage is found in the only extant 'Body
and Soul' debate in Provençal, which dates from the fourteenth century, and may well
show the influence of the *Mireour/Somme le Roi*. See the edition by Kastner, 'Débat',
lines 1069–1075. See also *Puis ke homme deit de ci partyr*, ed. Reinsch, 'Mitteilungen',
p. 76, lines 27–30, although here the 'recipients' are not personified.

[51] Usurers appear in poems such as *La Patrenostre a l'userier* and *Le Credo a l'userier* from
Paris, Bibliothèque nationale, MS. fr. 837, edd. Barbazan & Meon *Fabliaux et Contes*,
IV.99–114, or Ilvonen, *Parodies*, pp. 59–103; see also the long passage condemning
usury in Robert le Clerc, *op. cit.*, stanzas 144–162 *et passim*.

[52] Cf. Ecclesiasticus 14:3–20. Mediaeval examples include: Hugo de Berzé op. cit., 722–
772. *Corps, en toi n'a point de savoir*, ed. Bartsch, *La langue et la littérature françaises*, pp.
547–554, st. 14. *Un samedi par nuit*, ed cit., P-text 277–286 (and parallel in B).
Worcester fragments, ed. Buchholz, B, 12–13; C, 35. R. Morris, op. cit., Vol. 2, no.

which was gaining popularity in the thirteenth century and was to become even more widespread in the genre of the *danse macabre* in the following centuries.

A complete investigation of the ramifications of the 'worms'-motif would be beyond the scope of this essay, but I should like to make a few observations concerning its appearances in the literature of France and England around the time of composition of the *Dit d'avarice*.

Although motifs of transience are common in the Bible, as has been pointed out by Gilson,[53] that of the worms devouring a body occurs only two or three times, in the books of Job and Isaiah.[54] Elsewhere, worms are seen as agricultural pests or unpleasant parasites; sometimes used as images of destruction or hell. King Herod is 'eaten by worms' in Acts xii.23, but this is a rather different matter, since they attack the king while he is still alive.[55]

The Latin Fathers in their turn do not refer to worms particularly often. A noteworthy early example is Caesarius of Arles, who, in a sermon on almsgiving, exhorts his congregation to contemplate the tombs of the rich, who are now *esca vermium*.[56] The worms are found in a sermon attributed to Columbanus,[57] in the writings of Anselm[58] and in an early Latin prose version of the *Address of the Soul to the Body*[59] before appearing in the *Meditationes piissimae* long attributed to Bernard of Clairvaux but more recently ascribed to William of Tournai.[60] Innocent III includes in his *De miseria* a section on the decay of the body in which he refers to worms several times, adducing biblical quotations to support his argument.[61] They do not, however, figure in the *De vanitate mundi* of Hugh of Saint Victor, which is widely regarded as one of the greatest influences on mediaeval poetry on death and transience.[62]

The motif of the worms seems to be most widespread in England and in northern France, where it appears frequently in the vernacular, often in connex-

---

XXIX, p. 183. *Noctis sub silentio*, ed. Wright, *Walter Mapes*, pp. 95–106, lines 68–71. Uc de l'Escura, *De mots ricos*, ed. Jeanroy, pp. 477–80.

53   Gilson, *Les idées et les lettres*, pp. 9–38.

54   The only two verses which are close to our theme are Job 21:26, on Death the Leveller, and Is. 14:11 prophesying the downfall of the King of Babylon. See also Job 17:14. It is interesting that MS. A should contain a French paraphrase of the Book of Job (fo 166r), but the two facts are probably connected only by the taste of the compiler of that manuscript.

55   This incident appears in the *Carmina Burana* Christmas Play (*ed. cit.*, 227): 'Postea Herodes corrodatur a uermibus'. Compare the belief that worms around one's heart could cause sudden death, quoted from a thirteenth-century sermon by F&B, II.277n.

56   Caesarius of Arles, ed. G. Morin, in Corpus Christianorum, CIII, pp.135–136 (Sermo XXXI).

57   P.L. 80, 237–238.

58   P.L. 158, 720.

59   ed. Batiouchkof, 'Le débat' text printed on pp. 576–578, and reproduced by J. Zupitza, 'Zu Seele und Leib', and Dudley, 'An early homily'.

60   P.L. 184, 489–492. See also (attrib.) Helinandus, *De cognitione sui*, in P.L. 212, 721–35, especially Cap. IX (col. 730).

61   Innocent III, *ed. cit.*, Lib. III, iv.

62   P.L. 176, 706–40.

ion with the 'Body and Soul' theme. In particular, it is found in numerous Old English pieces, in manuscripts dating back as far as that of the tenth-century Vercelli Homilies.[63] It has been suggested by J. E. Cross that a number of such motifs derive ultimately from the sermon by Caesarius of Arles we have mentioned,[64] possibly by way of the *Ad fratres in eremo* sermons, of whose provenance, however, we know nothing.[65] What is quite clear is that Old English poets seized upon the 'worms'-motif and others like it with considerable enthusiasm,[66] and that later English poems on death, as Eleanor Heningham points out, drew from their works concrete elements which only rarely occur in early Latin works.[67]

In twelfth-century England, two passages in *Vices and Virtues* warn of the fate of the body,[68] and a similar warning appears in Guischard de Beaulieu's Anglo-Norman *Sermon*.[69] A twelfth-century homily for St Andrew's day from Cambridge, Trinity College, MS. B.14.52 shows the soul consigning the body it has just left to the chewing of the worms.[70] The worms appear in the twelfth-century Worcester 'Body and Soul'-fragments and in subsequent Middle English and Anglo-Norman treatments of the 'Body and Soul'-debate.[71] It is interesting to note that most of the earlier versions of this debate seem to be of Insular origin.[72] Several thirteenth-century English lyrics also contain the 'worms'-motif,[73] as do at least two Latin poems which very probably originated in England.[74] Finally, we should mention the occurrences of the 'worms'-motif in the Anglo-Norman verse sermon *Oyez, Seigneurs, sermun*, which its editor dates to shortly before

---

[63] *Die Vercelli-Homilien*, ed. Förster, no. IV (pp. 85 and 97).
[64] Cross, '*The dry bones speak*', especially p. 434.
[65] See Dudley, especially pp. 225–226.
[66] See for example the following pieces: *Angelsächsische Homilien und Heiligenleben*, ed. Assmann, no. XIV, 29, 40–42. *The Blickling Homilies*, ed. Morris (EETS o.s. 73), VII (pp. 99–101) and X (pp. 111–113). Napier, *Wulfstan*, XXIX (pp. 139–141) (also printed by Dudley, *loc. cit.*), XXX (p. 145), XL, (p.187), XLVI (p. 240).
[67] Heningham, 'Old English precursors', especially 299n.
[68] ed. Holthausen (EETS o.s. 89), pp. 63, 137.
[69] ed. Gabrielson, laisse 4.
[70] ed. Morris, II.183, no. XXIX, p. 183.
[71] For bibliographical information on the 'Body and Soul' debate, see especially Woolf, *The English Religious Lyric in the Middle Ages*, pp. 89–102. Texts include: Worcester fragments, *ed. cit.*, B, 41; C, 28, 38–50; D, 1, 24; Oxford fragment (*ibid.*) 16. *Un samedi par nuit*, ed cit., P-text 428–438 (and parallels in B and C). *Þe desputisoun bitwen þe bodi and þe soule*, ed. Linow, lines 54, 86, 165.
[72] See the list given by Wright, pp. 321–4.
[73] See Brown, *English Lyrics of the XIIIth Century*, 10A, 34; 10B, 34; 19, 36; 20, 21; 29A, 47; 30, 4; 51, 48.
[74] See *Cur mundus militat*, in *Oxford Book of Medieval Latin Verse*, ed. Raby, 284, which appears in the *Summa Iustitiae* attributed to Grosseteste, and contains the phrase 'O esca vermium!' Woolf, *The English Religious Lyric*, p. 91, classed *Noctis sub silentio* (see ed. cit., 174, 217 for our motif) as a twelfth-century Anglo-Latin piece, along with *Nuper huiuscemodi uisionem somnii*, the edition of which I have not been able to consult, but which probably also makes reference to the worms if, as Woolf states, *Un samedi par nuit* is a translation of it.

1250,[75] and *Le Besant de Dieu* (1226/7) by Guillaume le Clerc, who undoubtedly spent much of his life in England but was also influenced greatly by the *De miseria* of Innocent III.[76]

Worms appear in Old French literature not only in 'Body and Soul'-poems,[77] but especially too in the various versions of the *Dit des trois morts et des trois vifs*,[78] which appeared late in the thirteenth century, and has been shown by Rotzler to have originated in France rather than in England as had been previously supposed.[79] The late twelfth-century poem *Miserere* by the Renclus de Moiliens refers to worms in st. 20, 10–12, and they also appear briefly in the Walloon *Poème moral* (ca 1200), and in works by Robert le Clerc and Rutebeuf;[80] but in general the worms do not seem to feature as prominently in France as they do in England, being absent from the works of poets such as Hélinant, Hugo de Berzé, and Guiot de Provins. In Provençal literature the incidence of the 'worms'-motif is even lower. There are only two explicit mentions of them: namely, Peire Cardenal's line 'E-l cors es sai vianda dels lonbrix',[81] and Sordello's 'E ses aver serem de verms pastura',[82] both dating from the thirteenth century. Other forms of the theme of transience are by no means uncommon in Provençal poetry, but lurid descriptions of corpses or of hell-fire do not seem to have enjoyed the same popularity in southern France as they did further north.[83]

While bearing in mind Rotzler's caveat concerning the uncertain origins of mediaeval 'transience'-topoi,[84] it appears highly probably in the light of this evidence that the motif of the worms could have passed from Old and Middle English literature into the vernacular literature of northern France by way of the Anglo-Norman tradition, rather than being independently extracted from Latin sources by poets in France.

Returning to our text, the poet moves on from the three-part division of the body, soul, and wealth to focus on the fate of the soul, whose eternal torments are presented in the very physical imagery of filth, decay, hunger and thirst, as was

[75] Tanquerey, *Deux Poèmes moraux anglo-français*. See *Sermon*, 1183–94.
[76] ed. Ruelle: see pp. 8–9 for references to England; and lines 181–2 and 343–48 for the worms.
[77] Though *Un samedi par nuit* and most other 'Body and Soul' poems contain the 'worms' motif, *Cors en toi n'a point de savoir* does not.
[78] See for example Baudouin de Condé, *ed. cit.*, XVII, 12, 19–21; Anon. III (see Rotzler, *Die Begegnung*, p. 35); Anon. V (long version) (*ibid.*, p. 40).
[79] *Ibid.*, p. 45.
[80] *Le Poème Moral, ed. cit.*, 1718; Robert le Clerc, *op. cit.*, st. 117, 12; Rutebeuf, ed. F&B, XLVII, 25–26. See also Baudouin de Condé, *ed. cit.*, XI, 19–32; XVII, 12, 19–21; *Moult est cil fous ke trop se fie* ed. Reinsch, op. cit., pp. 59–61, lines 54, 61–2, 81, 104–106; *Le Mireour du monde, ed. cit.*, p. 155; '*Le Miroir de Vie et de Mort* par Robert de l'Omme (1266)', ed. Långfors, especially 2nd prologue, 12, and Text, 595–8.
[81] Peire Cardenal, *ed. cit.*, LII, 35.
[82] ed. Boni, XXI, 44.
[83] A description of hell exists in Provençal (see Bartsch, *Denkmäler*, pp. 310–14), but such pieces are very rare. We have already mentioned that the only extant 'Body and Soul' poem in Provençal dates from the fourteenth century.
[84] Rotzler, *Die Begegnung*, p. 15.

usual at this period.[85] In the thirteenth century this argument is even more widespread than that of the decay of the body and is used in almost every poem warning against vice. In twelfth- and thirteenth-century French sculptures, devils, serpents, and other beasts are usually shown tormenting the dead sinner's soul after the Last Judgment;[86] skeletons and corpses do not appear until a later date.

In stanza XII, we return from the otherworld to the present life, and to the generally wicked state of the world condemned at the opening of the poem. In particular, this passage connects with the opening of stanza III: everybody desires wealth. The entire poem up to this point is, as it were, summed up in this stanza, and in particular in the epigrammatic line *avoir et aver porrira*, which suggests in the word-play *avoir–aver* the close identification of the miser with his money, and alludes at once to the corruptibility both of earthly treasure (as in Matthew vi.19–21), and of the body of its owner.

The next stanza (XIII) takes the reader by surprise with its sudden emphasis on the lot of the minstrels, coming as it does after the very general criticisms of society voiced in the poem up to this point. The use of *sermonner* referring to the activity of the *menestrels* is felicitous, in that it succeeds in conveying a sense both of moral authority on their part and of boredom or resentment on that of the listeners.[87] It becomes clear that the poet, far from being an ascetically minded moralist, prophesying doom for a sinful world, is motivated largely by self-interest, or at least by strong personal feelings. The abrupt close of the poem just when some specific accusations of society might be expected, leaves the modern reader somewhat disappointed, but the poet obviously feels he has said as much as is necessary or expedient.

Rather than being a true 'sermon', examining the evils of the world and attempting to suggest a cure – as do, for example, the poems of Baudouin de Condé, the *Sermon* by Peire Cardenal[88] or Hélinant's *Vers de la mort* the *Dit d'avarice* uses the language of asceticism in order to express an individual's bitterness about the state of the world and, especially, his lot as a poet. He has a jaundiced view of the rich, and identifies with the poor man who is ignored and the minstrel who is told to try his luck elsewhere. The rhetoric is not really that of the preacher aiming to make converts, but that of an invective or threat. It seems unlikely that the writer expects to elicit any payment from his audience by

---

[85] See for example *Thibaut de Marly, Les Vers*, ed. Stone, *passim*, and Robert le Clerc, *ed. cit.*, stanzas 2, 10, 216, 257.

[86] Sculptures at Aulnay (Charente-Maritime), Blars (Lot), Chanteuges (Haute-Loire) and Conques (Aveyron) show various beasts (lions, snakes, dragons) tormenting the soul of the miser. Numerous others show devils as the torturers; see for examples the list given by Bréhier, 'La sculpture romane en Auvergne', especially p. 395.

[87] Tobler-Lommatzsch gives the meanings of 'predigen' or 'schwatzen', and Godefroy 'prêcher' and 'discourir'.

[88] Peire Cardenal, *ed. cit.*, LV.

means of this poem, but rather that he is dwelling on the futility of the rich man's life-style and the horrible nature of his future punishment as a parting-shot.

AUTHORSHIP

MSS. A and B were both used by Auguste Scheler in editing the works of Baudouin and Jean de Condé, although his principal manuscripts were Paris, Bibliothèque de l'Arsenal, MS.3524 (then Belles-Lettres 317) and Brussels, Bibliothèque royale, MS. 9411–9426, neither of which contains the Dit d'avarice.[89] Scheler also refers to several other manuscripts, but the Dit d'avarice is not mentioned in the published descriptions of any of them.

However, because of the position of the Dit d'avarice among works by Baudouin de Condé, especially in BN fr. 12467, it is necessary to consider whether this piece too could be attributed to Baudouin. The theme of avarice is quite widespread in Baudouin's works, and the religious and moralising tone of the piece seems, at least on a first reading, to be similar to that found in poems by Baudouin.[90] On closer inspection, though, the treatments of the theme are so different as almost to exclude the possibility of Baudouin's authorship of the Dit d'avarice.

It has been noted that the form of the Dit d'avarice is related to the twelve-line strophe of two of Baudouin's dits, but since this form is widely used from the twelfth century onwards, it cannot be argued from this similarity that the Dit d'avarice need be connected with Baudouin de Condé or his school. Finally, one must bear in mind that almost all of Baudouin de Condé's recognised poems bear his name in at least one manuscript, and that many of them contain his 'signature' in the text itself. There does not, therefore, seem at present to be sufficient evidence to justify the suggested attribution of the Dit d'avarice to Baudouin de Condé.

It is, however, possible that the poem may come from the Artois, since there are many parallels with Robert le Clerc's Vers de la mort, especially in lines 31–6, which share the rhyme-words amasse, lasse, trespasse with Robert's stanza XLVII:

> Mors tient por fiens quanqu'on amasse.
> Car, s'aucuns a de vie espasse,
> N'i puet il lonc tans demorer.
> Dont est mout fols qui plus se lasse
> Por aquerre avoir qui trespasse
> Dont l'ame estuet sans fin plorer.

---

[89] Scheler, op. cit., I.xxv–xxviii.
[90] See, for example, ed. cit., nos I, III, XVI.

See also the next stanza of Robert's poem, which contains the lines:

> Bien se doit clamer ame lasse
> Qui compre çou qu'avers amasse
> Quant infer l'en estuet avoir.

Other parallels with Robert include the topoi of decline of the world, of the insatiability of the miser, of the worries of the rich man, and of the worms eating the body, which we have seen above.

The *Dit d'avarice* may possibly be linked with the school of Rutebeuf. The use of the language of the Ile-de-France, though only a very weak indicator at this period, at least does not contradict this theory. More importantly, as Faral and Bastin point out, the *Dit d'avarice* shares two pairs of lines with the poem by Rutebeuf *Por ce que li mondes se change*, though in both cases the order of the couplet is reversed.[91] There is another close parallel with Rutebeuf in lines 2 and 5 of the *Dit*, which echo *La voie de Tunes*, a crusade-poem drawing heavily on the themes of transience:[92]

> Li mauvais demorront, nes couvient pas eslire
> Et s'il sunt *hui mauvais*, il seront *demain pire*
> De jour en jour iront *de roiaume en empire*.

The *Dit d'avarice* lacks the topicality of Rutebeuf's writing, and is probably to be considered the later of the two poems.

---

[91] F&B, I.384n and 388n. Lines 70–71 of the *Dit d'avarice* are the same as Rutebeuf, ed. F&B, XVII, 21–22; and *Dit*, lines 73–74 correspond to Rutebeuf XVII, 157–8.
[92] XXV.129–31. My italics.

Understanding and misunderstanding in *La Male Honte*

A. E. COBBY

While many old French fabliaux survive in Anglo-Norman manuscripts,[1] only three explicitly connect their action to the British Isles, and each of these plays with language. *Les Deux Angloys et l'Anel*[2] pokes fun at the French spoken by two Englishmen, whose accent causes them to be given a donkey (*asnel*) to eat instead of a lamb (*agnel*) and provokes much mirth along the way. *Le Roi d'Angleterre et le Jongleur d'Ely*[3] prefaces its defence of jongleurs with an exchange in which the jongleur deliberately misunderstands each of the king's questions. He takes the king's words in the most literal sense and thereby thwarts each attempt to learn facts about him:

> – Dont estez vus? ditez saunz gyle.
> – Sire, je su de nostre vile.
> – Où est vostre vile, daunz Jogler?
> – Sire, entour le moster.
> – Où est le moster, bel amy?
> – Sire, en la vile de Ely.
> – Où est Ely qy siet?
> – Sire, sur l'ewe estiet.
> – Quei est le eve apelé, par amours?
> – L'em ne l'apele pas, eynz vint tousjours
> Volenters par son eyndegré,
> Que ja n'estovera estre apelée.   (43–54)

At the same time the king is made to look stupid, for when he complains,

> – Tot ce savoi je bien avaunt,

---

[1] According to the corpus of Nykrog, *Les Fabliaux*, pp. 311–24. The *Nouveau recueil complet des fabliaux*, edd. Noomen and van den Boogaard (hereafter NRCF) omits *Le Roi d'Angleterre et le Jongleur d'Ely*.

[2] *Recueil général et complet des fabliaux des XIIIᵉ et XIVᵉ siècles*, edd. Montaiglon & Raynaud (hereafter MR), II.178; *Twelve Fabliaux*, ed. Reid, p. 11.

[3] MR, II.242.

the jongleur retorts,

> – Don qe demandez com enfant?   (55–6)

This text shows the potential for humour of a situation where speakers refuse to agree on the meaning of words and of phrases, and use words to block communication. But, like *Les Deux Angloys*, it does not develop this potential, presenting no more than a joke which is neither subtle nor particularly funny. It is, however, noteworthy that both tales link Englishness with misunderstanding, be it deliberate or unwitting.

The fabliau of *La Male Honte*[4] builds a much more substantial joke upon a similar theme. It tells how an Englishman named Honte dies and, according to custom, leaves his wealth, in a bag – *une male*[5] – to the king. When his friend takes the bag to court, the king thinks he is having shame wished upon him and will none of it. The fabliau recounts at length the misunderstanding between the two, which persists until a courtier succeeds in breaking the deadlock. It ends with a satirical point which, depending on the version, attributes shame to the king, to the English, or to *vilains*.

The text survives in two versions, one signed 'Guillaume', the other attributed in one of its three manuscripts to Huon de Cambrai;[6] the relationship between the two is the subject of disagreement. Previous comparison of the two versions has been based on consideration of common verses and of details of the plot;[7] I propose here to analyse the authors' use of the ambiguous phrase *la male honte*, showing how our understanding of the phrase is regulated as the misunderstanding between the protagonists progresses.

---

4   Edited several times: *Fabliaux et contes*, ed. Barbazan & Méon, III.204 and 210; MR IV.95 and V.95; *Huon le Roi, [etc.]*, ed. Långfors; *Fabliaux*, edd. Johnston & Owen, p. 51 (Guillaume's version); Rychner, *Contribution*, II.16; and forthcoming in NRCF, vol. V. My discussion will use Rychner's edition, which prints in parallel Långfors's text of Guillaume (based on Paris, Bibliothèque nationale, MS. fr. 2173 with emendations from Paris, Bibliothèque nationale, MS. fr. 19152) and editions of the three manuscripts of Huon, Paris, Bibliothèque nationale, MSS. fr. 837 (A) and fr. 12603 (F), and Bern, Burgerbibliothek, MS. 354 (B). The text, though much edited, is little studied; the only analyses of any length are Rychner, *Contribution*, I.21–8, and Spencer, 'The *courtois* – *vilain* nexus'.
5   Tobler-Lommatzsch, *Altfranzösisches Wörterbuch*, s.v., glosses the word as 'Mantelsack, Felleisen, Koffer'. A drawing in MS. fr. 2173, fo 93c, depicts a man carrying on his shoulder what is clearly a small trunk; but, as both versions of the fabliau state that the *male* is hung (*qui la pent*, Guillaume 17; from the *villain's* neck, Huon A 28, 135, B 119, F 109), 'bag' is clearly the better sense.
6   Whether this Huon is to be identified with Huon le Roi (de Cambrai) is uncertain: see *Huon le Roi [etc.]*, ed. Långfors, pp. xiii–xv. I speak for convenience of 'Huon's version' even though only MS. A attributes the text to him. Similarly, when I speak of 'Guillaume' I do not mean to imply that the extant fabliau is necessarily identical with the original of this version.
7   *Huon le Roi [etc.]*, ed. Långfors, pp. xii–xiii; Rychner, *Contribution*, I.21–8.

Guillaume's version opens with a clear and separate presentation of the two elements, *la male* and *Honte*.

> Uns preudons morust qu'ot non Honte:
> Honte ert li preudom apelez.
> Quant vint qu'il fu si adolez
> Et que il vit qu'il ne vivra,
> Un sien compere en apela:
> 'Comperes, dist Honte, prenez
> Mon avoir, que vos la veez,
> En cele male qui la pent.'
> . . .
> Honte mourut de cel malage.   (10–17, 25)

That Honte is a man's name is forced home by repetition, and the physical reality of the bag is impressed upon us by the use of the demonstrative *cele* and by the vivid *qui la pent*. Accordingly, when we hear

> Maintenant prent la male Honte,   (27)

there can be no doubt in our mind that this is Honte's bag – an interpretation supported by the verb *prent*. It is important that the audience should be given a firm grasp of this concrete sense, for it is not the only meaning of the phrase. *La male honte* is also an idiomatic formula of Old French, meaning 'foul shame',[8] and this is how the king will understand it. He is so used to hearing the phrase as a unit, with one meaning only, that he cannot analyse it and see that it could bear a different interpretation: he is conditioned to take it as a formula. The audience too is familiar with the usual, formulaic sense; it is therefore essential that the local, literal meaning be put very firmly before us, lest our pre-existing linguistic knowledge blind us as it blinds the king.

When the *vilain* arrives at court the phrase becomes a formula of another kind. Now it is he who becomes so accustomed to using it as a unit having only one sense that he cannot conceive of its having a different meaning; nor does it occur to him to separate its elements, or that others could understand it differently from himself. For him, *la male Honte* means 'Honte's bag' as unambiguously as it means 'foul shame' for the king. For the audience to appreciate this, the essential ambiguity of the phrase must be carefully maintained. This is achieved at the expense of some unnaturalness in the *vilain*'s speech:

> Sire, fait il en son language,
> La male Honte vos aport:
> Ge li oi couvent a sa mort
> La male Honte vos donroie.
> Prenez la qu'il la vos envoie:
> Sire, prenés la male Honte!   (34–9)

---

8   Spencer believes this translation is insufficiently strong ('The *courtois-vilain* nexus', p. 291, n. 21). The precise meaning is not important for the present discussion.

He encourages the king's misinterpretation by his inarticulateness: he uses the phrase three times in five lines, without once explaining who Honte was, and he does not disjoin the formula even when the result sounds forced (for example, in line 37 *sa male* or *la* would sound more natural). We thus have put before us, simultaneously and repeatedly, the form of words which we know from the common formula meaning 'foul shame', and the concrete sense 'Honte's bag'.

The king does not for a moment doubt that the phrase is the formula he knows and that the *vilain* is wishing shame upon him. His conditioning is so strong that he disregards the words *aport, donroie, envoie, prenez*, all of which would suggest a physical entity. He hears only the phrase *la male honte*, and he responds to it in a way which shows clearly the sense he is giving to it, speaking of *honte* unambiguously and without a qualifier:

> Mais tu aies honte touz diz!
> De honte me puist Deus desfendre!   (42–3)

The misunderstanding is now clearly established; each speaker is entrenched in his own interpretation of the phrase, whilst we can see both points of view.

The formula is not again disjoined until the confusion begins to be resolved; before that it is used many times, and often ambiguously. The *vilain* next uses the formula in soliloquy, together with unequivocal references to Honte and his wealth:

> Ha las! fait il, or me recort
> Que mes comperes me proia,
> Quant il mourut et defina,
> Que cest avoir au roi donasse;
> Volentiers encore i parlasse
> Et donroie la male Honte,
> . . .
> Encor serai ge si estouz
> Que li donrai la male Honte.   (52–7, 64–5)

He again attempts to give the bag to the king, and this time stresses the physical nature of his gift as plainly as he can:

> Sire, sire, la male Honte
> Vos raport ge encore et offre:
> D'esterlins i a plain un cofre.   (72–4)

Yet still he does not disjoin the formula, showing that he is as far as the king from seeing that there is an alternative interpretation of his words. The king for his part is so set in his own formulaic understanding of the phrase that he does not even notice the physical description; prejudice triumphs over evidence.

The next occurrences of the phrase are spoken by the narrator as he represents the king's reaction. They show a subtle ambiguity, both supporting our knowledge of the facts and conveying the king's misapprehension:

> Del vilain a tel duel et ire,
> Qui la male Honte li baille   (78–9)

> Dou roi qui vers lui s'aïroit
> Quant li offroit la male Honte.   (90–1)

Then the balance is tipped towards the concrete meaning again in preparation for the *vilain*'s third attempt:

> Li vilains revint touz chargiez
> De la male Honte qu'il porte.   (100–1)

Once more he repeats the phrase, no fewer than four times:

> Sire, sire, la male Honte,
> Fait li preudons, quar recevez,
> Car par droit avoir la devez.
> La male Honte vos remaigne,
> S'en donnez a vostre compaigne.
> La male Honte est grans et lee,
> Si la vos ai ci aportee.
> Uns miens comperes, ce sachiés,
> La vos envoie et vos l'aiés,
> Car vos d'Engleterre estes rois:
> La male Honte aiés, c'est drois.   (104–14)

Line 109 is unambiguously physical; in combination with the actual presence of the bag, this should lead any hearer to consider the possibility that there is more to the phrase than its formulaic meaning. The other three references to *la male Honte*, however, are more abstract than in any other of the *vilain*'s speeches, so that the balance between the two senses is now as total as the misunderstanding between the protagonists.

The failure of communication is so complete that it can only be remedied by the intervention of a third party, who uses the phrase with perfect ambiguity:

> Sachiés que est la male honte.   (127)

The king takes up this ambiguity, asking the *vilain*:

> Que dis tu de la male honte?   (131)

Now at last the *vilain* explains – we may assume – clearly, speaking of Honte alone and identifying him openly:

> Dont li conte cil et devise
> Com la male Honte ot emprise

> Et com Honte, ses bons compere,
> Li pria par l'ame sa mere
> Qu'aprés sa mort li aportast.   (135–9)

It is now the king's turn to use the formula:

> Or te doins ge a bele chiere
> La male Honte a ta partie,
> Car par droit l'as bien deservie,   (146–8)

and the narrator confirms:

> Ainsint ot cil la male Honte.   (149)

An epilogue both reasserts the ambiguity and finally disjoins the formula completely:

> Ce dist Guillaumes en son conte
> Que li vilains en a portee
> La male Honte en sa contree,
> Si l'a aus Englés departie.
> Encore en ont il grant partie:
> Sans la male ont il asez honte
> Et chascun jor lor croist et monte.
> Par mavés seignor et par lache
> Les a la honte pris en tache.[9]   (150–8)

In its attempt to extract a jibe from the formula, this whole passage (from line 146) is forced; the king fails to see the ambiguity of his words, completely forgetting his previous understanding of the formula (there is no sense that he is cursing the *vilain* here), and the narrator says first that the English have the bag, then that they have shame without it. We shall return to this point after discussing Huon's version of the fabliau.

Before we turn to this, the ambiguous uses of *la male honte* at the point of resolution deserve attention. In these lines (127, 131) there is no presupposition as to the meaning of the phrase; that is their point. In view of this it is interesting that in both cases (and they are separated by only one couplet, so that attention is drawn to the phenomenon) the phrase is at the rhyme, and that it rhymes with *honte*, used without the article and definitely meaning 'shame':

> Mes ençois que li faciez honte   (128)

> Tu m'en avras fait mainte honte.   (132)

The word *honte* was last used alone during the establishment of the confusion whose resolution is announced in this passage (40–3). In one of its occurrences

---

[9]   BN fr. 19152: *Les a honte mis en s'ataiche* (*Huon le Roi [etc.]*, ed. Långfors, p. 64).

there (*si a grant honte*, 40) it again rhymes with *la male Honte*, this time spoken by the *vilain*: this rhyme forms a transition between his first speech, which presents the concrete meaning of the formula, and that of the king, who twice uses the word *honte* meaning 'shame'. These rhymes suggest at first sight that the rhyme-words are not synonymous, but form a *rime équivoque*.[10] This would encourage one to read *la male Honte* in all three cases, and would thus undermine the balance in the words of the king and the courtier. To test this hypothesis on a similar work the fabliau of *Estormi* was examined, and found to have many rich rhymes and equivocal rhymes.[11] A number of the latter, however, are not technically *rimes équivoques*, but rather use the same word twice in the same sense, with one or both instances being part of an idiom or a common formula of the language. Thus, for example,

> L'un aprés l'autre,
> qu'ainc n'en sot mot li uns de l'autre,   (85–6)

n'en sot mot: sanz dire mot (173–4), *ce poise mi: d'entor mi* (323–4). This would suggest that such formulas function at the rhyme in the same way as compound words, to which they are indeed comparable in that they have a fixed form and make one semantic unit. It seems, then, that the rhyme *la male honte: honte* is as valid as *la male Honte: honte*, and the ambiguity required by the resolution scene is maintained.

Guillaume's version of the fabliau, then, shows a careful regulation of understanding and ambiguity. The audience's pre-existing linguistic knowledge is tempered by a vivid presentation of the literal meaning of the phrase *la male Honte*; throughout the misunderstanding between the *vilain* and the king the formula is always used as a unit; resolution proceeds from a point of perfect ambiguity; and only at the end does the author himself appear confused. There are only a few moments of unnaturalness in direct speech, and everything is concentrated upon the pun: circumstantial narration is kept to a minimum, and the longest interval between occurrences of the formula is seventeen lines (40–56). There is thus little to distract attention from the point of the fabliau, and the conflicting demands of obscurity for the protagonists and clarity for the audience are carefully managed.

Huon's version is by no means as skilful. It does not, as does Guillaume's, confine disjunction of the formula to the beginning and end of the fabliau, but uses the separate elements also during the period of misunderstanding. Balance is not

---

[10] Elwert, *Traité de versification*, § 28, writes of the *rime du même au même*: 'on ne la rencontre qu'assez rarement chez les poètes du Moyen Age, sans que pour autant elle ait été évitée ou interdite'.

[11] *Fabliaux français du moyen âge*, ed. Ménard, I.29; also in MR, I.198, and NRCF, I.1. Of the first hundred couplets (a passage of comparable length to *La Male Honte*) sixty-nine have rich rhymes, while the complete text of 630 lines contains twenty-nine equivocal rhymes (many more if compound words such as *enfoui: foui* (429–30) are included).

maintained between the two senses: though the king sees only one meaning, the *vilain*'s words are designed to express both, and plausibility is damaged by the resulting confusion.[12] Nor is the inherent ambiguity of the phrase played upon so effectively. It is as if someone were retelling a joke he had heard, without the care which comes from constructing *ex nihilo*. The following discussion will be based on MS. F, with significant divergences in the other manuscripts noted in their place.[13]

Like Guillaume's version, Huon's opens with an exposition conveying the custom of leaving wealth to the king and the identity of Honte:

> Del vilain dont je di le conte
> On l'apeloit un [sic] païs Honte.   (9–10)

MS. B, like Guillaume, stresses the name by repetition, a useful insurance against inattention or mishearing, which would be disastrous. It also has a line with no parallel elsewhere, which makes a witty point out of a formulaic opening:

> Saignor, vos qui honte cremez,
> A cest fablel bien entendez.   (1–2)

In this way the two meanings of *honte* are established very early, and by a means not found in any of the other texts.

The physical reality of the bag is next made clear, and its role in the story:

> Parti en .II. pars son avoir:
> Ce que li rois en doit avoir
> A mis en une soie male.
> Cil qui le vis ot taint et pale
> Si le querqua un sien compere,
> Sor Dieu et sour l'ame son pere,
> Que presenter l'alast au roi,
> Que s'ame ne fust en desroi.
> Quant cil fu mors, si s'en tourna,
> La male prist, si le carcha,
> Dessi a Londres ne s'areste,
> La u li rois tenoit sa fieste.
> Au mieus qu'il pot entre en la sale
> Et a son col porte la male,
> Qui molt estoit grande et velue.   (13–27)[14]

---

[12] Cf. Rychner, *Contribution*, I.26–7. Rychner attributes the desire for ambiguity to the *vilain* ('qui, visiblement, connaît le double sens de *male honte* et en use', p. 27). Since he has no motive for doing so, and a strong disincentive, namely being beaten, I would see this as being rather the intention of the author.

[13] Neither Lǎngfors nor Rychner offers a conclusion as to the relation between the manuscripts; they both tend to see them as representing three different traditions (*Huon le Roi [etc.]*, ed. Lǎngfors, p. x; Rychner, *Contribution*, I.23).

[14] v. 26 supplied from B; missing in F.

The *vilain*'s first speech conforms to that in Guillaume by mentioning *la male Honte* three times (twice in MS. A, which omits the last two lines):

> Rois, je t'aport la male Honte;
> La male Honte recevés,
> Que par droit avoir le devés.
> Par saint Thumas le boin martir,
> Jel vous ai fait si bien partir
> Que je cuit que vous en aiés
> Le plus, si ne vous esmaiiés:
> La male Honte est grans et lee
> Que je vous ai chi aportee!   (30–8)

The speech is, however, much less finely tuned. The *vilain* is still less articulate than Guillaume's; he does not even make the confused allusion to his dead friend, *ge li oi couvent*. His first words are ambiguous, but the last couplet is distinctly unfortunate at this point, for it expresses the concrete meaning far too clearly. Conditioned as the king is to take the words in their formulaic sense, he could hardly cling to his interpretation after hearing this.

The king's response, too, is less subtle than in Guillaume. His words, as they must, make his interpretation clear, but instead of returning shame to the *vilain* he simply rejects the gift:

> Donner me volés trop malvais mes,
> Qui male honte me promés.   (43–4)[15]

The *vilain* now removes *la male Honte* (53) and vows he will not leave until the king has taken it, using the phrase even in reported soliloquy (59). Here MS. B adds a reference to *la male* alone, which weakens the passage by disjoining the formula prematurely, adding an unnecessary clarification where potential ambiguity is all-important.

The *vilain*'s second speech shows a better balance, being perfectly ambiguous:

> La male Honte encor t'atent;
> Si ne me voeil de chi mouvoir
> Si l'aiés faite rechevoir.
> La male Honte par raison
> Doit demourer en vo maison.   (78–82)

But this should have preceded the excessive clarity of the physical description *grans et lee*, as Guillaume's more abstract first speech precedes the concrete detail

---

[15] v. 43 supplied from B; corrupt in F.
[16] From v. 81 (A and F). Rychner believes the omission is deliberate (*Contribution*, 1.22), whereas Långfors (*Huon le Roi [etc.]*, p. xi) thinks it is accidental and that A in other respects represents the original; Rychner's argument on the grounds of coherence is convincing.

in the second, *d'esterlins i a plain un cofre*. At this point A omits an episode.[16] MSS. F and B continue with another soliloquy by the *vilain*:

> Mar vi, fait il, la male Honte,
> Tant en avrai anui et honte.
> Cis mauvais rois que me demande,
> Que si laidengier me commande
> Et molt est grans et plains de visces?
> Mes par saint Jaque de Galice,
> S'il ne reçoit demain la male
> N'en orai mais parole male
> Ne plus ne l'en ferai proiiere,
> Ains m'en retournerai arriere.   (95–104)[17]

This speech makes the *vilain* seem wilfully and incomprehensibly obtuse in his dealings with the king: incomprehensibly, because he has twice been beaten for failing to disjoin the formula. He proves here not only that he can do so but that he knows the meaning of the common noun *honte* and of the adjective *male*. The polysemy of the latter word is pointed up (in F only) by the rhyme, while the rhyming together of *la male Honte* and *honte* stresses the proximity of the two uses, and the man's blindness to the implications.

This is the only instance in Huon of this rhyme, and it has none of the subtlety of those in Guillaume; it neither contributes to ambiguity nor marks any kind of transition. For the *vilain* does not gain insight from his words. He sets off again with the bag:

> La male Honte a son col pent,   (109)

and once more speaks to the king:

> Si vous aport a boine estrine
> La male Honte – et puis l'encline.
> Ne voeil vers vous de riens mesprendre:
> Tost me feriés ardoir u pendre
> U revancier tout men linage.
> Si aimme mieus en mon corage
> Que vous la male Honte aiiés
> Que mors en fuisse ne plaiiés.
> La male Honte vous remaingne,
> Sel departés a vo compaingne
> Et as chevaliers de vo table.   (121–31)[18]

Again, the speech is badly judged. On the one hand the king can hardly fail to see the reality of the bag which is being pointed out to him (*et puis l'encline*). On the other, the *vilain* persists in using the fixed phrase and abstract language, as if

[17] v. 100 supplied from B; missing in F.
[18] A rejoins FB at v. 129.

he were deliberately forgoing the obvious means of clarification. The poet's desire for ambiguity has led him to forget to motivate the misunderstanding.

The impression of wilfulness on the part of the *vilain* is enhanced by the following scene. After a long interlude,[19] which contains no uses of the formula but slackens the pace and defers the dénouement, the *vilain* is asked for an explanation. With one last repetition of his refrain, he obliges:

> Sire, fait il, la male Honte
> Vous aport chi plaine d'avoir,
> Si m'en devés boin gré savoir.
> En la tere de Cantorbile
> Mest uns vos hons a une ville;
> Ja ne vous ert ses nons celés:
> Honte ert el paiis apelés.
> Quant gisoit el lit mortel,
> Si me manda a son ostel
> Pour che, biaus sire, que je ere
> Et ses amis et ses comperes.
> Si parti son avoir par mi:
> Vostre part vous envoiie chi
> En une male qui fu soiie.
> N'ai mais talant en vo court voise:
> Tant i m'an batu le dos [sic]
> Que tous en ai froissié les os.
> Or recevés la male Honte,
> Sire, tenés de l'avoir vo conte.
> La raison vous ai descouverte.   (166–85)

MS. B ends slightly differently:

> Veez ici la male Honte,
> Ne ne tenez de ce nul conte.
> La male Honte aiez en chief,
> Que vos n'en doignois ja relief;
> La raison vos ai descoverte.   (181–5)

There is no verisimilitude in this *volte-face*, unless we are to believe that the *vilain* was deliberately playing a joke on the king. This interpretation might be supported by the words *ja ne vous ert ses nons celés*, a formula familiar from the romance, where it signifies openness and honesty.[20] Here it seems plainly ironic, since the point of the preceding 170 lines is precisely the concealment of this name. But the motivation is poor whichever way we look at it. If the *vilain* has indeed been deliberately tricking the king, his action is unexplained and inex-

---

[19] Thirty-six lines in F (130–65).
[20] For example, Chrétien de Troyes, *Le Roman de Perceval*, ed. Roach, line 8831. Further comparable examples are given in Tobler-Lommatzsch, *Altfranzösisches Wörterbuch*, s.v. *celer*.

plicable. If, as is more likely, the author has merely been using him to express both meanings of *la male honte*, his obtuseness and his ability to explain alike make no sense. Like that of the courtier which precedes it, moreover, this speech rambles – a fatal flaw in a punch-line. The misunderstanding was ill begun and poorly continued, and its resolution cannot but be unsatisfactory.

In MS. A the *vilain*'s speech is slightly different. It is less coherent in that it omits all mention of Honte's being a man's name; on the other hand, it improves upon FB by placing here the description of the bag as *granz et lee* (119). There follows in all the versions a brief scene in which, as in Guillaume, the king gives *la male Honte* to the *vilain*. Only B has the donation in direct speech; the other texts thus avoid the implausibility in Guillaume of the king's shift in his understanding of the formula. A, on the other hand, labours the pun; it adds a speech by the *vilain* which explicitly contrasts *la male* and *male honte*:

> La male praing je voirement
> A tout l'avoir qui est dedenz;
> Mes je pri Dieu entre mes denz
> Que male honte vous otroit!
> Si fera il, se il m'en croit,
> Autre que celi que je port
> Quar ledengié m'avez a tort.   (144–50)

It is quite clear that the *vilain* understands the meaning of the phrase and thus the previous ambiguity of his words; but in A it is not as implausible as in FB that, knowing both senses, he should have allowed the misunderstanding to continue. For one thing he is beaten only once; for another, his use of the formula is more coherent than in FB, preserving ambiguity throughout his two attempts to give the king the bag, and only in the explanatory speech giving the latter a physical reality (*plaine d'avoir, granz et lee*) and disjoining the formula. Even so this final speech distracts from the original thread of the fabliau for the sake of a satirical point. Like the version of Guillaume, all three manuscripts of Huon end on a satirical note, though the butt differs; all these epilogues will be considered presently.

Disregarding for the time being the direction of the satire, we should give some attention to the relation between the three manuscripts of Huon's version. Both Långfors and Rychner see them as independent *remaniements*, and this would indeed seem to be the case. F and B, though different in many details, do not diverge substantially until the end. Långfors believes A is closest to the original (with an involuntary omission of the *vilain*'s third approach to the king), because it contains the author's name.[21] Rychner, on the other hand, maintains that A shows signs of deliberate abbreviation, and that the name of Huon is an addition to this manuscript only.[22] Analysis of the handling of the central formu-

---

[21] *Huon le Roi [etc.]*, ed. Långfors, p. xi.
[22] Rychner, *Contribution*, I.23.

la has shown a greater coherence in A than in FB, and this would suggest that A is the earlier. However, it is clear that in the rest of its narrative – in particular in its having only two episodes, which cannot, as Rychner shows, simply be seen as a lacuna – it is less coherent. Moreover, the superior use of the formula springs in large measure from the very omission of the third episode: there are fewer inappropriate occurrences of the formula because the formula occurs less often. In placing the *granz et lee* couplet later, A improves upon FB; the other details do not lend weight to A's anteriority. The speech of the *vilain* at the end, which A alone has, is a labouring of what will become obvious in the epilogue.

If we now compare F and B with Guillaume, as both Långfors and Rychner have done, we find contradictory evidence here too. Långfors suggests that Guillaume's version derives from a manuscript close to F,[23] Rychner that the textual coincidences could indicate that it derives from one close to B, though on other grounds he suggests that Huon as a whole is probably later than Guillaume.[24] F shares exclusively with Guillaume two lines in the epilogue, which Rychner shows could well belong to the shared original.[25] B, on the other hand, has Guillaume's repetition of *Honte* at the beginning, abbreviates the speech of the courtier (though it has neither the pithiness nor the rhyme-play of Guillaume), and, like Guillaume's version, has the king give the bag to the *vilain* in direct speech.[26] Since B and Guillaume are in the main so different, their similarities here – of which only one is literal – should be attributed not to a direct filiation in either direction, but at most to contamination: the redactor of B may have heard Guillaume's version and enhanced his own poem with a few remembered touches.

Huon's version, it is plain, exploits much less fully than Guillaume's the ambiguity of the phrase *la male Honte*, neither being as dramatically convincing as Guillaume's nor balancing obscurity and clarity so evenly. One of the subtleties of Guillaume, we saw, was his use of equivocal rhyme to stress ambiguity. In fact, the differences in the use of rhyme between the two versions are remarkable. Guillaume has far fewer rich rhymes than Huon: fifteen in seventy-nine couplets against fifty-two in a hundred.[27] A higher proportion of these is equivocal in Guillaume,[28] but the most significant difference is in the placing of keywords at the rhyme. Of Guillaume's five equivocal rhymes, three rhyme *honte* together; Huon has this rhyme only once. Guillaume uses the formula *la male honte* twenty times, of which nearly half – nine – are at the rhyme. Words in this

[23] *Huon le Roi [etc.]*, ed. Långfors, p. xiii.
[24] Rychner, *Contribution*, 1.24–5, 28.
[25] *Ibid.*, 1.24. The lines are F 197–8 and Guillaume 157–8.
[26] Rychner's fourth point (the verbal identity of B 139–40 and Guillaume 107–8, and the slight differences in AF) is too insignificant to contribute to the argument.
[27] In F; the corresponding figures in the other manuscripts are 43 in 79 couplets in A, 48 in 103 in B.
[28] Guillaume 5 (⅓ of the rich rhymes, 1/16 of the total couplets); A 4 (1/11 and 1/20 respectively); F 6 (1/9 and 1/17), of which two are not equivocal but identical; B 4 (1/12 and 1/26).

position are stressed by the rhythm of the line, by being followed by a pause, and by the very fact of rhyming. Moreover, in oral delivery rhyme-words were least likely to be lost to the audience if noise intruded, for they could most easily be reconstructed. Guillaume's heavy concentration of *la male honte* at the rhyme thus contributes to the effect of his fabliau. Huon, on the other hand, has fewer uses of this all-important phrase (sixteen in MS. F, which is a third as long again as Guillaume)[29] and places it at the rhyme much less frequently: only four times in F, a quarter of the occurrences.[30] Just as Guillaume and Huon differ in the care with which they distribute the disjoined and undisjoined formula, so too they show unequal skill in their exploitation of rhyme: in Guillaume little use is made of complex rhyme except where it can contribute to ambiguity or stress, while Huon shows virtuosity with no purpose outside itself.

Such concentration of effort is typical of Guillaume. We have seen how his fabliau unfolds more briskly than Huon's, how he omits all unnecessary narration, and above all how carefully he meets the demands of ambiguity. This is true not only of his distribution of the formula *la male honte*, but also of his phrasing. He does not once use the phrase *male honte* without the article: whenever he speaks of 'foul shame' his words allow the interpretation 'Honte's bag', and on five occasions both meanings are actualised at once. The manuscripts of Huon, on the other hand, use *male honte* between one and three times, yet never use *la male honte* with dual meaning. When Guillaume wants to be unambiguous he uses the single word *honte*, proper or common noun, which, unlike the formula, cannot serve obscurity and is better kept for clarity. He uses the man's name four times at the beginning, where it is important, against Huon's once or twice; later he speaks seven times of *honte* or *la honte*, which Huon uses a maximum of twice. In Guillaume all is focused upon the pun and the development of misunderstanding, while Huon tries to steer a path between the two meanings and does justice to neither. All these points of superiority would suggest that Guillaume's is the earlier version; he is the man who thought of the pun and worked it out with his eye firmly fixed upon the climax, whilst Huon seems to have retold the tale, trying to use all the resources of the pun at once and thus sacrificing verisimilitude, undermining the dénouement, and diminishing the effect of the fabliau.

In all the foregoing discussion we have eschewed consideration of the fabliau's satirical element. The epilogues of the three manuscripts of Huon and the version of Guillaume draw varying satirical interpretations from the preceding narration. In Guillaume the *vilain* distributes *la male Honte* to his compatriots:

> Ce dist Guillaumes en son conte
> Que li vilains en a portee
> La male Honte en sa contree,
> Si l'a aus Englés departie.

[29] 11 in A, which is the same length as Guillaume; 16 in B.
[30] 3 times in A, 5 in B.

Encore en ont il grant partie:
Sans la male ont il asez honte
Et chascun jor lor croist et monte.
Par mavés seignor et par lache
Les a la honte pris en tache.   (150–8)

MSS. A and F of Huon attribute shame primarily to the king:

Lors a li vilains reportee
La male Honte en sa contree;
A mainte gent l'a departie,
Qui en orent molt grant partie;
Sanz la male ot il trop de honte
Et chascun jor li croist et monte,
Mes, ainz que li anz fust passez,
Ot li rois de la honte assez.   (A, 151–8)

Et li vilains a raportee
La male Honte en sa contree;
A mainte gent l'ont departie,
Encore en ont mainte partie;
Sans la male ont il assés,
Car chascun jour lor croist viltés.
Par malvais seignor et par lasque [31]
Nous a li honte pris en tasque;
Ains que li ans fust trespassés
Ot li rois de la honte assés.   (F, 191–200)

There is disagreement as to the interpretation of A's version. Långfors and Rychner invert the last two couplets,[32] opposing the wealth distributed by the *vilain* and the shame suffered by the king. Spencer, by contrast, defends the order of the manuscript, understanding *il* (155) as referring to *mainte gent*.[33] In this reading A would have fundamentally the same sense as Guillaume's version, but for the more pointed reference to *li rois*. MS. F conforms closely to the version of Guillaume, but for the pronoun *nous*. MS. B, on the other hand, is quite different, assigning shame solely to *vilains*, and implicitly to all *vilains*, English or not:

A itant li vilains s'en part,
Toz liez s'en vint en son païs;
Si a mendé toz ses amis
Et les vilains de la contree:
Male honte lor a donee.
Onques nus frans hom point n'en ot;
N'i a vilain qui ne s'en lot,

---

[31] MS: *par m. sejour*; the emendation is Spencer's ('The *courtois-vilain* nexus', p. 284) and is evident.
[32] *Huon le Roi [etc.]*, ed. Långfors, p. xii; Rychner, *Contribution*, I.23.
[33] Spencer, 'The *courtois-vilain* nexus', pp. 282–4.

Trestuit en furent parçonier.
Por ce dit an en reprovier,
Qui fu trové par icest conte:
Que vilain aient male honte!   (196–206)

Where all the other versions make some play on the distinction between *la male Honte* and *honte*, B alone uses the unambiguous phrase *male honte* here, abandoning all attempt at a dual reference.

Just as the manuscript readings diverge, so too do the interpretations of critics. On the assumption that specific political satire is intended, inconclusive attempts have been made to identify the English king referred to, and thereby to date the poem.[34] A different approach is that of Spencer, who views the entire fabliau as an allegory which partly attacks *vilains*, partly preaches the reconciliation of social extremes; for him, its basis is neither anti-English satire nor linguistic comedy, but the social and moral opposition between *courtois* and *vilain*.[35] In the face of such divergence of interpretation, both by the redactors of the various versions and by modern scholars, can our analysis of the development of the fabliau's central pun lead to any conclusions concerning the original role of satire in the poem?

The salient characteristic of the handling of the formula *la male honte* in all the epilogues is that of confusion. In each case the formula itself, and the foregoing tale, suffer violence for the sake of a satirical point. The authors of all the versions except B[36] force logic by attributing to the recipients of the king's gift first *la male Honte*, then shame without the bag. The reference to the king's own shame is likewise confused, particularly in the versions of Huon; the redactors seem to confuse the king of the fabliau and that of history.[37] Rychner attributes this confusion to the superimposition on Huon's tale of '[une] intention satirique et venimeuse', which, he says, also accounts for the attempt to make the *vilain* expressly wish shame upon the king.[38] It is true that Huon has a stronger satirical vein, and that, as we saw, this leads to an imperfect handling of ambiguity. But in Guillaume too the satirical point is a superimposition, as is evident from its incoherence as well as from the fact that the fabliau is complete without it. Guillaume's version demonstrates a characteristic of many fabliaux: a moral is attached to a tale which has no need of it.[39] Huon's, on the other hand, in this respect as in so many others, shows signs of reworking: knowing that the fabliau he was retelling ended satirically, Huon attempted to imbue his entire

---

[34] The king is variously identified as Henry III or as John: cf. MR IV.234; *Huon le Roi [etc.]*, ed. Långfors, pp. xiii–xv; *Fabliaux*, edd. Johnston & Owen, p. 100; Rychner, *Contribution*, I.27, n. 1.

[35] Spencer, 'The *courtois-vilain* nexus', pp. 286–90.

[36] With reference to the epilogues of Huon, one should indeed speak of versions rather than of manuscripts.

[37] Rychner, *Contribution*, I.27.

[38] *Ibid.*

[39] Cf. *Fabliaux*, edd. Johnston & Owen, pp. xiii–xviii.

poem with this meaning, and diminished it as he did so. Nevertheless the satire remains no more than an overlay. The very fact that the butts differ shows that it is not fundamental to the fabliau: what is common, and therefore original, is the working-out of the pun, and satire is merely grafted on to this.

Satire against *vilains* is no more fundamental to the tale than political satire. The final scene of B states clearly that the king gives *la male Honte* to the *vilain* and to his heirs:

Je la doin toi et ton lignage
Et la t'otroi en eritage, (193–4)

and the epilogue confirms this. Though the expression is more coherent than that of the other versions, the satire is not supported by the rest of the tale. For, while it is true that the *vilain* is presented in this version, as in all the rest, as stupid, so too is the king; and we would be entitled to expect greater perspicacity from him than from his subject. It is important for the misunderstanding and for comedy that each should be as narrow-minded as the other; the *vilain's* stupidity may derive from his station, but the king's social superiority does not give him greater insight.

If political satire against the English is not the *raison d'être* of the fabliau, what then is the relevance of its being set in England? In contrast to *Les Deux Angloys et l'Anel*, its intrigue could as well take place in France – or elsewhere – as in England.[40] Yet both versions localise it clearly in England. Since this is surely an original element of the fabliau, we should look for its explanation in the tale's essential feature, namely the title-formula, and consider whether there is in it anything which could only apply to England.

The name *Honte* has puzzled critics, and has clearly been dictated by the needs of the pun. Långfors explained it as the Flemish 'De Hont', Reid as the English 'Hunt', which is more plausible because it is English.[41] Spencer is undoubtedly right to say that the author would not necessarily expect a French audience to appreciate an allusion to an English surname.[42] But I think it not unreasonable to suggest that the pun first came to a poet's mind because he knew both that such a name existed and that in the French spoken in England the Francien [ō] was pronounced [ū].[43] Perhaps when he first heard the name 'Hunt' it amused him by its similarity, on Anglo-Norman lips, to *honte*. The confusion provided a starting-point for his pun and so for his fabliau. Later *remanieurs* (or, indeed, the same man) drew more out of the pun, applying the mediaeval habit of thought which interpreted the literal in terms of the figurative; but essentially

---

[40] The custom of leaving wealth to the king was not peculiar to England: see *Huon le Roi [etc.]*, ed. Långfors, pp. xii–xiii.

[41] *Ibid.*, p. x, n. i; Reid, review of Johnston & Owen, p. 125; cf. Bédier, *Les Fabliaux*, p. 311; Spencer, 'The *courtois-vilain* nexus', p. 289.

[42] Spencer, 'The *courtois-vilain* nexus', p. 289.

[43] Fouché, *Phonétique historique*, II.360; cf. *The Anglo-Norman Voyage of St Brendan*, ed. Waters, pp. cxlix–cli.

the Englishness of the fabliau derives not from a satirical intention, but from the punning possibilities of Anglo-Norman as heard by a native of France. Seen in this light, the fabliau partakes of one of the standard French attitudes to England in the middle ages: the English were renowned for their comical language.[44] In *Les Deux Angloys*, this theme is obvious and is simplistically presented; in *La Male Honte*, it is treated with much greater subtlety, for it provides the impulse for a work which bases on it a comedy finer and less restricted than any mere chauvinistic mockery.

[44] Cf. Rickard, *Britain*, pp. 171–8.

The *Estoires d'Outremer*:
history or entertainment?

MARGARET JUBB

The *Estoires d'Outremer et de la naissance Salehadin* survives in three manuscripts. Two – Paris, Bibliothèque nationale, MSS fr. 770 and 12203, are late thirteenth-century or early fourteenth-century, and the third, Paris, Bibliothèque nationale, MS. fr. 24210, is fifteenth-century.

The *Estoires*, at least in part, is a historical narrative, and it is clearly related to the maze of texts in Old French, the Ernoul-Bernard *abrégé*, and the continuations to William of Tyre, which draw on the lost chronicle of Ernoul. The narrative opens, like that of the *abrégé*, with a brief outline of crusade history, beginning in 1099. The account, again like that of the *abrégé*, then becomes increasingly detailed. Up to the year 1185, indeed, the *Estoires* and the *abrégé* agree quite closely, even though this agreement allows for more divergence than does any other agreement between two texts in the whole Ernoul corpus. After the year 1185, however, the *Estoires* diverges markedly from the *abrégé*. In particular, the narrative after Henry of Champagne's death in 1197 is so condensed and chronologically confused as to be largely incoherent. The *Estoires* ends with a mention of the successfully repulsed Saracen attack on Jerusalem in 1229–1230, and the absolution of Frederick II by Pope Gregory IX in August 1230. This is precisely the point at which the first recension of the Ernoul-Bernard *abrégé* had also ended.[1]

Into the main historical narrative, the compiler of the *Estoires* makes two major fictional interpolations. The first of these, *La Fille du comte de Pontieu* (hereafter *Fille*), is abruptly inserted just after Reynald of Châtillon has been introduced into the main narrative. This colourful and entirely fanciful interpolation, which exists independently elsewhere,[2] relates at some length how Saladin was descended from the French noble house of Ponthieu. The second major interpolation, the *Ordre de chevalerie* (hereafter *Ordre*), occurs in only one of the extant manuscripts of the *Estoires*, BN fr. 770. It leads on quite smoothly from the account of the battle of Beaufort in the main narrative. Hugh of

---

[1] Morgan, *The Chronicle of Ernoul*, pp. 145–6.
[2] See *La fille du comte de Pontieu*, ed. Brunel.

Tiberias is taken prisoner by Saladin and prevailed upon to initiate his captor into the mysteries of christian knighthood. The *Ordre*, like the *Fille*, exists independently elsewhere.[3]

In addition to the inclusion of these two fictional interpolations, the *Estoires* also differs from the *abrégé* and related texts in including some apparently serious historical narrative, from an unidentifiable source, dealing with Saladin's war against the queen of Turkey and her allies, King Elxelin of Nubia and the caliph of Baghdad. This material comprises several episodes, which are interwoven into the main narrative.

Another idiosyncracy of the *Estoires* is the inclusion of an exemplary story about a penitent king of Damascus. This occurs in the course of the biblical/geographical passages describing the Holy Land, and is triggered by the mention of Samaria, over which the king in question is said to have ruled. Similar stories exist independently elsewhere.[4]

Finally, the *Estoires* also includes two anecdotes about Saladin – his criticism of the christian offertory, and the dispute which he institutes on his death-bed between the three world-religions – which are not found in the *abrégé*. They both form part of the popular *légende de Saladin*, and have been preserved independently elsewhere.[5]

To date, comparatively little critical attention has been paid to the *Estoires*. In a fleeting reference to the text, in 1859, the *RHC* editors of the Old French continuations to William of Tyre[6] recognised at once its affinity with and distinctness from the Ernoul-Bernard *abrégé*. After a very long period of scholarly neglect, the question of the *Estoires*'s relation to the *abrégé* and the continuations was taken up by Morgan in 1973. She made the interesting suggestion that the *Estoires* may derive independently from old sources and so be only indirectly related to the *abrégé*.

I began preparation of my Ph.D. dissertation (an edition and critical study of the *Estoires*) with a view to investigating this question further, and to determining the precise significance of the *Estoires* as a historical source. The conclusions to which I came seemed at first rather negative. In short, it is extremely unlikely that the *Estoires* derives any more directly from Ernoul than does any other

---

[3] For the verse version, see *L'Ordène de chevalerie*, ed. W. Morris; for the prose versions, see 'Les Rédactions', ed. Kjellman.

[4] See *Barlaam et Josaphat*, ed. Mills, pp. 46–9. For an even closer parallel, see *Gesta Romanorum*, ed. Oesterley, pp. 498–500; *The Exempla of Jacques de Vitry*, ed. Crane, pp. 16–17.

[5] On the criticism of the christian offertory, Paris, 'La légende de Saladin', p. 294, refers to one of the continuations of the *Chanson de Jérusalem* (Paris, Bibliothèque nationale, MS. fr. 12659, fos 360–2. The debate between the three religions is related in Tours MS. 468 (*ancien* 205), fo 161r, quoted by Lecoy de la Marche, *Anecdotes historiques*, p. 64, n. 1.

[6] Académie des Inscriptions et Belles-Lettres, *Recueil des historiens des Croisades* (hereafter RHC). The abbreviation always refers to the series *Historiens Occidentaux*.

extant text. Its significance as a historical source for scholars of the crusades is hence very limited.

The significance of the *Estoires* is considerable nevertheless. It is a curiosity which, quite apart from its entertainment value, offers much which is of interest to the student of literary history.

First, there is the prominence accorded in the narrative to flagrant legend. The modern reader is perhaps tempted, because of this, to rank the text immediately as *histoire romancée*, an entertaining adventure-story set against a historical backcloth, rather than as a serious chronicle.

It is necessary, however, to consider the *Estoires* in its contemporary context before any serious weight can be given to this conclusion. The modern division between history and fiction was, of course, not current in the middle ages. It was considered perfectly valid for the chronicler to use his imagination to transform real events. Nevertheless, a distinction was made between history-writing and story-writing in this respect. The historian might use fiction, but he would do so in order to convey some piece of reality or truth. If not actually true, his story could, at least, conceivably have been true. Pure fiction did not contain this grain of truth. Conrad of Hirschau expressed it thus: 'Fabula est quod neque gestum est nec geri potest.'[7]

Seen in this light, the fictional interpolations of the *Estoires* do not necessarily disqualify it as a work of history. Undoubtedly, Saladin's behaviour towards those he defeated inspired in the Christians an involuntary respect for him. To justify a truthful portrait of Saladin as a chivalrous and good man, though a pagan, a chronicler might well include the legends we find in the *Estoires*. The *Fille* reflects the strength of a noble, christian nature over a pagan nature, and, furthermore, explains Saladin's magnanimity to the Franks, from whom he is supposedly descended. The inclusion of the *Ordre* is justified by Saladin's subsequent chivalrous behaviour. Moreover, some of the glory for the same is thereby reflected on to the christian institution instead of its all devolving upon a pagan, however admirable he may have been. The king of Nubia episodes, even if they have no historical validity, also contain a grain of truth. Saladin did indeed wage war against his co-religionaries, and did conquer other lands – Egypt, Mosul, Aleppo, Damascus – besides Jerusalem. The episodes thus present an essentially true picture of his all-conquering ambition and make his conquest of Jerusalem seem the more inevitable.

Contemporary theory about historiography justified the inclusion of such fictional episodes, not only because they contained a grain of truth, but also because they served as an entertaining diversion. Digression was a constant of ancient and mediaeval historiography and was justifed *ad recreationem lectoris*.[8] What would strike a modern reader as an extraordinary hotchpotch of material,

---

[7] Conrad of Hirschau, *Dialogus super auctores*, in *Accessus ad autores*, ed. Huygens, p. 76, line 149.
[8] See Lacroix, *L'Historien au moyen âge*, p. 189.

hardly deserving of the name of history, would have been quite acceptable in the thirteenth century. If a digression not only served as *divertissement*, but also had an exemplary value, then it was so much the better. Clearly, the *Ordre* has such a value; indeed, its principal object is a didactic exaltation of the ideals of knighthood. The story of the penitent king of Damascus might also have been countenanced, in a work of history, for its diverting and its exemplary value.

These fictional interpolations alone are not sufficient, then, to call into doubt the status of the *Estoires* as a serious work of history. The factual shortcomings of the historical narrative, however, are a different matter. It is one thing to interpolate fictional episodes into an otherwise factual, historical narrative, but quite another to modify the factual narrative itself to such an extent that it too becomes a fiction, and one, moreover, without a compensatory grain of truth.

To illustrate the factual shortcomings of the historical narrative, we might consider the *Estoires*'s idiosyncratic treatment of the third crusade, in which English and French joined forces against Saladin. So careless of factual accuracy is the compiler that he even makes an error over the dating of the capture of Jerusalem, his hero Saladin's crowning achievement, and the event which launched the third crusade. In fact, Saladin encamped before Jerusalem on 20 September 1187 and the city surrendered on 2 October. Yet we read in the *Estoires*:[9] 'Salehadins sist tout adiés devant Jherusalem dusc'a l'entree de fevrier', and later (fo 349vb): 'celui jor estoit vendredis et si estoit Quaresmes'.

The *Estoires*'s geography is no better than its chronology. The compiler frequently substitutes well known place-names, likely to strike a chord with his public, for lesser known, but factual, originals. Thus, relating Richard the Lionheart's shipwreck and subsequent capture in 1192, the *Estoires* has:[10] 'Dont vint en la tiere de Roumenie et quant il vint en un chastiel ki estoit l'empereour d'Alemaigne viers Bouloigne la Crasse . . .' In fact, Richard's boat was wrecked near Aquileia.[11] Whether by *Roumenie* the *Estoires* is designating the Italian province of Romania, or Anatolia, the region between the Black Sea and the Mediterranean, its geography is fanciful. The identification of the castle where Richard was detained as Bologna is also curious. The *abrégé* and continuations do not name the castle, but it is thought to have been the fortress of Dürnstein on the Danube.

The treatment of this episode reveals another characteristic of the *Estoires*: the telescoping of detail, even at the cost of some internal confusion. According to the *Estoires*, Richard falls straight into the hands of Emperor Henry VI. The *abrégé*[12] and continuations[13] both correctly have the duke of Austria as intermediary.

Elsewhere the *Estoires* shows a similar concern to simplify the narrative by

---

9 Fo 349rb. All folio-references to the *Estoires* are to BN fr. 770.
10 Fo 352va.
11 *La Chronique d'Ernoul*, ed. de Mas Latrie, p. 297.
12 *Ibid.*
13 *RHC*, II.201.

keeping the number of principal figures to a minimum. Whereas the *abrégé* [14] and continuations [15] state correctly that Philip Augustus left the duke of Burgundy in command of his army, the *Estoires* [16] has Philip delegating authority to Henry of Champagne. In view of subsequent history, when Henry of Champagne was very definitely Richard's man, this is an important change and one which makes for political nonsense.

Coherence is further prejudiced in the *Estoires*, [17] when Richard calls Henry of Champagne and laconically tells him 'k'il fust rois'. Henry became king of Jerusalem by virtue of his marriage to Isabel of Montferrat. Admittedly, Richard played a large part in arranging this marriage, but no mention has been made of the event in the *Estoires*. Indeed, the last thing our text has had to say on the subject of the succession was that Sibylla was queen of Jerusalem. It has mentioned neither the death of Sibylla and her children, nor the succession of Isabel and her second husband, Conrad of Montferrat, nor the subsequent death of Conrad.

The laborious details of royal successions and of political relations between the English and French patently concern the compiler less than the creation of a fast-moving and entertaining narrative. In order to court his public's sympathy, he not only simplifies political reality; he may also on occasion deliberately traduce it. Thus, in contrast to the accounts of the *abrégé* and continuations, the *Estoires* [18] represents the King of France as undisputed leader of the crusading army. After the capture of Acre, we read: 'li rois de France douna au roi Ricart le moitié de tout le gaaing'.

Elsewhere, errors on points of historical fact may not have been made with deliberate intent, but they are equally revealing of the *Estoires*'s preoccupations. Referring to events in Europe in 1210, the compiler writes as if the king of England were still Richard. [19] In fact, Richard died in 1199, and the king was now his brother John. For the compiler and his public, however, a preoccupation with the adventures of Saladin meant that the king of England in their minds was Richard, simply because Richard was king in Saladin's time. A preoccupation with Richard was a consequence of their greater preoccupation with Saladin.

There is an even more glaring error illustrative of this same phenomenon. The besieged citizens of Jerusalem are said to use 'le grant tresor dou roi Richart d'Engletiere' [20] to help pay their ransom. The treasure in question was extremely famous and was sent not by Richard I, but by his father, Henry II, penitent for the death of Thomas Becket.

The tendencies which are apparent in the *Estoires*'s treatment of the third

---

14 *La Chronique d'Ernoul*, ed. de Mas-Latrie, p. 277.
15 *RHC* II.182.
16 Fo 351va.
17 Fo 352rc.
18 Fo 351rb.
19 Fo 353rc.
20 Fo 349vb.

crusade are even more marked in the concluding part of the historical narrative. After the death of Henry of Champagne in 1197, chronological confusion and factual inaccuracy render the text virtually useless from an informative point of view. With the departure of his hero Saladin from the scene, the compiler appears to have been anxious to conclude his tale as quickly as possible.

There is a further possible explanation for the extreme concision of the *Estoires*. Up to 1197, the *abrégé* presents a great variety of materials – history, topographical digressions, biblical stories – all included to serve the ends of good narrative with wide appeal. After that point, however, it becomes less entertaining and presents an unrelieved, and often quite tedious, report of events, usually in chronological order. The *Estoires*'s source was, we infer, like the *abrégé* on this point. Up to 1197, the compiler of the *Estoires* needed to make only fairly minor abbreviations in order to speed up the pace of what was already a varied and entertaining narrative. Thereafter, he has evidently had to modify his weighty source very extensively in order to make a good story-line. He omits entirely the dry account of relations between Armenia and Antioch, and retains only the most dramatic and colourful episodes from his source, such as the death of Richard the Lionheart, the battle of Bouvines, the fourth crusade, and the siege of Damietta. The latter, with Pelagius as the villain of the piece, allowed him to give vent to anti-clerical sentiment, and thus would be assured of appeal to a lay audience.

Indeed, this latter part of the *Estoires*'s narrative, with its kaleidoscopic succession of scenes, seems deliberately to court the attention of an unlearned audience. The compiler takes some extraordinary liberties with the chronology of his source, with a blatant disregard for factual accuracy. For instance, after relating the pope's appeal to Frederick II in 1219, he makes an abrupt flashback to the fourth crusade. This is then linked into the succeeding narrative by equating the crusaders left behind in Venice with the Germans waiting for Frederick II to lead them on crusade to the East. The result is indefensible as serious, informative history.

All the available evidence shows that the *Estoires* was written in north-eastern France in the early thirteenth century.[21] There was in this region at the period in question a considerable interest in vernacular historiography, and in crusade historiography in particular. The region had provided much of the manpower for the crusades, and there was a special interest in the deeds of relatives who had gone beyond the seas. The chronicles of Villehardouin,[22] Robert de Clari,[23] and Henri de Valenciennes[24] were written primarily to inform this lay interest.

---

[21] For the history of BN fr. 770 and 12203, see *La Fille du comte de Pontieu*, ed. Brunel, pp. xxxiv–xxxix. For the evidence of an art-historian, see Morgan, *The Chronicle of Ernoul*, p. 15, n. 16.

[22] G. de Villehardouin, *La Conquête de Constantinople*, ed. Faral.

[23] Robert de Clari, *La Conquête de Constantinople*, ed. Lauer.

[24] H. de Valenciennes, *Histoire de l'empereur Henri de Constantinople*, ed. Longnon.

It seems unlikely, however, that the compiler of the *Estoires* wrote with the same intention uppermost in his mind. His extremely abbreviated historical narrative cannot be entirely explained away by attributing to him the purpose of the original author of the Saint-Denis *Historia regum Francorum*.[25] The latter said that he wrote not for scholars, but for those who were too busy with their own affairs to acquire more than a concise, clear outline of historical events. Concise the *Estoires* may be, but its outline of events is far from clear. The desire to entertain evidently far outweighed the desire to inform.

The deciding factor, ultimately, is not the inclusion of entertaining, fictional episodes in itself, but the elaboration of these episodes as compared to the condensation of the rest of the narrative. Ancient and mediaeval historiography did, admittedly, on occasion countenance the inclusion of fabulous material for no other purpose than that of pure entertainment. The passage in the thirteenth-century *Fet des Romains* describing the trials undergone by Cato and his soldiers in the Libyan desert, the patently fabulous effects of snake-venom, and the legendary origins of the snakes give a particularly striking example of the taste for and sanctioning of the marvellous in a work of history. However, the compiler of the *Fet des Romains* does acknowledge the fabulous nature of this material and presses on with the historical narrative.[26] As a historiographer, his purpose is to record the events of the past, primarily with an informative and didactic end in view. The desire to provide entertainment is only secondary.

The *Estoires*, on the other hand, seeks to provide entertainment above all else, and not only in the fictional interpolations, but throughout the text. The compiler has responded to a general interest in and admiration for the figure of Saladin, and has collected a variety of material, historical background and legend, all to the end of providing an exciting adventure-story. It seems probable that he wrote his work, as Philippe Mouskés did his *Chronique rimée*, with the primary aim *pour resgoïr*.[27]

The audience which he aimed to please would be accustomed to hearing *chansons de geste*, *romans*, *fabliaux*, and exemplary *contes*. Several features in the *Estoires* show the compiler's awareness of this contemporary literary universe. Thus, in the course of one of the episodes about Saladin's war with the king of Nubia, he writes, in connexion with a place besieged by Saladin: 'Cele ille tint Bourriaus dont on parole tant el roumant de Guillaume d'Orenghe.'[28] Later in the same episode, the *Estoires* makes reference to the *Roman d'Alexandre*. These references are undoubtedly made in a calculated attempt to stimulate the interest of the audience.

The compiler of the *Estoires* also seeks to stimulate interest in his tale by borrowing proper names from the literary world of epic and romance. Many of the place-names in the king of Nubia episodes have no identifiable historical

25 See Schmitz, *Histoire de l'ordre de Saint Benoît*, V.232.
26 *Li Fet des Romains*, edd. Flutre & Sneyders de Vogel, p. 604.
27 Philippe Mouskés, *Chronique rimée*, lines 42–3 (ed. de Reiffenberg, p. 4).
28 *La Prise d'Orenge*, lines 601 and 1684 (ed. Régnier, pp. 67 and 112).

counterparts, though they do have fictional counterparts in other mediaeval texts. The *Chanson de Roland* is a particularly rich source, giving for example, Baligant, Moriane, and Oliferne.

On one occasion, the compiler of the *Estoires* actually modified the historical material he is recounting in the light of literary tradition. I refer to his account of the death of Andronicus Comnenus. The *abrégé*[29] and the continuations[30] describe how the deposed emperor is mounted on a donkey and stoned to death by the populace. The *Estoires*, however, gives an entirely different version: Andronicus is tied by the hands and feet to two horses, and dragged along the ground. This punishment recalls that meted out to the archetypal traitor, Ganelon, in the *Chanson de Roland*. Less concerned with a faithful transmission of information, as available in his main source, than with thrilling his audience, the *Estoires*'s compiler has apparently modelled his account on that of the well-known epic. His version, stripped of the graphic, though tedious, detail found in the *abrégé* and continuations, but resonant with the associations of epic, would doubtless have been assured of a more immediate appeal.

The work to which the *Estoires* has most often been compared, because of its very evident courting of applause, is the so-called *Chronique d'un menestrel de Reims*.[31] Like the *Estoires*, this work is less concerned with giving a coherent, informative record of events than with achieving a varied, entertaining narrative. Although it includes much historical material about events in the Latin kingdom of Jerusalem, and in Flanders, this is interspersed with legend (Saladin's visit to the Hospitallers, the story of Richard the Lionheart and his minstrel Blondel), downright fiction (Henry II strangling himself to death with the reins and braces of his horse), a fable, and popular proverbs which judge the actions of princes in the light of commonsense wisdom.

Certainly, there are parallels between the two works, in content and in aim, but there are considerable differences in structure and in tone. The *Estoires*, episodic though it is in structure, is nevertheless united round the central theme of Saladin's career. The *Chronique d'un menestrel de Reims*, by contrast, presents not a sustained narrative, but rather a kaleidoscopic succession of diverting anecdotes. Whereas the *Estoires* ranges in tone from the epic (in the historical narrative) to the courtly (in the *Fille* interpolation), the work of the *menestrel* ranges from epic to farce. Both works seek to excite and entertain; the work of the *menestrel* seeks also to amuse. This is a diverting collection of anecdotes, akin to fabliaux, whereas the *Estoires* is perhaps ultimately best described as a historical adventure story, centreing on the figure of Saladin.

We find in the *Estoires* a fascinating example of the interpenetration of fiction and history-writing in the vernacular, in an age when vernacular prose historiography itself was in its infancy. In certain respects, it is reminiscent of the rhymed

[29] *La Chronique d'Ernoul* ed. de Mas-Latrie, p. 94.
[30] RHC II.21–2 *La Continuation de Guillaume de Tyr*, ed. Morgan, pp. 28–9.
[31] *Récits d'un menestrel de Reims*, ed. de Wailly.

chronicle of Philippe Mouskés. This also drew on multiple sources, often fabulous rather than historical, using epic poems, for instance, as a source for its 'history' of Charlemagne. In its very prose form, however, and in explicitly pejorative remarks, the *Estoires* reflects the contemporary distrust of verse and the desire for a realistic, credible narrative.[32] It reflects also the widespread interest in crusade-history, and in the figure of Saladin in particular. Finally, it provides a source and an inspiration for the compiler of the fifteenth-century *Saladin*,[33] who seizes upon the romanesque elements in the *Estoires* and develops them into a veritable *roman courtois*, with Saladin as its hero.

In the latter text, we see the ultimate result of the christians' veneration for Saladin. A possibility latent in the concept of the *Estoires*, the grouping of a body of legend about the figure of Saladin, has here been fully realised. The Saracen's *vaillance*, *largesse*, and *courtoisie* have exalted him in the popular imagination to the stature of the exemplary, all-conquering Alexander. Thus we read: 'Et disoient aulcuns que Alixandre n'eust sceu plus largement faire en son temps'.[34] Even as Alexander had become a hero of romance, so too in his turn has Saladin. In this text, we are clearly in fabulous realms, free from the intruding, restricting framework of historical fact. There is a total disregard of chronology, not just the vagueness which characterises the *Estoires*. The passage from the first to the third crusade is effected very simply, by the identification of the pagan Dodequin, from the first crusade, with Hugh of Tiberias from the third, and likewise by the identification of Baldwin of Bourc with Baldwin IV, and of Tancred who took part in the first crusade with Tancred the king of Sicily at the time of the third.

Henry James's characterisation of romance, as dealing with 'experience disengaged from the conditions that we normally know to attach to it',[35] very aptly fits *Saladin* but is certainly not applicable to the *Estoires*. A large part of the latter consists of a fairly accurate, though admittedly sometimes rather garbled account of actual historical events. Those historical events have sometimes been abbreviated and modified to make for a more exciting narrative, resonant on occasion with the associations of epic. However, they are not deliberately disregarded in order to give a more exotic romance flavour, as in the English romance *Richard Cueur de Lyon*.[36] Even though he was writing, like the compiler of the *Estoires*, fairly hard upon the events which he recounts, the English author had not hesitated to 'abolish' Eleanor of Aquitaine and provide Henry II with an Eastern princess for a queen. He thus gave himself occasion for a colourful, romanesque description of the princess's arrival in a magnificent Eastern galley.

By comparison, the compiler of the *Estoires* treats his historical material very

---

[32] Thus we read (fo 330rc): 'Sor cele mer fu çou que Nostre Sire fist de l'aighe vin, quant il fu as noces de Sainte Eglyse, mais non pas d'Archedeclin, *si com on dist en ces roumans rimés*. Archedeclin fu uns asaieres de vins.'

[33] *Saladin*, ed. Crist.

[34] *Ibid.*, p. 99.

[35] From the Preface to *The American*; quoted by Stevens, *Medieval Romance*, p. 17.

[36] Cited *ibid.*, p. 231.

conservatively. The possibility of creating a romance of Saladin already existed in the thirteenth century, as witness the number of colourful legends which circulated about him.[37] Perhaps a passage of time was necessary, however, before the necessary transformation of historical events could occur, and indeed before these could lose their very strong topical appeal. The *Estoires* bears witness to a transitional stage between historiography and romance, when the renown of Saladin was such that he already merited the centre of the stage in a historical *chanson d'aventures*, but before the historical background had faded sufficiently to allow a *roman courtois* to emerge.

The originality of the *Estoires*'s compiler lies in his selecting and assembling the startlingly diverse elements which make up his text. The resultant narrative gains over the closely related *abrégé* in pace, variety, and excitement, even where it loses in coherence and accuracy. Its fictional interpolations, like those of the Rothelin compiler of the continuations,[38] are fascinating evidence of how the crusades had become for many in the thirteenth century an exciting literary topos, rather than a matter of urgent religious or political concern. Finally, what we find in the *Estoires* is not a work which fits into a very clearly definable genre, but one which lies at the crossroads of several – historiography, *chanson d'aventures*, and embryonic romance – and which consequently throws light on the development and complex interrelations of all three.

[37] Paris, 'La légende de Saladin'.
[38] Morgan, 'The Rothelin continuation'.

France, England, and the 'national crusade', 1302–1386

NORMAN HOUSLEY

It has long been almost an article of faith among historians of the crusading movement that the development of national feeling in thirteenth- and four-teenth-century Europe was one of the factors which caused a decline in crusading enthusiasm. Palmer A. Throop, whose *Criticism of the Crusade* shaped the think-ing of a generation of crusade historians, wrote that 'the new nationalism looked upon the holy war in the Levant as a costly and futile foreign adventure . . . Nationalism was too powerful a force in the late thirteenth century to be over-come by the old appeals to sacrifice all for a distant land.'[1] The reasoning behind such generalisations is extremely dubious: nationalism and crusading zeal were not simple phenomena and the relationship between them was complex and changing. Certainly rulers in the fourteenth century took it for granted that they had a prior claim to the personal service and resources of their subjects, lay or clerical; by 1335 Alfonso IV of Aragon was arguing that before proclaiming a general passage to the East, the pope was obliged to summon 'all the kings and princes of the world' to secure their assent to the taxes needed.[2] But this was sovereignty, not national feeling, and the reason why Alfonso and other Western kings felt compelled to exercise their growing control over their subjects to the detriment of the crusade was that they feared the loss of manpower and revenue which the continuing appeal of holy war might bring about. When that appeal was actually in harmony with both sovereignty and national feeling, all three powerfully reinforced each other. In such cases the old antithesis between na-tionalism and the crusade is revealed to be the reverse of the truth.

As historians are now beginning to realise,[3] this was most clearly evident in the kingdoms of Spain and Eastern Europe. For the Castilians, Poles, Hungarians, and – to some extent – the Aragonese and the Swedes, *defensio fidei* and *defensio*

---

[1] Throop, *Criticism*, p. 286. For examples of his influence, see Runciman, 'The decline', p. 638; Prawer, *Histoire*, II.390–1. To save space, references to secondary works will be kept to a minimum.

[2] *Documenta selecta*, ed. Vincke, no. 509. Here and usually elsewhere in this article, translation from primary sources is my own work.

[3] For example, Linehan, 'Religion'; Knoll, 'Poland'.

regni went hand in hand in the fourteenth century. In these countries the enemies who menaced both *ecclesia* and *regnum* were Moors or pagans. The holy wars being waged there had their roots in the eleventh and twelfth centuries; they were perfectly respectable in juridical terms, and the Avignonese Curia was normally prepared to issue the bulls needed to convert the military efforts of the kings and their peoples into crusades. But there were two other national kingdoms in fourteenth-century Europe whose rulers strove to achieve the same conversion, the difference being that they were fighting either against each other or against other christian opponents. Their efforts to bring about a 'national crusade' were much more protracted, succeeding only when the Roman Church bifurcated in the Great Schism. The process has never been studied and reveals another aspect of the way in which national feeling and crusading ideas influenced each other.

Why did the French and English courts want to elevate their conflicts in Western Europe to crusading status, and why did they consider this to be a viable goal? Although the answer to the first part of the question varied according to circumstances, the key-point is the advantage to be gained from the association: the way in which it facilitated, or made less expensive, the recruitment of soldiers; the additional sources of revenue which it opened up; the extra strength which it bestowed on the government's case if internal opposition to the war developed; and the prestige which it offered in the field of international diplomacy. As for viability, by 1300 crusading by the papacy and its allies against christian lay powers had been a feature of political life in the West for a century.[4] The justification for these campaigns lay in the arguments that the christian foes of the Holy See were impeding a crusade to the Holy Land, or inflicting damage on the Church and, directly or by implication, threatening the integrity of Catholic belief. At both courts it was clear that if the French and English kings could plausibly deploy such arguments against their christian enemies, and persuade the Curia to accept these, they too could make use of the advantages of the crusade.

The foregoing gives the impression of a calculated manipulation of crusading ideas and institutions. It is more in keeping with the sources to interpret the actions of the individuals concerned as those of hard-pressed or desperate men who regarded the association of their national cause with the crusade not as forced, but as wholly natural. This was especially the case as the Anglo-French conflict deepened in intensity in the 1340s and 1350s, with the involvement in one form or another of all social groups and a growing feeling that the enemy was threatening the entire nation – including the Church – and must be combated with every means, actual or potential, at the disposal of the government.[5] It is

---

[4]   Housley, *Italian Crusades*.
[5]   Allmand, *Society at War*. For an up-to-date bibliographical guide to the voluminous literature on the development of national sentiment in France and England, see Guenée, *States and Rulers*, pp. 261ff. I have found most useful Guenée, 'Etat et nation'; Genet, 'English nationalism'.

also clear that it was not only material benefits which rulers hoped to extract from their efforts; they also banked on securing the spiritual benefits of increased prayers and masses, and on winning God's backing for a cause declared to be his.

Association of royal policy with the crusade came more easily to the French than to the English. In the first place, the Capetian court had a much fuller and more varied crusading tradition than its Plantagenet rival. As has often been pointed out, between 1226 and 1285 three French kings died on crusade. By the early fourteenth century this degree of dynastic and national commitment to the defence of the Holy Land and of the Church in the West was fully appreciated and commented on at the French court.[6] Again, the development of national sentiment was closely entwined with the richest burgeoning of this commitment, between 1248 and 1300, in the expeditions of Louis IX, Charles of Anjou, and Philip III. In promoting crusades in East or West, the popes poured praise on the piety and might of France's knighthood. Thus Charles of Anjou's successful crusade against Manfred and Conradin was depicted not only by Charles and the French chroniclers, but also by Pope Clement IV, as a victory for France, while Martin IV in 1282/3 appealed for crusading recruits by arguing that the Sicilian revolt had dealt a blow to national pride.

From about 1301 publicists and counsellors at Philip IV's court began to make active use of these themes, to develop and expound them in a series of arrogant and far-reaching claims which were, nonetheless, only the extrapolation of ideas outlined in the preceding decades: that Philip the Fair was 'the most Christian king', that the French excelled all other nations in their devotion to the Church and the crusade, and that French policies were intimately linked to the recovery of Palestine. These themes have received much attention from historians, and it has been plausibly suggested that they were taken up as a response to the anti-French propaganda coming from Boniface VIII.[7] Robbed of papal support, the French court employed its indigenous crusade-tradition to good effect, as Frederick II had earlier tried to do.

This was very much a second best. It meant that, when Flanders rebelled in 1302, Philip IV could not hope for a crusade along the lines of that proclaimed against the rebel Sicilians twenty years earlier. All he could do was to employ crusade-ideals for propaganda purposes in order to quash internal objections to war taxation. This he did, and a sermon written by an anonymous French cleric, probably after the crushing defeat at Courtrai in July 1302, remains one of the best examples of royal employment of crusading ideas. The *Sermo cum rex Franciae est processurus ad bellum* opens with a popular quotation from I Maccabees, which itself epitomises the link between holy war and nationalism: 'They have come before us to despoil us and our wives and our sons, and to rob us. We shall in truth be fighting for our souls and our laws, and God will destroy [our enemies]

6   For example, *Recueil*, ed. Bouquet *et al.*, XXI.512–15.
7   See especially Strayer, 'France'; Hillgarth, *Ramon Lull*, pp. 106–13; Schein, 'Philip IV'.

in front of our eyes'.[8] In a text pitted with quotations from Maccabees, the cleric goes on to describe the historic achievements of French kings on behalf of the Church and to condemn the Flemings' rebellion; but the core of the sermon lies in a series of linked statements which have often been quoted, and properly so: 'He who wages war against the King [of France] works against the whole Church, against Catholic doctrine, against holiness and justice, and against the Holy Land.'[9]

The *Sermo* of 1302 shows clearly that there were two ways in which royal policy could be most effectively linked to the crusade – by arguing that a conflict was itself worthy of crusade-status, in that its goal was defence of the Church, and by depicting it as the essential preliminary to a crusade to the East. The second argument was markedly easier to employ, and after the accession of Clement V in 1305 circumstances favoured its use, since the breach between France and the papacy was healed and projects for a *passagium* to recover the Holy Land were again actively promoted. The pace accelerated after 1313, when a festive Cross-taking ceremony at Paris inaugurated more than twenty years of French crusade-planning; the papal curia began to experience the full weight of French diplomatic effort, and one of its demands was that the Christian opponents of the French should be branded as *impeditores passagii transmarini*, similar to Markward of Anweiler in 1199 and the Sicilians in 1283.[10]

At the Pentecost-assembly of 1313 the count of Flanders refused to take the Cross to accompany Philip IV to the East, and war resumed in 1314, continuing intermittently through the reigns of Louis X, Philip V, and Charles IV. It posed one of the most formidable obstacles to French crusade-plans, and there is clear evidence that in 1319 Philip V tried to persuade John XXII to authorise full-scale crusade-preaching against the Flemings. The king must have been encouraged by the fact that John XXII was prepared to take a tough line towards Flanders, one reason being that the chances of at least a minor French crusade, a *passagium particulare*, appeared good, with a surge of enthusiasm amongst the French nobility and the appearance of a champion in the person of Louis of Clermont.

In 1317 the papal correspondence about Flanders was being permeated by arguments and language which echoed those of thirteenth-century crusades against christians. In August the pope accused the Flemings of several offences traditionally associated with the worst enemies of the Church, including that of delaying a crusade to the East.[11] In March 1318 French envoys called for papal support against the rebels, possibly including the crusade among their demands. The pope prevaricated, on the grounds that peace was still possible, adding however that if Flemish stubbornness continued, to the detriment of the crusade,

---

8   Leclercq, 'Un sermon', p. 168. The quotation is from I Maccabees iii.19–22.
9   Leclercq, 'Un sermon', p. 170. Cf. Kantorowicz, *The King's Two Bodies*, pp. 249–55; Schein, 'Philip IV', p. 122.
10 Housley, *Italian Crusades*, pp. 64, 75–6. For the phrase, see the Continuator of William of Nangis, *Chronique latine*, ed. Géraud, II.11.
11 *Lettres*, edd. Coulon & Clémencet, no. 367, and cf. no. 197.

then the French cause, which was God's too, would enjoy papal backing.[12] By March 1319 John was threatening the Flemings with excommunication and interdict, which were often first steps towards a crusade,[13] but on 26 March he wrote to Philip that he had turned down his pleas for help on the grounds that 'the said petition could not have been granted by us without offending justice and the dignity of the Church'.[14]

That Philip V wanted a crusade against the Flemings becomes clear from a reply which he wrote in July 1319 to a request from Louis of Clermont for royal pressure on the Curia to sanction a *passagium* to the East. The king wrote that if it proved impossible to make peace with the Flemish rebels, he intended to ask the pope for aid against them. This aid would include crusade-indulgences, privileges, legacies, and subsidies. If the pope refused to grant them, Philip would ask for them on Louis' behalf for the *passagium* to the East.[15] This letter, which postdates John's March rebuff, shows that Philip still entertained hopes that pressure on the pope might succeed. If the king submitted this renewed demand (which he probably did not, as a peace-treaty was sealed in August 1319), it was unsuccessful.[16] The reason for the French failure in 1317–1319 was a combination of papal scepticism about French sincerity on the subject of the crusade with understandable reluctance to alienate the Flemings for a dispute which was not central to papal goals. In a period when French and papal policies were slowly drifting apart, such papal reluctance was one of the chief obstacles to the development of a full-scale national crusade in France.

To contemporaries, however, who viewed with alarm the way in which the Curia acceded to French demands on taxation and Franco-papal collaboration on such matters as the Imperial title, there seemed a real danger of a return to the days of Clement IV and Martin VI. From this point of view one of the many measures which John XXII incorporated into his package of crusade-privileges to Philip VI in July 1333 is of great interest. By this time, the Curia had come to accept that those who maintained order at home during a crusade were entitled to receive spiritual rewards, and John agreed to grant the crusade-indulgence to twelve regents who would be selected by Philip VI to govern France during the king's absence on crusade in the East. To a hundred others who would stay behind for the same reason the pope granted the indulgence provided that they made a financial contribution to the expedition, and to all who defended France 'in person or in another way' he promised partial indulgences.[17] To some extent this was a logical development of the well-established practice of granting Church-protection to crusaders' lands, the clause following John's formal placing of the *regnum* under the guardianship of St Peter. But it could easily be miscon-

---

[12] *Ibid.*, no. 530.
[13] *Ibid.*, no. 800.
[14] *Ibid.*, no. 830.
[15] *Titres*, ed. Huillard-Bréholles, I.282–3, no. 1633, and see also p. 263, no. 1526.
[16] For the whole sequence of events, see also Tyerman, 'Philip V', pp. 18–19.
[17] *Lettres secrètes*, edd. Coulon & Clémencet, no. 5207.

strued as papal acceptance of the Capetian-Valois propaganda-theme that the defence of France was a holy task. Pierre Dubois, for example, had earlier suggested granting crusade-indulgences to those who helped restrain warmakers in the West.[18]

By the end of 1335 Philip VI's crusade-project had foundered on the twin rocks of financial impracticability and impending conflict with England. In the years that followed, the idea that France's Christian enemies were impeding her crusading efforts made its last contribution to French propaganda in the idea that Edward III's aggression had crippled the *passagium*. In 1340, for instance, replying to Edward III's challenge to a duel, Philip VI asserted that the English king's wilful and unjust war had held up the crusade and that it constituted an affront to the Church.[19] However, it is undeniable that the propaganda which the French extracted from the postponed *passagium* was surprisingly thin, certainly by comparison with what Guillaume Nogaret or Pierre Dubois would have made of such events. Possibly Philip VI was wary of referring to a project whose postponement lay heavily on his conscience and gave rise to much popular indignation against him. By 1340 too French territory was under threat, and the alternative and more potent theme of *defensio regni* could be employed.

So far, this discussion has dealt solely with France: I have been unable to detect comparable trends in English thinking until the propaganda-conflict of 1335–1340. There are obvious reasons for this sluggishness. Crusading endeavour in thirteenth-century England had not become entwined with national pride or achievement, nor had these been associated with crusading against Christians. In England *crux cismarina* meant primarily Henry III's expensive and fruitless involvement in the 'Sicilian business', part of the background to the bitter and divisive barons' war of 1263–1267.[20] Worse, on two occasions in the thirteenth century, crusading-ideas and institutions were dragged into civil conflicts.[21] Nevertheless, persistent Anglo-French hostility provided a framework on to which religious antagonism could be transposed, given the right setting. When Prince Louis and an army of French invaded England in May 1216 in support of the baronial party, 'many', according to the Waverley annalist, 'both nobles and commoners, took the sign of the Lord's cross on their breast in order to throw Louis and the French out of England, preferring to have a king from their own country rather than a foreigner'.[22] The key factor here was confusion in papal policy, which enabled both John and the baronial supporters to depict themselves as the protagonists of a holy cause. Throughout the Avignon period, by contrast, the Curia was distinctly pro-French, and this, together with the comparative weakness of the recent English crusade-tradition, made the achievement of a 'national crusade' problematic.

---

[18] *De recuperatione*, ed. Langlois, pp. 9–10.
[19] Walsingham, *Historia anglicana*, ed. Riley, I.229–30.
[20] Powicke, *King Henry III*, chs 9–12.
[21] Lloyd, 'Political crusades'.
[22] *Annales de Waverleia*, in *Annales monastici*, ed. Luard, II.287.

During the early phase of the Hundred Years' War this weakness worked, paradoxically, to Edward III's advantage. Since the English government had put forward no plans for *passagia* to the East, as the French court had repeatedly done over the previous two decades, it was not tainted by failure. Edward could publicise the claim that he had genuine crusade-aspirations which Philip VI was impeding, neatly making use of a well-worn French argument and casting the French in the unfamiliar role of *impeditores*. This argument was employed on several occasions in the late 1330s; and while Edward could hardly be expected to back up his claim with preparations while the nation was at war, there are signs that it placed him in an awkward situation once peace had been restored: Walsingham related that knights from Spain, Cyprus, and Armenia came to the Smithfield tournament of 1362 to ask the king to aid their countries against the Muslims.[23] As one would expect, these protestations of crusading zeal were supported by the complementary theme that Philip VI's crusade plans had acted as a cover for warlike preparations against England. In 1340, for instance, Edward III commented that Philip was attacking England 'with the ships which he had pretended to be preparing for a holy passage overseas'.[24]

From about 1340, both courts transferred the thrust of their propaganda from arguments based on Philip VI's crusade-plans, to the theme of the enemy threat to *regnum* and *ecclesia*.[25] At the same time, as the conflict grew fiercer and demanded heightened national burdens,[26] both Churches were called on to make substantial contributions to the war-effort. These have received considerable attention in the case of England but much less, unfortunately, in that of France. The English Church was expected to pay heavy war-taxes, recently estimated at over 400,000 pounds for the province of Canterbury in the fourteenth-century phase of the war.[27] From 1369 onwards, in a notable infringement of clerical status and canon-law, clerics had to take part in military arrays;[28] and from the start of the war they had to function as 'involuntary political propagandists' on behalf of the Crown. This meant in particular a stream of requests for the holding of special prayers, masses, sermons, vigils, and processions in connexion with military campaigns.[29]

It is hard to believe that English clerics acquainted with I Maccabees did not at times insert in their special prayers quotations implying that Edward III was

[23] Knighton, *Chronicon*, ed. Lumby, I.476; Walsingham, *Historia anglicana*, ed. Riley, I.201, 296–7; *Lettres*, edd. Vidal and Mollat, no. 2981.
[24] Walsingham, *Historia anglicana*, ed. Riley, I.219. Cf. Canon of Bridlington, *Gesta Edwardi III*, ed. Stubbs, p. 132; Knighton, *Chronicon*, ed. Lumby, I.476.
[25] Hewitt, *The Organization*, pp. 158ff.; Allmand, *Society at War*, pp. 142ff.
[26] Harriss, *King*, ch.14, especially pp. 314–20; Henneman, *Royal Taxation . . . 1322–1356*, chs 4–8.
[27] McHardy, 'The English clergy', pp. 171–2.
[28] McNab, 'Obligations'.
[29] Jones, 'The English Church'; McHardy, 'Liturgy and propaganda', pp. 215–27, and 'The English clergy', *passim*.

fighting for a holy cause.[30] Did they go further and appropriate crusading institutions, especially indulgences, to the national war-effort? The granting of forty
days' indulgence to all who attended these occasions was standard and fully in
line with episcopal powers and regular practice,[31] but one passage in Henry
Knighton's chronicle suggests that such indulgences were also offered to comba-
tants specifically for military service against the French. In 1360, because of the
French attack on Winchelsea in the previous year, all English males between the
ages of sixteen and sixty were arrayed for the defence of the country against a
possible French assault. Knighton added that 'the archbishops and bishops
granted great indulgences throughout their sees to all who journeyed to the coast
to defend the kingdom against its enemies, and allowed each of them to choose
his own confessor at will'.[32] Significant as this sentence is in its portrayal of
military activity being rewarded with partial indulgences, it also shows clearly
the difficulties which English prelates faced in attaching firm crusade-status to
their cause. To bestow the full crusade-indulgence would have entailed a direct
assault on papal authority, and this they did not dare to launch.

These limitations were the more frustrating in that from the accession of
Clement VI in 1342, the English had to deal with four popes whose sympathy for
the enemy-cause was undeniable and irksome. For the next thirty-six years, while
it worked for peace with consistent energy, the Curia also geared its diplomatic
and financial policies to help the Valois war-effort. English irritation took the
retaliatory form of legislation against papal provisions, while military victory
gave rise to the ironic verses quoted by Knighton:[33]

> Ore est le pape devenu Franceys,
> e Jesu devenu Engleys.
> Ore serra veou qe fra plus,
> ly Pape ou Jesus.

As archbishop of Rouen, Clement VI had negotiated with John XXII for Philip
VI's crusade. He thus knew of, and may even have proposed, the indulgences
granted in 1333 to people who defended France during the general passage, and
in 1338 he preached a *collatio* on a characteristic text from I Maccabees: 'Arm
yourselves and be valiant, men, and be prepared for the morning, so that you may
fight against the nations which are gathered together to destroy us and our holy
place'.[34] By 1344 some Englishmen had begun to fear that this highly partisan
pope might go to the lengths of launching a crusade against them.

The context was the peace-talks which took place at Avignon in the autumn-
months of the year. Relations between the English government and the Curia
over provisions and taxation had become very strained, and the English envoys

---

[30] Cf. *Vitae paparum avenionensium* edd. Baluze & Mollat, II.304–5; see also below, p. 190.
[31] Jones, 'The English Church', p. 21; McHardy, 'Liturgy and propaganda', p. 220.
[32] Knighton, *Chronicon*, ed. Lumby, II.110.
[33] *Ibid.*, II.94.
[34] Wood, *Omnino partialitate cessante*, p. 182. The quotation is from I Maccabees iii.58.

noted with growing unease the enfeoffment of Louis de la Cerda with the Canary Islands in November and the grant of crusade-status to the expedition being planned to conquer the islands and convert the natives to Christianity. They suspected that the crusade was really intended for England:[35]

> It was public knowledge at the Curia that this prince would lead a big army and fleet to the islands in the following summer, and that both the pope and the king of France were making very substantial preparations of sailing ships and galleys, at their own expense, on his behalf. As a result of all this the English and the supporters of the king of England considered the very likely possibility [uerisimilem coniecturam] that when all the foregoing had been prepared, the prince would invade the island of Great Britain with the help of the pope and the king of France, under the pretence that it was one of the Fortunate Islands [the Canaries] and in rebellion against the Apostolic See.

Not surprisingly, the peace-talks broke down and the English resumed the offensive in the spring of 1345.[36]

This chain of events is not easy to interpret. English fears were almost certainly unjustified in this instance, since the real background to Louis's enfeoffment was the accelerating interest shown in the Canaries in the early 1340s; it is hard to believe that Clement VI would have written to the Iberian monarchs, trying to enlist their support for Louis, had he really been planning an invasion of England.[37] Was this, then, another instance of English propaganda, designed to bring about the collapse of the talks and to justify further anti-papal moves in England? It is true that the peace-talks were doomed to failure and that both sides were ready for renewed conflict. But an invasion of England masquerading as a crusade would have been in accordance with a string of recent events, such as the diversion of a Franco-papal crusade-flotilla into the Guelph-Ghibelline struggle in 1319, Philip VI's transfer of his crusade-fleet to the Channel in 1336–7, and French siphoning of a crusade tenth into the Anglo-French conflict between 1335 and 1344.[38] Together with Clement VI's partisan activity and the unfortunate timing of the enfeoffment, this consideration makes English fears comprehensible, even if the envoys knew nothing of the pressure exerted on John XXII by Philip V in 1317–1319.

In reality, although Clement VI was lavish in his provision of financial assistance to the French court, there is no evidence that either he or Innocent VI sanctioned the employment of crusade-institutions against the English: the repercussions of such an action would clearly have made the Statutes of Provisors

---

[35] Adam Murimuth, Continuatio chronicarum, ed. Thompson, p. 163. Cf. Wood, Omnino partialitate cessante, pp. 185–7.

[36] Perroy, The Hundred Years War, pp. 116–18.

[37] Lettres, edd. Déprez et al., nos 1314–15; see also nos 1348–9.

[38] Housley, The Italian Crusades, pp. 100–1; Tyerman, 'Philip VI', p. 25; Housley, The Avignon Papacy, pp. 178–85.

and Praemunire seem trivial.[39] Crusading did, however, become a feature of internal political life in France from 1361 to 1369, entering it from a rather different direction, that of the *routier*-threat and attempts to counter it by issuing indulgences. Beginning in January 1361, when a force of mercenaries seized Pont-Saint-Esprit and threatened the papal court at Avignon, the Curia adopted the practice of granting plenary indulgences, usually *in articulo mortis*, to people who took up arms against the companies' combination of looting and protection racketeering. Usually this took the form of the issue of Urban V's bull *Cogit nos*.[40]

This, of course, was not a 'national crusade', nor was it directed specifically against the English. Indeed, the stimulus of indulgences was called for precisely because the French Crown was incapable at this time of organising resistance to the companies. Opposition to their activity was inherently localised and fragmented, taking the characteristic shape of *ad hoc* leagues of seigneurs, urban communities, and royal seneschals or baillis. The tradition, ecclesiastical and popular, in which the anti-*routier* movement functioned was that of the eleventh- and twelfth-century Peace of God, rather than that of the 'national crusade' of, for example, Charles of Anjou in 1264–1268. The *routiers* were commonly dubbed 'the English' by those whom they tormented, because Edward III created the circumstances in which they could operate. However, not all were Englishmen, and the companies did not execute royal policy.

Ironically, the temporary collapse of national monarchy in France had opened the way for what the Capetian publicists had worked towards but never quite achieved: a clear statement by the papal Curia that the *defensio regni Francie* was a holy task, without reference to a planned *passagium* to the East. The correspondence of Pope Urban V is pervaded by an understandable sense of horror at the devastation of the *patria*: 'they are striving to destroy the kingdom of France not only in a hostile fashion, but in that of the pagan infidels'.[41] For the English, the danger was that, as Charles V reconstructed royal authority and contemplated the renewal of the war against England, the French court might effect the subtle transfer of the anti-*routier* crusade to the level of the national conflict, in the same way as it had made the anti-Moorish crusade into an instrument of French policy in 1365.[42]

It is perhaps in this context that we should interpret a petition which Charles V presented to the Curia *ca* 1368. The French king objected to papal attempts to restrict such indulgences as were granted to opponents of the *routiers* to those who died in battle or of wounds received there. He argued that the mercenaries were schismatics, and by implication heretics, and that they should be subjected to the full rigours of the crusade: anybody who fought them, *ubicunque existant*, who provided money for the struggle or who supplied the royal forces, should

[39] Pantin, *The English Church*, pp. 81–7.
[40] Housley, 'The mercenary companies'.
[41] *Lettres*, edd. Lecacheux and Mollat, no. 1500.
[42] Housley, 'The mercenary companies', pp. 275–6.

enjoy the full indulgence of the crusader. All nobles and prelates who had ignored or abused papal processes against the *routiers* and their *fautores* should themselves be condemned as fautors.[43] Urban V did not accede to these requests in full, but in January 1369 he both extended the plenary indulgence *in articulo mortis* for another two years and granted unspecified partial indulgences to the categories of contributor which Charles V had mentioned. This decree was to be published throughout France in cathedrals and parish-churches.[44]

Like other fourteenth-century rulers granted less than the full apparatus of the crusade, Charles V wanted more, plainly because it would be more profitable. But the timing of the petition makes one suspect that there was more to it than that. If, as seems highly likely, this document was presented to Urban V in the final months of 1368, then it was drawn up at the point when Charles, accepting the appeals of his Gascon sub-vassals, was deliberately heading towards renewed war with England. The pope's letter of January 1369 was published after Charles V's proclamation that he had the right to hear Gascon appeals.[45] It could be argued that Charles was simply adding weapons to his armoury lest he should have to deal with the *routier*-problem at the same time as fighting the English; but, as the renewal of war would effectively end this problem by giving the companies proper employment again, it is hard to avoid the conclusion that when he submitted his petition Charles was really thinking ahead to the reconquest of Gascony and the reduction of its English garrisons. These would have contained large numbers of former *routiers*, now soldiers of the English king but still classifiable as opponents of the crusade.

This is hypothetical: I know of no traces of the administration of indulgences to finance the reconquest of Gascony in 1369–1374 or of the bestowal of the indulgence *in articulo mortis* to Charles V's soldiers.[46] But, besides being fully in line both with the French court's hard-pressed financial position in 1368-9,[47] and with earlier attempts to secure indulgences against its christian enemies, the suggestion does flow quite naturally from Charles V's justifiable view that the *routier*-problem was not only originally caused by the English but was sustained by the Prince of Wales's activities in the 1360s. In 1369, for example, he argued that, if the ransom due for his father's release had not been paid, it was because of the disruption caused by the king of England's mercenaries.[48] It is also worth noting that, of all the Avignon popes, Urban V was the most likely to have declared a crusade against the English, under the useful cover of the anti-*routier* approach. Not only was he prepared to go further than either Clement VI or Innocent VI in backing the Valois cause,[49] but he was as desperate as Charles V

[43] Denifle, *La Désolation*, II.505.
[44] *Ibid.*, II.506–7.
[45] Perroy, *The Hundred Years War*, pp. 159–62; Delachenal, *Histoire de Charles V*, IV, ch. 4.
[46] Delachenal, *Histoire de Charles V*, IV, chs 6–13 *passim*. It is worth pointing out that evidence for such procedures is generally slight in this period.
[47] Henneman, *Royal Taxation . . . 1356–1370*, pp. 255ff.
[48] *Ibid.*, p. 253.
[49] Palmer, 'England, France'.

to find a solution to the problem of the mercenaries. In September 1368 the pope was compelled to reissue indulgences against a fresh incursion by the companies into the Comtat Venaissin.[50]

Even if this interpretation of these documents is valid, it would remain the only instance in the period 1302–1378 of a pope sanctioning the use of crusading institutions by either France or England against a national enemy. Crusade-related propaganda was adroitly used; revenue, arms, and shipping intended for the crusade to the East were diverted into the Anglo-French war; the national Churches' material and spiritual resources were rigorously harnessed to the needs of the Crown; and indulgences were offered to those who took up arms against the threat of French invasion in England and against the depredations of the routiers in France. However, the full apparatus of the crusade – the measures for which Philip V petitioned in 1317–1319 and Charles V in 1368 – remained unattainable. The full crusade-indulgence, the intensive administration of vows, and the official preaching of the Cross with its associated privileges could be obtained only by persuading the papal curia to issue the relevant bulls; and this it would not do. The fact is striking evidence of the continuing and unquestioned control exercised by the Curia over the making of a crusade. Equally striking, however, is the fact that papal resistance was the only consideration which held a national crusade back. The other preconditions – in terms of governmental goals and thinking, the readiness of the vast majority of the clergy to co-operate with their rulers, and popular acceptance of crusading against a national enemy – were all fully developed by 1378.

These two points mean that the Great Schism, vitally important as it was, nevertheless exercised only the function of a catalyst. The Schism gave the Anglo-French conflict an added dimension, such that popular feeling held the national enemy to be schismatic; and by turning previous papal policy on its head, it also rapidly introduced crusading-institutions into the very struggle from which they had so long been excluded. For one of the means proposed to end the Schism was the *uia facti*, which Pierre d'Ailly in 1381 characterised as 'the way of those who say that in this case it is necessary to proceed against the schismatics by excommunicating them and taking military action against them'.[51] With the existence of a long tradition of crusades against schismatics and excommunicates, and an immediate background of crusading in Italy under Urban V and Gregory XI, acceptance of the *uia facti* almost inevitably involved the crusade. Thus in November 1378, less than two months after his election, Urban VI sent the archbishop of Canterbury the bull *Nuper cum uinea*, with its grant of crusading-indulgence and privileges to all who took the Cross to fight against Clement VII and his supporters. Urban ordered the crusade to be preached throughout England.[52]

[50] Denifle, *La Désolation*, II.517.
[51] Swanson, *Universities*, p. 46.
[52] *Concilia*, ed. Wilkins, III.138–40; see also Lunt, *Financial Relations*, pp. 535ff.

The timing of *Nuper cum vinea* was inauspicious. Richard II was a minor; the King's Council and parliament were divided; John of Gaunt and Archbishop William of Courtenay were at odds over the recent breach of sanctuary in Westminster Abbey; and, above all, the country was war-weary. Events in Flanders, on the other hand, forced the government to consider an expedition. The Flemish cloth-manufacturing towns were of central importance to the English wool-trade, and taxes on wool exported to Flanders via the Calais staple vital for government-finance. After the marriage of Louis of Mâle's daughter, Margaret, to Philip the Bold of Burgundy in 1369, England faced the danger of a Flanders dominated by the French. The Schism, which caused Urbanist Ghent to rebel against the Clementist Louis in 1379/80 and again in January 1382, offered a way out of this difficulty, since rebel leaders were prepared, under the right conditions, to accept English suzerainty. It also induced an immediate crisis, because Louis sealed off the Bruges–Calais road and forced England to suspend the staple in May 1382.[53]

These considerations forced the English government to plan a Continental expedition, and therefore to show interest in Urban VI's proposed crusade. Nevertheless, negotiations between English envoys and the Roman curia, in the winter of 1381/2, show that the former were prepared to accept a crusade only on their own terms. Among other demands, they insisted that the crusade-bull should be directed specifically against the schismatic kingdoms of France, Scotland, and Castile rather than against Clement VII (presumably because this would be more popular), and that Urban VI should donate some of the proceeds of cameral taxation in England towards the crusade. The grant of indulgences was not enough: 'Wars are not waged through indulgences, nor can these meet the cost of wages these days'.[54] By the time Parliament met, in October 1382, ambitious plans for an Anglo-German offensive had been abandoned and two alternative projects were mooted: an expedition to aid the Flemish rebels, and a crusade to Castile led by John of Gaunt, who in 1371 had acquired by marriage a claim to the Castilian throne. Apart from John's powerful personal support, the Castilian project had the strategic appeal of bringing a major neighbour of France into the English camp.

The proponent of the *voie de Flandre* was Henry Despenser, bishop of Norwich. Despenser, aptly dubbed *episcopus bellicosus* by a contemporary, had already secured a crusade-bull, *Dudum cum vinea*, in March 1381.[55] Events in Flanders in 1382 persuaded the London capitalists to give his project their backing, and, although John's opposition prevented the October parliament from giving its sanction to Despenser's crusade, the battle of Roosebeke (27 November 1382), in which the Flemish militia was heavily defeated by a French army, forced the government to accede to it. Recruitment thus proceeded in the spring

---

[53] Perroy, *L'Angleterre*, pp. 167–75.
[54] *Ibid.*, pp. 392–404, especially pp. 399, 403.
[55] *Wykeham's Register*, ed. Kirby, II.198–206; Lunt, *Financial Relations*, pp. 535–6.

of 1383, despite the continuing hostility of John of Gaunt and the aristocracy generally, who viewed a campaign led by a bishop as an affront to their natural rights of war-leadership. The first true 'national crusade' preached in England thus occurred against a backcloth of indecisiveness, disquiet, and barely suppressed factional animosity.

Nevertheless, the preaching of the crusade aroused great enthusiasm. This was partly due to the rare generosity of the indulgences offered to those who enlisted or gave money[56] and to the energy displayed by Despenser's preachers (who worked on a commission-basis), but it was also the result of the crusade's unprecedented fusion of national sentiment and religious zeal. In the first point of his *ordinationes pro cruciata publicanda* Despenser stated that his crusade was on behalf of God, Church, and kingdom,[57] and the archbishop of Canterbury made much the same comment in a letter of April 1383: 'The Church cannot have peace without the Realm, nor can the well-being of the Realm be secured except through the Church, and it is both meritorious to fight for the Faith and fitting to fight for one's Lord.'[58] The preaching of the crusade in fact marks the culmination of the English Church's contribution towards the national war-effort in the fourteenth century: all its resources were placed at Despenser's disposal, and he stage-managed ceremonies at St Paul's and Westminster Abbey which emphasised the dual character of the enterprise.[59]

Thomas Walsingham and Henry Knighton, among others, testified to the resultant fervour. Knighton wrote that 'he collected ... an inestimable and incredible amount of money in gold and silver, together with jewels, necklaces, rings, plate, figures, pearls, and other ornaments, especially from ladies and other women, for it was said that one lady alone gave him 100 pounds', adding that 'in this way the kingdom's secret treasure, which lay in the hands of women, was placed in danger'. Recruitment, as usual with fourteenth-century crusades, took several forms: some paid men-at-arms and archers to fight on their behalf, while others decided to go in person.[60] Walsingham wrote that 'almost nobody' refused to give money or take the Cross, and such great sums were collected and carried to Despenser that the poorest of England's bishops was able to carry out a project which his detractors had described as impossible.[61] Most striking, however, is Froissart's claim that a large Gascon tun was filled with money collected for the crusade in the diocese of London alone.[62]

Crusade-enthusiasm on this scale has few parallels in the fourteenth century – perhaps only that displayed in Italian cities when indulgences were preached for the Smyrna crusade in 1344/5.[63] Moreover, it spilled over into the expedition

[56] Housley, *Avignon Papacy*, pp. 128–43.
[57] Knighton, *Chronicon*, ed. Lumby, II.201.
[58] *Concilia*, ed. Wilkins, II.177.
[59] *Westminster Chronicle*, edd. Hector and Harvey, pp. 32, 38.
[60] Knighton, *Chronicon*, ed. Lumby, II.198–9.
[61] Walsingham, *Historia anglicana*, ed. Riley, II.85.
[62] *Oeuvres de Froissart*, ed. Kervyn de Lettenhove, X.207.
[63] Housley, *The Avignon Papacy*, pp. 146–8.

itself. The army, which made the crossing to Calais in May 1383, operated in an atmosphere of crusading zeal: when it marched on Gravelines it was preceded by a *vexillum sanctae crucis*; it received exhortatory pre-battle speeches which stressed that its cause was God's; it attributed its successes to divine assistance manifested through miracles. When news of its early successes reached England, large numbers of individuals, including clerics and London apprentices, spontaneously took the Cross and joined the army in Flanders, much to the irritation of Despenser, who had no use for them.[64]

It is important to lay emphasis on this enthusiasm because historians have devoted much attention to contemporary criticism of Despenser, both during and after his crusade. It is true that John Wyclif, the Lollards John Aston and John Corringham, and others condemned the whole enterprise: but their views had little popular resonance.[65] As for the proceedings against Despenser in the autumn of 1383, these focused on the bishop's own shortcomings, which were largely responsible for the crusade's ultimate failure. The crusade proved to be a scandal not because it was a perversion of the idea of holy war but as a result of abuses in the preaching of its indulgences and the fact that a good chance to inflict a defeat on the French, who forced Despenser to abandon his Flemish allies, had been lost through incompetence in the field. The expedition was anomalous in its structure, not in its character as a *cruciata*.[66] No doubt many wistfully reflected on what might have been achieved had an army raised in such popular circumstances been led by the Black Prince.

One indication that Despenser's crusade was not as scandalous as some have supposed is John of Gaunt's revival of the *voie d'Espagne* in 1386. At Aljubarotta in August 1385 the Portuguese defeated the Castilians, and there were hopes that an English expedition would be able to conquer Castile. John secured Richard II's permission to lead an army to the Iberian peninsula, and he began to utilise the bulls which Urban VI had sent him in 1383. The crusade was proclaimed at St Paul's in February 1386, and the preaching campaign began in April. As in 1382/3, generous indulgences were offered in exchange for cash-payments, but the response was certainly less impressive. Walsingham's comment was that 'by frequent granting, these indulgences and pardons were so cheapened and tarnished in the popular view, that there were few who gave anything in this renewed Cross-taking'.[67] This indicates that a combination of frequency and abuses had eroded enthusiasm in England.

Clement VII was no less willing than was Urban VI to use the crusade against the rival obedience and its supporters: in 1382 he granted indulgences to those who undertook to follow Louis of Anjou to southern Italy, where France hoped

64 Walsingham, *Historia anglicana*, ed. Riley, II.88–96; Pantin, 'A medieval treatise', pp. 359–61; *The Westminster Chronicle*, edd. Hector & Harvey, pp. 40, 44.
65 Siberry, 'Criticism'; see also Perroy, *L'Angleterre*, p. 188n.
66 Aston, 'The impeachment'.
67 Walsingham, *Historia anglicana*, ed. Riley, II.143; see also Perroy, *L'Angleterre*, ch. 6; Russell, *The English Intervention*, ch. 17; Lunt, *Financial Relations*, pp. 544–8.

to entrench its influence in the same way as Despenser and John of Gaunt planned to do in Flanders and Castile.[68] Indeed, if these crusades were on a smaller scale than might have been expected in the light of developments before 1378, it is not because of hesitancy on the part of either obedience about using the *via facti*, but because the initial stages of the Schism coincided with a quiet phase in the Anglo-French war. By the time hostilities began again in earnest, in 1415, the *via facti*, and by implication the crusade, were generally discredited in favour of peaceful solutions. Crusading against the supporters of a rival obedience continued to occur in Italy, but it played no further part in the Hundred Years' War.[69]

Attempts to forge a clear link between national interests and the crusade thus never bore full fruit in either France or England in the fourteenth century. A comparison with the papal-Angevin crusades against the last of the Staufen is revealing. From 1263 to 1268 Charles of Anjou and the Curia created and maintained a satisfactory working-relationship, because Urban IV and Clement IV were resolved to use the crusade to destroy Manfred and Conradin, and Charles was ambitious and strong enough to execute this policy. Problems arose – notably in persuading Louis IX to support the crusade, finding the money needed, and controlling Angevin ambitions – but there was an underlying consensus on what had to be done.[70] By contrast, between 1302 and 1378 neither the French nor the English could persuade the popes to back them fully; and after 1378 they were not in a position to use papal pliability to best effect.

Apart from a brief period in 1382–1386, the French and English governments never succeeded in making the crusade an instrument of royal policy and national endeavour,[71] but they did take many steps in that direction. In a period when national sentiment was felt more and more strongly, when English contemporaries were accepting William of Courtenay's identification of the needs of Church and state, and when the papacy had been preaching crusades against its Christian enemies for more than a century, such steps were not only natural but almost inevitable.[72] It was purely fortuitous that the late fourteenth century did not experience the extraordinary event of armies of French and English soldiers, *crucesignati* against each other, clashing on the battlefield.[73]

---

[68] Valois, *La France*, II.24.
[69] Lunt, *Financial Relations*, pp. 559–62.
[70] Jordan, *Les origines*.
[71] By contrast, the Iberian and East European kings did succeed in this, because their lands bordered on those of Moors and pagans: Housley, *The Avignon Papacy*, pp. 50–74.
[72] Considerations of space have precluded any treatment of analogous trends in Scotland, but see MacQuarrie, *Scotland*, pp. 70ff.
[73] Ironically, in 1390 the Genoese witnessed the curious spectacle of crusaders from rival obediences embarking together to fight the Muslims in North Africa: Setton, *The Papacy*, I.333.

Counselling the king:
perceptions of court politics in poetry of the reign of Richard II

M. E. J. HUGHES

In a poem from the last year of Richard II's reign, an anonymous poet offers what appears to be a series of little snippets of domestic and agrarian wisdom: if you fail to crop a bush, it will grow wild; if you do not mow the green grass, it will take over the whole field; a large bag must be sown up and made smaller, otherwise it will get holes in it. The poem is, of course, the famous allegorical satire against King Richard's ministers, Sir John Bushey, Sir Henry Greene, and Sir William Bagot.[1] It is one of the wittiest of the many political poems which survive from the end of the fourteenth century.[2] It focuses its attack not on the king himself but rather on his 'bad counsellors', blaming the corrupt practices and the inefficiency manifest in the government of the country on Richard's advisers. This limitation of radicalism is typical of much political verse of the middle ages: *Rex ut salvetur, falsis maledictio detur!*, exclaims a poet almost exactly a century before Bushey, Bagot, and Greene came under attack;[3] in a poem of 1338–1340, 'Ens el mois de Setembre ...', on the theme of the French wars, the anonymous poet depicts the king, Edward III, presiding peacefully over his London court until one of his counsellors, Robert of Artois, *comencha la guerre et l'orible hustin* with France which was to cause the death of many a *bon chevalier*;[4] and a third poet, writing in the reign of Edward II, laments that the abuses of the taxation system could be remedied 'ac were the king wel avised, and wolde worche bi skile'.[5]

---

[1] *Political Poems and Songs*, ed. Wright, I.363–6.
[2] There are several anthologies of such political verse. The most useful is still *Historical Poems*, ed. Robbins. *Political Poems and Songs*, ed. Wright, contains many valuable Latin examples.
[3] *Political Songs of England*, ed. Wright, pp. 182–7: edited from London, British Library, MS. Harley 2253.
[4] *Political Poems and Songs*, ed. Wright, I.1–25. This poem is commonly called *The Vows of the Heron*; it is edited from Bern, Burgerbibliothek, MS. 323.
[5] *Political Songs of England*, ed. Wright, pp. 323–45, at p. 338. The poem is known as *The Simonie*. An edition from a different manuscript, and a discussion of the poem's date, is given by Ross, 'On the evil times', p. 174.

Indeed, we can identify a satiric motif of attack, recurring throughout the four-teenth century, against the king's counsellors.[6]

In this essay, I should like to ask what conclusions can be drawn about this apparent tradition of poetic attacks against members of the king's inner circle of advisers. Should we see such poems as evidence of the perennial, and historically verifiable, problems which confronted the mediaeval kings of England: those of finding good counsellors, of keeping channels of information open between the court and powerful political lobbies, and of assessing the importance and influ-ence of various social groups?[7] or should we see the consistency of such attacks against members of court throughout the middle ages as evidence of a literary tradition, emerging as much out of theoretical notions of kingship and popular satiric verses about rulers as out of any perception of the contemporary situation at a particular time?[8]

The theme of the bad counsellor, misadvising the ruler of the day or conceal-ing important information from him, is, of course, only one of many political themes which are introduced into fourteenth-century verse. The complementary theme of the king who fails to look for, or take, advice, being *redeles*[9] or *sine consilio*,[10] also appears. There is, too, a good selection of poems which wholehear-tedly support the king, his advisers and his decisions, such as the proudly jingois-tic verses of Laurence Minot. Indeed, satires against bad counsellors represent only one side of a complex discussion of decision-making at court which the whole corpus of fourteenth-century verse provides. Satire and eulogy, jingoism and bitterness, personal complaint and general history: these contrasting styles and tones of writing are all brought into play in poetry about court-politics. It is clear that the poets who composed such diverse accounts of the king and his

---

6 For example, see *Political Songs of England*, ed. Wright, pp. 72–121, and Gower's 'Tri-partite Chronicle', in *Works*, ed. Macaulay, IV,iv.1.

7 A good deal of research has been done on this topic. See Tuck, 'Richard II's system of patronage', p. 7 (where the author describes the personal involvement of Richard in deciding petitions of a delicate political nature); Thomson, *The Transformation*, pp. 284–7; and, for a more detailed account of the structure and organisation of the king's inner council, see Baldwin, *The King's Council*.

8 The following lines were written in the reign of Henry III: *Regis a duersarii sunt hostes bellantes, / Et consiliarii regi adulantes, / Qui uerbis fallacibus principem seducunt, / Linguis-que duplicibus in errorem ducunt* (*Political Songs of England*, ed. Wright, p. 99). Walter Map suggests the other side of the same coin when he points out that those who surround the king are never sure of their position: *Multitudo certe sumus infinita, uni soli placere contendens: et hodie sumus una multitudo, cras erimus alia . . .': De nugis curialium*, ed. James, rev. Brooke & Mynors, p. 2. The theme of foolish courtiers and inadequate counsellors is, however, not peculiar to mediaeval literature; it is commonplace in Classical Latin satire, notably in Persius's famous fourth *Satire*.

9 See 'Abuses of the Age 1', in *Historical Poems*, ed. Robbins, no. 56 (p. 144), from London British Library, MS. Harley 913. See also the poem known as 'Richard the Redeless', in *The Vision of William*, ed. Skeat, I.603–28, especially p. 606.

10 *Political Songs of England*, ed. Wright, p. 182. Gower writes of the 'immature counsel of fools' in his 'Tripartite Chronicle': *Works*, ed. Macaulay, div. 1, line 15.

ministers must have belonged to a variety of political lobbies and held a range of political opinions.

Furthermore, even if we were to single out the poems on the theme of the bad counsellor as a type of sub-species of court satire, we should still find a multiplicity of apparent purposes and persuasions underlying the attacks. In some poems, the monarch of the day is shown weakly or erroneously leading the country to war through ill counsel;[11] in others, it is on account of bad advice that the king makes peace.[12] In certain poems the king's foreign-policy advisers are shown as the enemies of domestic prosperity;[13] but in other poems corruption in court-circles at home is blamed for the poor conditions suffered by soldiers overseas.[14] Not only did those ministers who advised the king come under attack in verse long before the accession of Richard II, but we can see that the medium of poetry was used by a variety of political lobbies in the search for a means of expressing their grievances.[15]

The fact that such a diversity of opinions is expressed in verse during the fourteenth century (and, indeed, from the Conquest onwards) is very interesting; so, too, is the fact that poetry, often using highly contrived devices, such as allegory, personification, or word-play, should become a medium for political expression at all. Several scholars have asked why this should be. Janet Coleman, for example, suggests that verse of political complaint shares many of its techniques with poetic romance but differs in its 'confrontation with moral dilemmas constituting the "real" and the "now".'[16] Dr Coleman briefly touches on the reasons why she feels that verse was particularly suitable for political purposes: the metrical line permits statements of a 'more epigrammatic' nature than a prose-line allows; and it is characteristic of verse complaints that they combine the specificity of real events with the generalities of abstract truths.[17] V. J.-Scattergood believes that the wide currency of verse as a medium for all types of subject – astrology, topography, alchemy, hunting, and so on – makes the exist-

---

[11] Political Songs of England, ed. Wright, p. 182: 'Grantz mals ly fist aver gravesque ruinas, / celi qe ly fist passer partes transmarinas.' This poem was written in the reign of Edward I.

[12] This theme becomes especially prominent after the peace with France, ratified in 1360. See Piers Plowman, ed. Schmidt, p. 312, on Langland's treatment of the theme, and also the further discussion below.

[13] Political Songs of England, ed. Wright, p. 183: 'Ne puet estre que tiel consail constat Deo carum . . .'; see also ibid., p. 197: 'Thos kingis ministris beth i-schend . . .' Both these poems were written in the reign of Edward I.

[14] Political Songs of England, ed. Wright, p. 335: 'Ac o shrewe in a court many man may shende.' On soldiers as the source of rumours about the mismanagement of the wars in France, see Barrie, War, p. 33; Hewitt, The Organization, ch. 7.

[15] The vast majority of these political poems are anonymous. For attempts to identify 'typical' versifiers, see Scattergood, Politics and Poetry, pp. 14–18: Owst, Literature and Pulpit, pp. 210–36.

[16] Coleman, Medieval Readers and Writers, p. 97.

[17] Ibid., p. 98; see also Peter, Complaint and Satire, p. 9; and, on the tone of these poems, Kinney, 'The temper'.

ence of political poetry unsurprising.[18] However, Stephen Medcalf, writing specifically about the political poetry of the reign of Richard II, has a further suggestion: he comments that certain traditional poetic modes, such as the allegorical vision or the verbal ambiguity, permit quite complex social or political ideas to be put forward; and they even allow the poet to describe a political situation whose ethics are extremely complicated.[19]

Indeed, if we pursue Dr Medcalf's suggestion further, we find that much late fourteenth-century verse is generated by a desire to marry contemporary political grievances, on the one hand, with the most general notions of the function performed by a king, on the other. In other words, references to the political situation were fused with rather aphoristic expressions of theories of kingship in order to bring a moral dimension into specific complaint-literature. For example, in a poem preserved in three manuscripts and dating from around 1388,[20] the king is alleged to be ill-informed about his country and ignorant of its plight: 'The kyng knowyth not alle, / non sunt qui vera loquuntur.'[21] The poem contains what appear to be specific references to contemporary events, not only lamenting the injustices of the lawcourts and the decline in public order (both traditional themes of mediaeval satire),[22] but also alluding to the flight of Robert de Vere and Michael de la Pole in 1388.[23] The poem concludes with the wish that, as he grows older, the king will become aware of his people's state: 'Ful welle that he knowe, / quanto dolet Anglia luctu. / O rex, si rex es, rege te, vel eris sine re rex, / Nomen habes sine re, nisi te recteque regas rex.'[24] The account of the problems caused by the king's youth and his bad counsellors merge into an expression of the most abstract notion of kingship, the matter (res) of being the king. The fact that this is expressed in Latin adds to its aphoristic tone.[25] In a later poem, probably composed at the turn of the century, 'For drede ofte my lippes y steke . . .',[26] the poet complains of the inequalities of the judicial system in England,

---

[18]   Scattergood, Politics and Poetry, p. 14.
[19]   Medcalf, 'Piers Plowman and the Ricardian age', p. 653.
[20]   Political Poems and Songs, ed. Wright, I.270–8, at p. 273. On manuscripts and the dating of the poem, see ibid., p. 270.
[21]   The poem is macaronic throughout, and the Latin tags are often used to marry contempory events with accepted general wisdom.
[22]   See Mann, Chaucer and Medieval Estates Satire, pp. 86–91.
[23]   This apparent allusion is used by Wright to date the poem. The poem describes 'Jacke and Jacke Noble' fleeing to regna remota: Political Poems and Songs, ed. Wright, I.274.
[24]   Ibid., p. 278. The same Latin couplet appears in the Prologue to Piers Plowman. One of the most useful discussions of this theory of kingship is Baldwin, The Theme of Government.
[25]   Auerbach, Literary Language, provided a major study of the kinds of uses to which Latin was put during the middle ages and suggested its qualities of epigrammatic and aphoristic expression.
[26]   Historical Poems, ed. Robbins, pp. 39–44. The poem probably dates from just after the deposition of Richard and is among those preserved in Oxford, Bodleian Library, MS. Digby 102. On the manuscript, see the Introduction to Twenty-Six Political and Other Poems, ed. Kail.

especially the judgement of petitions presented to the king and his court, but he adds, rather hastily:

> A kyng may not al aspie:
> Summe telle hym soþ, summe telle hym les.
> Þe whete fro þe chaf 3 try3e,
> So mowe 3e leue in rest & pes.
> I speke not in specyale
> Of oo kyngdom the lawe to telle,
> I speke hool in generale
> In eche kyngdom the law to telle.[27]

Then, to make his point clear, the poet comments that two things contribute to the supremacy of a country: 'Wys counseil, and good gouernance'.[28] A further example of such juxtaposition of contemporary reference and moral didacticism may be found in the long account of the events of 1399, 'And as I passid in my preiere . . .', which was composed in about September of that year.[29] Richard II is described as *redeless*, and his counsellors are derided as mere ghosts, who have never seen the field of battle (25–6). Had the king himself ruled the kingdom, murder and corruption would not have been rife (76–7), but he chose counsellors who were young and heady with power: 'The cheuyteyns cheef that 3e chesse euere / Weren all to yonge of 3eris to yeme swyche a rewme' (88–9). The point of the poem, however, is to act as a warning, 'ffor kyngis and kayseris comynge here-after' (85).

The literary quality of fourteenth-century political verse is increased when an ethical or a political dilemma is suggested by the poet. *Piers Plowman* is the prime example of a text in which a poet attempts to show that conflicting notions of the king's role put him in a position in which decision-making and the taking of counsel are extremely difficult. It is interesting that Langland reveals this conflict at greater length in the C-text, written in 1385/6,[30] than in either of the earlier versions of the poem. It is also interesting that Langland shows the problematic nature of the issue of how the king should take advice in a poetic style which features several of the most contrived 'literary' devices. The passage with which I am concerned is C.IV.156–507, a debate between two allegorical characters, Mede and Conscience,[31] and particularly Mede's attack on

---

[27] *Historical Poems*, ed. Robbins, pp. 40–1.
[28] *Ibid.*, p. 44.
[29] This poem is known as *Richard Redeless*, and it has been suggested that the poet may have been influenced by Langland's *Piers Plowman*, but the connections are tenuous. The poem is edited by Skeat (see above, n. 9) and in *Political Poems and Songs*, ed. Wright, I.368–417.
[30] For the evidence of the dates of the three versions, see *Piers Plowman*, ed. Schmidt, pp. xii–xvi.
[31] Although there are several more recent editions of the C-text, I shall be using the Skeat-edition (see above, n. 9), since it is still the most useful parallel edition containing all three versions of the text.

Conscience for being a bad counsellor (C.IV.232–84). The verb to counsel ('counseille') and the noun 'counsail' are repeated again and again during Mede's attack. Conscience, she says, has defamed her before the king, for 'culde ich nevere no kyng ne consailed so to done' (C.IV.233). It is Conscience, asserts Mede, who disheartens many soldiers (C.IV.237) and misadvises the king: 'Cay-tiflyche thow, Conscience consailedist the kyng leten / In hus enemys honde hys heritage of Fraunce' (C.IV.243–3). Then, in some lines which have no parallel in the earlier versions of the poem, Mede adds some general advice to kings:

> 'For-thy ich counsayle no kyng eny counsayle aske
> At Conscience, yf he coueyteth to conquery a reome.
> For sholde neuere Conscience be my constable,
> Were ich a kyng ycoroned by Marye,' quath Mede,
> 'Ne be mareschal of my men ther ich moste fyghte!'   (C.IV.254–8)

It was through Conscience's counsel, Mede argues, that the king abandoned France and sold his rights 'for a lytel moneye' (C.IV.264–5).

In this passage, we find a series of conflicts: between the role of the two disputants, Mede and Conscience, as representatives of abstracts and their char-acterisation in the narrative as figures advising a king on a specific matter; between the contemporary preoccupation with King Edward's peace with France (which had been ratified in 1360 and by which the king forfeited his rights to the French throne) and a hypothetical notion of how a king – any king – ought to behave; between the ironic comment on the way the political world operates through bribery and corruption and the statement of economic reality – soldiers will only fight if they are paid. Indeed, Mede's arguments are put forward with as much force as Conscience's response. What we find here is that the ambiguitites inherent in the style of the passage – the allegory, word-play, and dialogue – raise questions both of a literary and of a political nature. The problems which we face in interpreting the passage – Who is speaking? Is the character expressing the author's opinion or acting as 'devil's avocate'? Is the speaker a counsellor or an abstract? Does the speaker realise all the implications of what he or she is saying? – suggest a complex relationship between political expediency and moral abso-lutes.[32] Mede's argument suggests that Langland has perceived, and has at-tempted to illustrate, society's paradoxical demand that a king should be a successful warrior, leading his country to military glory, while he should also ensure peace and justice at home, following his 'conscience'. One of the chief problems for any fourteenth-century English king was the need to maintain a fighting army at the same time as he controlled the financial burden being placed

[32] The wisdom of the Treaty of Bretigny was still a major issue in the reign of Richard II. For a mediaeval account of the peace, see *Anonimale Chronicle*, ed. Galbraith, pp. 46–9; for a discussion of the personification of meed in mediaeval literature, see Yunck, *The Lineage*.

on the tax-payers.[33] Equally, he had to repay services fairly, without seeming to favour or bribe his courtiers or advisers. Society demanded a careful balance: the king must be successful on the battlefield but not a danger to domestic prosperity; he must reward but not favour; and he must be practical without abandoning an abstract notion of 'the right'. Much fourteenth-century satire attacks the king for failing to achieve this kind of balance.

Like Langland, the poet of the 'Dialogue of Mede and Muchethank',[34] written probably a little after the C-text of *Piers Plowman*, chooses the debate-form in order to show this awkward balance demanded of the king. While Langland seems sympathetic to the ruler's difficulties, however, the poet of 'Mede and Muchethank' suggests that those who counsel the king cause corruption to spread both on the domestic front and in the wars abroad. The trait noted above of criticising counsellors, rather than the king, is also characteristic of this poem. The narrator of the poem sees two men disputing. The first is 'but in mene array'; the other, however, is 'clothed in gawdy gren' (10–11). The manner of dress of the disputants is of some significance, since it suggests immediately that one character's philosophy is more successful (at least in material terms) than the other's. The first man, badly clothed, turns out to be a travelling man (a foot-soldier), representing 'muchethank'. The other is a member of the court, a 'yes-man', or rather a 'yes- and no-man': he claims to please his lord with fripperies: '[I] fede hem forth with nay and ȝay' (28). He represents *mede*. The familiar criticism of counsellors' inability to give good advice because they live sinful lives[35] recurs here:

> In wikked lyuer no good counsayle,
> Is coward of kynde nyȝt and day.
> Good lyuere dar fende and assayle,
> And hardy in dede brouȝt to bay.
> I wolde thou were brouȝt to assay
> At nede a wys counseil to rede.
> Were thou as hardy as thou are gay.
> Ȝe were wel worthy to haue good mede.   (73–80).

Furthermore, the bad counsel of the courtier has perpetuated war: 'Thou woldest evere more were werre', accuses the soldier, 'for profyt and pilage thou myght glene' (67–8). The juxtaposition of the reality of the war with France, which leaves 'men of armes / In fight, in presoun, and distresse' (51–2), and the theor-

---

[33] On the close relations between war and economic prosperity, see Thomson, *The Transformation*, pp. 65–72: see also *ibid.*, p. 149, on the dual demands of defence and finance.

[34] *Twenty-Six Political and Other Poems*, ed. Kail, pp. 6–9. The poem is edited from MS. Digby 102. On this manuscript, see many references in Scattergood, *Politics and Poetry*; Mohl, *The Three Estates*, p. 108, on the supposed 'democratic' tendencies of the author of some of the Digby poems (though probably not the dialogue under discussion).

etical discussion of what it takes to be a good counsellor illustrates the common tendency of late fourteenth-century political verse to extract the moral from the contemporary political argument – in this case about whether to resume hostilities in France – and also the tendency to appeal to a notion of how the king ought to take advice in order to show the present situation as a deviation from a universally accepted ideal.

In these poems, the poets criticise the king's counsellors, but in doing so they seem to set themselves up as alternative counsellors. It is significant that, despite the anonymity of these poems, they almost invariably suggest an individual poetic voice, often expressing strong opinions in the first person. The authority implied for this alternative advice is the authority of general, accepted wisdom, and of a universally approved ideal of kingship. The comic side of this satiric posture is the poem with which I began this essay, the allegorical satire against Richard's ministers (see above, n. 1). Here, the appeal to accepted wisdom is very domestic. The king's counsellors must be treated just as one would treat the farm or objects around the house. The ideal of kingship which underlies so much contemporary verse is replaced by an ideal of husbandry.

In conclusion, one can say that mediaeval political verse about the king and his advisers is double-edged: it contains both specific complaint and also general theory in the tradition of the 'Mirror for Princes' genre. These two elements are kept in play through literary devices and modes of composition which contribute to the poeticism of the texts – devices such as allegory, debate, and word-play. In some cases, the interplay of complaint and theory serve to underline the corruption of the king's counsellors, but in others, notably the passage from *Piers Plowman*, they suggest the ethical and practical complexity of contemporary politics.

Gillion de Trazegnies:
a fifteenth-century Burgundian Eliduc?

FRANCES HORGAN

Once upon a time, a knight maligned by his enemies left his home and his wife
and took service with the king of Exeter. His valour was great, and he rose
quickly to become warden of the land. Now the king had a beautiful daughter
who fell in love with the knight and he with her. For a time he resisted his
passion, thinking of his wife at home, but at length his feelings overcame him,
and he took ship with the princess for his native land. At sea a great storm blew
up, and a sailor accused the knight, saying that his treason to his wife would
bring about all their deaths. On hearing that her lover was married, the princess
fell into a deathlike swoon and after the ship had landed was carried by the
knight to a chapel in the forest near his home. Thinking the princess dead, the
knight rejoined his wife but could not conceal his grief. Some days later, the wife
discovered the princess in the chapel and realized the cause of her husband's
sorrow. With the aid of a magic flower, she restored the girl to life and withdrew
to a convent so that her husband and the princess could marry. This they did,
and they lived happily for many years until at length they too entered religion,
and the princess was received with honour by her husband's first wife.

Marie de France's *Eliduc*, composed in all probability in England in the last
third of the twelfth century, is perhaps the most famous literary treatment of a
theme which recurs, under various guises, in a number of mediaeval works,
ranging from the final part of *Tristan* to the anonymous *Beuves de Hamtone*, and
which has been taken up in our own time by John Fowles.[1] Gaston Paris first
drew attention to the theme of the 'man with two wives' in an article in which
he discussed three versions: *Eliduc*, the legend of the count of Gleichen, and
Gillion de Trazegnies.[2] J. E. Matzke later identified the presence of the same theme
in a number of other works, including *Le Fresne*, *Ille et Galeron*, *Galeran de
Bretagne*, *Beuves de Hamtone*, *King Horn*, and *Tristan*.[3] More recently, W. Ann

---

[1] In *The Ebony Tower*, (1974): Morse, John Fowles.
[2] Paris, *La poésie*, pp. 109–30.
[3] Matzke, 'Source and composition', and 'The lay of *Eliduc*'.

Trindade has re-examined this group of stories,[4] and the theme has been discussed in passing by several other scholars.[5]

By reducing these stories to their essentials, Matzke demonstrated that many had their origins in the reduplication of a tale of exile and winning a bride. In *Ille et Galeron*, for example,[6]

> A youth unknown and deprived of his heritage arrives at a court where he distinguishes himself by his bravery and is raised to an important office. In consequence a princess falls in love with him and the two are married. Presently they are separated. The knight journeys to another court where similar scenes are re-enacted, but he remains steadfast to his first love.

This outline, with minor modification, holds good for *King Horn* and *Beuves de Hamtone*. In addition to the basic outline, certain details are present in all three works: in each case, the hero defeats rejected suitors for the hand of the princess, and in all but *Beuves* the hero, on leaving the court of the second lady, promises to return if help should be needed.[7]

Matzke also noted the presence in a number of the stories of what he called the 'resemblance theme: the hero's attraction to the second lady is the result of her resemblance to the first. This theme is prominent in *Fresne*, *Galeran de Bretagne*, and the final part of *Tristan*, and may account for the similarity between the names of the two ladies in *Eliduc* (Guildeluëc and Guilliadun) and *Ille* (Galeron and Ganor). Sometimes, as in *Galeran de Bretagne*, the 'resemblance-theme' is interwoven with the exile-formula, while in *Fresne* this formula is absent.

Trindade agreed with Matzke that 'the "beginning of the legend" is the result of a common narrative technique, the process of repetition, one of the simplest ways of extending a narrative sequence'.[8] She suggested, however, that two distinct types of narrative pattern are discernible, and that 'the first type ... is based on a simple formula of repetition or doubling, while the lays of *Fresne* and *Eliduc* represent the modification of the first type through introduction of a different story pattern, one lacking any element of reduplication, but presenting

---

4   'The man with two wives'.
5   Notably by Schoepperle, *Tristan and Isolt*, pp. 158–77; Loomis, 'Problems'; Newstead, 'Isolt'.
6   Matzke, 'The lay of Eliduc', p. 214.
7   This is not to suggest that these romances are adequately summarised by such an outline, but in each case, the hero's involvement with the two ladies follows a similar pattern. Beuves de Hamtone, for example, is sold to Saracen sailors and taken to the court of King Hermin. There, his valour wins him the favour of the king and the love of his daughter, Josiane. After many adventures, the two are married but are soon separated. Beuves then arrives in the town of Civile, whose lady is being attacked by rejected suitors. He defeats the enemies and agrees, under duress, to a formal marriage with the lady on condition that she release him if Josiane reappears within seven years. Just in time, Josiane does reappear, and the two are reunited.
8   Trindade, 'The man with two wives', p. 468.

the two ladies in functional opposition to the husband'.[9] The 'different story pattern' she found in the Irish tale of 'The wooing of Fithir and Dáirine', where the king of Leinster, having married Dáirine, elder daughter of King Tuathal, tells her father that she is dead and takes the second daughter, Fithir. On finding her sister still alive, Fithir dies of shame, whereup Dáirine dies of grief. Trindade supposes that the Breton *Guildeluëc ha Guilliadun* may have been 'a short narrative modelled either directly on some version of the Fithir and Dáirine story or on a Tochmarc tale of the same type, in the same way that an *aithed* story, cognate perhaps with Diarmuid and Gráinne . . . may have suggested to the first Welsh Tristan poets the framework of the celebrated legend'.[10]

Matzke had already considered the absence of reduplication in *Eliduc*, and had suggested that Marie's lay reproduces only the second half of a reduplicated original. His argument is plausible, for the correspondences between *Eliduc* and *Horn* and *Ille* are undoubtedly striking. Like those heroes, Eliduc occupies an important position at the court of his king: *il aveit la tere a garder* (34). He is married to a noble lady from whom he is separated because he is maligned by jealous courtiers (cf. *Horn*). He goes to a foreign court, where he rises through his valour to become guardian of the land and wins the love of a foreign princess, who makes advances to him. He defeats rejected suitors for her hand, leaves the foreign court and promises to return if needed. It is certainly not impossible that in some earlier incarnation Eliduc was a youth deprived of his heritage who won for himself the favour of the king of Brittany and the hand of his daughter before the malicious tongues of his enemies drove him from the court. Admittedly, Guildeluëc does not appear to be the king's daughter, but this difference of detail does not affect the narrative structure.

Trindade's thesis is perhaps weakened by her attempt to associate *Eliduc* with *Fresne* in opposition to *Ille*, *Horn*, *Beuves*, *Galeran* and *Tristan*. She ignores the fact that *Eliduc* is linked to *Ille*, *Horn*, and *Beuves* by the prominence of the exile-formula, while in *Fresne* and to a large extent in *Tristan*, this formula is absent. Nevertheless, her remarks, in so far as they concern *Eliduc*, are pertinent. It is true that in the tale as we have it there is no element of reduplication and the two ladies are presented 'in functional opposition to the husband'. Whether or not this is the result of contamination by an Irish analogue must remain a matter for conjecture.

There is another striking difference between *Eliduc* and the other stories we are discussing: Eliduc alone of all the heroes betrays his first love. Horn remains true to Rimenhild; Beuves's marriage to the lady of Civile is purely formal; Ille only marries Ganor when Galeron has freed him for quite unconnected reasons; and even Gurun and Tristan are faithful in spirit to Fresne and to Yseut la Blonde.

---

[9] *Ibid.*, p. 467.
[10] *Ibid.*, p. 473.
[11] Marie de France, *Lais*, ed. Ewert, pp. 127–57.

We come now to *Gillion de Trazegnies*,[12] a romance in French prose composed in Burgundy in the mid-fifteenth century and dedicated to Philip the Good. The hero, a knight of Hainaut, marries Marie d'Ostrevant, a cousin of Count Baudouin of Hainaut. The couple live happily together for many years but have no children. Eventually Gillion prays for a child, promising that if his prayer is granted he will make a pilgrimage to the Holy Land. Not long after, Marie becomes pregnant and Gillion at once departs. On his way home, he is captured and imprisoned by the sultan of Babylon, whose beautiful daughter, Gracienne, falls in love with him and converts secretly to christianity for his sake. One day, when the sultan is doing battle with Ysoré de Damas, a rejected suitor for the hand of Gracienne, the princess releases Gillion and sends him to her father's assistance, having first made him swear to return to prison after the battle. As a result of his valour, Gillion wins the favour of the sultan, and is eventually entrusted with the command of his armies. Meanwhile, Amaury des Mares has fallen in love with Marie d'Ostrevant, who refuses to contemplate a second marriage while there is a chance that her husband is still alive. Amaury goes in search of Gillion, and on finding him tells him that his wife is dead. He does not live to profit from his treachery, however, but is killed as he flees from a battle. Gillion, whose relations with Gracienne had remained *justes et loyales* while he thought that Marie was still alive, now resolves never to return to Hainaut, and he eventually marries the princess. Meanwhile his twin sons have grown up and set off in search of their father. When they find him and he learns that Marie is not dead, Gillion departs immediately for Hainaut, accompanied by Gracienne, who announces her intention of becoming the servant of Gillion and Marie. But on their arrival Marie will not hear of such a sacrifice and decides to enter a convent. Gracienne's love for Marie is such that the two take the veil together, and Gillion enters a monastery. The two women die a year later, on the same day, and Gillion, responding to a plea from the sultan to return, is killed in battle in the East. A triple tomb is constructed, where the heart of Gillion now rests between the bodies of his two wives.

The author tells us that his work is translated from 'ung petit livret en parchemin, escript d'une tresanchienne lettre moult obscure en langue yta-lyenne' (fo 1v). We are not surprised by this declaration, but nor do we take it seriously. Claims of this sort are a conventional device of the fictionalised bio-graphy so popular at the Burgundian court. Nevertheless, it is unlikely that the romance did not have a source: this is the era of the *mise en prose*, when large numbers of early verse narratives were turned into prose. In fact, although no verse *Gillion* has survived, a close examination of the prose reveals traces of octosyllables, and it seems probable that the romance is based on an octosyllabic poem composed around the middle of the fourteenth century.[13]

Our concern here is less with the immediate source of *Gillion* than with its

---

[12] *Histoire de Gilion de Trasignyes*, ed. Wolff; *Gillion de Trazegnies*, ed. Horgan.
[13] *Gillion de Trazegnies*, ed. Horgan, pp. cv–cxii.

ultimate derivation. It is clearly related to the other versions of the story of the 'man with two wives'; our aim will be to define the relationship more precisely.

First, let us note the clear dependence of the romance upon Matzke's exile-formula. Once again, the hero, who holds an important position in his own land, is separated from his wife and goes to a foreign court where his valour wins him both the favour of the sultan and the love of a princess. He defeats rejected suitors for the hand of the princess and, when he eventually leaves the sultan's court, promises to return if he should be needed.

In his study of *Gillion de Trazegnies*,[14] Alphonse Bayot noted these details, which for him recalled *Eliduc*. He made a detailed comparison between the two works and concluded not merely that they were related but that the younger work depended directly on the older.[15] His argument is not wholly convincing, however, first because many of his points of resemblance are commonplace (both Gillion and Eludic are brave knights, for example, and both Marie and Guildeluëc are of noble birth), and secondly because he failed to point out that many of the elements found in *Gillion* and *Eliduc* are in fact common to a number of the stories we are discussing.

There are, of course, major differences between *Gillion* and *Eliduc*.

(a) Eliduc is aware that he is acting wrongly in abandoning Guildeluëc for Guilliadun, whereas Gillion only marries Gracienne because he believes his first wife to be dead.

(b) Eliduc accepts Guildeluëc's sacrifice and lives happily for a time with Guilliadun, whereas Gillion and his two wives both retire immediately to convents.

(c) A number of episodes in *Eliduc*, and in particular the apparent death and miraculous restoration to life of Guilliadun, are quite absent from *Gillion*.

(d) The setting is quite different: *Eliduc* takes place in Britain whereas most of *Gillion* is set in the orient.

(e) The hero's adventures are differently motivated: Eliduc is sent away from the court as a result of malicious accusations by his fellow-courtiers, where-as Gillion makes a voluntary pilgrimage to the Holy Land.

Bayot does not attempt to conceal the extent and importance of these differences, but he suggests that they can all be explained by the desire of the author to christianise the work and to make his hero above reproach. Now, if the author wanted a moral reversal of *Eliduc*, he had no need to invent one: there was one to hand in the shape of *Ille et Galeron*. Whether or not *Ille* was conceived as an 'anti-Eliduc' (a problem which has not been satisfactorily resolved),[16] it is un-questionably true that Gautier's romance is susceptible of such an interpretation.

---

[14] Bayot, *Le Roman de Gillion de Trazegnies*.
[15] *Ibid.*, pp. 65–7.
[16] See Matzke, 'Source and composition'; Hoepffner, 'Le roman d'*Ille et Galeron*'; Fourrier, *Le courant réaliste*, pp. 278ff.

So is *Gillion* perhaps a fifteenth-century *Ille* rather than a fifteenth-century *Eliduc*?

Let us consider the structure of the two works. *Ille* is an excellent example of Matzke's reduplicated story. *Eliduc*, on the other hand, lacks any element of reduplication. In *Ille*, the two ladies are simply a natural consequence of the reduplication; in *Eliduc* they appear together 'in functional opposition to the husband'. Structurally, *Gillion* is far closer to *Eliduc* than to *Ille*. The exile-formula is clearly present, but not in reduplication; and, as in *Eliduc*, the absence of reduplication might be explained by the hypothesis that the tale as we now have it is in fact the second half of a reduplicated original. The fact that Gillion wins Marie through his valour, and that Marie is a *proche parent* of Baudouin of Hainaut may be a vestigial survival of a lost first part. Similarly Marie and Gracienne, far from being mere consequences of the doubling process, are functionally identical with Guildeluëc and Guilliadun. The author's numerous and lengthy digressions do not mask the basic structure perceived by Gaston Paris when he commented that 'l'âme du récit . . . c'est l'union parfaite dans laquelle vivent les deux femmes'.[17] We may also note the striking similarity between the denouements of *Gillion* and of *Eliduc*.

To set against this structural correspondence is the fact that Gillion, unlike Eliduc but like Ille, Horn, and Beuves, is faithful to his first love. Or is he? Certainly in fact, but less obviously in spirit. Consider the following passage:

> Alors Gillion encommença de regarder la pucelle. Le coer lui encommença tous a fremir et ne sot plus que faire pour ung dart d'amours que ly lancha avoec une estinchelle ardant jusquez au coer. Mais tantost apprés lui vint ung soudain souvenir par coy en pou d'eure le fist changier et muer sa pensee, quant il lui vint en memore de sa tres-desiree moullier.   (fo 20r)

We are irresistibly reminded of Eliduc in similar circumstances:

> Tut est murnes e trespensez,
> Pur la belë est en esfrei,
> La fille sun seignur le rei,
> Que tant ducement l'apela,
> E de ceo ke ele suspira.
> Mut par se tient a entrepris
> Que tant ad esté al païs,
> Que ne l'ad veüe sovent.
> Quant ceo ot dit, si se repent:
> De sa femme li remembra.   (314–23)

Comparisons such as this lend weight to Bayot's assertion that the differences between *Gillion* and *Eliduc* are the result of the author's desire to christianise his work.

---

[17] Paris, *La Poésie*, p. 124.

Our contention that *Gillion* is closer to *Eliduc* than to any other version of the story of the 'man with two wives' should not blind us to the presence in *Gillion* of a number of elements from the other versions. The search for the missing spouse, for instance, which is nowhere to be found in *Eliduc*, appears in *Gillion* when Amaury des Mares sets off in search of the hero; it may be paralleled by the searches for Galeron and Beuves in *Ille* and *Beuves de Hamtone*. It is interesting that in both *Gillion* and *Beuves* the period of seven years is seen as crucial: the count of Hainaut assures Marie d'Ostrevant that she may lawfully remarry when her husband has been absent for seven years (fo 38v), while Beuves agrees to a formal marriage with the lady of Civile on condition that she release him if his first wife reappears within seven years.[18] Similarly, Gillion's return to Egypt after the death of his two wives may have been suggested by Ille's return to Rome after Galeron's decision to enter a convent.

It is also clear that the story of *Gillion* as we have it has attracted the theme of the enamoured Muslim princess, a familiar figure in mediaeval epic and romance who makes a very early appearance in the *Historia ecclesiastica* of the Anglo-Norman chronicler Ordericus Vitalis.[19] Ordericus describes the three-year captivity (1100–1103) of Bohemond, prince of Antioch, in the dungeons of the Danishmand emir, and attributes his eventual release to the influence of the emir's daughter, Melaz (though contemporary accounts do not bear him out). The role played by Melaz is remarkably similar to the one played by Gracienne. She visits her father's Frankish prisoners and converses with them about the christian faith. Later, when civil war breaks out between the emir and his brother, she arms the Franks and sends them to her father's assistance, having first extracted a promise that they will not avail themselves of the opportunity to escape. There the similarity ends, however, because after the emir's victorious return Melaz defies her father and converts openly to christianity.[20]

The presence of such additional elements does not obscure the essential similarity of structure that links the fifteenth-century romance with Marie's lay. Whether, as Alphonse Bayot suggested, the author of *Gillion* used *Eliduc* as a source is less clear. It is certainly a possibility, but not one that is susceptible of proof: even Bayot's step-by-step comparison fails to convince. Nevertheless, although the exact nature of the relationship between the two works is impossible to determine, its existence cannot be denied: *Gillion de Trazegnies* may justly be described as 'a fifteenth-century Burgundian *Eliduc*'.

---

[18] See Boje, *Über Beuve de Hamtone*, p. 39.
[19] See Metlitzki, *The Matter of Araby*, pp. 161ff.
[20] Ordericus Vitalis, *Ecclesiastical History*, trans. Forester, III.307ff.

The use of examples in some sixteenth- and seventeenth-century French grammars and observations on the French language

WENDY AYRES-BENNETT

INTRODUCTION

Examination of the examples employed by a grammarian – of their type, source, presentation and use – throws light on at least three important questions.[1] First, the choice of examples provides valuable insights as to what norm or preferred usage is being promoted in the grammar; secondly (and following on from the first question), it suggests what theoretical model is being espoused by the grammarian; thirdly, it provides some clues as to how a grammatical tradition is built up as successive generations adopt (or reject) the examples used by their intellectual forebears. The aim of this essay is to provide some modest, preliminary observations about the significance and the role of the examples in the major sixteenth- and seventeenth-century grammars and collections of remarks on the French language. While the main focus will be on grammars and *remarques* published in France, those intended for native speakers of English will also be considered as representative of the intense interest abroad at this time in the French language. For convenience, we may divide the period under consideration into three broad phases, following Chevalier:[2]

I   1530–1562. During this time we find the first grammars of French appearing in France: Sylvius or Dubois (1531), Meigret (1550), Robert Estienne (1557), and Ramus (1562). Two important grammars were published in England: Palsgrave (1530) and Du Wes (?1532).

II   1562–1660. Alongside the grammars published in France aimed primarily at foreigners – Henry Estienne (1582), Maupas (1607), Oudin (1632), Irson (1656) – and teaching grammars in England – for example, Desainliens or Holyband (1573, 1576), Bellot (1588), Erondell (1615), Sherwood

---

[1] For comments on the role of examples in texts selected from Graeco-Roman times to the present day, see Chevalier, 'Le jeu des exemples', and 'Exemples'.

[2] Chevalier, *Histoire de la syntaxe*.

III

(1634), Mauger (1653) –, there appeared for the first time collections of *remarques* which analysed details and finer points of usage (Vaugelas 1647).

1660–1709. This period saw the proliferation of collections of observations (Bouhours (1674, 1675, 1692), Ménage (1672, 1676), d'Aisy (1685), etc.) and notes on Vaugelas's *Remarques* (Th. Corneille (1687), Académie Française (1704)), the publication of the seminal Port-Royal *Grammaire générale et raisonnée* (1660), which gave rise to a whole series of philosophically based grammars in the following century, and the continuation of teaching grammars produced abroad, which occasionally assimilated some of Port-Royal's ideas, but essentially continued to follow the established grammatical tradition – Festeau (1667), Miege (1678), Berault (1688), etc.. These teaching grammars also increasingly took cognisance of the pronouncements of Vaugelas and Bouhours and of other teaching grammars, published elsewhere abroad, such as Chiflet (1659).[3]

SOURCES OF THE EXAMPLES

The source of the examples naturally provides crucial information about the norm being promoted. For instance, it is important to note whether the examples are actually attested ones or whether they have been fabricated – that is, created for the particular need of the rule being illustrated as tokens, on the grounds that hundreds of a similar kind could be invented. In the first case, we would need to ask how the information has been collected, whether the source is written or spoken language, whether it is contemporary or not, and whether the examples are attributed. In the second case, we must consider how plausible or genuine the examples seem, what register they are aiming to mirror, or whether they are intended to be 'neutral'. Both approaches depend on a long tradition. Casewitz and Charpin point to Priscian's reliance on quotations in his *Institutiones grammaticae*, a work which contains more than 4,800 citations from mainly 'Classical' sources, covering more than five centuries of usage. The most recent of them pre-date the publication of his work by some 350 years, but they are all treated as contemporary and include 1,246 citations from Virgil, 504 from Terence, 359 from Cicero, 271 from Plautus, 215 from Lucan, and 170 from Horace.[4] Conversely, Robins mentions the use made by Thomas of Erfurt of the useful sentence *Socrates albus currit bene*.[5] Equally, both methods have their drawbacks. The first type of attested examples may lend a spurious authenticity to a rule if, for instance, the example is unrepresentative of general usage or is archaic. On the

---

[3] Chiflet's grammar itself had already assimilated many of Vaugelas's observations, although it was essentially intended to be a grammar for foreigners (see below).
[4] Casewitz & Charpin, 'L'héritage', p. 67.
[5] Robins, *A Short History*, p. 82.

other hand, artificially created examples may lack credibility, and their 'neutrality' may be problematic. In Wagner's words, 'En l'absence d'une documentation de base, étagée par niveaux, et d'un corpus raisonnablement extrait d'elle, ce français commun de tout le monde, défini *in abstracto, n'est le français de personne.*'[6] Cellard summarises the difficulties surrounding the choice of examples in the following terms: 'Au faux aristocratisme du collectionneur de belles phrases répond le faux populisme du fabricant de phrases banales'.[7]

What of our grammarians? Two general statements can be made about the first grammars published in France. The examples are generally made up, sometimes in a rather unsatisfactory way, and the lack of space devoted to syntax, the concentration on concerns of pronunciation and morphology in the analysis of the parts of speech and their accidents, means that the examples tend to be short and atomistic. Only the immediate context of a word being discussed is considered, and little or no attention is paid to sentence-construction, since it is thought that longer phrases and sentences are formed by a simple process of addition.

Dubois is as dependent on Latin in his choice and presentation of examples as he is throughout the whole of his grammar. His preferred form of French does not mirror any group of French speakers, but is rather that which is closest to Latin, and all his examples are furnished with Latin translations: 'Ita enim quoties postponimus substatiuã, loquimur nostri & vestri amici, nos & vos amis: nostrae & vestrae literae, nos & vos lettres' (p. 111). Meigret, in recording the usage of *gens bien appris*, introduces a clearer notion of degrees of acceptability with its normative implications, a prescriptive flavour which was to become increasingly important, as I shall show: 'Ę pour comęncer aoz interrogatifs: qi ne confessera qe çete façõ de parler a' tu ouuęrt çete porte? ne soęt plus propr' ę plus elegante qe, esçe toę qi as ouuęrt çete porte?' (fo 51r). Robert Estienne, in explaining the use of tenses in French, employs a very common device of substitution of elements in model sentences, which are presumably to be learnt by heart: 'I'avoye faict quãd vous veintes. I'eu faict quand vous arrivastes. I'eusse faict si tu me l'eusse escript. I'ay eu faict auant qu'il arriuast' (p. 41).[8]

The examples in these first French grammars also prove the close dependence of the grammarians on one another and demonstrate direct influences. To trace all the details of the interdependence of the grammarians goes beyond the scope of this essay, but some obvious cases can be cited. Both Robert Estienne and Ramus draw heavily on Meigret's material. Robert Estienne copies many of Meigret's rules and examples somewhat slavishly, and Ramus, while highly orig-

---

6 Wagner, *La Grammaire française*, II.105.
7 'Grammairiens d'avant et d'arrière-garde (3 mars 1974)', in *La Vie du language: Chroniques 1971–1975 'Le Monde'* (Paris 1979), pp. 182–5 (p. 183).
8 Cited here from the 1569 Paris edition. Note that, of all the early French grammarians, Robert Estienne is the only one to make a typographical distinction between his text and the examples. A full list of grammars cited is given at the end of this paper (pp. 230–1).

inal in methodology, favouring a formal analysis of the language, nevertheless shows a lack of concern for originality in his choice of illustrative material and adopts many of Meigret's examples, even when their correctness is by no means certain.[9]

Here are two representative cases:

Meigret (1550)	Robert Estienne (1557)	Ramus (1562)
il ęt bon, il ęt nęcessęre de bien viure: aosi ęt il auât y a, ny a: come il y a infiniz homes męchans: il ny a hom' ao monde. (fo 56r)	... car Il se met le plus souuent deuant le Verbe: Il dit, Il fait, Il est bon, Il est necessaire, Il y a infinis hommes, Il n'y a homme. (p. 30)	comę, Il e' bon, Il e' nesserę dę bien vivrę, Il faut bien vivrę. Lę semblablę e' dęvant i a, ni a, comę Il i a infinis omę' męçans, Il ni a omę au mondę bien vivant. (p. 99)
je prize bien la męzon qe vou' m'auez vęndu, ę mieus, qe laqęlle vou' m'auez vęndu ... (fo 58r)	Ie prise bien la maison laquelle m'auez vendue: ou, que m'auez, & c. (p. 32)	comę, J'eimę lę çęval cę vou' m'ave' done, Ję prizę la mezon cę vou' m'ave' vendue. (p. 88)

Evidence of a grammarian's knowledge of a predecessor may emerge in a more indirect way. For instance, Brunot points out that, while Meigret makes no overt mention of Sylvius, his choice of amer as his example when he is criticising those grammarians who try to alter forms suggests a possible allusion to the author of the Isagωage.[10]

Grammars written for the English obviously may have recourse to translation and comparison with English in the presentation of their examples.[11] The first two grammars intended for the English-speaking public stand in strong contrast to each other in their choice of illustrative material. Palsgrave's work is somewhat unusual for a grammar published abroad, in that, as well as having short made-up phrases to illustrate the parts of speech and their accidents, together with lists of elements as in his exemplification of the use of luy (Qui yra? luy; cest luy; il ne scayt luy; aides luy; asteure luy; pour luy; et luy; que luy; háy luy miserable. Ilz monterent a cheual luy, sa fame et son train),[12] he also includes in more complex cases quotations from literary authorities (or sometimes proverbs). One can only speculate that the novelty of his enterprise made him feel obliged to support his pronouncements with attested examples from authors of renown. Those authors most frequently cited in support of his rules include Alain Chartier and Jean

---

[9] See Brunot, Histoire, II.151–2.
[10] Brunot, Histoire, II.139. For Meigret's dependence on Priscian in his examples, see Hausmann, 'Louis Meigret', p. 345.
[11] For example, Palsgrave translates many of his examples by way of clarification, and Du Wes provodes an interlinear translation of all his examples and dialogues.
[12] Palsgrave (1530), p. 336.

Lemaire de Belges, as well as Guillaume de Lorris (*Roman de la Rose*), Octavien de Saint-Gelais, Jean Meschinot, Guillaume Alexis, and Jean Froissart.[13] Palsgrave's choice of examples illustrates two recurrent problems. First, his selection of literary examples is often dated: note that there is no living French poet in the above list.[14] Secondly, the volume of examples illustrating the wealth of grammatical detail means that the work is not easy to refer to. As a result, Palsgrave's work never enjoyed great popularity, despite its obvious merits. By contrast, Du Wes's more concise *Introductorie* was very successful. Du Wes adopted what was to become the standard format for teaching grammars: a brief grammatical section with short examples, followed by illustrative dialogues, in this case tailor-made for the Princess Mary, his pupil. There is thus a contrast between the grammatical part, where the language is treated as a decontextualised object with artificial examples, and the dialogues, in which the language is presented in a lively way as used in certain contexts. No indication is given as to how the transition is to be made from one section to the other – that is, from viewing language as a system in the abstract to its spontaneous use in daily life, or, indeed, from a knowledge of the model to the creative use of language in novel situations.[15]

In the period 1562–1660 this format for English teaching-grammars of French – comprising paradigms to be learnt by heart, exercises, and dialogues, which constantly covered the same centres of interest such as *le lever* – became well established. Often proverbs, golden sayings, letters, prayers, and polite formulas were also appended. As Peter Erondell makes clear in *The French Garden* (1605), a work specifically designed for 'English Ladyes and Gentle-women', the (here very brief) rules of grammar and pronunciation are to be viewed as preparation for the dialogues, the two parts together constituting a complete method ('To the Reader'). To highlight the differences between the two languages, the examples and dialogues of these grammars are generally furnished with a literal translation. Desainliens (or Holyband, as he styled himself) argues that to give an elegant translation would be to corrupt the French, citing the following examples:

> *Hath no bodie asked after mee?*
> N'a personne demandé pour moy?
> *And the Frenchman sayeth,*
> Personne ne m'a il demandé? yet:
> *Make the fier (sic) burne:*
> Faites brusler le feu:

---

[13] He also makes mention of other commentators on French – Tory, Barclay, Jacobus Vallensis, Du Wes.

[14] This problem becomes acute in the eighteenth century, when the grammarians look to writers from the previous century for their data.

[15] Cf. the comments on Mauger's use of examples in Bouton, *Les Grammaires françaises*, pp. 153–4.

> *And our phrase is,* faites du feu: *or,*
> allumes le feu.
>> (*The French Schoole-maister*, 'A Warning to the Reader').

No norm is specified in these grammars, but, since more importance is attached to the dialogues than to the rules, the tone is conversational. Occasionally, however, the language used in the dialogues may appear rather stilted and formal, as is the case in the third dialogue, entitled 'Du Voyageur' in Robert Sherwood's *The French Tutour* (1634).[16] Here is the opening:

Casannier: Je n'approuve point la peregrination: premierement pource que nous n'avons que faire de sçavoir ce qui se fait ailleurs, ains avons assez à soigner, & nous occuper chez nous.

Eudoxe: Le circuit de la terre n'a il pas esté fait pour le manoir & habitation de l'homme? pourquoy donc en devrions nous ignorer les estres & parties? N'oserons-nous pas aller admirer les oeuvres divines & incomparables qui y sont, pour en loüer l'ouvrier? (p.190)

In the case of James Bellot's *The French Methode* (1588), which is a straightforward grammar of French without dialogues, the examples frequently have a formulary or aphoristic tone. The following are typical examples from the section 'Of Construction' and demonstrate well the artificial character of the illustrative material:

> Le poure content, est plus riche que ne sont les autres.
> Le Lion, l'Ours et le Thoreau, sont forts.   (fo R2r)

Some examples are evidently intended to convey moral instruction at the same time as linguistic coaching:

> Tout trompeur sera trompé,
> Le deuoir de tout homme est de bien faire.   (fo R2v)
>
> Pierre est vn bon homme: mais il se promet beaucoup,
> Marie est belle: mais elle se farde.   (fo S2r)

Of particular interest from this period are Desainliens's two highly popular works, *The French Schoole-maister* (1573),[17] intended for private study, and *The Frenche Littelton* [1576], composed for use in Desainliens's school. In the first work Desainliens's adopts the more usual order, beginning with the rules of grammar and pronunciation and then moving on to the dialogues, proverbs, prayers, graces, and vocabulary. In contrast to the artificial examples cited above or the literary tone of the examples in certain subsequent discussions, the illus-

---

16 This work survives only in its second edition (dated 1634).
17 Lambley, *The Teaching*, p. 419, suggests that the work was first published in 1565, but that no surviving copy is known of this edition.

trations of French usage have a lively conversational ring. The section headed 'Deuis familiers pour parler en tous lieux & places' opens thus: 'Haus François leues vous, & alles a l'eshole: vous seres batu, car il est sept heures passées: abilles vous vistement, dites vos prieres, puis vous aures vostre desiuner' (p. 63). On the other hand, in *The French Littelton* Desainliens starts with the dialogues and places the rules and explanations at the end, to be used only 'as occasion requireth' in conjunction with actual examples.[18] This is perhaps the clearest example of the conversational method, with the emphasis being on the spoken word in use. Yet the work is also intended as preparation for reading the New Testament, M. de Lavnay, 'Sleidans commentaries in Frenche' and Philippe de Commins (sic), who 'when he is corrected, is very profitable and wise' ('The Epistle'). Once again there is a vast difference between the lively scenes created in the dialogues and the mechanical nature of the examples in the grammar itself, with their drills of learning by substitution; for instance –

ne: ie ne veux point de cela: il ne fait pas ce qu'il ha dit: ie ne voy personne: ie ne dy rien: il n'y ha aucun danger: ne le veistes vous jamais? ie ne le vei oncques.   (fo Oiiijr).

Perhaps the most successful grammar for the English in the following century was Claude Mauger's *The True Advancement of the French Tongue* (1653), which, after running to numerous editions, continued to enjoy popularity when published together with Paul Festeau's grammar as the *New Double Grammar French–English and English–French* (1672). Mauger prefers to rely on translation and numerous examples rather than on explanations, and his examples are notably idiomatic. For instance, to illustrate the use of the definite article, he chooses a sentence beginning with *c'est*: 'C'est une terrible chose de tomber entre les mains du Dieu vivant'.[19] In addition, as Bouton suggests, the examples at times testify to a sense of humour, finesse, opportunism, and even a desire for historical objectivity. Whereas in the 1693 edition of Mauger–Festeau the example 'Le Roy de France a *toujours* été heureux depuis qu'il a fait la guerre' is found, by the 1696 edition the example has become 'Le Roy n'*a pas toujours* été heureux depuis qu'il a fait la guerre', thus reflecting the current political situation.[20]

What was happening on the other side of the Channel at this time? The grammars intended for foreigners continue the trend of looking to past generations for support. Henri Estienne (1582) reproduces a Latin version of his father's grammar, but in adding his own notes and comments to it he foreshadows the work of the writers of observations; already there are signs that the examples are gaining in importance as they become more numerous and somewhat longer.

[18] Peter Du Ploich also put the dialogues before his few grammatical rules in the first edition of his *Treatise in English and Frenche right necessary and proffitable for al young children* (c.1553), but the order was reversed in the 1578 posthumous edition: Lambley, *The Teaching*, p. 133.

[19] Chevalier, *Histoire de la syntaxe*, p. 572.

[20] Bouton, *Les Grammaires françaises*, p. 44.

It is, however, with the grammars of Maupas and Oudin that we begin to find alongside the short examples, which illustrate the uses of the parts of speech and continue to display the devices of commutation and variation of context, longer ones, as gradually more attention is paid to syntax and word-order. For instance, in his discussion of the use of tenses in French, Maupas moves beyond the rather bald statements typical of the early grammars and includes more complex sentences such as 'L'an mil cinq cens quatre-vingts & dix le Roy obtint victoire de ses ennemis, gagna la bataille d'Yvri, peu de temps apres la ville de Paris se mit en son obeissance' (p. 294); 'Vous seriez plus à vostre ayse que vous n'estes si vous m'eußiez voulu croire' (p. 305). Note, however, that the examples are still artificially created. In Maupas's opinion, sentence-construction and style are best learnt together with the grammatical rules; he therefore intersperses longer examples in his grammar rather than favouring separate dialogues.[21] Oudin's *Grammaire françoise rapportée au langage du temps* (1632), intended to expand and update Maupas's grammar, depends heavily on Maupas in the grammatical analysis, but favours a Parisian and Court norm and uses different examples.[22]

The interdependence of grammarians in France and the borrowing of examples even cross genres and schools. Although Vaugelas's *Remarques sur la langue françoise* (1647) are aimed at those native speakers who wish to refine their usage of the finer points of grammar and style, Vaugelas nevertheless uses certain examples found in Oudin's teaching-grammar for foreigners.[23] On the whole, however, Vaugelas's approach to examples is strikingly different, and is in part influenced by Malherbe's work. Malherbe, of course, never produced a formal grammar of French, but rather recorded his linguistic comments as annotations to Desportes's work.[24] In Vaugelas's *Remarques* we find an at times rather uneasy mixture of examples culled from literary sources and from the spoken word of the Court in accordance with Vaugelas's definition of *le bon usage*, which serves as the norm for his observations: 'C'est la façon de parler de la plus saine partie de la Cour, conformémemt à la façon d'escrire de la plus saine partie des Autheurs du temps' (Preface, II.3). It is probable that the starting-point for Vaugelas's observations was the careful examination of Malherbe's *Oeuvres* and the collection of examples he deemed unworthy of Malherbe or of those words and expressions he considered meritorious of particular praise.[25] Many of the examples in the *Remarques* are therefore derived from Malherbe and from other literary sources, especially Coeffeteau and Amyot, although the wording may be slightly changed to avoid the charge of being over-critical of great writers. Vaugelas states very clearly his views on when it is appropriate to name the source of an example,

---

21 See the *épître* to the second edition of the work (published in 1618 and now entitled *Grammaire et syntaxe françoise*), cited in Winkler, *La Doctrine*, p. 10.

22 Surprisingly, even the translation of Maupas by W[illiam] A[ufield] (London 1634) sometimes varies the examples, for no apparent reason.

23 See Winkler, *La Doctrine*, p. 4.

24 See Brunot, *La Doctrine*.

25 See Ayres, 'A study', pp. 23–4.

adopting the respectful attitude of the *honnête homme*. Any author whose usage is censured is not specifically named. If the author is considered worthy of praise he is named if dead, but not if still alive for fear of being accused of flattery (Preface, XV.1). Thus the observation entitled *Exemple d'vne construction estrange* opens: 'Vn de nos plus celebre Autheurs [=Malherbe] a escrit, *l'auenture* [Malherbe, *le fait*] *du lion & de celuy qui vouloit tüer le Tyran, sont semblables.*' Vaugelas then concludes: 'La question est, si cette expression est vicieuse, ou elegante. Les opinions sont partagées. Pour moy, ie ne m'en voudrois pas seruir' (p. 193). Side by side with these literary examples, however, we find others which are supposed to mirror the spoken language of the Court. A remarkable feature of the *Remarques* is that it contains for the first time discussion of how data should be collected and a naive response elicited from informants: *De quelle façon il faut demander les doutes de la langue* (p. 505). It is in the collections of observations such as Vaugelas's that individual examples take priority. Rather than starting with a general statement and illustrating it with a token example, the writers of these observations start from specific examples and may or may not go on to make a more general statement. There is an implied criticism of those who try to make language appear more regular than it is (also, perhaps, of the fabrication of not very authentic examples) in Vaugelas's repeated assertion of the beauty of idiomatic expressions such as *perdre le respect à quelqu'vn* (pp.*462–*463)[26] and of Quintilian's phrase *aliud est latinè, aliud grammaticè loqui*, in which the emphasis is placed on knowing how to speak the language idiomatically in context as opposed to having an abstract knowledge of the language-system.

Vaugelas's reputation was such that his examples permeated into the grammatical tradition and were constantly repeated. Ironically, Vaugelas's influence was so great that his advocation of a contemporary norm for good usage was forgotten in the zeal to retain his pronouncements to the letter. Indeed, his examples even find their way into different types of analyses of French: for instance, with the works of Irson (1656) and Chiflet (1659), Vaugelas's rules and examples, based on the usage of the Court and the best authors, enter teaching-grammars. Irson's work, an elementary and practical grammar, nevertheless includes a résumé of many of Vaugelas's observations, retains his examples, and juxtaposes basic rules of French pronunciation and spelling with lists of famous authors, orators, poets, grammarians, etc., who may be consulted as authorities. Chiflet's *Essay*, used by the Jesuits right up to 1709, is aimed at two different groups of people: foreigners, who are advised to omit the observations and concentrate on the main points, where the examples are usually fairly brief and the differences between French and other languages highlighted; and those wishing to perfect their French usage, who must also read the observations, where Vaugelas's examples once more appear. Chiflet stresses the importance of choosing and using one's examples wisely if one wishes to formulate accurate rules:

---

[26] The asterisk indicates the second set of pagination of a duplicated series of pages.

> Car il y en a quelques-uns qui s'embroüillent, en cherchant le vray point de l'étendüe & des limites de la Regle qu'ils veulent establir: & apres s'estre bien debatus, desesperant d'en voir le fond, ils vous renvoyent à l'usage. D'autres fondent leurs preceptes sur quelques petit nombre d'exemples, qui leur viennent en l'esprit, sans examiner plus avant ce qui est de l'usage contraire, dans le reste de la Langue; & par ce moyen ils forgent des Regles plus fausses qui vrayes.   (Preface)

Once again there is evidence of a move away from learning isolated words to looking at them in some sentence-form, so that construction and vocabulary can be learnt at the same time.

In the following period the number of collections of observations and remarks multiplied rapidly. A noteworthy feature of the many writers adopting Vaugelas's model is that, unlike Vaugelas, they name their sources, especially those criticised – perhaps from a desire to prove their erudition and wide reading and to add authority to their judgments. For instance, Bouhours, in his *Doutes sur la langue françoise* (1674), when quoting various authors and opinions on each question, attributes the quotations and usually gives a page-reference; in addition, his work includes an index of the works cited, which range from the 1627 edition of Montaigne's *Essais* to *Le Renversement de la morale de Jesus-Christ* published in 1672, and embrace some of the major authors of the first half of the seventeenth century – Balzac, Voiture, Pascal and Arnauld d'Andilly. In the 'Avertissement' to his *Remarques nouvelles* he argues that authors of repute may be criticised, so that they are not copied in their mistakes, 'Car les plus excellens ouvrages ne sont pas exempts de fautes'; and in the *Suite* he justifies criticising authors by name on the grounds that he himself does not have Vaugelas's authority. Bouhours provides a clear statement of his attitude to examples in the 'Avertissement' to his *Remarques nouvelles*. Since he attaches great importance to the value of examples in helping people to improve their style, where his authorites do not provide an appropriate example he makes one up. Typically now, the context of a word under discussion is taken into consideration:

> Pour autoriser un mot, j'ay rapporté quelquefois des périodes toutes entiéres, afin qu'on vît mieux l'usage du mot; car cela ne se voit point clairement, à moins qu'on ne sçache ce qui suit & ce qui précede, & comment le mot est enchassé dans le discours.

The extreme case of citing examples from literature is found in Ménage's work. While Ménage ostensibly defers to contemporary usage, he includes attributed examples from a very wide range of authors, including Villon, Crétin, Rabelais, Marot, Jodelle, Du Bellay, and Pasquier. Ménage is the erudite, adducing numerous references and quotations. The observation entitled *Suis-je senté-je; Perds-je, perdé-je* opens in typical fashion:

> Malherbe dans les Plaintes d'Alcandre pour la captivité de sa Maistresse, a dit,

Mais parmi tout cet heur, ô dure destinée!
Que de tragiques soins, comme oiseaux de Phinée
    Sens-je me devorer!
Bertaut dans une de ses complaintes a dit de mesme,
    Or sens-je combien de plaisirs
    Sont amers à ma souverance.   (*Observations*, I.101–3)

Quotations are then added from M. de S. Arnaut, M. Sarasin, Villon, and the authors of the *Grammaire générale* in support of the forms *sens-je*, *perds-je*, etc.

The authors of observations and remarks also adopt many of Vaugelas's examples, adding their own comments. More than a quarter of Ménage's first volume of *Observations*, for instance, is intended to complete or criticise Vaugelas's comments, whether he is explicitly acknowledged or not. This adoption of Vaugelas's examples is most evident in two new types of work. First, there appeared compilations such as d'Aisy's *Genie de la langue françoise* (1685), which, after a short summary of French grammar, contains an ordered presentation of Vaugelas's, Bouhours's, and Ménage's observations.[27] Secondly, Thomas Corneille (1687) and the Académie (1704) preferred simply to annotate Vaugelas's observations and examples rather than producing original works.[28] In all these works we see the beginning of the lack of concern paid to considerations of time and space which is so typical of the following century.[29]

Despite all the changes occuring on the Continent, the French grammars published in England continued to follow the same models as their predecessors. Thus Berault in his *New, Plain, Short, and Compleat French and English Grammar* (1688) employs mostly simple declarative sentences which he has invented to illustrate a certain point in his examples – for example, *La France est un bon Pais, La Bourgogne produit de bon vin, Le Paradis est un lieu fort agréable, l'Enfer est épouvantable* (p.120) – and includes substitution-drills to illustrate how to vary a verb – *je suis vôtre Amy; je ne suis pas vôtre Amy; suis je vôtre Amy?*, etc. (p. 135). Both Festeau and Miege adopt the grammar- and dialogue-format, although neither of them attaches as much importance to the dialogues as do their predecessors.[30] Miege reiterates the importance of considering a wide range of examples before formulating rules:

Some Grammars are immethodical, and the Rules thereof as it were wrapt up in a Cloud, being more like Prophesies than Grammar Rules. In others you will find Exceptions turned into Rules, and Rules into Exceptions. An easie and common Mistake amongst Grammarians, when grounding their

---

[27] Such compilations continued to appear, culminating in Girault-Duvivier's *Grammaire des Grammaires* (published in 1812), which analyses the grammatical classics.
[28] See *Commentaires*, ed. Streicher.
[29] For the conservative attitude of eighteenth-century grammarians, see Seguin, *La Langue française*, pp. 63–4.
[30] Festeau, *Lecteur Dobonnaire*: 'Ie ne vous donne pas beaucoup de Dialogues, parce que les petits exercices que j'ay donnez sur les Regles, & qui sont des Phrases bien Françoises, suppleent à ce defaut'.

Precepts upon a few Examples that come into their mind, they make little or no Inquiry into the contrary Use.   ('The Preface to the Reader')

Once again, we are led to believe that certain examples – for example, 'j'aime mon salut eternel plus que tous les biens perissables' (p. 177) – are not only aimed at linguistic instruction. The examples in a grammar may be as instructive about the main preoccupations of an age as they are about the state of the language.

With the appearance of the Port-Royal *Grammaire generale et raisonnée* in 1660 we find a new attitude to the choice and use of examples which stands in stark contrast to the approach of Vaugelas and his followers. Whereas Vaugelas had started from individual examples which included words and phrases causing difficulty, Arnauld and Lancelot start from general, logically based rules and then illustrate them with examples. Examples such as *la terre est ronde, Dieu est infini, tout corps est divisible, le tout est plus grand que sa partie* (pp. 94, 102)[31] can no longer be considered as simple examples; rather, they are models or tokens representing the canonical form of construction, that is, an affirmation, comprising a subject and verb, to which all other examples are reduced. It is now well known that there are parallels between Arnauld and Lancelot's lack of attention to surface phenomena and Chomsky's distinction between 'deep' and 'surface' structure in our century.[32] Examples which deviate from the paradigm are to be rewritten to make them conform, for instance by expanding them. *Dieu invisible a creé le monde visible* (pp. 68–9) comprises three judgments and is thus deemed to be an elliptical form of *Dieu qui est invisible a creé le monde qui est visible*. As a result, many of the examples, which are typically short and in content have a logico-theological bias, appear artificial. No mention is made of the norm being promoted; the examples are anonymous artefacts. The desire to formulate general rules entails the complete removal of language from context, the alienation of the speaker. Here language is treated as an object, and the token examples have little to do with language in use. The type of grammar therefore clearly dictates the tone of the examples. Discourse only reappears briefly in the discussion of the *syntaxe figurée* or *figures de construction* (pp. 158–60), where examples which apparently infringe the general rules, such as *il est six heures*, are explained with reference to rhetorical devices. In short, Arnauld and Lancelot show a complete lack of concern for collecting data or examples; their aim is simply to provide general rules which will explain the behaviour of a wide range of languages, for which artificial examples may stand as representative. This approach was also destined to be highly influential in France for years to come.[33]

[31] Cited here from the third edition (dated 1676).
[32] See Lakoff, 'La grammaire'.
[33] Note that, despite the difference in their approach, they nevertheless occasionally cite Vaugelas's examples: for instance, for past participle agreement (pp. 139–41).

THEORETICAL MODELS

From the discussion above it should already be clear that the choice of examples reflects not only the linguistic norm represented in the grammar, but also the choice of theoretical model: that is, the type and volume of examples selected, their organisation, and their use are equally symptomatic of the type of grammar. For instance, the volume of examples and their positioning in the grammars and observations of our period point to a constrast between inductive and deductive models, between data-orientation and theory-orientation. The most obvious case of this is the difference between Vaugelas's approach and that of the Port-Royal grammarians, but on a more modest scale the same contrast could be drawn between Desainliens's two works – the one moving from the grammar to the dialogues, the other from the dialogues to the rules. As Cellard points out, grammarians have to be wary of falling into the trap of circularity caused by adducing examples to support a rule or observation, after having derived the rule from those same examples, or to use his words, 'de tirer l'exemple de la règle, après avoir tiré la règle de l'exemple'.[34]

Perhaps the most important questions to ask when considering what the examples chosen suggest about the writer's approach are why the examples are included and how are they used. In some cases, the examples virtually constitute the definition, or at least are essential to the definition because it is inadequate on its own. For instance, Sherwood's explanation of the positioning of subject-pronouns is unsatisfactory, since it does not indicate when it is appropriate to place the pronoun after the verb. Only the examples clarify that subject-pronouns follow the verb in the interrogative:

> The nominative cases of pronounes are sometimes set immediately after the verbe; as, *Feray-je mal afin que bien en vienne?* shall I do evill, that good may come thereof? *Crois-tu qux Prophetes?* beleevest thou the Prophets? *Viendrez-vous avec nous?* will you come with us?   (p. 98)

As for the use of *aucun*, Sherwood conveys this only through his examples with their English translation:

> *Aucun* is thus used; *Ie ne connoy aucun de cette ville*, I know not any of this city, *avez vous accointance aucune avec cet homme?* have you any acquaintance at all with that man? ...   (p. 109)

In other cases the examples complement or supplement the definition, or they may be included to clarify a particularly difficult point. This seems to be true of Oudin's use of examples in his section entitled 'Des autres constructions & arrangemens des verbes'; for instance:

[34] Cellard, p. 184.

On met aussi par occasion, tout vne phrase entiere, qui demonstre le sujet de l'action, entre le nominatif & son verbe: *Le Prince ayāt conneu le merite de vostre parent, a commandé qu'on le reçoiue honorablement*: Ie ne trouue pourtant pas à propos d'y mettre vn simple aduerbe: cōme, *mon valet souuent reuient tard*: il est mieux de dire, *mon valet reuient souuent*, &c. . . . (p. 210)

Once again, we may point to the difference in the use made of examples between the collections of observations, where they are usually central to the discussion and could not possibly be skipped over, and Arnauld and Lancelot's work, where they feature far less prominently.

Also informative about the grammarian's attitude to the language is the treatment of exceptions and of constructions deemed 'incorrect'. The handling of exceptions may suggest the degree of respect the grammarian has for the language as it is actually used and whether a descriptive or a prescriptive approach is favoured. While most of the elementary grammars merely ignore exceptions for practical reasons, as we have seen, for the writers of remarks exceptions to the rules are frequently cherished as idiomatic expressions testifying to the individuality and beauty of the language, whereas for the Port-Royal grammarians apparent exceptions are to be reduced to the rule wherever possible.[35] By the eighteenth century, as Rickard indicates, exceptions caused grammarians great embarrassment, and stringent efforts were made to 'rationalise' them.[36] These differing attitudes to exceptions are well summarised in Chevalier's conclusion: 'le grammairien-rhéteur renvoie à l'art toutes sortes de tours ... le grammairien-logicien raisonne à l'écart des faits qu'il torture à sa fantaisie'.[37]

From Meigret on, we find the notion of good usage, with its normative and prescriptive implications, appearing in French grammars. The ideal of 'correctness', of promoting the best or the most elegant usage, finds its culmination in Vaugelas's *Remarques*. Many of the grammarians include 'faulty' constructions in their grammars side by side with the correct version, together with a warning that they represent unacceptable French usage. For instance, Maupas comments on foreigners' usage of examples like *l'ay acheté ce chappeau pour trois escus* and concludes 'ce stile n'est ni Latin, ni François' (p. 281); and Miege cites, for instance, *Je veux & promet d'accomplir ma promesse* (p. 206) as an example of a badly constructed sentence. The authors of observations often start with a 'faulty' construction which has appeared in the writings of an author otherwise recommended as an authority. Such 'wrong' constructions are problematic for them, since they may seem to undermine the authority of their preferred authors. The question of whether 'faulty' construction should be included is perhaps particu-

---

[35] See Chapter X, 'Examen d'vne Regle de la Langue Françoise: qui est qu'on ne doit pas mettre le Relatif aprés vn nom sans article', which 'explains' apparent exceptions to Vaugelas's rule (pp. 79–87).

[36] Rickard, *Embarrassments*.

[37] Chevalier, *Histoire de la syntaxe*, p. 727.

larly significant in the case of elementary grammars and teaching-grammars for foreigners. Grammarians of our period do not hesitate to warn the reader against incorrect usage by including proscribed sentences (often because of their method of contrasting French with other languages), and do not consider whether this is a pedagogically sound procedure – that is, whether the students are not equally likely to remember the criticised version as the preferred one. Indeed, the practice of juxtaposing 'wrong' usage with 'good' usage has a long history in France and survives today, for instance in grammars adopting the format *ne dites pas . . . dites*.

CONCLUSION

In broad terms, we can conclude that, whereas the examples in the early grammars published in France were typically artificially fabricated and short, reflecting the lack of attention paid to syntactic problems in the sixteenth century, by the end of the seventeenth century two main 'schools' had emerged in France: the data-orientated writers of observations, who focused on actual, attested examples, increasingly derived from literary sources, and who were concerned with the finer details of good usage; and the theory-orientated rationalists, who tended to neglect idiomatic expressions and to promote general, logically based rules which could be illustrated with token examples. As for grammars of French published in England, the preferred format – comprising a grammatical section with short, made-up examples, and dialogues illustrating lively discourse – highlights a problem common to all the works under consideration, albeit in a less obvious way in other grammars: namely, how the transition is to be made from knowledge of the system and the assimilation of short representative examples to the ability to use languages creatively in novel situations. Chevalier rightly concludes that from the seventeenth century on (and, one might add, from the earliest grammars of French on) a constant feature of all grammars has been 'la *discordance* entre les règles de base avec leur corpus d'exemples et les possibilités multiples du discours'.[38] If in content the examples in a grammar may reflect their time by mirroring the socio-cultural or political climate or suggesting the major preoccupations of the age, certain trends and problems nevertheless recur throughout the years and indeed continue to be a feature of grammatical writing today.[39]

[38] Chevalier, 'Exemples', p. 202.
[39] For instance, if Grevisse in *Le Bon usage* clearly follows the literary, conservative tradition, Ruwet in his *Théorie* employs artificial token examples to illustrate his rules. This article was submitted to the editor, in 1985 and so fails to take account of the literature published between submission and publication of the article.

GRAMMARS CITED IN CHRONOLOGICAL ORDER

Where two dates are given, the first indicates the date of the first edition, the second the edition cited here.

PALSGRAVE, J. (1530) *L'esclarcissement de la langue francoyse* ([London] 1530), cited here from *L'Éclaircissement de la langue française par Jean Palsgrave, suivi de la Grammaire de Giles de Guez*, ed. F. Génin, 2 vols (Paris 1852)

DUBOIS, J. (1531) *Iacobi Sylvii Ambiani in linguam gallicam Isagωge, vnà cum eiusdem Grammatica Latino-gallica, ex Hebraeis, Graecis, & Latinis authoribus* (Paris 1531)

DU WES, G. [1532?] *An introductorie for to lerne to rede to pronounce, and to speke French trewly* ([London, ?1532])

MEIGRET, L. (1550) *Le tretté de la grammere françoeze* (Paris 1550)

ESTIENNE, R. (1557, 1569) *Traicté de la Grāmaire Françoise* (Paris 1550)

[RAMUS, P. (P. de la Ramée)] *Gramere* (Paris 1562)

DESAINLIENS, C. [HOLYBAND] (1573)

  The French Schoole-maister (London 1573)

[1576] *The Frenche Littelton* (London 1566*)

ESTIENNE, H. (1582) *Hypomneses de gall. lingua, peregrinis eam discentibus necessariae: quaeda vero ipsis etiam Gaallis multum profuturae* ([Geneva] 1582)

BELLOT, J. (1588) *The French Methode, wherein is contained a perfite order of Grammar for the French Tongue* (London 1588)

ERONDELL, P. (1605) *The French Garden: for English Ladyes and Gentlewomen to walke in. Or, A Sommer dayes labour* (London 1605)

MAUPAS, C. (1607) *Grammaire françoise* (Blois 1607)

OUDIN, A. (1632) *Grammaire françoise, rapportée au langage du temps* (Paris 1632)

SHERWOOD, R. (1634) *The French Tutour: By Way of Grammar exactly and fully teaching all the most necessary rules, for the attaining of the French tongue*, 2nd edn (London 1634)

[VAUGELAS, C. F. de] (1647) *Remarques sur la langue françoise vtiles à ceux qui veulent bien parler et bien escrire* (Paris 1647)

---

* The date on the title page, 1566, is almost certainly a misprint for 1576.

MAUGER, C. (1653)   *The true advancement of the French tongue* (London 1653)

IRSON, C. (1656)   *Nouuelle Methode pour apprendre facilement les principes et la pureté de la langue françoise* (Paris 1656)

CHIFLET, L. (1659, 1668)   *Essay d'vne parfaite grammaire de la langue françoise* (Paris 1668)

ARNAULD A., & LANCELOT, C. (1660, 1676)
                                 Grammaire generale et raisonnée, 3rd edn (Paris 1676)

FESTEAU, P. (1667)   *A New and Easie French Grammar: Or, A Compendius way how to Read, Speak and Write French exactly, very necessary for all Persons whatsoever* (London 1667)

MÉNAGE, G. (1672)   *Observations de Monsieur Menage sur la langue françoise* (Paris 1672)

[BOUHOURS, D.] (1674)   *Doutes sur la langue françoise, proposez a Messieurs de l'Academie françoise par vn gentilhomme de province* (Paris 1674)

BOUHOURS, D. (1675)   *Remarques nouvelles sur la langue françoise* (Paris 1675)

MÉNAGE, G. (1676)   *Observations de Monsieur Ménage sur la langue françoise. Segonde partie* (Paris 1676)

MIEGE, G. (1678)   *A new French grammar; or, a New Method for Learning of the French Tongue* (London 1678)

CORNEILLE, Th. (1687)   *Remarques sur la langue françoise de Monsieur de Vaugelas . . . Avec des notes de T. Corneille* (Paris 1687)

[D'AISY, J.] (1685)   *Le Genie de la langue françoise* (Paris 1685)
BERAULT, P. (1688)   *A New, Plain, Short and Compleat French and English Grammar* (London 1688)

BOUHOURS, D. (1692)   *Suite des Remarques nouvelles sur la langue françoise* (Paris 1692)

ACADÉMIE FRANÇAISE (1704)
                                 Observations de l'Académie françoise sur les Remarques de M. de Vaugelas (Paris 1704)

Elizabeth and Essex:
the ring and the rhetoric

GILLIAN JONDORF

I first became interested in Gauthier de Costes de la Calprenède (1614–1663) in his capacity as one of the earliest French playwrights to choose subjects from modern English history. In that respect he was a follower of Antoine de Mont-chrestien, whose play on Mary, Queen of Scots, *L'Ecossaise* (1601), seems to have had some influence on La Calprenède's play about Lady Jane Grey, *Ieanne Reyne d'Angleterre* (1638).[1]

The relations between La Calprenède, English history, and English literature are not entirely clear. La Calprenède wrote three plays on English subjects. One of these, a tragi-comedy called *Edouard* (1640), deals with an amorous episode in the life of Edward III, but the only 'historical' elements that an English reader would recognise in it are the gallantry of the king who founded the Order of the Garter and the wickedness of Edward's mother, Isabella, and her lover, Mortimer. In the other two plays, La Calprenède was dealing with much more recent history. He deals with it, however, in an idiosyncratic way. In *Ieanne Reyne d'Angleterre*, by starting his action at a very late point, when Mary Tudor's supporters have already practically won the day, and omitting any reference to the Wyatt-rebellion or to the religious divisions in the country, La Calprenède produces a play very different from either the Jane Grey play by Dekker and Webster, *The Famous History of Sir Thomas Wyat* (1607), or John Banks's play *The Innocent Usurper* (1694).[2] In *The Famous History* (thought to be a corrupt

---

[1] There are at present (1986) no modern editions of La Calprenède's plays. I have used photo-copies of the following editions: *Ieanne Reyne d'Angleterre. Tragedie* (Paris 1638), the only edition; *Le Comte Dessex. Tragedie* (Paris 1650), the second edition (the first was 1639). References are by act- and scene-number. In discussing seventeenth-century plays, I have used modern English spelling for the names of English historical figures, no matter how they are spelled by dramatists, although it is with reluctance that I discard La Calprenède's *Soubtantonne*. I have also corrected La Calprenède's *Dessex* to *d'Essex*.

[2] Dekker, T. and Webster, J., *The Famous History of Sir Thomas Wyat*, London 1607. There is a facsimile of the first edition (Tudor Facsimile texts, 122: Edinburgh 1914). The play can also be read in *The Dramatic Works of Thomas Dekker*, ed. Bowers, I.

and mutilated version of a lost earlier play on Jane Grey in two parts, by Dekker and others) the focus is divided between the rather cloyingly virtuous and adoring couple Jane and Guildford Dudley, and Wyatt, who, after supporting the accession of Mary Tudor as the legitimate heir designated by Henry VIII, changes his mind about her when he learns that she is likely to marry Philip II of Spain. Fearing that this will reduce England to a neglected dependency of Spain, he transfers his allegiance to Jane and leads an unsuccessful rebellion to try to restore her to the throne. Wyatt's role is potentially the most interesting part of the play, but it is not very fully developed. The main impression created by the play is of chop-and-change, of swift reversals of fortune and swift changes of loyalty; only Jane and Guildford are constant, but this cannot save them in a tumultuous world in which they have been exploited and betrayed.

Banks's play makes scant reference to Wyatt, but, in contrast to the earlier writers, Banks shows the whole of Jane's reign, starting just before the death of Edward VI and continuing through Jane's imprisonment and trial to the moment of her execution. Jane is shown as reluctant usurper, dutiful daughter and enthusiastically tender wife. In the last act the religious element becomes very prominent, for Jane is offered the chance of saving her own life and her husband's if she will renounce her Protestant faith, as her evil father-in-law Northumberland has already done. Jane reacts to this proposition with horror ('I have seen a Bassalisk!') and becomes a martyr for the reformed religion.

Such a view of the Act of Supremacy and its consequences would hardly suit a French public, and La Calprenède does not refer to the religious question at all. Nor does he show us Jane's parents, whereas these are prominent in Banks – particularly Jane's mother, the duchess of Suffolk, conspicuously modelled on Lady Macbeth and going splendidly mad in Act IV. On the other hand, Banks does not show Mary and Elizabeth Tudor at all, while they are of central importance in the French play. Indeed, the main interest for La Calprenède is in the difficult decision to be made by Mary, who must choose whether to act expediently, as Elizabeth argues, for her own safety and that of the realm, or whether to let her pity for Jane, and her wish to be a magnanimous ruler with hands less bloodstained than her father's, triumph over the *raison d'état* urged by Elizabeth.

In short, there is little resemblance between Banks and La Calprenède here, yet Banks certainly knew of La Calprenède, for his first play, *The Rival Kings* (1677), was derived from La Calprenède's historical romance *Cassandre* (1642–1645).[3] Even if Banks could not read French (*Cassandre* appeared in a translation by Sir Charles Cotterell in 1667), at least he knew of La Calprenède's existence and might have known of the subjects of his plays.

There is more similarity between the two plays about Elizabeth and Essex, La Calprenède's *Le Comte d'Essex* (1639) and Banks's *The Unhappy Favourite* (1681

Banks, J., *The Innocent Usurper, or The Death of the Lady Jane Grey* (London 1694). The play was banned from performance and there is no modern edition.

3   There is a modern edition in the form of a Slatkine reprint (Geneva 1978).

or 1682).[4] Walther Baerwolff noted that the few textual resemblances are not conclusive and can be attributed to the similarity of the material and the conventionality of the passages where they occur;[5] he suggested, however, that there are striking likenesses between the two plays in the analysis of Elizabeth's conflict and the fact that 'die Liebe zeigt sich in der französischen wie in der englischen Bearbeitung der Staatsraison überlegen'. Essex, he says, is similarly characterised by both writers, being in both plays boastful and something of an *Eisenfresser*. Also, both plays use the apocryphal story of the ring, given by Elizabeth to Essex as a pledge, with the promise that if he sent it to her when in danger she would save him. La Calprenède, who says he used oral sources to supplement the historical record, is the first writer in any language to use the story of the ring. By the time Banks's play appeared, an elaborate version of the story (differing in many details from La Calprenède's) had been published as a novel by an anonymous 'Person of Quality', under the title *The Secret History of the most renowned Queen Elizabeth and the Earl of Essex* (London [1680?]). This seems to have been Banks's main source, but he also uses the incident of Elizabeth giving Essex a box on the ear (though changing the time and reason for it) – a real event which is not cited by the 'Person of Quality' or by La Calprenède, who if he knew of it perhaps thought it unseemly.

Neither of these plays gets much acclaim from literary historians and critics (except G. P. Snaith, whose enthusiasm for *Le Comte d'Essex* it is a pleasure to acknowledge).[6] Both plays seem to me rather odd. I believe that in both cases, coincidentally, this oddness arises from a disjunction between some of the writer's likely intentions and his rhetorical forms. I shall consider this first in the case of Banks, where it struck me first, and hope then, by looking at La Calprenède, to arrive at some conclusions about the evolution of rhetoric in seventeenth-century French tragedy.

Banks's *The Unhappy Favourite* is the first of his historical tragedies on English themes, to be followed by a play on Anne Boleyn, one on Mary, Queen of Scots, the Jane Grey play already mentioned, and a revision of the Mary Stuart play (which, like *The Innocent Usurper*, had been banned by the censor). Before turning to English history, Banks had written three heroic tragedies.

When *The Unhappy Favourite* opens we learn that the countess of Nottingham (whose love Essex has spurned), Burleigh, and Raleigh are all enemies of the queen's favourite, Essex, but a scheme to impeach him for misconduct of the campaign against Tyrone's rebellion in Ireland is angrily rejected by the queen.

---

4   Banks, J., *The Unhappy Favourite, or The Earl of Essex* (London 1682): this is the date on the title-page; the play has been edited in this century with an introduction and notes by T. M. H. Blair, who mentions the possibility of an earlier publication-date. The text he gives is a reduced facsimile of the first edition. References are to this edition, by act- and page-number as scene-divisions are not marked.
5   Baerwolff, *Der Graf von Essex*, pp. 25–7.
6   Snaith, 'Aspects', is the only modern monograph on La Calprenède's theatre. I am grateful for the author's permission to refer to it.

Essex, however, imprudently and disobediently comes home to clear himself, to the consternation of his friend Southampton and of the countess of Rutland (secretly married to Essex). The queen expresses anger at his arrival and receives him coldly, though inwardly moved. Later they are briefly reconciled, but she is still determined to strip him of his offices; this provokes the short-tempered Essex to anger, and his insolence in turn provokes the queen into hitting him. Essex's reaction to this humiliation is to organise an unsuccessful uprising of his followers, for which he is tried and condemned to death. With characteristic bad judgment he entrusts to his enemy, the countess of Nottingham, the ring which should invoke Elizabeth's aid. The countess withholds the ring and gives Elizabeth a false account of Essex's last message. Essex is executed and the countess's action is revealed through a letter which Essex sent to Elizabeth by a more reliable messenger (his wife) before his execution. The queen is inconsolable and banishes the countess of Nottingham but offers friendship to the widowed countess of Rutland.

The *Unhappy Favourite* and *The Innocent Usurper* were probably written within a year or two of each other, and both show strong rhetorical patternings. In *The Innocent Usurper* the most prominent patterns consist of one series of images and allusions drawn from Milton's *Paradise Lost*, another relating to the gigantomachy (overlapping somewhat with the first, since both giants and fallen angels are brought down because of pride and rebellion), and another on the theme of the crown. In *The Unhappy Favourite* there are *Paradise Lost*-allusions again, also a string of Roman allusions, and a series of identifications with mythological characters – the mythological *Doppelgänger* varying with the point of view of the speaker: thus Burleigh is variously likened to Lucifer, Aesculapius, St Christopher, and the 'Phrygian monster' who ate seven virgins a week, and Elizabeth is likened to the Sun, Circe, and Juno. There is also a recurring image of a tall tree (Essex) with lesser plants looking up at him, or ivy throttling him (Burleigh and Raleigh), or a vine clinging to him (the countess of Rutland). This all seems familiar territory to a straying *seizièmiste*. These patterns, I am tempted to say, are the vehicle of the play's content. The Adam–Eve–Serpent figure expresses fittingly the relationships between Essex (whose sin is disobedience), the countess of Rutland, and the countess of Nottingham, who destroys their chance of happiness and at the end is cursed by the 'Bright Goddess of the Day', Elizabeth. The images define the characters, and the comparisons vary because, for example, Adam is differently seen by Eve and by the Serpent. Furthermore characters can take over and distort one another's rhetoric. So Nottingham, transmitting a deliberately false account of Essex's last message to Elizabeth, takes over and transforms his imagery. Here is what Essex says as he gives Nottingham the ring:

> Hold generous Madam, I receiv'd it on
> My Knees, and on my Knees I will restore it.
> Here take it, but consider what you take:

'Tis the Life, Blood, and very Soul of *Essex*.
I've heard that by a skillful Artist's Hand,
The Bowels of a Wretch were taken out,
And yet he liv'd; you are that Gallant Artist,
O touch it as you would the Seales of Life,
And give it to my Royal Mistress Hand,
As you wou'd pour my Blood back in its empty Channels,
That gape and thirst like Fishes on the Ouse
When streams run dry, and their own Element
Forsakes 'em; if this shou'd in the least miscarry,
My Life's the purchase that the Queen will have for't.   (v.59)

Here is Nottingham's account, borrowing and transforming the images of blood and entrails:

        . . . I've seen a Lyon
That has been play'd withall with gentle stroaks,
Has at the last been jeasted into madness;
So of a sudden started into Passion
The furious Earl, his Eyes grew fiery red,
His words precipitate, and speech disorder'd;
Let the Queen have my Blood said he, 'tis that
She longs for, pour it to my Foes to drink,
As Hunters when the Quarry is run down,
Throw to the Hounds his Intrails for Reward.
I have enough to spare, but by the Heav'ns
I swear, were all my Veins like Rivers full,
And if my Body held a Sea of Blood,
I'de loose it all to the last innocent drop,
Before I'de like a Villain beg my life.   (v.61)

Essex's speech has indeed been 'disorder'd' by this false reporter, whom Essex had erroneously addressed as 'charitable Messenger'.

However, although Banks's use of rhetoric seems to me both rich and clever, I do not think that a study of it would give an adequate account of the play. A wealth of rhetoric there certainly is, enough to gladden the heart of a sixteenth-century humanist, but there is something else as well. What Banks is on to is the shifting of moods and feelings between people, and he conveys this partly, but only partly, through the clumsy device of the aside (which he abuses).

It is not easy to say how else he does it, particularly as it can co-exist with large dramatic effects such as Elizabeth boxing Essex's ear or the countess of Rutland rushing in with an ill-timed confession of her marriage to Essex. A look at these two scenes, the ear-boxing and the confession, will illustrate the point. As a historical incident, well vouched for, the ear-boxing is easy to understand. It happened when, in the course of an argument about who should be appointed as Lord Deputy in Ireland, Essex in exasperation turned his back on the queen and, according to Raleigh, said that her conditions were as crooked as her carcase. It is hardly surprising that the queen lost her temper, hit him, and told him he might go and be hanged. Banks has transposed the incident to a very different context. Essex has defended, to the queen, his conduct in Ireland, and accused Cecil and Raleigh of plotting his ruin. The queen is angered by his truculence but pardons him; however, it seems that she is about to remove his offices from him, and this provokes another outburst from Essex. The angry queen calls him 'Audacious Traytor', and that is the last straw for Essex, who furiously and with bitter sarcasm reminds her of his exploits in her service and finishes: 'This *Essex* did, / And I'll remove the Traytor from your sight.' Before he can leave, the queen comes up to him and gives him a box on the ear, saying: 'Stay Sir, take your Reward along with you'. If the historical Elizabeth hit Essex because she was an uninhibited termagant, why does Banks's Elizabeth do it? Partly, I suppose, because the historical Elizabeth did it, although two years earlier than the time portrayed in the play. In the incident as Banks gives it, it seems to me that she hits him because he has not reacted with obsequious gratitude to her magnanimity in pardoning him and sparing his life, but also because his insolence is making her look a fool and making it difficult for her to justify in public her favourable treatment of him. But we can only arrive at this reading of Elizabeth, or indeed at any detailed interpretation of her behaviour, by a kind of intuition. It is the same in the scene with Rutland. This is in Act IV, after a scene in which, on his way to trial, Essex (who since we last saw him really has become a traitor, seizing the queen's privy councillors and trying to call the citizens of London to arms) has yet another interview with the queen in which she gives him her personal forgiveness although she cannot halt the trial. She gives him the ring and they part on excellent terms. With deplorable timing, the countess of Rutland rushes in, not realising that an appeal to Elizabeth is at the moment quite unnecessary. Furthermore, since it involves confessing that Essex and she are married, it has an effect very different from the one intended. It is not made explicit that the queen's state of agitation and her distaste for being touched by the countess (who hangs on to her skirt) are caused by jealousy. Elizabeth does not say 'He loves you!' or anything like it, but again we are surely to understand, without being told, that that is what is filling her mind as she struggles to tear herself away from the suppliant countess, unable to bear contact with her, and cursing as a 'vile Insect' Essex's unborn child, for whom the countess has implored her pity.

What I am saying is that this is not just a play about a clash beween *maximes d'état* and the maxims of the heart, a moral and political dilemma. It is a play involving complex states of feeling, and it is through these states of feeling that the tragic is attained. It is not to *raison d'état* that Essex is sacrificed, since Elizabeth will save him if he sends the ring, being prepared to flout the *maximes d'état* if he will humble himself. The case against Essex, based on his Irish campaign, is full of holes. Had Elizabeth given him the ring as soon as he came back from Ireland, we might read the gift as an expression of her doubts about his guilt and a recognition that the trial might not be fair; but Banks makes her give the ring after Essex's uncontrovertible acts of treason, when he seized the privy councillors and attempted to raise London in an armed revolt. Whether or not Essex committed treason in Ireland, he has certainly done so in London. Elizabeth gives the ring because at that moment the balance of her feelings has tipped in Essex's favour and in favour of the 'Pitty' which love arouses in her. The feelings operating in the play, and determining events, are not large, single, easy-to-label ones like 'Hatred', 'Vengeance' or 'Love', but complex and hard to define. These feelings are often misread by other characters. The countess of Nottingham, at Elizabeth's request, devises refinements of cruelty to make Essex's execution a more painful punishment for him; one of these is to arrange for Southampton to be pardoned, at the last minute and in Essex's presence. The countess has misjudged her victim, and Southampton's pardon is a comfort, not a torment, to Essex, who felt he had destroyed his friend and is relieved to see him spared – it is Southampton who is harrowed at losing his chance to die with Essex.

The secret underside of the play, dealing in unexpressed emotions, is oddly out of keeping with its rhetorical explicitness and systematisation. It is as though there were two plays going on at once here, one of large public utterances and gestures, the other of *tropismes* and nuances. The inner play is carried by the outer, rhetorical play, if only because the action and structure of the play are expressed in that outer rhetorical framework: but the two are very different from each other.

This odd co-existence arises in all probability from the fact that Banks is using the forms and language of heroic tragedy but doing something new with them. Blair identifies the 'something new' as being the writing of tragedies dealing with real, recent historical figures rather than with the remote or legendary figures of Banks's first three plays.[7] Allardyce Nicoll links the 'something new' with the 'she-tragedy'.[8] I think it does have to do with both of these, but in a particular way.

It has to do with the 'she-tragedy' because that is essentially a tragedy appealing to sympathy by showing heroines tormented by injustice, by cruelty, or by thwarted or misplaced love. These predicaments can be, and are, proclaimed in long formal speeches and through the rather clumsy (and easily abused) techniques of asides, but even more pathos and a more challenging appeal to sympathetic understanding can arise almost in the interstices of the text, especially with good enough actresses – and there seem to have been plenty of notable (and beautiful) actresses in the theatre at the time.

The importance of the choice of recent historical figures, rather than of what Banks himself (in the dedicatory letter to *Vertue Betray'd*, his Anne Boleyn play) refers to as 'the improbable and Romantick Actions of Princes remote, both by distance of time and place', is twofold. First, it seems to guarantee the authenticity of the outward events – Essex *was* Elizabeth's favourite, he *was* married in

[7] J. Banks, *The Unhappy Favourite*, ed. Blair, especially pp. 13, 14.
[8] Nicoll, *History*, p. 156.

secret (although it was no longer a secret in 1600), he *was* executed; although the ring-episode is almost certainly fictitious, it belongs to that category of historical legend known to us all, like Edward III picking up the countess of Salisbury's garter, Raleigh putting his cloak over the puddle, or the duke of Clarence drowning in a butt of Malmsey. So, as with any play dealing with well known 'real' events, there is simultaneous acceptance of the events and questioning as to motives. Nero murdered Britannicus – why? Lady Jane Grey, the innocent usurper, was executed – why? Elizabeth pardoned Southampton but not Essex – why? In *The Unhappy Favourite* the most interesting answers to the questions are implicit, not explicit.

Secondly, along with a knowledge of supposed facts goes a rough and ready knowledge of the people. The author can both exploit this and suggest that it is incomplete. We think of Elizabeth as imperious and autocratic; this is confirmed by Banks when she scolds Burleigh:

> How durst you seem t'interpret what's my Pleasure!
> . . . Leave me to act without your saucy Aid,
> If I have any Royal Power.   (II.17)

Yet we also see her vacillating, tortured by a love which she never expresses except to herself – and to us through the asides. We know that she boxed Essex's ear – a manifestation of that same imperiousness; but here we see the action provoked by emotional exasperation and distress.

Furthermore, if we are sufficiently persuaded by this revelation of motivation and character, we shall accept the more readily some tampering with the facts as we thought we knew them. The box on the ear is a good example – it happened in a very different context, but we accept its placing here because a plausible motivation is suggested (though not made fully explicit). The handling of the ring-episode is less happy. If there ever was a ring, it was surely given, at the latest, before Essex went to Ireland. Since the play begins just before Essex's ill-judged return (but omits his tempestuous irruption into the queen's bedroom on arrival), we can only see the ring being given if it is given later. A dramatic point is made thereby, since we see Essex receive it on his knees and later adopt the same posture, deliberately and reverently, when he entrusts it to the countess of Nottingham, but this timing does strain credulity, as Lessing pointed out.[9]

The combination, then, of large historical figures expressing themselves in formal rhetorical utterances, and shifting relationships and conflicts conveyed through an unspoken language of actions and implications, works unevenly, with one element sometimes stealing the scene at the expense of the other, or the rhetorical design conflicting with psychological *vraisemblance*. An example of this can be seen in the handling of Acts III and IV. In the first half of Act III are two contrasting but symmetrical scenes; in the first the countess of Nottingham tells the queen lies (we presume) about 'what all the World / Says of that proud

---

9   Lessing, *Hamburgische Dramaturgie*, V.153–4.

Ingrateful Man', the earl of Essex. In the second the countess of Rutland tries equally hard to convince Elizabeth of Essex's virtue and loyalty. The scenes go beyond rhetorical patterning into psychological exploration, for the queen notices both that the countess of Nottingham is being 'malitious' and getting very excited about it and that the countess of Rutland is in love with Essex and therefore equally biased and equally excited. Yet later on – as if these scenes *did* have only rhetorical, and not narrative, value – the queen appears to have learnt nothing from them. in Act IV she is shattered by the countess of Rutland's revelation that she is married to Essex – as though she had had no warning of their attachment – and later she sends the countess of Nottingham to report on Essex in the Tower – as though she did not know of her 'malitious' bias against him. Another example of the collision between rhetorical design and psychological consistency can be seen in the countess of Rutland's conduct. She is explicitly warned by Southampton, early in the play, not to reveal her marriage in the hope of moving the queen to pity, because it will have the opposite effect:

> Led by vain Hopes, you fly to your Destruction;
> There wants but that dread Secret to be known,
> To tumble you for ever to Despair,
> And leave you both Condemn'd without the Hopes
> Of the Queens Pitty, or Remorse hereafter.   (II.16)

But she does reveal the 'dread Secret', at a moment when there is no pressing need to do so, since Essex has not yet been condemned and has in fact just received the ring as token of the queen's forgiveness (though his wife does not know this). Psychologically the scene does not make much sense since we are not shown why the countess at that moment feels impelled to ignore Southampton's excellent advice. In terms of dramatic rhetoric, however, the scene is well placed, for after the happy scene of trust and hope just past, it is a satisfying contrast to have the countess's frantic entrance. Essex on his knees in noble submission, receiving the ring and comparing himself to the 'Remnant of mankind that saw / The Rain-bow Token in the Heavens' at the birth of 'a new smiling World', is followed by his wife on her knees in desperate appeal, comparing herself to 'A despis'd Plant beneath the mighty Cedar' and receiving, instead of pity, the queen's curse. So far from watching the rainbow from an ark as the floodwaters go down, she is

> like a miserable Wretch, that thinks
> H'as scaped from drowning, holding on a Rock
> With fear and Paine, and his own weight opprest,
> And dasht by ev'ry Wave that shrinks his hold.   (IV.54)

If we think of this scene in terms of 'character', it makes the countess seem a heedless fool, endangering her husband by her lack of self-control. If we think of it in terms of rhetorical design, it is superb.

Another example of the triumph of the patterned rhetoric can perhaps be seen at the end of the play. Part of the ring-story which 'every schoolboy knows' (or at least every reader of *1066 and All That*) is that, when Elizabeth discovered after the execution that Essex had tried to send her the ring but that the countess of Nottingham had not brought it to her, she exclaimed: 'God may forgive you but I never shall', or, in the wording of the 'Person of Quality', 'Whether Heaven will pardon thy Crimes, I know not; sure I am, I shall never forget them.' It is slightly surprising that Banks does not use this gift of a line; but he has perhaps demonstrated that he knows of it by adapting it earlier in the play when he makes Elizabeth say (in an aside addressed to 'just Heav'n' shortly before she gives Essex her pardon and the ring): 'And youl forgive me, tho the World may not' (IV.52). Instead, Elizabeth's last words to the countess of Nottingham are perhaps dictated by the rhetorical pattern (the countess as serpent, destroying the Edenic happiness of Essex and Rutland and now cursed by the Deity) rather than by the traditional story or by the intricacies of the personal relationships lurking behind the stylised speeches:

> Begon – Fly to that utmost Verge of Earth,
> Where the Globe's bounded with Eternity,
> And never more be seen of Humane kind,
> Curst with long Life and with a fear to dye,
> With thy Guilt ever in thy Memory,
> And *Essex* Ghost be still before thy Eye.
>   . . . let her live
> Howling to th'Seas to rid her of her pain,
> For she and I must never meet again –
> Away with her.   (V.76)

In turning now to La Calprenède, I emphasise again that if the comparison is helpful it is not because of direct influence between the plays – it is partly in order to avoid giving that impression that I am dealing with them in reverse chronological order. While it is not impossible that Banks knew La Calprenède's play or at least knew of it, what is more pertinent is that La Calprenède's play can, like Banks's, be seen as transitional; and this perhaps, as with Banks, explains some of its peculiarities.

The play starts after Essex's return from Ireland. He is accused by Elizabeth not of disobedience (in his conduct of the Irish campaign and his precipitous return from Ireland), but of treason, for she holds treasonable letters allegedly written by Essex to the Irish rebel leader, Tyrone, which Essex denounces as forgeries and tears up (somewhat similar letters were produced at Essex's first trial, 5 June 1600, and declared by Essex to be forgeries). Essex is arrested, tried (his trial occupying the third act of the play) and condemned. He entrusts Elizabeth's ring to Lady Cecil, a discarded mistress whom he now claims to love; she appears to be on the point of taking it to the queen to save Essex's life, but is intercepted by her husband, Essex's enemy Robert Cecil, and the ring does not reach Elizabeth. After Essex's death, Lady Cecil, dying of grief and remorse, confesses to Elizabeth, who announces that her own death is imminent.

Perhaps the main source of unease for the reader in Le Comte d'Essex is uncertainty: first as to Essex's guilt or innocence, and secondly as to whether or not we are to believe him when he tells Lady Cecil that he still (or again?) loves her. Elliott Forsyth says: 'Essex se révèle comme un être vaniteux qui n'est peut-être pas entièrement innocent du crime dont il est accusé, et qui semble exploiter sans scrupule l'amitié des femmes devenues sensibles à son charme.'[10] G. P. Snaith, although a most sympathetic reader of La Calprenède, sees the uncertainties, especially as to Essex's guilt, as weaknesses in the play.[11]

It would be possible to argue that the uncertainty is a deliberate device by La Calprenède to force the reader or spectator to enter actively and critically into the world of the play. I must say I do not believe that this is so, but it is a possible way of reading the play.

My own interpretation is that Essex's execution is to be seen as a mistake and Essex as an honourable and innocent man (though proud and short-tempered). One reason why I am persuaded of this is that it is quite clear that Raleigh and Cecil resent his power, seek to belittle his exploits – called 'services légers' by Cecil (II.1) – and want him destroyed. This surely disposes us to think him innocent, and at the same time it accounts for one troubling feature – the fact that the queen thinks he is guilty. She, we can assume, is misled by the 'trames perfides' woven by Essex's enemies, of which Essex speaks in his vigorous self-defence in the opening scene.

Secondly, since Essex is the eponymous hero, it is likely that his death is intended to move us; if we were to react with pity to the death of a traitor, it would have to be because we understood, and approved, the motives of his treachery; because we saw him as freedom-fighter rather than villain. That is not the case here, for, although Elizabeth is capable of anger and haughtiness, and although Southampton abuses her (in a speech in I.5 to which I shall return), there is nothing in the play to make us believe that she is a tyrant from whom the nation needs liberating. Elizabeth herself, in her self-accusing final speech, mentions only one specific crime she has committed, and that is not a crime against the English people but the execution of Mary, Queen of Scots.

Thirdly, Essex repeats his assertion of innocence when alone, speaking of:

> l'entretien
> D'un coeur plein d'artifice [Raleigh] et d'un homme de bien [Essex].
> Ces laches ennemis d'un genereux courage,
> Qui contre un innocent ont desployé leur rage.   (II.4)

It would surely violate the conventions of drama if a villain did not admit his villainy when alone.

[10] Forsyth, La Tragédie française, p. 377.
[11] Snaith, 'Aspects', pp. 70–1.

As to whether he is to be believed when he tells Lady Cecil that he loves her, there is negative evidence in his favour in the sense that there is nothing to suggest he does not mean it; unlike Banks's Essex he is not married, nor does he ever claim to love Elizabeth; and surely Lady Cecil's remorse after Essex's death would have a very different and rather sinister colouring if Essex was false in his declarations and Lady Cecil right to disbelieve them.

Finally, Southampton's love and loyalty are unfaltering and it does not seem plausible to me that we are to suppose them to be misplaced.

If Essex is meant to be innocent, I think there are two quite different reasons why La Calprenède has failed to make this entirely clear. One has to do with his organisation of the historical material, the other with a difficulty of fit, comparable to that discussed in the case of *The Unhappy Favourite*, between rhetoric and other elements.

I must here give a brief account (based mainly on *The Dictionary of National Biography*) of the historical material. The sequence of events in 1600–1601 was that after his return from Ireland Essex was tried before a special court, held in Essex House on 5 June 1600; apparently no full record of the proceedings was kept, but the charges arose from his conduct of the Irish campaign: he was charged with having concluded a 'dishonourable and dangerous' treaty with Tyrone and with 'contemptuous leaving of his government' to come back to London to justify himself. Essex was sentenced to dismissal from all his offices of state and was to remain a prisoner in Essex House at the queen's pleasure.

He was set at liberty on 24 August but seems to have become increasingly frustrated at having no access to the queen or the court, and a few months later he hatched his foolhardy plot to seize Whitehall, force an audience with Elizabeth, and demand the dismissal of her councillors and the summoning of a parliament.

He tried to carry this out in February 1601, failed because he did not get the popular support he had counted on, gave himself up at Essex House, and was taken to the Tower (8 February). On 19 February he and Southampton were brought before a commission of twenty-five peers and nine judges in Westminster Hall. Both were sentenced to death, but Southampton was pardoned by the queen. Essex was executed on 25 February, the queen having exhibited great reluctance to sign the death-warrant, and even recalled the first warrant, but signed a second time on 24 February.

It can easily be argued that Essex was not guilty until after the first trial, and that it was the upshot of the first trial that provoked him to form his unlucky conspiracy, which led to the second trial and the death-sentence. Banks preserves this outline more or less, although the ear-boxing scene in effect takes the place of the first trial; but La Calprenède obscures it, conflating the two trials into one, at which Essex is accused both of the Irish misdemeanours (including treasonable communication with Tyrone) and the detention of the privy councillors and attempted armed revolt. He has thereby created some awkwardnesses. For instance, Essex must be assumed to have staged the revolt (of which he is accused in his trial) before the opening of the play, for he is arrested by the end of the first act and so has no opportunity to do so within the time-span covered by the action; (whereas in *The Unhappy Favourite* the revolt is supposed to take place between Acts III and IV). So why not make Elizabeth mention this, instead of the dubious Irish letters, when she attacks him in the first scene? The answer must, I think, be that this would give us too strong an impression of Essex's guilt. Again, in order to sustain our faith in Essex's innocence, there must be a defence against the charges relating to the uprising – and there is one, offered by Southampton, although it is distressingly feeble. It consists of claiming that Essex's private army of two hundred men was for legitimate and necessary self-defence, and that the alleged seizing of the councillors was a respectful and hospitable gesture. This may seem like further clumsiness on La Calprenède's part, but the very proffering of this weak defence is to my mind part of the evidence that La Calprenède wants us to think Essex innocent. The defence is poor, but at least it is there, and no doubt it is the best that can be done.

If the murkiness as to Essex's guilt or innocence is due partly to La Calprenède's handling of the historical material, there is one other source of doubt, and that is the speech of Southampton in the only scene (I.5) where he is alone with Essex. He talks of the power and capriciousness of kings and goes on:

> Et de vouloir chocquer cette grandeur auguste
> Est un dessein fatal autant qu'il est iniuste.
> Helas! que plust à Dieu que vous eussiez suivis
> Et le meilleur exemple et le meilleur advis,
> Et qu'estant satisfait d'une fortune haute
> Vous n'eussiez point commis une si grande faute.

One could argue that the 'faute' referred to by Southampton is an error of judgment (annoying the queen) rather than a crime; but I should prefer to suggest that what has happened here is, as in Banks, a certain mismatching between rhetorical forms and other forces operating in the text. There are plainly several rhetorical elements in this play broadly similar to those of earlier, humanist tragedy. There are, for example, commonplace observations like those made by the queen's confidant Alix (V.2) on 'le destin des princes'. There are stylised monologues where a character proclaims his or her progress through contrasting states of feeling. Thus the queen in the first forty-four lines of her long speech in II.2 declares herself to be experiencing, successively, vindictive anger at Essex, anticipation of pleasure at his death, anticipation of the end of her love for him, love renewed by the recollection of past love, horror at the idea of Essex's death, a reminder that his life is a threat to her own, willingness to be killed by him rather than bring about his death. We hear these moods succeeding one another very rapidly; the aim is not to give a realistic glimpse into the movements of a mind, but to display in stylised and condensed form the various contradictory directions in which Elizabeth's feelings can be understood to be pulling her. There are also recurrent words and images: Essex's laurels, blood in various senses, the 'infame eschafaut', the Crown, a catalogue of Essex's exploits. There are patterned phrases: the most conspicuous is Essex's 'un homme comme moy' (expressing his sense of being what a Cornelian hero would call 'une âme peu commun'), which occurs first in I.1: 'Et vous vous faites tort d'accuser sans raison / Un homme comme moy de quelque trahison'. It is echoed by Raleigh – 'un homme de ma sorte' (II.4) – used again by Essex in the trial scene (III.1), then by Southampton to Raleigh when he comes to plead for Essex – 'un homme comme luy' (IV.3) – and finally by Essex on his way to execution as the final half-line of his futile appeal to the bystanders:

> Qu'un de mes compagnons, qu'un soldat charitable,
> Donne à son General un trespas honorable;
> Et ne permette pas s'il est homme de bien,
> Qu'un homme comme moy. Mais vous n'en ferez rien . . .   (V.1)

There are scenes of formalised debate, such as the one (II.1) where the monarch listens to two counsellors giving conflicting advice. An earlier specimen of this can be seen in Jacques de la Taille's *Alexandre* (Act II), where a 'Prophete Chaldean' urges Alexandre to leave Babylon, and the philosopher Aristarque urges him to say, and a later, more complex version is the scene in Corneille's *Cinna* (II.1), where Auguste consults Maxime and Cinna as to whether he should abdicate. Here, Cecil urges severity towards Essex while 'Le Comte de Salsbury' (a 'ghost'-character since Robert Cecil, younger son of William Cecil, first Lord Burleigh, was in fact Earl of Salisbury) urges the claims of dispassionate justice and also reminds the queen of Essex's courage and loyalty and his hitherto spotless reputation.

But, while constructing these formal rhetorical patterns, La Calprenède seems also to be wanting to create a sense of likeness to life and a bond of common humanity between his audience and his characters (and this is one of the directions in which French tragedy was developing in the 1630s and 1640s). This means that the rhetorical stylisation may be disrupted in various ways. Elizabeth, for instance, at the end of the set piece of 'monarch between opposing counsellors' (II.1), announces that she has a headache and will have to take a rest:

> Adieu, ce nouveau soing me donne un mal de teste
> Dont l'importunité me trouble à tout propos,
> Et me force de prendre un moment de repos.

The almost abstract quality conferred by rhetorical design may be momentarily disturbed by a realistic note, as when Essex makes a gibe about Elizabeth's age:

> Elle doit maintenant avoir de la prudence,
> Qu'elle quitte l'amour, son aage l'en dispence,
> Donne luy ce conseil.   (II.5)

The frequency of half-lines and unfinished sentences is also part of the antirhetorical side of the play. Half-lines are not worked into a pattern which formalises the very disruption of formal pattern (as is often done by Corneille); they simply transmit a momentary sense of the uncertain rhythms and incomplete forms of real dialogue.

If we have, in this play, a sense that rhetoric is discontinuous or fragmented, at times it is the other way round and rhetorical shaping triumphs over psychological coherence, rhetoric having a kind of impetus of its own which can cut across the integrity of 'character-portrayal'. This brings us back to Southampton, whose speeches to Essex in 1.5 I have referred to above as casting doubt on Essex's innocence.

Southampton represents the loyal but not uncritical friend of a great man (like Lucile, Marc Antoine's confidant in Garnier's *Marc Antoine*). His first speech is principally a moralising meditation on the perils of greatness and of royal favour, and it is in keeping with its edifying tone that it should rebuke Essex for having let his *outrecuidance* lead him into committing a 'grande faute' (unspecified). The speech has a generalising tendency:

> La puissance des Roys ne peut estre bornee,
> Leur caprice à leur gré fait nostre destinee;
> Nous sommes leur jouët, et l'inconstante main
> Qui nous hausse aujourd'huy nous rabaisse demain.

As this quotation makes clear, the edifying content of the speech is an adaptation of commonplace developments on Fortune and her turning wheel. Such developments are addressed to someone who has already demonstrated, by words or deeds, a tendency to regard himself as exempt from Fortune's whims, so the notion that a *faute* has already been committed, even if only by the expression of self-confidence (as in Essex's preceding speech), is normal for such a context. Southampton's is almost a choric voice here, as it is again in his next speech, where he gives a portrait of Elizabeth ('Cet esprit remuant, superbe, ambitieux . . .'), the formal nature of the speech being emphasised by its use of pattern:

> L'honneur, le droict, le sang, contre une telle amorce
> Sur ce coeur orgueilleux, n'ont iamais eu de force,
> Et pour se maintenir dans cet illustre rang
> Elle a foulé l'honneur, et le droict, et le sang.

To defend *Le Comte d'Essex* against all charges of inconsistency, unevenness or lack of clarity would probably be as difficult as defending the Earl of Essex against charges of treason and insubordination; it can, however, be maintained that the faults of this play are the products of the moment of its creation, looking back to a rhetorical drama and forward to one where the rhetoric would be more disguised and the emphasis more firmly on psychological coherence and vraisemblance.

A seventeenth-century Hiberno-Breton hagiological exchange

DAVID N. DUMVILLE

The seventeenth century saw the development of new attitudes to hagiology among the more historically minded of Europe's Catholic scholarly élite. One has only to think of the early Bollandists to appreciate some of the developments which had been set in train.[1] Various individual works of hagiological scholarship stand out from the pre-Bollandist era; one such endeavour will be considered here. But collaborative efforts too may be seen in the earlier seventeenth century. In particular, we associate the activities of a remarkable series of Irish ecclesiastics with the work of collecting, publishing, and writing commentary upon their predecessors' hagiographical writings.[2] Among these, Franciscans were notably prominent. Not all the ventures which were planned by Irish scholars of the early seventeenth century could be brought to fruition: but to mention John Colgan's massive *Trias Thaumaturga* (Leuven 1647) and his uncompleted *Acta Sanctorum Hiberniae* is to remind oneself of the enterprising scale on which hagiologists of the period could plan and execute their work.[3] Part of Irish cultural history in the era of Counter-reformation concerned the recovery of Ireland's mediaeval religious history.

Here we shall be concerned with two interlocking episodes in seventeenth-century hagiological research. Since the late fifteenth century a new interest had been taken in the history of what was then the Duchy of Brittany.[4] A succession of scholars, of very varying abilities and critical attitudes, had laboured to gather and publish materials relating to the region's history and culture. By the mid-1620s at the latest, it would seem, a plan had formed in the mind of Albert Le Grand, O. P., to create a collection of the Lives of the saints of Brittany.[5] A

---

[1] See Knowles, *Great Historical Enterprises*, for a convenient, introductory account.
[2] Jennings, *Michael Ó Cléirigh*; Sharpe, *Medieval Irish Saints' Lives*.
[3] See *Father John Colgan O. F. M.*, ed. O'Donnell; *Acta Sanctorum Hiberniae*, I, ed. Colgan, published in 1645, dealt with the saints of only the first quarter of the year.
[4] On Pierre Le Baud who was prominent at the beginning of this process, see the brief bibliographical notice by Fleuriot, *Les Origines*, p. 245.
[5] See his own account: *Les Vies*, ed. Le Grand (5th edn), pp. x–xj. Some of the notes which he collected (including those on St Vio) are preserved in Rennes, Bibliothèque municipale, MS. 267.

substantial volume, *Les Vies, gestes, mort et miracles des Saints de la Bretagne Armorique*, was published at Nantes in 1636. His motives were both religious and patriotic. He tells us that 'Mon principal dessein est d'écrire les Vies de tous les Saints de Bretagne venus à mon connoissance';[6] he did so, 'rendant ce service à l'Eglise et à ma patrie, à la confusion des ennemis'.[7] The body of his massive work does not appear overtly polemical, but the preface ('Avertissement au lecteur'[8]) has a different tone: 'J'interdis absolument la lecture de ce livre aux Athées, aux Libertins, aux Indifférents, aux Heretiques . . .';[9] 'La fin que je propose n'est autre que l'honneur de Dieu, la gloire de ses Saints, vostre utilité et édification, et la confusion des ennemis de l'Eglise'.[10] The style and the method of his writing were modest:[11]

> Mon stile, au reste, est simple et historique, autant que le sujet le peut permettre. S'il ne vous semble assez élegant, je vous reponds pour excuse, que le François m'est comme estranger, estant, comme j'ay déjà dit, natif de Morlaix, Ville située au coeur de la Basse-Bretagne, dont le langage naturel est le Breton. Vous remarquerez aussi que, là où l'Histoire semble Apocrife et de peu de Foy, toutesfois appuyée de la tradition immemoriale, je produits les raisons de part et d'autre, et laisse la chose indecise. Mesme, quand il se rencontre des opinions contraires entre les Autheurs, si ce ne sont contradictions notoirement manifestes, je ne m'arreste pas à les accorder, parce que ce seroit un travail de grande haleine et de peu d'utilité; non plus aussi à soustenir les uns et refuter les autres, mais j'en laisse la decision au judicieux Lecteur, et ce d'autant que ce n'est pas icy une dispute de Controverse, mais une simple Histoire, ennemie de toute obscurité; d'ailleurs, que je ne veux blesser la venerable Antiquité.

Apart from an occasional quotation in Breton or Latin, the work is in French throughout. The author's sources were likewise in Breton, French, and Latin; they were a mixture of printed, manuscript, and oral, and were combined by Le Grand within the limits which he described in the paragraph just quoted.

In 1628 Le Grand received from the Vicar General of the French Congregation of his Order a mandate to proceed with his work by investigating ecclesiastical archives for appropriate source-materials: the document was reproduced in the eventual publication.[12] It seems that his sources of information were drawn from a wide circle of Breton acquaintance. This Dominican scholar appears to be

6 *Les Vies*, ed. Le Grand (5th edn), p. xj.
7 *Ibid.*, p. xij.
8 *Ibid.*, pp. x–xiij.
9 *Ibid.*, p. xij.
10 *Ibid.*, p. xiij.
11 *Ibid.*, p. xij.
12 *Ibid.*, p. xiv.

scrupulous in giving references to his sources: they were usually listed in italics at the end of each Life. Sometimes these references are infuriatingly vague.[13]

Not at all vague, but still less full than one might wish, are two references to an unusual witness. In 1629, the year after Le Grand received the mandate from his Vicar General, he gained information which connected Breton and Irish saints' cults. First, under the heading 'La Vie de S. Sané, Evesque Hybernois, Titulaire de la paroisse de Plousané en Leon, le 6 Mars', Le Grand gave an account with a significant Irish content:[14] he quoted names and a phrase in Irish, and referred also to various writers who took the Irish position in the dispute about the mediaeval meanings of *Hibernia* and *Scotia*.[15] It becomes apparent, as the narrative continues, that St Sané of Plousané has been identified with St Senán of Scattery Island;[16] one chapter recounts a miraculous episode concerning a Protestant bishop in Ireland in the time of Queen Elizabeth I.[17] At the end of the Life Le Grand noted his sources:[18]

Cette Vie a esté par nous recueillie du Breviaire de Leon, qui en a l'Histoire en neuf Leçons, le 6 Mars, et un extraict autentique des Archives manuscrites de Nostre Dame d'Inis-Kaha et Killsenan au territoire d'Aruest au Comté de Kierri, Diocese d'Artfarten, Province de Mommoine en l'Irlande, à moy tranmis par le R. P. Frere Vincent Du-Val de Sainte Marie, Vicaire Provincial d'Hybernie, l'an 1629, et de la tradition qu'on en a en la Paroisse de Plousane.

Who, then, was this 'R. P. Frere Vincent Du-Val de Sainte-Marie'?

Further information comes from another of Le Grand's accounts, that of St Vougay. Under the heading 'La Vie de Saint Vouga, ou Vio, Evesque et Confesseur, le quinzième Juin', he writes of one '*Vouga*, lequel, pour sa probité & bonne vie, fut premierement fait Chanoine en l'Eglise d'Armacan, & enfin Canoniquement éleu Archevesque dudit lieu & Primat d'Hybernie'.[19] An ascetically motivated and miraculously aided flight from his responsibilities brought him to Brittany where he remained until his death *ca* A.D. 585.

---

[13] Cf. Conduché, 'Méthodes', p. 662.

[14] *Les Vies*, ed. Le Grand (5th edn), pp. 79–84.

[15] In § I he referred particularly to Thomas Messingham and to '*Hugues Cauello*, Archevesque d'Armacan, Primat d'Hybernie' (*ibid.*, p. 79). On Messingham (*fl.* 1624; rector of the Irish College at Leuven) see Jennings, *Michael Ó Cléirigh*, pp. 26–8, and Silke, 'The Irish abroad, 1534–1691', pp. 620, 628; on Hugh Mac Caghwell (Aodh Mac Aingil), *ob.* 1626, see Jennings, *Michael Ó Cléirigh*, pp. 24–6; Millett, 'Irish literature in Latin, 1550–1700', pp. 563, 575–6; Silke, 'The Irish abroad, 1534–1691', pp. 621, 630, 632. On the *Scotia/Scotti* controversy, see Mooney, 'Father John Colgan, O. F. M.', pp. 17–21.

[16] See Grosjean, 'Trois pièces', pp. 222, 225, 228–30. Cf. Gougaud, *Les Saints*, pp. 167–9.

[17] *Les Vies*, ed. Le Grand, p. 83 (§ XIII).

[18] *Ibid.*, p. 84.

[19] *Ibid.*, pp. 222–4.

The Armagh element in this Life is unexplained,[20] but it is again due to Le Grand's Irish informant. His notice of his sources reads as follows.[21]

Cette Histoire a esté par nous recueillie d'une vieille Chronique de Bretagne, écrite à la main, et d'un vieil Legendaire, aussi manuscrit sur vellin, que j'ay veu en l'Abbaye de Saint Matthieu en bas Leon, et des recherches des Antiquitez des Eglises de Leon, par Messire Yves Le Grand, Chanoine de Leon, Recteur de Plou'neventer et Aumônier du Duc François II. Le vieil Legendaire Choral de l'Eglise Cathedrale de Leon et les memoires authentiques d'Armacan en Yrlande, à moy transmis par le R. F. Vincent du Val de Sainte Marie, de l'Ordre des Freres Prédicateurs, Vicaire Provincial d'Hybernie.

It was evidently a Dominican network of information which transmitted these Irish reports to Albert Le Grand: but how the two men were brought into contact is not known.

1629, the year to which Du Val's transmission of information about St Senán is attributed by Le Grand, was one in which considerable activity was under way in the plan of the Irish Franciscans at Leuven to collect and publish the Lives of Irish saints. Indeed, in that very year, Michael Ó Cléirigh, O. F. M., made a number of copies of texts about St Senán.[22] Unfortunately, it remains to be determined how much (if any) effect this activity had on other ecclesiastical groups in Ireland. For the moment, one must say that insufficient is known about relationships between the Orders to allow one to speculate about the possible impact of the Franciscan enterprise on an Irish Dominican.[23]

One may, however, suspect that Du Val's information came to Le Grand in writing. Perhaps the word *transmis* – used on both occasions – need not imply this. But Le Grand's forms of two ecclesiastical place-names imply that he had misunderstood what he had read: he refers to the *Diocese d'Artfarten* and *l'Eglise*

---

[20] Who St Vio was supposed to be is a mystery (Gougaud, *Les Saints*, pp. 173–4, avoided the question; but cf. Loth, *Les Noms*, p. 126). In the list of Armagh successors of Patrick, only Feidlimid or Fiachra would appear to be candidates for identification, but neither seems very promising: see Lawlor & Best, 'The ancient list', p. 320. A century ago it was suggested (O'Hanlon, *Lives*, VI.668–71; cf. I.387, where the reference to 20 June is an error) that Vaux (Vogue) of Carnsore (Co. Wexford) was his Irish counterpart. Professor Ó Riain has commented, in a letter to me, that 'His feast was on another day, January 20, but, in any case, he is identical with Maedóc (>Mogue>Vogue). Could it be that Vouga's Irish 'Life', as reported by Albert Le Grand, is based on St Malachy's (Mael Maedóc's) tenure of Armagh?'

[21] *Les Vies*, ed. Le Grand, p. 224.

[22] Jennings, *Michael Ó Cléirigh*, pp. 86, 91, 94.

[23] From 1624 the University of Leuven had an Irish Dominican College (Holy Cross) as well as the famous Irish Franciscan house, St Anthony's, founded in 1606: Silke, 'The Irish abroad, 1534–1691', pp. 621–2.

d'Armacan where the names are abbreviations of Latin adjectival forms, *Artfertensis* and *Armacanus*, the nature of whose latinisation has been misperceived.[24]

Du Val appears from his name to have been a Frenchman: if so, his connexion with Le Grand would probably need to be explained by a shared phase in their careers in the Dominican order, at one of the Breton houses in which Le Grand had lived. However, it is not clear what would have caused a French Dominican to be 'Vicaire Provincial d'Hybernie' for his Order in 1629. There is in fact some evidence to suggest that in this case Du Val is a gallicisation of a name quite familiar in the Irish context.

It seems that at that period the name Du Val was commonly used by ecclesiastics whose family-name was Wall.[25] This has proved productive in the search for an identification. Vincent Wall, or Vincentius de Sancta Maria (Du Val), was indeed a member of the Dominican order in the 1620s. From 1619 to 1622 he was a matriculated student at the University of Salamanca,[26] another place which provided a haven for Irish ecclesiastics abroad.[27] In 1627 he was still (or again) in Spain, and by this time at least had achieved the rank of priest.[28] But by 1629 at the latest, on Le Grand's evidence,[28] he had acquired an Irish office. Perhaps it was he who in 1644 was the Vincent Wall promoted (with fourteen others) to a degree within the Order.[29]

Of Vincent Wall, his career, contacts, and interests, very little is therefore known. The surname, Wall, is found most commonly in Munster, and particularly at Limerick.[30] This would explain how the information about Scattery Island was available (and of interest) to him. It is more difficult to account for his access to Armagh sources.

If we allow the likelihood of a Munster background, Vincent Wall was perhaps in 1629 the Provincial's vicar for the province of Munster:[31] a number of Dominican houses could be found within the bounds of this archdiocese; but at which house Fr Vincent was first professed is at present a matter of speculation.

How Wall and Le Grand came into contact remains a problem. Generally speaking, Le Grand's sources tend to be relatively local. It is therefore open to one to speculate that Wall passed through eastern Brittany on his way from

[24] For the forms see *Les Vies*, ed. Le Grand (5th edn), pp. 84, 224. On Armacan, cf. the editors' annotation *ibid.*, p. 79, n. 6.
[25] I owe this observation to Fr Hugh Fenning, O.P. For further documentation of the equation of Duval and Wall, see Gallwey, *The Wall Family, passim*.
[26] Salamanca, Archivo Universitario, Libros de Matriculas, 324 (fo 12r), gives (for example) the information for 1619/20. I owe this reference and others to the generosity of Fr Thomas S. Flynn, O.P.
[27] An Irish College was founded at Salamanca (where the university acted as a magnet) in 1592: see Silke, 'The Irish abroad, 1534–1691', p. 616; cf. pp. 618–19, 622, 624–5.
[28] *Spicilegium Ossoriense*, ed. Moran, I.160.
[29] Fenning, 'Irish material', p. 313 (and n. 195), 274.
[30] Again, I owe this formulation to Fr Hugh Fenning.
[31] This is Fr Hugh Fenning's deduction.

Spain to Ireland in 1627 x 1629. It is known that at this period shipping plied
between Ireland and the Breton ports of Saint Malo and Nantes:[32] such may have
been the route by which a report from Wall reached Le Grand; perhaps the
Breton had asked the Irishman, as he made his way home to a new job in Ireland,
to keep his eyes open for information about Breton saints supposedly of Irish
origin.[33]

[32] Silke, 'The Irish abroad, 1534–1691', pp. 612–14.
[33] For this context in Brittonic hagiography, see Kenney, *The Sources*, pp. 181–2. In my
search for the identity of Vincent Du Val de Sainte-Marie, O.P., I have been aided by
Dr J.A. Bergin (Manchester), Monsignor Leonard Boyle (Rome), Dr Brendan
Bradshaw (Cambridge), Dr Donatien Laurent (Brest), Professor Brian Ó Cuív
(Dublin), Professor Pádraig Ó Riain (Cork), and Dr Richard Sharpe (Oxford). A
critical role was played by the two Dominican scholars (of St Mary's Priory, Tallaght,
Dublin) acknowledged in nn. 25–26, to whom I am greatly indebted.

Bibliography

ACKERMAN, R. W., 'English rimed and prose romances', in *Arthurian Literature in the Middle Ages*, ed. R. S. Loomis (Oxford 1959), pp. 480–519

ALEXANDER, J. J. G., 'The Benedictional of St Aethelwold and Anglo-Saxon illumination of the Reform period', in *Tenth-century Studies*, ed. D. Parsons (Chichester 1975), pp. 169–83 and 241–5

ALLMAND, C. T., *Society at War: the Experience of England and France during the Hundred Years War* (Edinburgh 1973)

ARNOLD, Thomas (ed.), *Henrici Archidiaconi Huntendunensis Historia Anglorum* (London 1879)

ASSMANN, B. (ed.), *Angelsächsische Homilien und Heiligenleben* (Kassel 1889)

ASTON, M., 'The impeachment of Bishop Despenser', *Bulletin of the Institute of Historical Research* 38 (1965) 127–48

AUERBACH, Erich, *Literary Language and its Public in Late Latin Antiquity and in the Middle Ages* (London 1965)

AYRES, W., 'A study in the genesis of Vaugelas's *Remarques sur la langue françoise*: the Arsenal manuscript', *French Studies* 37 (1983) 17–34

BAERWOLFF, W., *Der Graf von Essex im deutschen Drama*, Inaugural Dissertation (Tübingen 1919)

BALDWIN, A. P., *The Theme of Government in Piers Plowman* (Cambridge 1981)

BALDWIN, J. F., *The King's Council in England during the Middle Ages* (Oxford 1913)

BALLAIRA, G., *Per il catalogo dei codici di Prisciano* (Turin 1982)

BALUZE, E. & MOLLAT, G. (edd.), *Vitae paparum avenonensium* (4 vols, Paris 1914–22)

BAMMEL, Caroline P. Hammond, *Der Römerbrieftext des Rufin und seine Origenes-Übersetzung* (Freiburg i.B. 1985)

BAMMEL, C. P. Hammond, 'Products of fifth-century scriptoria preserving conventions used by Rufinus of Aquileia', *Journal of Theological Studies*, N. S., 30 (1979) 430–62 *and* 35 (1984) 347–93

BARBAZAN, Étienne, *Fabliaux et contes des poètes françois des XI, XII, XIII, XIV et XVe siècles, tirés des meilleurs auteurs* (new edn, by M. Méon, 4 vols, Paris 1808)

BARNIE, John, *War in Medieval Society. Social Values and the Hundred Years War 1337–99* (London 1974)

BARTSCH, K., *Denkmäler der provenzalischen Litteratur* (Stuttgart 1856)

BARTSCH, K., *La Langue et la littérature françaises* (Paris 1887)

BASTIN, Julia (ed.), *Recueil général des Isopets* (2 vols, Paris 1929–30)

BASTIN, J., 'Trois "dits" du XIIIe siècle', *Revue Belge de philologie et d'histoire* 20 (1941) 467–507

BATIOUCHKOF, T., 'Le débat de l'âme et du corps', *Romania* 20 (1891) 1–55, 513–78

BAUER, Clemens *et al.* (edd.), *Speculum Historiale. Geschichte im Spiegel von Geschichtsschreibung und Geschichtsdeutung* (Freiburg 1965)

BAUMGARTNER, Emmanuèle, *Le Tristan en prose* (Geneva 1975)

BAYOT, A. (ed.), *Le Poème moral* (Brussels 1929)

BECKER, G. (ed.), *Catalogi bibliothecarum antiqui* (Bonn 1885)

BÉDARD, É. & MAURAIS, J. (edd.), *La Norme linguistique* (Québec 1983)

BÉDIER, Joseph (ed.), *Les Chansons de C. Muset* (Paris 1912)

BÉDIER, Joseph, *Les Fabliaux: études de littérature populaire et d'histoire littéraire au moyen âge* (4th edn, Paris 1925)

BEER, R., 'Bemerkungen über den ältesten Handschriftenbestand des Klosters Bobbio', *Anzeiger der kaiserlichen Akademie der Wissenschaften zu Wien* (phil.–hist. Klasse) 48 (1911) 78–104

BELFOUR, A. O. (ed.), *Twelfth Century Homilies in MS. Bodley 343*, I (London 1909)

BELPERRON, P., *La Croisade contre les Albigeois 1209–1249* (2nd edn, Paris 1967)

BESSINGER, J. B. & CREED, R. P. (edd.), *Franciplegius: Medieval and Linguistic Studies in Honor of Francis Peabody Magoun, Jr* (New York 1965)

BISCHOFF, B. & BROWN, V., 'Addenda to *Codices Latini Antiquiores*', *Mediaeval Studies* 47 (1985) 317–66

BISCHOFF, B., *Die südostdeutschen Schreibschulen und Bibliotheken der Karolingerzeit*, II (Wiesbaden 1980)

BISCHOFF, B. & HOFMANN, J., *Libri Sancti Kyliani* (Würzburg 1952)

BISCHOFF, B., *Mittelalterliche Studien. Ausgewählte Aufsätze zur Schriftkunde und Literaturgeschichte* (3 vols, Stuttgart 1966–81)

BISHOP, E., *Liturgica historica* (Oxford 1918)

BISHOP, T. A. M., 'An early example of Insular-Caroline', *Transactions of the Cambridge Bibliographical Society* 4 (1964–8) 396–400

BISHOP, T. A M., *English Caroline Minuscule* (Oxford 1971)

BISHOP, T. A. M., 'Notes on Cambridge manuscripts', part VII, *Transactions of the Cambridge Bibliographical Society* 3 (1959–63) 413–23

BLAIR, T. M. H. (ed.), *J. Banks: The Unhappy Favourite* (New York 1939)

BLOCH, M., *Les Rois thaumaturges* (Strasbourg 1924)

BLOCH, R., *Medieval French Literature and Law* (Berkeley, Cal. 1977)

BOGDANOW, F., *The Romance of the Grail* (Manchester 1965)

BOLLANDUS, J. *et al.* (edd.), *Acta Sanctorum* (Antwerp etc. 1643–)

BONI, M. (ed.), *Sordelli: Poesie* (Bologna 1954)

BONILLA Y SAN MARTIN, A. (ed.), *Libros de Caballerías* (2 vols, Madrid 1907–8)

BOUQUET, M. *et al.* (edd.), *Recueil des historiens des Gaules et de la France* (24 vols, Paris 1737–1904)

BOUTON, C.-P., *Les Grammaires françaises de Claude Mauger à l'usage des Anglais (XVIIe siècle)* (Paris 1972)

BOWERS, F. (ed.), *The Dramatic Works of Thomas Dekker* (4 vols, Cambridge 1953–61)

BRALL, Artur (ed.), *Von der Klosterbibliothek zur Landesbibliothek. Beiträge zum zweihundertjährigen Bestehen der Hessischen Landesbibliothek Fulda* (Stuttgart 1978)

BRÉHIER, L., 'Les traits originaux de l'iconographie dans la sculpture romane de l'Auvergne', in *Medieval Studies in Memory of A. Kingsley Porter*, ed. W. R. W. Koehler (2 vols, Cambridge, Mass. 1939), II.389–403

BRETT, Caroline (ed. & transl.), *The Monks of Redon*. Gesta Sanctorum Rotonensium *and* Vita Conuuoionis (Woodbridge 1989)

BROOKE, C. N. L., *The Church and the Welsh Border in the Central Middle Ages* (Woodbridge 1986)

BROWN, Carleton (ed.), *English Lyrics of the XIIIth Century* (Oxford 1932)

BRUNEL, C. (ed.), *La Fille du comte de Poitiers, conte en prose: versions du XIIIe et du XVe siècle* (Paris 1923)

BRUNOT, Ferdinand, *Histoire de la langue française des origines à nos jours* (2nd edn, Paris 1966–)

BRUNOT, Ferdinand, *La Doctrine de Malherbe d'après son commentaire sur Desportes* (Paris 1891)

BUCHHOLZ, R. (ed.), *Visio lamentabilis. Die Fragmente der Reden der Seele an den Leichnam in zwei Handschriften zu Worcester und Oxford* (Erlangen 1890)

BULLOUGH, D. A., 'The Continental background of the Reform', in *Tenth-century Studies*, ed. D. Parsons (Chichester 1975), pp. 20–36 and 210–14

BULLOUGH, D. A., 'The educational tradition in England from Alfred to Ælfric: teaching *utriusque linguae*', *Settimane di studio del Centro italiano di studi sull'alto medioevo*, Spoleto 19 (1972) 453–94

BUSBY, K., *Gawain in Old French Literature* (Amsterdam 1980)

CARMAN, J. N., *A Study of the Pseudo-Map Cycle of Arthurian Romances* (Lawrence, Kansas 1973)

CASAS HOMS, J. M. (ed.), 'Una gramàtica inèdita d'Usuard', *Analecta Montserratensia* 10 (1964) 77–129

CASEWITZ, M. & CHARPIN, F., 'L'héritage gréco-latin', in *La Norme linguistique*, edd. E. Bédard & J. Maurais (Québec 1983), pp. 45–68

CELLARD, Jacques, *Dictionaire du français non conventionnel* (Paris 1980)

CHASE, Colin (ed.), *Two Alcuin Letter-books* (Toronto 1975)

CHATILLON, J., 'Isidore et Origène. Recherches sur les sources et l'influence des *Quæstiones in Vetus Testamentum* d'Isidore de Séville', in *Mélanges bibliques rédigés en l'honneur de André Robert* (Paris [1956]), pp. 537–47

CHAVANNES, Félix (ed.), *Le Mireour du monde* (Lausanne 1845)

CHÉDEVILLE, A. & GUILLOTEL, H., *La Bretagne des saints et des rois* (Rennes 1984)

CHEVALIER, J.-C. (ed.), *Grammaire transformationnelle: syntaxe et lexique* (Lille 1976)

CHEVALIER, J.-C., 'Le jeu des exemples dans la théorie grammaticale', in *Grammaire transformationnelle: syntaxe et lexique*, ed. J.-C. Chevalier (Lille 1976), pp. 233–63

CHIBNALL, M., 'Orderic Vitalis and Robert of Torigni', in *Millénaire monastique du Mont Saint-Michel*, ed. R. Foreville, II (Paris 1967), pp. 133–9

CHRIST, K., *Die Bibliothek des Klosters Fulda im 16. Jahrhundert* (Leipzig 1933)

CLEMOES, Peter & HUGHES, K. (edd.), *England before the Conquest. Studies in Primary Sources presented to Dorothy Whitelock* (Cambridge 1971)

CLOETTA, Wilhelm (ed.), *Les Deux Rédactions en vers du Moniage Guillaume, chansons de geste du XIIe siècle* (2 vols, Paris 1906–11)

COLEMAN, Janet, *Medieval Readers and Writers* (London 1981)

COLGAN, John (ed.), *Acta Sanctorum veteris et maioris Scotiæ, seu Hiberniæ sanctorum insulae*, I (Leuven 1645; 2nd edn, by B. Jennings, Dublin 1948)

COLGAN, John (ed.), *Triadis thaumaturgae . . . acta* (Leuven 1647)

COLGRAVE, Bertram & MYNORS, R. A. B. (edd. & transl.), *Bede's Ecclesiastical History of the English People* (Oxford 1969)

CONDUCHÉ, D., 'Méthodes de travail d'Albert Le Grand, hagiographe breton', *Bulletin philologique et historique (jusqu'à 1610) du Comité des travaux historiques et scientifiques* (1966) 661–71

CONNER, Patrick W., *Anglo-Saxon Exeter: a Tenth-century Cultural History* (Woodbridge, forthcoming)

CORBETT, N. L. (ed.), *Joinville: Vie de Saint Louis* (Québec 1977)

COULON, A. & CLEMENCET, S. (edd.), *Lettres secrètes et curiales du pape Jean XXII relatives à la France* (4 vols, Paris 1906–72)

COURCELLE, P., *Les Lettres grecques en occident* (2nd edn, Paris 1948)

CRANE, T. F. (ed.), *The Exempla or Illustrative Stories from the* Sermones Vulgares *of Jacques de Vitry* (London 1890)

CRICK, Julia C., *The Historia Regum Britannie of Geoffrey of Monmouth*, III, *A Summary Catalogue of the Manuscripts* (Cambridge 1989)

CRIST, L. S. (ed.), *Saladin: suite et fin du deuxième Cycle de la Croisade* (Geneva 1972)

CROSS, J. E., ' "The dry bones speak": a theme in some Old English homiles', *Journal of English and Germanic Philology* 56 (1957) 434–9

CURTIS, R. L. (ed.), *Le Roman de Tristan en prose* (3 vols, Cambridge 1984–5)

DAICHES, David & THORLBY, A. (edd.), *The Mediaeval World* (London 1973)

DAVIS, G. R. C., *Medieval Cartularies of Great Britain* (London 1958)

DE COURSON, Aurélien (ed.), *Cartulaire de l'abbaye de Redon en Bretagne* (Paris 1863)

DEJEANNE, J. M. L. (ed.), *Poésies complètes du troubadour Marcabru* (Toulouse 1909)

DEKKERS, E. & GAAR, A., *Clavis Patrum Latinorum* (2nd edn, Steenbrugge 1961)

DELABORDE, H. F. (ed.), *Guillaume le Breton: Philippiad*, (Paris 1885)

DELACHENAL, R., *Histoire de Charles V* (5 vols, Paris 1909–31)

DELISLE, Léopold (ed.), *Chronique de Robert de Torigni, abbé du Mont-Saint-Michel, suivie de divers opuscules historiques* (2 vols, Rouen 1872–3)

DELISLE, Léopold, *Le Cabinet des manuscrits de la Bibliothèque impériale*, II (Paris 1874)

DEL MONTE, Alberto (ed. & transl.), *Peire d'Alvernha: Liriche* (Turin 1955)

DE MAS-LATRIE, L. (ed.), *La Chronique d'Ernoul et de Bernard le Trésorier* (Paris 1871)

DE MONTAIGLON, Anatole & RAYNAUD, G. (edd.), *Recueil général et complet des fabliaux, des XIIIe et XIVe siècles* (6 vols, Paris 1872–90)

DENIFLE, H., *La Désolation des églises, monastères et hôpitaux en France pendant la guerre de Cent ans* (2 vols, Paris 1899)

DEPREZ, E. *et al.* (edd.), *Lettres closes, patentes et curiales du pape Clément VI se rapportant à la France* (3 vols, Paris 1901–61)

DE LUBAC, H., *Exégèse médiévale*, I (Paris 1959)

DE REIFFENBERG, F. (ed.), *Philippe Mouskés: Chronique rimée* (3 vols, Brussels 1836–45)

DEUFFIC, Jean-Luc (ed.), 'Calendrier à l'usage de l'abbaye de Landevennec', *Britannia Christiana*, Bibliothèque liturgique bretonne, fasc. 5 (1985)

DE WAILLY, N. (ed.), *Récits d'un menestrel de Reims* (Paris 1876)

DEWICK, E. S. & FRERE, W. H. (edd.), *The Leofric Collectar (Harl. MS. 2961), with an Appendix containing a Litany and Prayers from Harl. MS. 863* (2 vols, London 1914–21)

DOBIACHE-ROJDESTVENSKY, O., 'Le Codex *Q.v.I.6–10* de la Bibliothèque publique de Léningrad', *Speculum* 5 (1930) 21–48

DOBLE, G., 'St Congar', *Antiquity* 19 (1945) 32–43, 85–95

DOBLE, Gilbert, *St Winwaloe*, Cornish Saints Series 4 (Shipston-on-Stour 1940)

DREVES, G. M. & BLUME, C. (edd.), *Analecta hymnica medii aevi* (55 vols in 58, Leipzig 1886–1922)

DU BOULAY, F. R. H. & BARRON, C. M. (edd.), *The Reign of Richard II. Essays in Honour of May McKisack* (London 1971)

DUDLEY, L. (ed.), 'An early homily on the body and soul theme', *Journal of English and Germanic Philology* 8 (1909) 225–53

DÜMMLER, Ernst (ed.), *Das Formelbuch des Bischofs Salomo III von Konstanz* (Leipzig 1857)

DÜMMLER, Ernst *et al.* (edd.), *Epistolae Karolini Aevi* (Berlin 1892–)

DUGDALE, William (ed.), *Monasticon anglicanum* (new edn, 6 vols in 8, London 1817–30)

DUINE, F., 'Mémento des sources hagiographiques de l'histoire de Bretagne', *Bulletin et mémoires de la Société archéologique d'Ille-et-Vilaine* 46 (1918) 245–457

DUMVILLE, D. N., 'An early text of Geoffrey of Monmouth's *Historia Regum Britanniae* and the circulation of some Latin histories in twelfth-century Normandy', *Arthurian Literature* 4 (1985) 1–36

DUMVILLE, D. N., 'Brittany and "Armes Prydein Vawr"', *Etudes celtiques* 20 (1983) 145–59

DUMVILLE, David N., *England and the Celtic World in the Ninth and Tenth Centuries* (O'Donnell Lectures: publication forthcoming)

DUMVILLE, David N., *Histories and Pseudo-histories of the Insular Middle Ages* (Aldershot 1990)

DUMVILLE, D. N., 'Maelbrigte mac Tornáin (†927), pluralist coarb' (forthcoming)

DUMVILLE, D. N., 'Some aspects of annalistic writing at Canterbury in the eleventh and early twelfth centuries', *Peritia* 2 (1983) 23–57

DUMVILLE, David N. (ed.), *The Historia Brittonum, 3: the 'Vatican' Recension* (Cambridge 1985)

DUMVILLE, D. N., 'The manuscripts of Geoffrey of Monmouth's *Historia Regum Britanniae*', *Arthurian Literature* 3 (1983) 113–28

DUMVILLE, D. N., 'The manuscripts of Geoffrey of Monmouth's *Historia Regum Britanniae*: addenda, corrigenda and an alphabetical list', *Arthurian Literature* 4 (1985) 164–71

DUMVILLE, David N., *Wessex and England from Alfred to Edgar* (Woodbridge 1992)

DUNBABIN, Jean, *France in the Making* (Oxford 1985)

EDBURY, Peter W. (ed.), *Crusade and Settlement. Papers read at the First Conference of the Society for the Study of the Crusades and the Latin East and presented to R. C. Smail* (Cardiff 1985)

EKWALL, Eilert, *The Concise Oxford Dictionary of English Place-names* (4th edn, Oxford 1960)

ELWERT, W. Theodor, *Traité de versification française des origines à nos jours* (Paris 1965)

EMANUEL, H. D., 'Geoffrey of Monmouth's *Historia Regum Britanniae*: a second variant version', *Medium Ævum* 35 (1966) 103–10

ESPOSITO, M., 'The ancient Bobbio catalogue', *Journal of Theological Studies* 32 (1931) 337–44

FARAL, Edmond (ed.), *G. de Villehardouin: La Conquête de Constantinople* (2 vols, Paris 1938–9)

FARAL, Edmond, *La Légende arthurienne: études et documents* (3 vols, Paris 1929)

FARAL, Edmond & BASTIN, J. (edd.), *Oeuvres complètes de Rutebeuf* (2 vols, Paris 1959–60)

FAWTIER, R., *The Capetian Kings of France* (London 1960)

FENNING, H., 'Irish material in the registers of the Dominican Masters General (1390–1649)', *Archivum Fratrum Praedicatorum* 39 (1969) 249–336

FISCHER, Hanns, *Schrifttafeln zum althochdeutschen Lesebuch* (Tübingen 1966)

FLETCHER, R. H., *The Arthurian Material in the Chronicles, especially those of Great Britain and France* (Boston, Mass. 1906)

FLETCHER, R. H., 'Two notes on the *Historia Regum Britanniae* of Geoffrey of Monmouth', *Publications of the Modern Language Association of America* 16 (1901) 461–74

FLEURIOT, Léon, *Les Origines de la Bretagne. L'émigration* (Paris 1980)

FLOWER, R., 'Laurence Nowell and the discovery of England in Tudor times', *Proceedings of the British Academy* 21 (1935) 47–73

FLUTRE, L.-F. & SNEYDERS DE VOGEL, K. (edd.), *Li Fet des Romains* (2 vols, Paris 1938)

FÖRSTER, M. (ed.), *Die Vercelli-Homilien* (Hamburg 1932)

FOREVILLE, R. (ed.), *Millénaire monastique du Mont Saint-Michel*, II (Paris 1967)

FORSYTH, E., *La Tragédie française de Jodelle à Corneille (1553–1640): le thème de la vengeance* (Paris 1962)

FOUCHÉ, Pierre, *Phonétique historique du français* (3 vols, Paris 1952–61)

FOX, J. H. *et al.* (edd.), *Studies in Eighteenth-century French Literature presented to Robert Niklaus* (Exeter 1975)

FRANK, István, *Répertoire métrique de la poésie des troubadours* (2 vols, Paris 1953–7)

FRAPPIER, J. (ed.), *Les Chansons de geste du cycle de Guillaume d'Orange* (2 vols, Paris 1955–65)

FRAPPIER, Jean (ed.), *La Mort le Roi Artu, roman du XIIIe siècle* (3rd edn, Paris 1964)

FREDE, H. J., *Kirchenschriftsteller: Aktualisierungsheft* (Freiburg 1984)

FREDE, H. J., *Kirchenschriftsteller: Verzeichnis und Sigel* (Freiburg 1981)

FREYMOND, E., 'Artus' Kampf mit dem Katzenungetüm. Eine Episode der Vulgata des Livre d'Artus, die Sage und ihre Lokalisierung in Savoyen', in *Beiträge zur romanischen Philologie. Festgabe für Gustav Gröber* (Halle a.S. 1899), pp. 311–96

GABRIELSON, A. (ed.), *Le Sermon de Guischart de Beauliu* (Skrifter utgifna af K. Humanistiska Vetenskaps-Samfundet 12, 5) (Uppsala 1909)

GALBRAITH, V. H. (ed.), *The Anonimalle Chronicle 1333 to 1381* (Manchester 1927)

GALE, Judith, 'John Joscelyn's Notebook: a Study of the Contents and Sources of British Library Cotton MS. Vitellius D.vii' (unpublished M.A. dissertation, University of Nottingham, 1978)

GALLWEY, Hubert, *The Wall Family in Ireland 1170–1970* (Naas 1970)

GASQUET, F. A. & BISHOP, E. (edd.), *The Bosworth Psalter* (London 1908)

GEARY, Patrick, *Furta sacra* (Princeton, N.J. 1978)

GENET, J.-P., 'English nationalism: Thomas Polton at the Council of Constance', *Nottingham Medieval Studies* 28 (1984) 60–78

GÉRAUD, H. (ed.), *Chronique latine de Guillaume de Nangis de 1113 à 1300 avec les continuations de cette chronique de 1300 à 1368* (2 vols, Paris 1843)

GEROULD, G. H., 'King Arthur and politics', *Speculum* 2 (1927) 33–51

GILDEA, J. (ed.), *Durmart le Gallois* (Villanova, Pa 1965)

GILSON, E., *Les Idées et les lettres* (Paris 1932)

GISI, M. (ed. & transl.), *Der Troubadour Guillem Anelier von Toulouse: vier provenzalische Gedichte* (Solothurn 1877)

GNEUSS, H., 'A preliminary list of manuscripts written or owned in England up to 1100', *Anglo-Saxon England* 9 (1981) 1–60

GÖLLER, K. H., 'König Arthur in den schottischen Chroniken', *Anglia* 80 (1962) 390–404

GOUGAUD, Louis, *Les Saints irlandais hors d'Irlande étudiés dans le culte et dans la dévotion traditionnelle* (Louvain 1936)

GOUGAUD, L., 'Mentions anglaises de saints bretons', *Annales de Bretagne* 34 (1919–21) 273–7

GRANSDEN, Antonia, *Historical Writing in England c. 550–c. 1307* (London 1974)

GREENWAY, D., 'Henry of Huntingdon and the manuscripts of his *Historia Anglorum*', *Anglo-Norman Studies* 9 (1986) 103–26

GRIFFITH, R. R., 'The authorship question reconsidered: a case for Thomas Malory of Papworth St Agnes, Cambridgeshire', in *Aspects of Malory*, edd. T. Takamiya & D. Brewer (Cambridge 1981), pp. 159–77

GROSJEAN, G., *Le Sentiment national dans la Guerre de Cent Ans* (Paris 1925)

GROSJEAN, P. (ed.), 'Trois pièces sur S. Senán', *Analecta Bollandiana* 66 (1948) 199–230

GUENÉE, B., 'État et nation en France au moyen âge', *Revue historique* 237 (1967) 17–30

GUENÉE, B., *States and Rulers in Later Medieval Europe* (Oxford 1985)

GUILLOTEL, H., 'Le premier siècle du pouvoir ducal breton (936–1040)', *Actes du Congrès national des sociétés savantes, Section de philologie et d'histoire jusqu'à 1610* 103 (1978) 63–84

HADDAN, Arthur West & STUBBS, W. (edd.), *Councils and Ecclesiastical Documents relating to Great Britain and Ireland* (3 vols, Oxford 1869–78)

HALLAM, E. M., *Capetian France 987–1328* (London 1980)

HAMILTON, N. E. S. A. (ed.), *Willelmi Malmesbiriensis monachi de gestis pontificum Anglorum libri quinque* (London 1870)

HAMMER, J., 'Geoffrey of Monmouth's use of the Bible in the *Historia Regum Britanniae*', *Bulletin of the John Rylands Library* 30 (1946/7) 293–311

HAMMER, J., 'Some additional manuscripts of Geoffrey of Monmouth's *Historia Regum Britanniae*', *Modern Language Quarterly* 3 (1942) 235–42

HAMMOND, C. P., 'A product of a fifth-century scriptorium preserving conventions used by Rufinus of Aquileia', *Journal of Theological Studies*, N.S., 29 (1978) 366–91

HAMMOND, C. P., 'The last ten years of Rufinus' life and the date of his move south from Aquileia', *Journal of Theological Studies*, N.S., 28 (1977) 372–429

HAMMOND, C. P., 'The Manuscript Tradition of Origen's Commentary on Romans in the Latin Translation by Rufinus' (unpublished Ph.D. dissertation, University of Cambridge 1965)

HANNING, R. W., *The Vision of History in Early Britain from Gildas to Geoffrey of Monmouth* (New York 1966)

HARRISS, G. L., *King, Parliament, and Public Finance in Medieval England to 1369* (Oxford 1975)

HAUSMANN, F.-J., 'Louis Meigret, humaniste et linguiste', *Historiographia Linguistica* 7 (1980) 335–50

HECTOR, L. C. & HARVEY, B. F. (edd. & transl.), *The Westminster Chronicle 1381–1394* (Oxford 1982)

HENINGHAM, E. K., 'Old English precursors of *The Worcester Fragments*', *Publications of the Modern Language Association of America* 55 (1940) 291–307

HENNEMAN, John Bell, *Royal Taxation in Fourteenth-century France. The Captivity and Ransom of John II, 1356–1370* (Philadelphia, Pa 1976)

HENNEMAN, John Bell, *Royal Taxation in Fourteenth Century France. The Development of War Financing 1322–1356* (Princeton, N.J. 1971)

HENRY, Albert (ed.), *Adenet le Roi: Berte aus grans piés* (Geneva 1982)

HENRY, Albert (ed.), *Les Oeuvres d'Adenet le Roi* (3 vols, Bruges 1951–6)

HEWITT, H. J., *The Organization of War under Edward III, 1338–62* (Manchester 1966)

HILKA, A. & SCHUMANN, O. (edd.), *Carmina Burana* (4 vols, Heidelberg 1930–70)

HILLGARTH, J. N., *Ramon Lull and Lullism in Fourteenth-century France* (London 1971)

HOEPFFNER, E. (ed.), 'Chanson française du XIIIe siècle (*Ay Dex! ou porrey jen trouver*)', *Romania* 47 (1921) 367–80

HOHLER, C. E., 'Some service-books of the later Saxon Church', in *Tenth-century Studies*, ed. D. Parsons (Chichester 1975), pp. 60–83 and 217–27

HOLMES, Urban T., *Adenet le Roi's Berte aus grans piés* (Chapel Hill, N.C. 1946)

HOLTHAUSEN, F. (ed.), *Vices and Virtues, being a Soul's Confession of its Sins, with Reason's Description of the Virtues. A Middle-English Dialogue of about 1200 A.D.* (2 vols, London 1888–1921)

HOLTZ, L., *Donat et la tradition de l'enseignement grammatical: étude sur l'Ars Donati et sa diffusion (IVe–IXe siècle) et édition critique* (Paris 1981)

HOUSLEY, N., *The Avignon Papacy and the Crusades, 1305–1378* (Oxford 1986)

HOUSLEY, N., *The Italian Crusades: the Papal–Angevin Alliance and the Crusades against Christian Lay Powers, 1254–1343* (Oxford 1982)

HOUSLEY, N., 'The mercenary companies, the papacy and the crusades, 1356–1378', *Traditio* 38 (1982) 253–80

HOWLETT, Richard (ed.), *Chronicles of the Reigns of Stephen, Henry II., and Richard I.* (4 vols, London 1884–9)

HUILLARD-BREHOLLES, M. (ed.), *Titres de la maison ducale de Bourbon* (2 vols, Paris 1867)

HUTTON, W. H., *Philip Augustus* (London 1896)

HUYGENS, R. B. C. (ed.), *Accessus ad autores* (rev. edn, Leiden 1970)

ILVONEN, Eero (ed.), *Parodies de thèmes pieux dans la poésie française du moyen âge* (Paris 1914)

JAMES, Montague Rhodes, *A Descriptive Catalogue of the Manuscripts in the Library of Corpus Christi College, Cambridge* (2 vols, Cambridge 1909–12)

JAMES, M. R. et al. (edd. & transl.), *Walter Map, De nugis curialium* (Oxford 1983)

JEANROY, A., 'Les "coblas" de Bertran Carbonel', *Annales du Midi* 25 (1913) 137–88

JENNINGS, Brendan, *Michael O Cleirigh, Chief of the Four Masters, and his Associates* (Dublin 1936)

JEUDY, C., 'Complément à un catalogue récent des manuscrits de Priscien', *Scriptorium* 36 (1982) 313–25

JEUDY, C., 'L'*Ars de nomine et uerbo* de Phocas: manuscrits et commentaires médiévaux', *Viator* 5 (1974) 61–156

JEUDY, C., 'Les manuscrits de l'*Ars de uerbo* d'Eutychès et le commentaire de Rémi d'Auxerre', in *Etudes de civilisation médiévale (IXe–XIIe siècles). Mélanges offerts à Edmond-René Labande* (Poitiers [1974]), pp. 421–36

JOHNSON, Charles (ed.), *Registrum Hamonis Hethe Diocesis Roffensis A.D.1319–1352* (2 vols, Oxford 1948)

JOHNSTON, R. C. & OWEN, D. D. R. (edd.), *Fabliaux* (Oxford 1957)

JONES, W. R., 'The English Church and royal propaganda during the Hundred Years War', *Journal of British Studies* 19 (1979) 18–30

JORDAN, E., *Les Origines de la domination angevine en Italie* (Paris 1909)

JORDAN, William C. *et al.* (edd.), *Order and Innovation in the Middle Ages: Essays in Honor of Joseph R. Strayer* (Princeton, N.J. 1976)

JUBINAL, A. (ed.), *Jongleurs et trouvères* (Paris 1835)

JUBINAL, A. (ed.), *Nouveau Recueil de contes, dits, fabliaux et autres pièces inédites des XIIIe, XIVe et XVe siècles* (2 vols, Paris 1839–42)

JUBINAL, A. (ed.), *Rutebeuf: Oeuvres complètes* (2 vols, Paris 1839)

KAIL, J. (ed.), *Twenty-six Political and Other Poems* (2 vols, London 1904)

KAMPF, H., 'Pierre Dubois und die geistlichen Grundlagen des französischen Nationalbewusstseins', *Beiträge zur Kulturgeschichte des Mittelalters und der Renaissance* 54 (1935) 65–111

KANTOROWICZ, E. H., *The King's Two Bodies: a Study in Medieval Political Theology* (Princeton, N.J. 1957)

KASTNER, L.-E. (ed.), 'Débat du corps et de l'âme en provençal', *Revue des langues romanes* 48 (1905) 30–64

KEDAR, B. Z. *et al.* (edd.), *Outremer: Studies in the History of the Crusading Kingdom of Jerusalem, presented to Joshua Prawer* (Jerusalem 1982)

KELLER, H. E., 'The *Song of Roland*: a mid-twelfth century song of propaganda for the Capetian kingdom', *Olifant* 3 (1975/6) 242–58

KENDRICK, T. D., *British Antiquity* (London 1950)

KENNEDY, E. D., 'Malory's King Mark and King Arthur', *Mediaeval Studies* 37 (1975) 190–234

KENNEDY, Elspeth (ed.), *Lancelot do Lac. The Non-cyclic Old French Prose Romance* (2 vols, Oxford 1980)

KENNEDY, E., 'The two versions of the false Guinevere episode in the Old French Prose Lancelot', *Romania* 77 (1956) 94–104

KENNEY, James F., *The Sources for the Early History of Ireland: Ecclesiastical. An Introduction and Guide* (New York 1929; rev. imp., by L. Bieler, 1966)

KER, N. R., *Catalogue of Manuscripts containing Anglo-Saxon* (Oxford 1957)

KER, N. R., *Medieval Libraries of Great Britain. A List of Surviving Books* (2nd edn, London 1964)

KER, N. R., 'The handwriting of Archbishop Wulfstan', in *England before the Conquest*, edd. P. Clemoes & K. Hughes (Cambridge 1971), pp. 315–31

KERVYN DE LETTENHOVE, H. (ed.), *Oeuvres de Froissart* (18 vols, Brussels 1876–7)

KEYNES, S., 'King Athelstan's books', in *Learning and Literature in Anglo-Saxon England*, edd. M. Lapidge & H. Gneuss (Cambridge 1985), pp. 143–201

KINNEY, T. L., 'The temper of fourteenth-century verse of complaint', *Annuale mediaevale* 7 (1966) 74–89

KIRBY, T. F. (ed.), *Wykeham's Register* (2 vols, London 1896–9)

KJELLMAN, H. (ed.), 'Les rédactions en prose de L'Ordre de chevalerie', *Studier i Modern Språkvetenskap* 7 (1920) 139–77

KLOTZ, Alfred & KLINNERT, T. (edd.), *P. Papini Stati Thebais* (Leipzig 1973)

KNOLL, P. W., 'Poland as *antemurale christianitatis* in the late middle ages', *Catholic Historical Review* 60 (1974) 381–401

KNOWLES, David, *Great Historical Enterprises [and] Problems in Monastic History* (Edinburgh 1963)

KNOWLES, David et al., *The Heads of Religious Houses: England and Wales 940–1216* (Cambridge 1972)

KOEHLER, Wilhelm R. W. (ed.), *Medieval Studies in Memory of A. Kingsley Porter* (2 vols, Cambridge, Mass. 1939)

KÖLBING, E. & KÖSCHWITZ, E. (edd.), *Hue de Rotelande: Ipomedon* (Breslau 1889)

KOETSCHAU, Paul et al. (edd.), *Origenes Werke* (12 vols, Leipzig 1899–1976)

KOSMER, E. V., 'Master Honoré: a reconsideration of the documents', *Gesta* 14/1 (1975) 63–8

KOSMER, Ellen V., 'A Study of the Style and Iconography of a 13th-century *Somme le roi* (British Museum MS. Add. 54180), with a Consideration of other illustrated *Somme* Manuscripts of the 13th, 14th and 15th Centuries' (unpublished Ph.D. dissertation, Yale University 1973)

LACROIX, Benoît, *L'Historien au moyen âge* (Montréal 1971)

LAISTNER, M. L. W., 'Some early medieval commentaries on the Old Testament', *Harvard Theological Review* 46 (1953) 27–46

LAKOFF, R., 'La grammaire générale et raisonnée, ou la grammaire de Port-Royal', in *History of Linguistic Thought and Contemporary Linguistics*, ed. H. Parret (Berlin 1976), pp. 348–73

LAMBLEY, K., *The Teaching and Cultivation of the French Language in England during Tudor and Stuart Times* (Manchester 1920)

LÅNGFORS, Artur (ed.), *Huon le Roi, Le Vair Palefroi, avec deux versions de La Male Honte par Huon de Cambrai et par Guillaume: fabliaux du XIIIe siècle* (2nd edn, Paris 1970)

LÅNGFORS, A., ' "L'Anglais qui couve", dans l'imagination populaire du moyen âge', in *Mélanges de philologie romane et de littérature médiévale offerts à Ernest Hoepffner* (Paris 1949), pp. 89–94

LÅNGFORS, A. (ed.), '*Le Miroir de vie et de mort* par Robert de l'Omme (1266): modèle d'une moralité wallonne du XVe siècle', *Romania* 47 (1921) 511–31

LÅNGFORS, Artur, *Les Incipit des poèmes français antérieurs au XVIe siècle*, I (Paris 1917)

LÅNGFORS, A., 'Notice du manuscrit français 24436 de la Bibliothèque nationale', *Romania* 41 (1912) 206–46

LÅNGFORS, A. (ed.), 'Une paraphrase anonyme de l'Ave Maria en ancien français', *Neuphilologische Mitteilungen* 7 (1905) 117–25

LANGLOIS, C. V. (ed.), *De recuperatione terre sancte* (Paris 1891)

LAPIDGE, Michael & SHARPE, R., *A Bibliography of Celtic-Latin Literature 400–1200* (Dublin 1985)

LAPIDGE, Michael & GNEUSS, H. (edd.), *Learning and Literature in Anglo-Saxon England. Studies presented to Peter Clemoes* (Cambridge 1985)

LAPIDGE, M., 'Some Latin poems as evidence for the reign of Athelstan', *Anglo-Saxon England* 9 (1981) 61–98

LAUER, Philippe (ed.), *Les Annales de Flodoard* (Paris 1905)

LAUER, Philippe (ed.), *Robert de Clari: La Conquête de Constantinople* (Paris 1924)

LAVAUD, R. (ed.), *Peire Cardenal: poésies complètes* (Toulouse 1957)

LAW, V., *The Insular Latin Grammarians* (Woodbridge 1982)

LAWLOR, H. J. & BEST, R. I. (edd.), 'The ancient list of the coarbs of Patrick', *Proceedings of the Royal Irish Academy* 35 C (1918–20) 316–62

LECACHEUX, P. & MOLLAT, G. (edd.), *Lettres secrètes et curiales du pape Urbain V (1362–1370) se rapportant à la France* (2 vols, Paris 1902–55)

LECKIE, R. William, Jr, *The Passage of Dominion: Geoffrey of Monmouth and the Periodization of Insular History in the Twelfth Century* (Toronto 1981)

LECLERCQ, J. (ed.), 'Un sermon prononcé pendant la guerre de Flandre sous Philippe le Bel', *Revue du moyen âge latin* 1 (1945) 165–72

LECOY, F. (ed.), *La Bible au seigneur de Berzé* (Paris 1938)

LECOY, F. (ed.), *Le Roman de la Rose* (3 vols, Paris 1965–70)

LECOY DE LA MARCHE, A. (ed.), *Anecdotes historiques, légendes et apologues, tirés du recueil inédit d'Etienne de Bourbon* (Paris 1877)

LÉCUYER, Sylvie (ed.), *Jehan et Blonde* (Paris 1984)

LE GRAND, Albert, *Les Vies des saints de la Bretagne armorique* (5th edn, Quimper 1901)

LEHMANN, P., *Die Parodie im Mittelalter* (2nd edn, Stuttgart 1963)

LEHMANN, P. (ed.), *Mittelalterliche Bibliothekskataloge Deutschlands und der Schweiz*, I (Munich 1918)

LEHMANN, P., [Review of W. A. Baehrens, *Überlieferung und Textgeschichte der lateinisch erhaltenen Origenes Homilien . . .*], *Berliner philologische Wochenschrift* 37 (1917) 43–9

LEHMANN, P., [Review of *Origenes Werke, IX. Band: Die Homilien zu Lukas*, ed. Max Rauer], *Berliner philologische Wochenschrift* 50 (1930) 1475–80

LELAND, John, *De Rebus Britannicis Collectanea*, ed. Thomas Hearne (2nd edn, 6 vols, London 1774)

LE MEN, R.-F.-L. & ERNAULT, E. (edd.), 'Le Cartulaire de Landévennec', *Mélanges historiques* 5 (1885) 535–77 [repr. *Britannia Christiana*, Bretagne monastique, fasc. 5/1 (1985)]

LE ROUX DE LINCY, A., *Le Livre des proverbes français* (2nd edn, 2 vols, Paris 1859)

LEVISON, W., 'Die Iren und die fränkische Kirche', *Historische Zeitschrift* 109 (1912) 1–22; repr. in *Mönchtum und Gesellschaft im Frühmittelalter*, ed. F. Prinz (Darmstadt 1976), pp. 91–111

LEVISON, W., *England and the Continent in the Eighth Century* (Oxford 1946)

LIEBERMANN, F. (ed.), *Die Heiligen Englands* (Hannover 1889)

LINDSAY, W. M., *Notae Latinae. An Account of Abbreviation in Latin MSS. of the Early Minuscule Period (c.700–850)* (Cambridge 1915)

LINDSAY, W. M., 'The Laon AZ-type', *Revue des bibliothèques* 24 (1914) 15–27

LINEHAN, P., 'Religion, nationalism and national identity in medieval Spain and Portugal', *Studies in Church History* 18 (1982) 161–99

LINOW, W. (ed.), *Þe desputisoun bitwen þe bodi and þe soule* (Erlangen 1889)

LITTLE, L. K., 'Pride goes before Avarice', *American Historical Review* 76 (1971) 16–41

LLOYD, S., ' "Political crusades" in England, c.1215–17 and c.1263–5', in *Crusade and Settlement*, ed. P. W. Edbury (Cardiff 1985), pp. 113–20

LÖSETH, E., *Le Roman en prose de Tristan, le Roman de Palamède et la Compilation de Rusticien de Pise. Analyse critique d'après les manuscrits de Paris* (Paris 1891)

LÖWE, Heinz (ed.), *Die Iren und Europa im früheren Mittelalter* (2 vols, Stuttgart 1982)

LONGNON, Jean (ed.), *Henri de Valenciennes: Histoire de l'empereur Henri de Constantinople* (Paris 1948)

LOOMIS, Roger Sherman (ed.), *Arthurian Literature in the Middle Ages. A Collaborative History* (Oxford 1959)

LOT, F., 'La date de l'exode des corps saints hors de Bretagne', *Annales de Bretagne* 15 (1899–1900) 60–76

LOT, Ferdinand (ed.), *Nennius et l'Historia Brittonum: étude critique suivie d'une édition des divers versions de ce texte* (2 vols, Paris 1934)

LOTH, J., *Les Noms des saints bretons* (Paris 1910)

LOWE, E. A., *Codices Latini Antiquiores* (11 vols + suppl., Oxford 1934–71)

LUARD, H. R. (ed.), *Annales monastici* (5 vols, London 1864–9)

LUMBY, Joseph Rawson (ed.), *Chronicon Henrici Knighton, vel Cnitthon, monachi Leycestrensis* (2 vols, London 1889–95)

LUNT, W. E., *Financial Relations of the Papacy with England 1327–1534* (Cambridge, Mass. 1962)

MACAULAY, G. (ed.), *The Complete Works of John Gower* (4 vols, Oxford 1899–1902)

MCHARDY, A. K., 'Liturgy and propaganda in the diocese of Lincoln during the Hundred Years War', *Studies in Church History* 18 (1982) 215–27

MCHARDY, A. K., 'The English clergy and the Hundred Years War', *Studies in Church History* 20 (1983) 171–8

MCNAB, B., 'Obligations of the Church in English society: military arrays of the clergy, 1369–1418', in *Order and Innovation in the Middle Ages*, edd. W. C. Jordan *et al.* (Princeton, N.J. 1976), pp. 293–314 *and* 516–22

MACQUARRIE, A., *Scotland and the Crusades 1095–1560* (Edinburgh 1985)

MANITIUS, M., *Geschichte der lateinischen Literatur des Mittelalters*, I (Munich 1911)

MANN, Jill, *Chaucer and Medieval Estates Satire* (Cambridge 1973)

MANN, Jill, 'Satiric subject and satiric object in Goliardic literature', *Mittellateinisches Jahrbuch* 15 (1980) 63–86

MARTIN, Henry & FUNCK-BRENTANO, F., *Catalogue des manuscrits de la Bibliothèque de l'Arsenal* (9 vols in 10, Paris 1885–94)

MARZAC, Nicole (ed. & transl.), *Richard Rolle de Hampole (1300–1349): vie et oeuvres, suivies du Tractatus super Apocalypsim* (Paris 1968)

MAUS, F. W., *Peire Cardenals Strophenbau in seinem Verhältniss zu dem anderer Trobadors nebst einem Anhang enthaltend. Alphabetisches Verzeichniss sämmtlicher Strophenformen der provenzalischen Lyrik* (Marburg 1884)

MEDCALF, S., ' "Piers Plowman" and the Ricardian age in literature', in *The Mediaeval World*, edd. D. Daiches & A. Thorlby (London 1973), pp. 643–96

MÉNARD, Philippe (ed.), *Fabliaux français du moyen âge*, I (Geneva 1979)

MENEGHETTI, M. L., *I fatti di Bretagna* (Padua 1979)

MERLET, René (ed.), *La Chronique de Nantes (570 environ–1049)* (Paris 1896)

MERLET, R., 'Les origines du monastère de Saint-Magloire de Paris', *Bibliothèque de l'Ecole des Chartes* 56 (1895) 237–73

MEYER, P. (ed.), *Histoire de Guillaume le Maréchal* (3 vols, Paris 1891)

MEYER, P. (ed.), 'Poésie pieuse en sixains de vers octosyllabiques', *Bulletin de la Société des Anciens Textes Français* 33 (1907) 44–53

MICHA, A., 'Etudes sur le *Lancelot* en prose', *Romania* 76 (1955) 334–41

MICHA, A. (ed.), *Lancelot: roman en prose du XIIIe siècle* (9 vols, Geneva 1978–83)

MICHA, A., 'La tradition manuscrite du *Lancelot* en prose', *Romania* 85 (1964) 293–318, 478–517; 86 (1965) 330–59; 87 (1966) 194–233

MICHA, A., 'Le Départ en Sorelois. Réflexions sur deux versions', in *Mélanges de linguistique romane et de philologie médiévale offerts à M. Maurice Delbouille*, edd. J. Renson & M. Tyssens (2 vols, Gembloux 1964), II.495–507

MICHEL, F. (ed.), *Jean Bodel: La Chanson des Saxons* (Paris 1839)

MIGNE, J.-P. (ed.), *Patrologiae [Latinae] Cursus Completus* (221 vols, Paris 1844–64)

MILLAR, E. G., *The Parisian Miniaturist Honoré* (London 1959)

MILLETT, B., 'Irish literature in Latin, 1550–1700', in *A New History of Ireland*, edd. T. W. Moody *et al.* (9 vols, Oxford 1976–), III.561–86

MILLS, L. R. (ed.), *Barlaam et Josaphat* (Geneva 1973)

MÖLK, Ulrich & WOLFZETTEL, F., *Répertoire métrique de la poésie lyrique française des origines à 1350* (Munich 1972)

MOHL, R., *The Three Estates in Medieval and Renaissance Literature* (New York 1933)

MOODY, T. W. *et al.* (edd.), *A New History of Ireland* (9 vols, Oxford 1976–)

MOONEY, C., 'Father John Colgan, O.F.M., his work and times and literary milieu', in *Father John Colgan, O.F.M., 1592–1658*, ed. T. O Donnell (Dublin 1959), pp. 7–40

MORAN, P. F. (ed.), *Spicilegium Ossoriense: being a Collection of Original Letters and Papers illustrative of the History of the Irish Church from the Reformation to the Year 1800*, I (Dublin 1874)

MORGAN, M. R. (ed.), *La Continuation de Guillaume de Tyr, 1184–1197* (Paris 1982)

MORGAN, M. R., *The Chronicle of Ernoul and the Continuations of William of Tyre* (Oxford 1973)

MORGAN, M. R., 'The Rothelin continuation of William of Tyre', in *Outremer*, edd. B. Z. Kedar *et al.* (Jerusalem 1982), pp. 244–57

MORIN, Germain (ed.), *Sancti Caesarii Arelatensis sermones* (2 vols, Turnhout 1953)

MORRIS, R. (ed.), *The Blickling Homilies of the Tenth Century* (London 1876–80)

MORRIS, William (ed.), *L'Ordène de chevalerie* (Hammersmith 1892–3)

MUIR, L. R., 'King Arthur: style Louis XVI', in *Studies in Eighteenth-century French Literature presented to Robert Niklaus*, edd. J. H. Fox *et al.* (Exeter 1975), pp. 163–71

MUSTANOJA, T. F. (ed.), *Les Neuf Joies Nostre Dame: a Poem attributed to Rutebeuf* (Helsinki 1952)

MYNORS, R. A. B. (ed.), *Cassiodorus: Institutiones* (Oxford 1937)

NAETEBUS, Gotthold, *Die nicht-lyrischen Strophenformen des Altfranzösischen* (Leipzig 1891)

NAPIER, A. (ed.), *Wulfstan* (Berlin 1883)

NICOLL, Allardyce, *A History of Restoration Drama, 1600–1700* (3rd edn, Cambridge 1940)

NOBLE, Peter S. & PATERSON, L. M. (edd.), *Chrétien de Troyes and the Troubadours. Essays in Memory of the Late Leslie Topsfield* (Cambridge 1984)

NOBLE, P. S., 'Chrétien's Arthur', in *Chrétien de Troyes and the Troubadours*, edd. P. S. Noble & L. M. Paterson (Cambridge 1984), pp. 220–37

NOOMEN, Willem & VAN DEN BOOGAARD, N. (edd.), *Nouveau recueil complet des fabliaux* (Assen 1983–)

NYKROG, Per, *Les Fabliaux* (new edn, Geneva 1973)

O DONNELL, Terence (ed.), *Father John Colgan, O.F.M., 1592–1658. Essays in Commemoration of the Third Centenary of his Death* (Dublin 1959)

OESTERLEY, H. (ed.), *Gesta Romanorum* (Berlin 1872)

OGILVY, J. D. A., *Books Known to Anglo-Latin Writers from Aldhelm to Alcuin* (Cambridge, Mass. 1936)

O'HANLON, John, *Lives of the Irish Saints, with Special Festivals, and the Commemorations of Holy Persons, compiled from Calendars, Martyrologies, and Various Sources relating to the Ancient Church History of Ireland* (8 vols, Dublin [1875]–[1904])

OMONT, Henri, *Bibliothèque nationale: Catalogue général des manuscrits français. Ancien supplément français* (3 vols, Paris 1895–6)

ORR, John (ed.), *Guiot de Provins: Oeuvres* (Manchester 1915)

OWST, G. R., *Literature and Pulpit in Medieval England. A Neglected Chapter in the History of English Letters and of the English People* (2nd edn, Oxford 1961)

PALMER, J. J. N., 'England, France, the papacy and the Flemish succession, 1361–9', *Journal of Medieval History* 2 (1976) 339–64

PANTIN, W. A., 'A medieval treatise on letter-writing, with examples, from the Rylands Latin MS. 394', *Bulletin of the John Rylands Library, Manchester* 13 (1929) 326–82 *and* 14 (1930) 81–114

PANTIN, W. A., *The English Church in the Fourteenth Century* (Cambridge 1955)

PARIS, G., 'La légende de Saladin', *Journal des savants* (1893) 284–99, 354–65, 428–38, 486–98

PARRET, H. (ed.), *History of Linguistic Thought and Contemporary Linguistics* (Berlin 1976)

PARSONS, David (ed.), *Tenth-century Studies. Essays in Commemoration of the Millennium of the Council of Winchester and* Regularis Concordia (Chichester 1975)

PARTNER, Nancy F., *Serious Entertainments: the Writing of History in Twelfth-century England* (Chicago, Ill. 1977)

PASSALACQUA, M., *I codici di Prisciano* (Rome 1978)

PAUPHILET, A., *Historiens et chroniqueurs du moyen âge* (Paris 1952)

PERROY, E., *L'Angleterre et le Grand Schisme d'occident* (Paris 1933)

PERROY, E., *The Hundred Years War* (London 1959)

PERTZ, Georg Heinrich *et al.* (edd.), *Monumenta Germaniae Historica inde ab Anno Christi Quingentesima usque ad Annum Millesimum et Quingentesimum, Scriptores* (Hannover 1826–)

PETER, J., *Complaint and Satire in Early English Literature* (Oxford 1956)

PETIT-DUTAILLIS, C., *The Feudal Monarchy in France and England from the Tenth to the Thirteenth Century* (London 1936)

PICKFORD, C. E., 'Miscellaneous French prose romances', in *Arthurian Literature in the Middle Ages*, ed. R. S. Loomis (Oxford 1959), pp. 348–57

PLANTA, J., *Catalogue of the Manuscripts in the Cottonian Library deposited in the British Museum* (London 1802)

POWICKE, F. M., *King Henry III and the Lord Edward: the Community of the Realm in the Thirteenth Century* (2 vols, Oxford 1947)

PRAWER, J., *Histoire du royaume latin de Jérusalem* (2 vols, Paris 1969–70)

PRINZ, F., *Frühes Mönchtum im Frankenreich* (Munich 1965)

PRINZ, F. (ed.), *Mönchtum und Gesellschaft im Frühmittelalter* (Darmstadt 1976)

RABB, T. K. & SEIGEL, J. E. (edd.), *Action and Conviction in Early Modern Europe. Essays in Memory of E. H. Harbison* (Princeton, N.J. 1969)

RABY, F. J. E. (ed.), *The Oxford Book of Medieval Latin Verse* (Oxford 1959)

RANDALL, L. M. C., 'The snail in Gothic marginal warfare', *Speculum* 37 (1962) 358–67

RAUER, Max, *Form und Überlieferung der Lukas-Homilien des Origenes* (Leipzig 1932)

RAYNAUD, G. (ed.), 'Les Congés de Jean Bodel', *Romania* 9 (1880) 216–47

RÉGNIER, C. (ed.), *La Prise d'Orange: chanson de geste de la fin du XIIe siècle* (2nd edn, Paris 1969)

REID, T. B. W., [Review of *Fabliaux*, edd. R. C. Johnston and D. D. R. Owen], *Medium Ævum* 27 (1958) 122–6

REID, T. B. W. (ed.), *Twelve Fabliaux from MS. fr. 19152 of the Bibliothèque Nationale* (Manchester 1958)

REINSCH, R., 'Mittheilungen aus einer französischen Handschrift des Lambeth Palace zu London', *Archiv für das Studium der neueren Sprachen und Literaturen* 63 (1880) 51–96

RENSON, Jean & TYSSENS, M. (edd.), *Mélanges de linguistique romane et de philologie médiévale offerts à M. Maurice Delbouille, Professeur à l'Université de Liège* (2 vols, Gembloux 1964)

REYNOLDS, L. D. & WILSON, N. G., *Scribes and Scholars. A Guide to the Transmission of Greek and Latin Literature* (2nd edn, Oxford 1974)

REYNOLDS, L. D. (ed.), *Texts and Transmission. A Survey of the Latin Classics* (Oxford 1983)

RICKARD, P., *Britain in Medieval French Literature 1100–1500* (Cambridge 1956)

RICKARD, P., *The Embarrassments of Irregularity: the French Language in the Eighteenth Century* (Cambridge 1981)

RILEY, Henry Thomas (ed.), *Chronica monasterii S. Albani* (12 vols, London 1863–76)

ROACH, William (ed.), *Chrétien de Troyes: Le Roman de Perceval, ou, Le Conte du Graal* (Geneva 1956)

ROBBINS, Russell Hope (ed.), *Historical Poems of the XIVth and XVth Centuries* (New York 1959)

ROBINS, Robert Henry, *A Short History of Linguistics* (London 1967)

ROBINSON, J. A., *The Times of Saint Dunstan* (Oxford 1923)

ROBSON, C. A. (ed.), *Maurice of Sully and the Medieval Vernacular Homily* (Oxford 1952)

ROLLASON, D., 'Lists of saints' resting-places in Anglo-Saxon England', *Anglo-Saxon England* 7 (1978) 61–93

ROSS, T. W. (ed.), 'On the evil times of Edward II. A new version from MS Bodley 48', *Anglia* 75 [N.F., 61] (1957) 173–93

ROTZLER, Willy, *Die Begegnung der drei Lebenden und der drei Toten* (Winterthur 1961)

RUELLE, Pierre (ed.), *Le Besant de Dieu de Guillaume le Clerc de Normandie* (Brussels 1973)

RUNCIMAN, S., 'The decline of the crusading idea', in *Relazioni del X Congresso Internazionale di Scienze Storiche*, III, Storia del medioevo (Florence 1955), pp. 637–52

RUSSELL, P. E., *The English Intervention in Spain and Portugal in the Time of Edward III and Richard II* (Oxford 1955)

RUWET, Nicolas, *Théorie syntaxique et syntaxe du français* (Paris 1972)

RYCHNER, Jean, *Contribution à l'étude des fabliaux: variantes, remaniements, dégradations* (2 vols, Neuchâtel 1960)

SALTMAN, Avrom, *Theobald, Archbishop of Canterbury* (London 1956)

SANDGREN, F. (ed.), *Otium et Negotium: Studies in Onomatology and Library Science presented to Olof von Feilitzen* (Stockholm 1973)

SAWYER, P. H., *Anglo-Saxon Charters. An Annotated List and Bibliography* (London 1968)

SCATTERGOOD, V. J., *Politics and Poetry in the Fifteenth Century* (London 1971)

SCHAPIRO, M., 'From Mozarabic to Romanesque in Silos', *Art Bulletin* 21 (1939) 313–74

SCHEIN, S., 'Philip IV and the crusade: a reconsideration', in *Crusade and Settlement*, ed. P. W. Edbury (Cardiff 1985), pp. 121–6

SCHELER, Auguste (ed.), *Dits et contes de Baudouin de Condé et de son fils, Jean de Condé* (3 vols, Brussels 1866–7)

SCHMIDT, A. V. C. (ed.), *Piers Plowman* (London 1978)

SCHMITZ, B., *Histoire de l'ordre de Saint Benoît* (7 vols, Maredsous 1942–56)

SCHMOLKE-HASSELMANN, Beate, *Der arthurische Versroman von Chrestien bis Froissart* (Tübingen 1980)

SCOTT, John (ed. & transl.), *The Early History of Glastonbury. An Edition, Translation and Study of William of Malmesbury's De Antiquitate Glastonie Ecclesie* (Woodbridge 1981)

SEEL, Otto (ed.), M. *Iuniani Iustini Epitoma historiarum Philippicarum Pompei Trogi. Accedunt prologi in Pompeium Trogum* (2nd edn, Stuttgart 1972)

SÉGUIN, J.-P., *La Langue française au XVIIIe siècle* (Paris 1972)

SETTON, Kenneth M., *The Papacy and the Levant (1204–1571)* (4 vols, Philadelphia, Pa 1976–84)

SHARPE, Richard, *Medieval Irish Sants' Lives* (Oxford 1991)

SIBERRY, E., 'Criticism of crusading in fourteenth-century England', in *Crusade and Settlement*, ed. P. W. Edbury (Cardiff 1985), pp. 127–34

SICKEL, T., 'Alcuinstudien', *Sitzungsberichte der kaiserlichen Akademie der Wissenschaften, philosophisch-historische Klasse* (Wien) 79 (1875) 461–550

SIEGMUND, A., *Die Überlieferung der griechischen christlichen Literatur in der lateinischen Kirche bis zum zwölften Jahrhundert* (Munich 1949)

SILKE, J. J., 'The Irish abroad in the age of the Counter-Reformation, 1534–1691', in *A New History of Ireland*, edd. T. W. Moody et al. (9 vols, Oxford 1976–), III.587–633

SIMONETTI, Manlio (ed.), *Tyrannii Rufini Opera* (Turnhout 1961)

SISAM, Kenneth, *Studies in the History of Old English Literature* (Oxford 1953; rev. imp., 1962)

SKEAT, W. W. (ed.), *Lancelot of the Laik* (2nd edn, London 1870)

SKEAT, W. W. (ed.), *The Vision of William concerning Piers the Plowman together with Richard the Redeless* (2 vols, London 1886)

SNAITH, G. P., 'Aspects of La Calpranède's Drama' (unpublished Ph.D dissertation, University of Cambridge 1983)

SPANKE, Hans, *Beziehungen zwischen romanischer und mittellateinischer Lyrik, mit besonderer Berücksichtigung der Metrik und Musik* (Berlin 1936)

SPENCER, R., 'The *courtois–vilain* nexus in *La Male Honte*', *Medium Ævum* 37 (1968) 272–92

SPILLING, H., 'Angelsächsische Schrift in Fulda', in *Von der Klosterbibliothek zur Landesbibliothek*, ed. A. Brall (Stuttgart 1978), pp. 47–98

STEFFENS, F., *Lateinische Paläographie* (2nd edn, Berlin 1929)

STENTON, F. M., *Anglo-Saxon England* (3rd edn, Oxford 1971)

STEVENS, John, *Medieval Romance: Themes and Approaches* (London 1973)

STONE, H. K. (ed.), *Thibaut de Marly: Les Vers* (Paris 1932)

STRAYER, J. R., 'France: the Holy Land, the Chosen People, and the Most Christian King', in *Action and Conviction in Early Modern Europe*, edd. T. K. Rabb & J. E. Seigel (Princeton, N.J. 1969), pp. 3–16

STRAYER, Joseph R., *Medieval Statecraft and the Perspectives of History* (Princeton, N.J. 1971)

STREICHER, J. (ed.), *Commentaires sur les Remarques de Vaugelas* (2 vols, Paris 1936)

STUBBS, William (ed.), *Chronicles of the Reigns of Edward I. and Edward II.* (2 vols, London 1882–3)

STUBBS, William (ed.), *Memorials of Saint Dunstan, Archbishop of Canterbury* (London 1874)

SWANSON, R. N., *Universities, Academics and the Great Schism* (Cambridge 1979)

TAKAMIYA, Toshiyuki, & BREWER, D. (edd.), *Aspects of Malory* (Cambridge 1981)

TANQUEREY, F. J. (ed.), *Deux Poèmes moraux anglo-français* (Paris 1922)

TATLOCK, J. S. P., *The Legendary History of Britain. Geoffrey of Monmouth's Historia Regum Britanniae and its Early Vernacular Versions* (Berkeley, Cal. 1950)

TAUSENDFREUND, Eduard G. H., *Vergil und Gottfried von Monmouth* (Halle a.S. 1913)

THOMPSON, Edward Maunde (ed.), *Adæ Murimuth Continuatio chronicarum. Robertus de Avesbury de Gestis mirabilibus regis Edwardi tertii* (London 1889)

THOMSON, J. A F., *The Transformation of Medieval England, 1370–1529* (London 1983)

THOMSON, R. M., 'Identifiable books from the pre-Conquest library of Malmesbury Abbey', *Anglo-Saxon England* 10 (1982) 1–19

THOMSON, R. M., 'The reading of William of Malmesbury', *Révue bénédictine* 85 (1975) 362–402

THOMSON, Rodney M., *William of Malmesbury* (Woodbridge 1987)

THOMSON, R. M., 'William of Malmesbury and the letters of Alcuin', *Medievalia et humanistica*, N.S., 8 (1977) 147–61

THROOP, P. A., *Criticism of the Crusade: a Study of Public Opinion and Crusade Propaganda* (Amsterdam 1940)

TOBLER, A. & LOMMATZSCH, E., *Altfranzösische Wörterbuch* (Berlin 1915–)

TOBLER, A., *Vermischte Beiträge zur französischen Grammatik*, I (Leipzig 1886)

TRIER, Jost, *Der heilige Jodocus, sein Leben und seine Verehrung* (Breslau 1924)

TUCK, J. A., 'Richard II's system of patronage', in *The Reign of Richard II*, edd. F. R. H. Du Boulay & C. M. Barron (London 1971), pp. 1–20

TYERMAN, C. J., 'Philip V of France, the assemblies of 1319–20 and the crusade', *Bulletin of the Institute of Historical Research* 57 (1984) 15–34

TYERMAN, C. J., 'Philip VI and the recovery of the Holy Land', *English Historical Review* 100 (1985) 25–52

ULLMANN, W., 'On the influence of Geoffrey of Monmouth in English history', *Speculum historiale*, edd. C. Bauer *et al.* (Freiburg 1965), pp. 257–76

ULRICH, J. (ed.), *Robert de Blois: Sämmtliche Werke* (Berlin 1889)

VALOIS, N., *La France et le Grand Schisme d'occident* (4 vols, Paris 1896–1902)

VAN HAMEL, A. G. (ed.), *Li Romans de Carité et Miserere du renclus de Moiliens, poèmes de la fin du XIIe siècle* (2 vols, Paris 1885)

VIDAL, J.-M. & MOLLAT, G. (edd.), *Benoît XII (1334–1342): Lettres closes et patentes intéressant les pays autres que la France* (3 vols, Paris 1913–50)

VIEILLIARD, J., 'Conseils aux éditeurs de textes français du moyen âge', *Revue d'histoire de l'église de France* 29 (1943) 275–8

VINAVER, E. (ed.), *Malory: Works* (Oxford 1971)

VINCKE, J. (ed.), *Documenta selecta mutuas civitatis Arago Cathalaunicae et ecclesiae relationes illustrantia* (Barcelona 1936)

WAGNER, R.-L., *La Grammaire française* (2 vols, Paris 1968–73)

WALLACE-HADRILL, J. M., *The Long-haired Kings and Other Studies in Frankish History* (London 1962)

WALLENSKÖLD, Axel (ed.), *Les Chansons de Conon de Béthune* (Paris 1921)

WALTHER, Hans, *Proverbia sententiaeque Latinitatis medii aevi. Lateinische Sprichwörter und Sentenzen des Mittelalters in alphabetischer Anordnung* (6 vols, Göttingen 1963–9)

WAQUET, Henri (ed. & transl.), *Suger: Vie de Louis VI le Gros* (Paris 1929)

WARD, H. L. D. & HERBERT, J. A., *Catalogue of Romances in the Department of Manuscripts in the British Museum* (3 vols, London 1883–1910)

WARNER, George F. & GILSON, J. P., *British Museum Catalogue of Western Manuscripts in the Old Royal and King's Collections* (4 vols, London 1921)

WARREN, F. E. (ed.), *The Leofric Missal* (Oxford 1883)

WARREN, F. E., 'Un monument inédit de la liturgie celtique', *Revue celtique* 9 (1888) 88–96

WATERS, E. G. R. (ed.), *The Anglo-Norman Voyage of St Brendan by Benedeit* (Oxford 1928)

WATSON, A. G., 'An early thirteenth-century Low Countries booklist', *British Library Journal* 7 (1981) 39–46

WHITELOCK, Dorothy, *History, Law and Literature in 10th–11th Century England* (London 1981)

WHITELOCK, Dorothy (ed.), *Sermo Lupi ad Anglos* (4th edn, Exeter 1976)

WHITELOCK, D., 'The appointment of Dunstan as archbishop of Canterbury', in *Otium et Negotium*, ed. F. Sandgren (Stockholm 1973), pp. 232–47

WHITELOCK, D., 'Wulfstan at York', in *Franciplegius: Medieval and Linguistic Studies in Honor of Francis Peabody Magoun, Jr*, edd. J. B. Bessinger & R. P. Creed (New York 1965), pp. 214–31

WIENBECK, E. *et al.* (edd.), *Aliscans* (Halle a.S. 1903)

WILKINS, D. (ed.), *Concilia Magnae Britanniae et Hiberniae* (4 vols, London 1737)

WINDAHL, C. A. (ed.), *Li Vers de la Mort* (Lund 1887)

WINKLER, Emil, *La Doctrine grammaticale française d'après Maupas et Oudin* (Halle a.S. 1912)

WINTERBOTTOM, Michael (ed. & transl.), *Gildas: The Ruin of Britain and Other Works* (Chichester 1978)

WOOD, D., '*Omnino partialitate cessante*: Clement VI and the Hundred Years War', *Studies in Church History* 20 (1983) 179–89

WOOLF, R., *The English Religious Lyric in the Middle Ages* (Oxford 1968)

WORMALD, Francis & ALEXANDER, J. J. G. (facs. edd.), *An Early Breton Gospel Book* (Cambridge 1977)

WORMALD, Francis (ed.), *English Kalendars before A.D.1100* (London 1934)

WORMALD, F., 'The English saints in the litany in Arundel MS. 60', *Analecta Bollandiana* 64 (1946) 72–86

WRIGHT, N., 'Geoffrey of Monmouth and Bede', *Arthurian Literature* 6 (1986) 27–59

WRIGHT, Neil (ed.), *The Historia Regum Britannie of Geoffrey of Monmouth, I, A Single-manuscript Edition from Bern, Burgerbibliothek, MS. 568* (Cambridge 1985)

WRIGHT, Neil (ed.), *The Historia Regum Britannie of Geoffrey of Monmouth, II, The First Variant Version: a Critical Edition* (Cambridge 1988)

WRIGHT, Thomas (ed.), *Political Poems and Songs relating to English History, composed during the Period from the Accession of Edw. III. to that of Ric. III.* (2 vols, London 1859–61)

WRIGHT, Thomas (ed.), *The Latin Poems commonly attributed to Walter Mapes* (London 1841)

WRIGHT, Thomas (ed.), *The Political Songs of England from the Reign of John to that of Edward II* (London 1839)

WULFF, F. & WALBERG, E. (edd.), *Les Vers de la mort par Hélinant, moine de Froidmont* (Paris 1905)

YUNCK, J. A., *The Lineage of Lady Mede* (Notre Dame, Ind. 1963)

ZANGEMEISTER, Karl (ed.), *Pauli Orosii historiarum adversum paganos libri VII* (Vienna 1882)

ZUPITZA, Julius (ed.), *Aelfrics Grammatik und Glossar*, I (Berlin 1880)

ZUPITZA, J., 'Zu "Seele und Leib" ', *Archiv für das Studium der neueren Sprachen und Literaturen* 91 (1893) 369–404

Index of manuscripts

TABULA MEMORIALIS

ADAMS, Pauline, Somerville College, Oxford, OX2 6HD
ASTON, Dr S.C., St Catharine's College, Cambridge, CB1 4SH
AUSTIN, Professor Lloyd, 2 Park Lodge, Park Terrace, Cambridge, CB1 1JJ
AYRES-BENNETT, Dr W.M., Queens' College, Cambridge, CB3 9ET
BAMMEL, Dr Caroline, Girton College, Cambridge, CB3 0JG
BAYLEY, Professor Peter, Gonville and Caius College, Cambridge, CB2 1TA
BENBOW, Gillian, 34 Ridgeway Close, Lightwater, Surrey, GU18 5XX
BOND, Monique & Graham, 23 D'Aguilar Road, The Gap, Brisbane, Australia 4061
BOYDE, Professor Patrick, St John's College, Cambridge, CB2 1TP
BOYLE, Dr Nicholas, Magdalene College, Cambridge, CB3 0AG
BRADBROOK, Professor Muriel, 91 Chesterton Road, Cambridge, CB4 3AP
BRADSHAW, Dr Brendan, Queens' College, Cambridge, CB3 9ET
BRETT, Dr Caroline, Department of History and Archaeology, The University, Exeter, Devon, EX4 4QJ
BRETT, Dr Katharina, 12 Harding Way, Cambridge, CB4 3RR
BROOKE, Rosalind and Christopher, Faculty of History, University of Cambridge, West Road, Cambridge, CB3 9EF
BROWN, Helen, 124 Edge Hill, Ponteland, Newcastle upon Tyne, NE20 9JL
BUBBEAR, Theresa, Foreign & Commonwealth Office, King Charles Street, London, SW1A 2AH
BYRNE, Sister Lavinia, I.B.V.M., St Mary's Convent, 47 Fitzjohn's Avenue, London, NW3 6PG
CASTOR, Dr Gwyneth, 29 Leam Terrace, Leamington Spa, CV31 1BQ
COBBY, Dr A.E., 8 Oxford Street, Edinburgh, EH8 9PJ
COOK, Professor Alan H., Selwyn College, Cambridge, CB3 9DQ
DAVIDSON, N.S., Dept of History, The University, Leicester, LE1 7RH
DAYRAS, Professor Solange, 20 rue A. de Neuville, F-75017 Paris
DE MOURGUES, Professor Odette, deceased
DUFF, Mary, 11 Sherlock Close, Cambridge, CB3 0HW
DUKE, Alison, 20 Thornton Road, Cambridge, CB3 0NW
DUMVILLE, Dr David N., Girton College, Cambridge, CB3 0JG
EALES, Richard and Karen, 44 The Crescent, Canterbury, Kent, CT2 7AW
FINCH, Dr Alison, Churchill College, Cambridge, CB3 0DS
FINDLAY (née MORGAN), Gwyn, 3 Lainson Street, London, SW18 5RS
FOSTER, Dr Meryl R., 21 Darlaston Road, Wimbledon, London, SW19 4LJ
GASKELL, J.P.W., Trinity College, Cambridge, CB2 1TQ

GILLIES, Sheila, 1 Marion Close, Cambridge, CB3 0HN

GROUBE, Kristin, 91 Middlepark Road, Russell's Hall, Dudley, W. Midlands, DY1 2LJ

HALL, Mrs V.E., Cambridge University Library, West Road, Cambridge, CB3 9DR

HOBSON, Dr Marian, Trinity College, Cambridge, CB2 1TQ

HORGAN, Dr Frances, 5 Church Close, Cottenham, Cambs., CB4 4SL

HOUSLEY, Dr Norman, Department of History, The University, Leicester, LE1 7RH

HUGHES, Dr M.E.J., Magdalene College, Cambridge, CB3 0AG

IMAGE, Françoise Bayliss, 73 Barton Road, Cambridge, CB3 9LG

IVES, Margaret C., 97 Bowerham Road, Lancaster, LA1 4HJ

JENKINS, Revd Christopher, Catholic Chaplaincy, Fisher House, Guildhall Street, Cambridge, CB2 3NH

JOLOWICZ, Poppy, Girton College, Cambridge, CB3 0JG

JONDORF, Dr Gillian, Girton College, Cambridge, CB3 0JG

JUBB, Dr Margaret, Department of French, The University, Aberdeen, AB9 2UB

KALLAS, Jemima, 27 Brondesbury Road, London, NW6 6BA

KAY, Dr Sarah, Girton College, Cambridge, CB3 0JG

KEEN, Helen, 19 Digby Crescent, London, N4 2HS

KEMNITJES (née WRIGHT), H.G., 2440 Prince Street, Berkeley, CA 94705, U.S.A.

LAW, Dr Vivien, Sidney Sussex College, Cambridge, CB2 3HU

LETHBRIDGE, Dr R.D., Fitzwilliam College, Cambridge, CB3 0DG

LYON, Dr P. Anne, 35 Sedley Taylor Road, Cambridge, CB2 2PN

McKENDRICK, Dr Melveena, Girton College, Cambridge, CB3 0JG

MANN, Professor Jill, Girton College, Cambridge, CB3 0JG

MORRIS, Dr Rosemary, Woodstone Farm, New House Lane, Ashdon, Saffron Walden, Essex, CB10 2LX

MOULTON, Fred, 40 Windsor Road, Cambridge, CB4 3JN

MULLALY, Elizabeth Helen, Waterside House, 17 Lower Street, Pulborough, West Sussex, RH20 2BH

NUTTON, Dr Christine Clements, 225 Sandpit Lane, St Albans, Herts., AL4 0BT

PEARCE, Dr Susan, Dept of Museum Studies, The University, Leicester, LE1 7RH

POUNTAIN, Dr Christopher J., Queens' College, Cambridge, CB3 9ET

RAINEY, Beth, Rare Books Dept, Durham University Library, Palace Green, Durham, DN1 3RN

RICKARD, Professor Peter, Emmanuel College, Cambridge, CB2 3AP

RUBERY, Dr Eileen D., Hill Top Farm, 133 High Street, Harston, Cambs., CB2 5UD

RYBAK, Dr Stephanie, Language Centre, University of Cambridge, Sidgwick Avenue, Cambridge, CB3 9DA

SAYCE, Olive, Somerville College, Oxford, OX2 6QL
SHENFIELD, Professor Gill, 1 Delta Place, Lane Cove, NSW 2066, Australia
SINCLAIR, Dr Alison, Clare College, Cambridge, CB2 1TL
SMAILES, Helen E., 1 Windsor Street, Edinburgh, EH7 5LA
SMITH, Dr Margaret S., Registrar's Office, The University, Leeds, LS2 9JT
SMITH, Sarah J., Yewlands, Ockham Road South, East Horsley, Surrey, KT24
    6RX
STEVENS, Professor John, Magdalene College, Cambridge, CB3 0AG
STEWART, Dr Mary, Robinson College, Cambridge, CB3 9AN
STOPP, Dr Elisabeth, Girton College, Cambridge, CB3 0JG
STRATHERN, Professor Marilyn, Dept of Social Anthropology, The University,
    Manchester, M13 9PL
THOMPSON, Dr Dorothy J., Girton College, Cambridge, CB3 0JG
VITEBSKY, Dr Piers, Scott Polar Research Institute, University of Cambridge,
    Lensfield Road, Cambridge, CB2 1ER
VLASTO, Dr Alexis, Selwyn College, Cambridge, CB3 9DQ
WRIGHT, Dr Neil, Department of Anglo-Saxon, Norse & Celtic, University of
    Cambridge, 9 West Road, Cambridge, CB3 9DP

Bolton School (Girls' Division), Chorley New Road, Bolton, Lancs., BL1 4PB
The Library, Churchill College, Cambridge, CB3 0DS
The Library, Emmanuel College, Cambridge, CB2 3AP
The Library, Girton College, Cambridge, CB3 0JG
The Library, Gonville and Caius College, Cambridge, CB2 1TA
The Library, Magdalene College, Cambridge, CB3 0AG
The Library, Pembroke College, Cambridge, CB2 1RF
The Library, St Catharine's College, Cambridge, CB2 1RL
The Library, Sidney Sussex College, Cambridge, CB2 3HU
The Library, Somerville College, Oxford, OX2 6HD
The Library, Trinity College, Cambridge, CB2 1TQ
The Library, Dept of Anglo-Saxon, Norse & Celtic, University of Cambridge, 9
    West Road, Cambridge, CB3 9DP
The Library, Faculty of Modern & Medieval Languages, University of
    Cambridge, Sidgwick Avenue, Cambridge, CB3 9DA